OVERSEAS INVESTMENT IN THE AGE OF HIGH IMPERIALISM

MICHAEL EDELSTEIN

Overseas Investment in the Age of High Imperialism
The United Kingdom, 1850–1914

METHUEN & CO. LTD

First published in Great Britain in 1982 by
Methuen & Co. Ltd
11 New Fetter Lane, London EC4P 4EE
0 416 34730 4
© 1982 by Columbia University Press

Printed in the United States of America

British Library Cataloguing in Publication Data

Edelstein, Michael
   Overseas investment in the age of high
   imperialism.
   1. Investments, British—History
   2. Capital investment—History
   I. Title
   332.6'7341   HG4538
ISBN 0-416-34730-4

To Mady, With Love

CONTENTS

LIST OF FIGURES

LIST OF TABLES

ACKNOWLEDGMENTS

Over the many years it took to write this book I have received generous support which it is my pleasure to acknowledge.

The modern economic history of the aggregate nineteenth-century British economy owes a special debt to Phyllis Deane and Carl Feinstein, and this study of U.K. overseas investment is no exception. Without their national expenditure, income, and product accounts, the dimensions of the century's aggregate performance would be subject to great uncertainty, and the existence and character of many important economic relationships would pass unnoticed.

My earliest indebtedness is to my teachers, William G. Whitney, the late Dorothy S. Brady, Richard A. Easterlin, Martin Wolfe, Lawrence R. Klein, the late Arthur H. John, and Moses Abramovitz. They bear no responsibility for the current product, but if there is merit in this work of quantitative economy history, it owes much to their compelling guidance.

A number of colleagues have read early drafts of parts of this manuscript and made valuable comments. These include Gary R. Hawke, Donald Mathieson, Cormac O'Grada, Peter Temin, Donald N. McCloskey, Keith Aufhauser, Carl Riskin, Thom Thurston, Roger Alcaly, David Gold, Robert B. Zevin, Robert W. Fogel, Jon Cohen, William P. Kennedy, Donald Dewey, and Herbert S. Klein. Their kindnesses have been above and beyond the call of collegial duty. In this regard I owe a very substantial debt to Stanley L. Engerman, a friend and most accessible and trenchant reader. There is not a chapter that has not been improved by his demanding scholarship.

I am particularly thankful for the opportunity to present parts of this study to economic history seminars at the University of Chicago, Harvard University, Yale University, Stanford University, the University of Pennsylvania, Cambridge University, and above all, the Columbia University Seminar in Economic History. It is said that if you can't stand the heat, get out of the kitchen, and there were certainly times when, awaiting one of these seminars, I would have preferred a cold buffet. Still, once in the seminar, these occasions were singular for penetrating questions and helpful suggestions.

For innumerable services over many years given with efficiency and much patience, I am grateful to three librarians of the Watson Business Library of Columbia University, Ken Doesschat, Maryrose Miller, and Jane Winland. For excellent typing I am very grateful for the services of Queens College Reprographics, Sara Nicoll, and Deborah Bell. The figures were expertly drawn by Chris Brest.

I would like to thank Princeton University Press, the Economic History Association, Academic Press, and the American Economic Association for permission to reproduce some of my work that has appeared in the following publications: Rigidity and Bias in the British Capitalist Market, 1870–1913, in D. N. McCloskey ed., *Essay on a Mature Economy: Britain after 1840*, Princeton: Princeton University Press, 1970; The Determinants of U.K. Investment Abroad, 1870–1913: The U.S. Case, *Journal of Economic History* (1974) 24:980–1007; Realized Rates of Return on U.K. Home and Overseas Portfolio Investment in the Age of High Imperialism, *Explorations in Economic History* (1976) 13:283–329; U.K. Saving in the Age of High Imperialism and After, *American Economic Review*, (1977) 67:282–87.

OVERSEAS INVESTMENT IN THE AGE OF HIGH IMPERIALISM

Tell [Smiley] I have two proofs
and can bring them with me.
John Le Carre
Smiley's People

PART I: INTRODUCTION

CHAPTER 1: **BACKGROUND**

Few would deny that Great Britain's immense capital export must be counted among the most important phenomena of British and world history in the late nineteenth and early twentieth centuries. Never before or since has one nation committed so much of its national income and savings to funding capital formation abroad or derived so much of its income from overseas assets. On average Great Britain placed 5.2 percent of its gross national product in net foreign lending, 1870–1913, and across these same years net property income from abroad rose from 5 percent to 8 percent of gross national product.[1] France and Germany were also active capital exporters during the late nineteenth and early twentieth centuries. However, France and Germany allocated a substantially smaller proportion of national income and product to overseas investment activity. The French rate of net foreign lending averaged 2 percent to 3 percent of national product and the German rate was somewhat less than 2 percent (Green and Urquhart 1976:244). An even stronger contrast with Britain's late Victorian behavior arises from a comparison with today's major capital exporters. In the mid-twentieth century Great Britain, France, Germany, Japan, and the United States commit less than 1 percent of their national products to net foreign lending (OECD 1974).

Very rough materials suggest that the first appearance of a significant net outflow of investment funds from Great Britain may have coincided with the beginnings of the British Industrial Revolution.[2] From the 1770s to the early nineteenth century net foreign lending averaged around 1 percent of national product. From the 1820s to the 1840s the rate of net foreign lending was somewhat higher, perhaps 1 percent to 2 percent. The rate climbed to 3.3 percent in the 1850s, rose again in the 1860s to 3.8 percent, and thereafter to World War I averaged, as just noted, 5.2 percent. Clearly, the nature of British accumulation processes shifted in the third quarter of the nineteenth century and circumstances then sustained this uniquely high outflow of British savings for four decades.

To many observers the causes of the surging capital export had strong domestic origins. Broadly speaking, the nineteenth- and twentieth-century literature on this topic offers three distinct views favoring a domestic impulse for the outflow. Perhaps the most famous view is that domestic rates of return tended toward unusually low levels. Eighteenth- and nineteenth- century economists such as Smith, Matlhus, Ricardo, Wakefield, Mill, Marx, and Marshall thought that there was a tendency for domestic British rates of return to decline secularly and, if not actually falling, the rates would have fallen in the absence of the overseas outlets to absorb the amount of savings generated.[3]

The cause of this tendency was either that the state of human knowledge offered a limited set of investment opportunities bearing a positive return or that diminishing returns to land would drive up the cost of investment opportunities, regardless of any other limit they might have. This tendency might be staved off by a number of domestic factors, technical progress being the most important. Despite the widely observed improvements in manufacturing, transportation, and agricultural technologies in Britain across the nineteenth century, it was presumed that the rate of invention or diffusion of new technologies was inadequate to occupy all of Britain's savings. Mid-twentieth-century studies of nineteenth- and twentieth-century technical change and productivity growth have often identified a British climacteric, starting either in the late 1870s or at the turn of the nineteenth century.[4] Frequently disputed, these studies may be thought to provide empirical evidence for the diminishing returns argument. Whether, in fact, this or any other potential source of diminished domestic opportunities affected the rate of return to British assets has yet to be tested. Strikingly, there has been no comprehensive empirical investigation of rates of return to home and overseas British assets covering the full 1870–1913 period.[5]

A second view favoring a domestic impulse for the massive capital outflow is most frequently associated with J. A. Hobson's work on underconsumption (1894:179–204, 1902:91, 99). Earlier in the nineteenth century Sismondi and Marx suggested that underconsumption played an important causal role in the business cycle.[6] Indeed, both Sismondi and Marx thought underconsumption might lead to foreign investment. However, Hobson, writing at the turn of the nineteenth century, gave the fullest articulation of the connection between underconsumption and foreign investment. And it is Hobson's views that occupy a central and largely unaltered role in Lenin's famous pamphlet on the origins and structure of early twentieth-century European imperialism (1915:216).

Hobson held that, because too little of the national income of Britain was allocated to wage earners who did most of the nation's consumption and too much to property owners who did most of the nation's savings, there was a strong tendency for a prosperous Britain to generate too little consumption and too much savings. The crucial assumption was that a substantial portion of British savings were sensitive to the factor income distribution but insensitive to rates of return. Given this invariance to rates of return and a tendency to generate too much savings, funds were inevitably pushed abroad searching for any sort of placement. Curiously, despite volumes on the theory and measurement of consumption behavior since Keynes brought the various components of aggregate demand into the center stage of business cycle behavior, Hobson's views have rarely been explicitly tested and never during the period with which he was most concerned, the decades around the turn of the nineteenth century. (An exception is Nemmers 1956).

The third and final stream of thought favoring a domestic explanation argues that British investors and capital market institutions were biased toward overseas borrowers and assets. As part of the Report of the Committee on Finance and Industry of 1931 (the Macmillian Report), it was argued that in the 1920s Britain's central capital market in London had limited facilities to aid medium-sized British manufacturing firms. As is sometimes the case, an idea concerned with one period crept into the interpretation of an earlier period. In 1965 J. Saville (1961:57) made a strong case for similar institutional rigidity and bias during the 1870–1913 years. Saville argued that facilities available to satisfy the expanding needs of domestic industry in London were quite slow in developing and grossly inadequate relative to the facilities available to governments and public utilities, home and foreign. The large investment banks of Germany, one of Britain's strongest competitors, offered far superior service to German industry. In perhaps the most widely read recent interpretive essay on the industrial development of Western Europe since 1750, D. Landes concurred with Saville and hinted at the additional role of rigid habits of capital market facilities and investors.[7]

Importantly, the hypothesis of capital market rigidity and bias is logically separate from the views that capital flowed abroad because of tendencies toward low domestic returns or too much savings. The latter hypotheses are essentially concerned with demand failure; the capital market rigidity and bias hypothesis is concerned with institutional failure. Taken solely on its own ground, the implication of the capital market failure hypothesis is that, in the absence of institutional rigidity and investor bias, there would have been plenty of domestic investment projects waiting to be serviced.

More recently, it has been argued that British investors were biased toward safety, not overseas assets per se. Inefficient diversification of high-risk projects led to the flow of funds toward conservative overseas investments (Kennedy 1974, 1976). Inefficient diversification of high-risk projects was and remains an important problem for all capital markets, largely the result of poor and unequal access to information about alternative investment opportunities. The contribution of the large investment banks in Germany and certain ramshackle arrangements in the United States was their role in diversifying the high risks of *some* technologically progressive firms, albeit ignoring many other firms and some entire regions. However, according to Kennedy, British capital markets were quite segmented; few, if any banks, investment houses, mutual funds, insurance companies, etc., attempted to surmount this segmentation through diversification or intermediation activities; the result was the insufficient funding of new industries such as electricity and automobiles.

The question remains, however, why such diversifying institutions did not bloom in Britain. One possibility is that the British public was so risk averse that financial intermediaries offering diversification of high risks had no market for their services.

Another plausible hypothesis is that there were so few risky domestic firms offering high, risk-adjusted returns that neither financial innovators nor the British public were strongly tempted. Finally, it is possible that domestic industry did not need special institutional arrangements, because retained earnings, private sources, and public capital markets left domestic industry relatively well funded. Obviously, each of these possibilities has quite different implications for the role of institutional or investor bias in motivating foreign investment.

Against these several views of domestic push causation, there is a prominent argument that places reliance on overseas pull factors as the dominant cause of the export of capital from Britain. In brief, the unusually high profits of railroad and other social-overhead investments in the emerging primary product economies of North America, South America, South Africa, and Australasia pulled British savings abroad. More natural resources, transportation, and industrial projects with high returns appeared abroad than at home. An eighteenth- or nineteenth-century economist favoring this view would probably stress that regions of recent settlement were so empty of labor and capital, relative to natural resources, that they were subject to increasing, not decreasing, returns (e.g., A. Smith 1776:87, 92–95). Twentieth-century observers might concur to some extent and add that much technical progress was embodied in the capital involved in filling these relatively empty corners of the globe (Abramovitz and David 1973). Some evidence on the timing of overseas investments in the United States and Australia suggests that overseas factors may have dominated the British capital outflow.[8] However, some of these tests are incomplete and subject to conflicting interpretation and thus suggest the need for further work. Furthermore, as noted earlier, there has been little direct study of rates of return to determine whether, in fact, overseas rates of return manifested eruptively high levels.

The purpose of this volume is to explore the motivations of Britain's capital export in the late nineteenth and early twentieth centuries. Toward that end chapter 2 continues this introduction by gathering together the main quantitative facts concerning the size, timing, and character of the capital export, 1860–1914. The general concern of part II is the microeconomics of British capital exports. Chapter 3 focuses on the institutional setting of British capital exports with particular emphasis on testing the hypothesis that the unusual size of Britain's capital export was due to certain biases in the organization of Britain's capital markets and investors. Chapter 4 quantifies the microeconomic behavioral structure of Britain's overseas investment. Primary attention is placed on the largest single borrower, the railway system of the United States. Using econometric techniques, an attempt is made to identify and weight the unique British and U.S. microeconomic forces governing the transfer. These results are then compared with what is known of the transfer to other major overseas receivers. Chapters 5 and 6 are concerned with one of the most important issues on the understanding of the capital export, the rate of return on home and overseas investment. The contribution of these chapters is to offer for the first time a consistent measure of returns covering a wide swath of home and overseas financial assets.

Part III considers the macroeconomic forces governing the aggregate long-term rate of U.K. net foreign lending. In chapter 7 a general model of national savings, overseas investment, and domestic investment is introduced. The principal theories offered to motivate the rise of overseas investment in the late nineteenth century—diminishing domestic investment opportunities, oversaving, and escalating overseas investment opportunities—are cast in terms of this simple model and their aggregate behavioral underpinnings are discussed. In chapter 8, the character of U.K. national savings behavior is specified and Hobson's theory of oversaving as a cause of the period's capital outflow is tested. Chapter 9 examines the role of domestic investment and return in aiding and abetting the flow of overseas lending. In chapters 10, 11, and 12, the influence of United States, Australian, and Canadian aggregate accumulation pressures on U.K. overseas lending is investigated. The various threads are drawn together in a chronological survey in chapter 13.

CHAPTER 2: **OVERSEAS INVESTMENT DURING THE PAX BRITANNICA: Size, Timing, and Character**

THE ORIGINS

Little is known about the exact size, timing, and character of British long-term lending to overseas regions prior to the nineteenth century. Rough evidence suggests, that, starting in the early seventeenth century, joint stock trading and colonizing companies, interloping merchants, and wealthy agrarians gathered a certain amount of long-term funds for overseas warehouses, shipping, port facilities, slaves, and plantations, located for the most part in the newly acquired East and West Indian colonies. The annual flow of these long-term overseas placements was regularly interrupted by the period's many wars with Holland, France, Spain, and Portugal, as well as the English Civil War of the mid-seventeenth century.

In the longer run, however, the pace and size of the overseas accumulation was most strongly tied to the success of British arms in these foreign wars and the extent of the European and North American market for sugar, coffee, spices, cotton, and other raw materials produced in the East and West Indies. Mercantilist policies in the colonial regions and the uncertain quality of foreign justice seem to have made sovereignty a necessary condition for these transoceanic direct investments; the literature of seventeenth- and eighteenth-century colonial development rarely speaks of British capital in Dutch or other's overseas colonies or vice versa. During these centuries it is likely that Britons also held a certain amount of foreign securities. London merchants and wealth were in fairly constant contact with Amsterdam, the principal international market for short-term capital and interest-bearing long-term debt of European governments. As a very rough guess Feinstein estimates that the stock of these overseas direct and portfolio placements may have amounted to £10–15 million by 1760, perhaps 1 percent of the nation's total assets.[1]

Nevertheless, Great Britain was probably a net debtor on

international account for most of the seventeenth and eighteenth centuries. The Dutch and other Europeans were substantial holders of the British government's debts both before and after its consolidation in the late seventeenth century. Furthermore, they were also equity participants in the British East India Company, founded in 1600, and the Bank of England, chartered in 1694. Various contemporary sources lead Feinstein to estimate Dutch and other foreign holdings at £30–35 million in 1760 (1978:71). Thus, at that date Britain was a net debtor of roughly £20 million and there is much evidence to suggest that this net debtor position characterized the British international position for at least the previous century or more.

Between 1760 and 1800 the *net* flow of international funds seems to have been strongly outward. Indeed, it is probably during these years that Great Britain became a net creditor on international account. By capitalizing the value of some rough estimates of property income from abroad, c. 1800, Feinstein finds that the £10–15 million of British holdings in 1760 grew to perhaps £35–40 million in 1800 (*Ibid.*). Furthermore, a number of contemporary sources suggest that foreign holdings of British assets diminished, dropping from £30–35 million in 1760 to perhaps £25–30 million in 1800. The net effect was therefore to turn Britain into a net creditor on international account to the extent of some £10 million, c. 1800. Using these stock estimates for 1760 and 1800, Feinstein hazards the guess that, although net foreign lending was negligible in the 1760s, annual net foreign lending averaged around 1 percent of Britain's annual gross domestic product, 1770–1800.

Importantly, these decades are often given as the strongest sustained period of British industrial and income growth in the eighteenth century. There is some evidence that a period of sustained growth in income per head occurred in the 1740s and 1750s, but the growth rates of the latter quarter of the eighteenth century were faster and their industrial base somewhat firmer (Deane and Cole 1969:80; Crafts 1976). From the late seventeenth century British trade with the Continent and her overseas colonies had been expanding, and there is good evidence that this participation in international trade accelerated in the 1780s and

1790s after the temporary downturn occasioned by the American War (Deane and Cole 1969:48–49). Any fair reading of the causes of the British Industrial Revolution would treat this eighteenth-century trade growth and its acceleration after 1780 as one of several causes and, certainly, an important effect of the surge in industrial output and incomes.[2] The growth of Britain's markets abroad afforded greater specialization and scale economies in certain British regions, and, along with Britain's military successes, technical change—partly induced by prior increases in market size—augmented overseas markets. Furthermore, population growth from the 1740s and increasing average incomes of some Britons dating from these same years meant a growing market for Continental and colonial producers in Britain.

The pace and character of these developments in trade, production, and military affairs could not help but influence the size of the market for British borrowers, lenders, and finanical intermediaries. Indeed, the extent and variety of London's financial services accelerated from the late 1760s, accompanied by a lessening segmentation of London's various short-and long-term financial markets (John 1953; Joslin 1954–1955; Eagly and Smith 1976:206). Additionally, Britain's wars in the late 1770s and 1790s and Holland's in the early 1780s and 1790s may have meant that British merchants had less access to the premier European money market in Amsterdam.[3] Thus, owing to these developments in trade, production, and finance across the eighteenth century and their acceleration in the last quarter of the century, it is very likely that an important part of the surging net outflow of British savings, 1770–1800, was in the form of much larger *British* participation in the *short-term* funding of Britian's burgeoning bilateral and multilateral trade. Certainly, there is strong qualitative evidence that British trade credits were central to the renewed growth of Chesapeake tobacco and British West Indian sugar after the conclusion of the American War, and Georgia and South Carolina cotton in the 1790s (Price 1973:733–35; Edwards 1967:83–96). Furthermore, these American and West Indian developments in trade and production were accompanied by expanded imports of slaves, a trade dominated by British merchants and credit (Curtin 1969:140).

How much of the 1770–1800 net outflow of capital constituted long-term commitments is conjectural. Surely, some of the continued growth of British West Indian exports reflects more plantation and slave investments not covered by colonial retained earnings and British trade credits, particularly the expansion of British West Indian cotton growing in the 1780s and early 1790s (Edwards 1967:83–96; Curtin 1969; 140). However, there is no evidence of an important British presence in the early long-term funding of the very rapid expansion of cotton plantations and slave holdings in the Georgia and South Carolina uplands following Whitney's invention of the cotton gin in 1793. D. North finds a significant U.S. capital import averaging perhaps £370,000 per year, 1790–1799, the overwhelming proportion funded by Britain (1960:587–88, 600). However, this U.S. capital import could easily be renewed trade credits in tobacco, new trade credits for upland Georgia and South Carolina cotton, and 1- to 2-year credits for slave imports into Georgia, South Carolina, and elsewhere. Some 80,000 slaves were imported, 1790–1800.[4] With slave prices averaging £45–50, credit for slave imports, and short-term funding of American international trade, there was probably little long-term participation (equity, mortgages) by British capital in America.

Thus, although there is little exact evidence on the size, direction, or character of Feinstein's late-eighteenth-century surge in net foreign lending, some useful conjectures do emerge from existing materials. It is likely the bulk of the outflow was short term, funding the accelerating level of Britain's international trade activities. The destination of any upsurge in long-term placements was probably the British West Indies; certainly some long-term funds flowed into new West Indian cotton plantations and slaves. Finally, at least part of this upsurge in net foreign lending involved a displacement of Dutch participation in British trade credit, based partly on the steady rise of British commercial and agricultural wealth, the growth and articulation of British financial institutions, and perhaps the deflection of older financial links with Holland during the period's various wars.

Considerable controversy surrounds the contribution of these overseas accumulations to the development of the domestic economy in the seventeenth and eighteenth centuries (Dobb 1947, ch. 5; Crouzet 1972:175-76; Cameron 1967:65). Clearly, if money from foreign investments was involved in the earliest stages of the British Industrial Revolution, say, in the four decades on either side of 1760, it was probably balanced *in the aggregate* by outflows of dividend and interest payments to the Continent. Given Feinstein's estimates of the 1760 international balance sheet, the rate of return on British holdings abroad would have to have been more than 2.5 times the rate of return earned by foreigners on British assets in order for the profits of Britain's overseas holdings to have a *net* impact on national totals of funds potentially available for investment in Britain's economy. Such a ratio is not implausible given that British-owned overseas assets were mostly in risky plantations, slave capital, and inventories, while foreign holdings of British assets were overwhelmingly in the British National Debt, whose yield hovered around 4 percent, 1740-1780 (Mitchell 1962:455). However, for the *net* flow of property income to have contributed, for example, 1 percent of gross domestic product, the rate of return on overseas holdings would have been near 20 percent on average.

Clearly, a 20 percent rate of return might have characterized the more successful overseas operations and trading expeditions, but did it characterize any substantial aggregate? Recent research on the average rate of return to the plantations and slave capital of the British West Indies places the average annual rate of return somewhere between 4 percent and 8 percent, exclusive of capital gains, c. 1775 (Sheridan 1968:56; R.P. Thomas 1968:34, 36). Slave prices in the American South and the British West Indies were fairly stable in the first half of the eighteenth century and then rose steadily (USBC 1975:1174). From 1748-52 to 1773-75, one source of price data suggests that the rate of capital gain was around 2 percent per annum. Thus, the most plausible upper bound for the realized rate of return on capital placed in the British West Indies was approximately 10 percent per annum, c. 1775. On the assumption that this 10 percent rate of return held for all other British-held assets abroad, the rate of return to the latter was roughly 2.5 times the rate of return to foreigner's holdings of British Consols, just that ratio that would mean the gross flows of property income in and out of Britain roughly balanced.

If the evidence that overseas profits had a powerful *net* aggregate effect on British savings supplies is called into question by these numbers, then it might be argued that the special role accorded overseas profits really stems from the fact that they were a concentrated potential source of savings in a period when capital markets in Great Britain were segmented heavily along geographic, social, and industrial lines.[5] Given this segmentation, it thus becomes important that the funds from abroad may have concentrated to an important extent in and around London, Bristol, Liverpool, Glasgow, and other western outports.[6] Furthermore, these ports had extensive trading and financial connections with their immediate hinterlands where much manufacturing in Britain took place (Edwards 1967; Minchinton 1954:78, 82–85).

Pollard's research has stressed the relatively small proportion of the early cotton and iron firms involved in fixed capital and the large amounts of short-term capital tied up in inventories of raw materials, goods-in-process, and finished items (1964). Hence, even though aggregate flows of property income from the colonies may have been counterbalanced by the outflow of interest to the Continent, some of the flows from the colonies landed in close proximity, geographically, socially, and industrially, to the growth sectors of the British economy and probably in some amount were used to fund inventory capital, if not fixed captial.[7] How much of the capital formation in Britain's growth sectors was funded from this source is quite uncertain. Given the lack of evidence on overseas and home mercantile short-term credit networks, no clear answer may ever emerge. It is well to remember, however, that the overseas commodity and slave trades of the middle and late eighteenth century were quite profitable and expanding. This probably meant high rates of reinvestment of profits within the trades. Hence, it is likely that only a fraction of overseas profits was shunted out of the trades and, then too, the new manufacturing sectors in and around the thriving British ports would be only one of a large number of alternative placements.

One must ask, of course, how imperfect British capital markets were in the third quarter of the eighteenth century. In a sense, to say there are segmented capital markets is to say that the rates of return to mobilizing capital across social groupings, industries, and regions were too low to evoke rapid development of new financial intermediaries and institutions to achieve the mobilization. Some barriers were slowly being eroded by a few banks before 1750 (Mathias, 1969:165–78; Anderson 1972:223–56). Might they have been eroded quicker without the hypothesized profits from abroad? Or, more specifically, would the country banks have developed sooner if the overseas profits that landed in England, Wales, and Scotland had been somewhat more restricted? The rapid development of the country banks after 1750 suggests high banking profits and an elastic supply of founding capital. (Pressnell 1956). The country banks were not a radical institutional solution in an environment of financial market backwardness. Essentially, the country bank movement was the diffusion to the countryside of an institution well known in London and the large towns. Hence, it seems reasonable to suggest that, whatever the role of overseas profits in funding some plants and inventories at some locations during the early British Industrial Revolution, neither the amount nor location was essential to the timing of the event.[8]

THE VOLUME AND RATE OF FOREIGN INVESTMENT IN THE NINETEENTH CENTURY

The various elements of Britain's nineteenth-century international capital transactions may be usefully displayed in the following accounting identity:

+ (annual purchases of foreign securities by individuals and firms resident in Britain)
− (annual sales of previously held foreign securities to residents of foreign countries by individuals and firms resident in Britain)
+ (annual direct investments abroad by individuals and firms resident in Britain)
− (annual direct and portfolio investment in Britain by residents of foreign countries)
+ (annual short-term lending to residents of foreign countries by individuals and firms resident in Britain)

- (annual short-term lending to residents of Britain by individuals and firms residents in foreign countries)
= (the *total net annual outflow* of British savings into foreign assets)

Unlike the state of knowledge of British foreign investment in the seventeenth and eighteenth centuries, our understanding of nineteenth-century capital exports benefits from good primary data sources and their thorough examination by several generations of scholars. These primary data sources permit the construction of annual series on the first item, annual purchases of foreign securities by individuals and firms resident in Britain, 1865–1914, and the last item, the total net annual outflow of British savings into foreign assets. Somewhat poorer data permit crude guesses at various dates of the remaining items.

Starting publication in 1864, *The Investor's Monthly Manual* presented monthly data on the total nominal value of new home and overseas security issues ("creations") offered in London and separate information on calls for cash payments ("money calls"). Just before World War I Paish and C. K. Hobson assembled these monthly data into annual series, C. K. Hobson extending his investigations back to 1870.[9] More recently, Simon sought to include new security offerings issued elsewhere in Great Britain and British subscriptions to new issues offered in foreign capital markets, to exclude all new issue sales placed with foreigners (1967). The result of his prodigious labors is a good estimate of the overwhelming majority of annual purchases of new foreign security issues by individuals and firms resident in Britain, 1865–1914, nominally valued (figure 2.1). The main drawback of Simon's estimates is that they are valued in nominal terms, not at the actual price paid by the first British purchaser. Securities were often sold at a discount, sometimes quite substantial. Thus, in a sense, Simon's series is conceptually closer to *ex ante* desired offerings than it is to executed market sales. Correcting for this factor would probably lower Simon's totals somewhat and increase their annual variability, but it would not significantly alter their trend or cycle timing. In any event, Simon found that the accumulated total of new issues, 1865–1914, came to £4082 million. This estimate is somewhat larger than Hobson's less comprehensive estimates, but it accords well with the estimates of

Figure 2.1

OVERSEAS INVESTMENT, 1816-1913

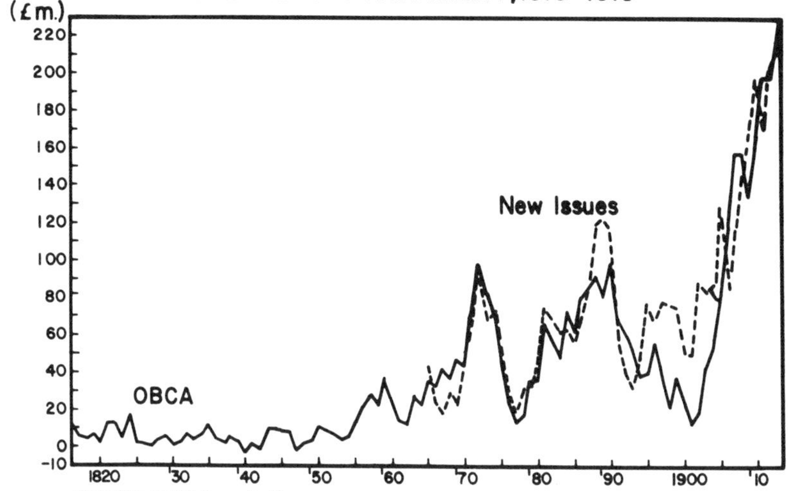

SOURCES: OBCA: Appendix I.
New Issues: Simon 1967: Table II.

the stock of British-held foreign securities in 1914 found in Paish and Feis.[10]

Although there are no annual estimates of the other items comprising the *total net annual outflow* of British savings into foreign assets, an indirect method is available. Government statistics and other sources allow the rough construction of all noncapital items in the international balance of payments, 1815–1914. The summation of these items leaves a residual that is commonly termed net foreign investment (NFI). If net annual additions to bullion reserves (G & S) are subtracted from NFI, the remaining figure is the net annual outflow of British savings into foreign assets, more usually termed the overall balance on current account (OBCA). C. K. Hobson produced a rough estimate of OBCA, annually, 1870–1912, from data on exports and imports of goods and services (including shipping services and earnings) and a crude guess at net property income from abroad (NIPA) based on Inland Revenue schedules (1914:164–205, esp. 204). In a Ph.D. thesis submitted to Cambridge University in 1935 and published in 1953, Cairncross revised C. K. Hobson's estimates of shipping

earnings and NPIA (1953:170-81). The most authoritative estimates of both NFI and OBCA are due to the work of Imlah
published in 1958 and revised in minor ways by Feinstein in 1972
and 1976. Imlah thoroughly reworked the 1870-1914 materials
and extended the various series back to 1815.[11] Feinsteins'
revisions affected the estimates of bullion accumulation, 1830-
1860, and NFI, 1899-1913 (1978:72; 1972:T37-38. The Imlah/
Feinstein estimate of the net annual outflow of British savings
into foreign assets (OBCA) is shown with Simon's new issue totals
in figure 2.1.

The first conclusion that emerges from figure 2.1 and other
materials is that total net overseas lending across the nineteenth
century was dominated by the purchase of long-term negotiable
securities. Although there are no *annual* data for new long-term
security issues, 1815-1865, Jenks estimated that the stock of
British-held overseas securities increased by £75-88 m., 1815-
1830, and with further purchases the outstanding stock of British-
held overseas securities stood at £195-230 m. in 1854 (1927:356-57,
412-13). The Imlah/Feinstein OBCA estimates show an accumulating sum of £100..7 m., 1815-1830, and a further increase of £116
m., 1831-1854.[12] The rough equivalence of these movements is
clear. The annual data presented in figure 2.1 suggest that, from
1865 to 1913, both the trend and the longer sweeps of new overseas
issues and the OBCA were quite close. Simon's estimate of total
new issues, 1865-1913, is £3878.6 m., while the accumulated sum
of Imlah/Feinstein's OBCA estimates over the same years is £3487
m.[13] Since at least part of this difference is due to the nominal
valuation of the new issue data and its likely overestimation of
actual sterling transactions, the rough equivalence in size and
timing of new long-term security issues and net overseas lending
for the 1865-1913, as well as 1815-1865, indicates that long-term
securities were the largest part of net foreign lending.

Perhaps the best evidence for the importance of new long-term
security purchases in the net flow of British savings abroad in the
nineteenth century stems from various rough estimates of the
stock of international short-term credits and liabilities. At one
time it was widely held that Britain's holdings of short-term assets
exceeded its short-term liabilities by a wide margin, and this

implied that Britain was a large net international creditor on short-term, as well as long-term, account (Great Britain 1931). Clearly, Britain was the world's largest *gross* short-term creditor. "Its short term overseas assets consisted primarily of acceptance claims on foreigners representing commercial and financial bills that had been accepted by London houses on their behalf . . . ," perhaps amounting to £215 m. just before WW I (Bloomfield 1963:71–72).

Far less is known about the extent of Britain's position as a short-term debtor. Britain had short-term liabilities in the form of foreign holdings of sterling bills, short-term loans to the London discount market, and colonial and foreign deposits in London banks. British-based data on these liabilities are limited, but in independent investigations Bloomfield and Lindert found useful information in the banking records of other nations. Both authors concluded that British short-term liabilities were quite substantial; indeed, the data presented by Bloomfield and Lindert permit a guess that gross British short-term liabilities totaled more than £100 m. at the end of 1913 (Bloomfield 1963:71–73; Lindert 1969:16–27). Hence, the *net* short-term credit position in 1913 was approximately £100 m. When it is considered that the total *net*, short- and long-term, stock of British overseas holdings estimated from OBCA data suggests a sum of £3932m. in 1913, and Simon's estimates of total money calls on new issues of overseas securities was £3878.6m., 1865–1913,[14] it seems quite clear that the overwhelming proportion of Britian's nineteenth- and early twentieth-century net placements abroad took the form of long-term negotiable assets.

Still, the discrepancy between new issues and the OBCA shown in figure 2.1 suggests that short-term and perhaps other long-term financing movements did not always take a minor role in the movements of the OBCA. Indeed, the timing of these decrepancies between the new issue and OBCA data suggests their proximal source. First, and probably most important, Lindert's study of key currencies in the pre-WW I decades shows that world accumulation of key foreign exchange currencies was unusually rapid, 1895–1905, precisely the years of the largest discrepency between new long-term issues and net foreign lending shown in figure 2.1

(Lindert 1969:24). Since sterling represented perhaps 40 percent to 50 percent of the world's foreign exchange reserves (Lindert 1969:18–19), it is reasonable to hypothesize that these years saw an unusual growth of short-term lending by overseas residents to Great Britain. This hypothesis is bolstered by the fact that a substantial number of colonial, American, and other foreign banks opened branches in London during these years. Thus, an unusually rapid accumulation of short-term liabilities seems a reasonable explanation for the largest and longest discrepancy in the new-issue and OBCA data of figure 2.1. Another contributing factor might have been repatriation of outstanding American railway issues. The reorganization of the American railway system in the early 1890s and the subsequent decision of several large American railways to increase dividend payout rates made American railway stocks and bonds very attractive, reasonably stable investments for American insurance companies and rentiers in the halcyon days of the turn-of-the-century American merger movement.

A second major conclusion illustrated by figure 2.1 is the break in the pace of overseas lending in the third quarter of the nineteenth century. From the Peace of Vienna to the midcentury the annual net outflow of British savings into overseas assets (OBCA) dawdled along with no apparent growth in volume over the trade cycle. Then, starting sometime in the mid-1850s the net outflow into overseas assets entered a period of sustained and rapid growth, possibly gaining momentum as World War I approached. In current prices the average annual net outflow of British savings into overseas assets (OBCA) hovered in the range of £4–6 m. from 1821 to 1850 (table 2.1). In the 1850s the average net outflow tripled; it doubled again in the 1860s; and then, from the 1870s to World War I, with some fluctuation, the average once again doubled. The deflated series shows the same trends (table 2.2).

A similar pattern appears when the net annual outflow is viewed in proportion to either gross national product (Y) or gross national savings and investment (GNA). Somewhat above 1 percent in the 1820–1850 period, OBCA/Y jumped to 2.8 percent in the 1850s, to 3.1 percent in the 1860s, and thereafter averaged 4.5

Table 2.1

Home and Foreign Investment, Savings, and National Income,
by Decade, 1831–1910
(current prices, millions of £ per annum)

Decade	Y	GNA	GDFI	II	NFI	OBCA	NPIA	GPS	GS
					Great Britain				
1831–40	371.7	46.5	38.5	3.5	4.5	4.5	6.7	--	--
1841–50	458.5	61.0	49.5	5.0	6.5	5.3	8.5	--	--
1851–60	609.1	81.5	58.0	3.5	20.0	17.1	14.1	--	--
					United Kingdom				
1861–70	1003.6	129.3	82.1	10.0	37.2	31.3	26.2	120.4	8.9
1871–80	1277.4	194.4	124.7	17.5	52.2	49.6	53.1	182.9	11.5
1881–90	1360.2	192.4	102.5	15.0	74.9	74.2	74.3	178.7	13.7
1891–1900	1634.2	216.2	145.4	21.0	49.8	44.6	97.2	200.5	15.7
1901–10	2085.7	297.2	190.2	9.5	97.5	94.5	132.0	284.7	12.5

Abbreviations: Y = gross national product; GNA = gross national investment = gross national savings;
GDFI = gross domestic fixed investment; II = net inventory investment; NFI = net foreign investment; OBCA = overall balance on current account (= NFI – increase in gold stock); NPIA = net
property income from abroad; GPS = gross private savings (= GNA–GS); GS = gross government saving.

Sources:
Y: 1831–60. Gross domestic product from Feinstein 1978: 91, plus NIPA (see below). 1861–1910.
    See Appendix 1.
GNA: GDFI + II + NFI.
GDFI, II, NFI: 1831–60. Feinstein 1978: 69, 91. 1861–1910. See Appendix 1.
NPIA, OBCA: 1831–60. Imlah 1958: 70–2, 1861–1910. See Appendix 1.
GPS: GNA – GS.
GS: See Appendix 2.

Table 2.2

Real Home and Foreign Investment, Real Savings, and Real National Income, by Decade, 1821-1910

(various price indices, 1900 = 100, millions of £ per annum)

Decade	y	gna	gdfi	ii	nfi	obca	npia	gps	gs
Great Britain									
1831-40	386.7	50.0	43.5	2.5	4.0	4.0	4.4	--	--
1841-50	477.4	64.9	55.7	3.5	5.7	4.8	6.1	--	--
1851-60	632.7	84.7	64.6	2.5	17.6	15.0	9.5	--	--
United Kingdom									
1861-70	954.6	137.5	89.8	7.0	40.7	34.2	17.3	129.1	8.4
1871-80	1193.1	187.4	123.3	12.5	51.6	49.0	36.0	176.8	10.6
1881-90	1283.8	210.4	115.1	11.5	83.8	83.3	62.5	194.9	15.5
1891-1900	1727.1	242.7	164.4	22.0	56.3	50.4	96.0	225.0	17.7
1901-10	2082.8	320.5	205.6	9.5	105.4	102.2	123.1	307.4	13.1

Abbreviations: Same as table 2.1, the lower case lettering indicating real (price deflated) quantities.

Sources:

y: 1831-60. Gross domestic product (GDP) from Feinstein 1978: 91 deflated by Deane's 1968: 104-7 implicit gnp deflator, plus npia (see below). 1861-70. gdp from the compromise index in Feinstein 1972: T18 corrected for Feinstein 1973, plus npia (see below). 1871-1910. Feinstein 1972: T14-5, corrected for Feinstein (1979).

gna: = gdfi + ii + nfi.

gdfi: 1831-60. Feinstein (1978: 91) deflated by Deane's (1968, 104-7) implicit gdfi deflator. 1861-1910. Feinstein 1972: T88-9 corrected by Feinstein 1979.

Table 2.2 (cont.)

Sources (cont.):

ii: 1831-60: Feinstein 1978: 69, deflated by Rousseau's wholesale price index (WPI) in Mitchell 1962: 473. 1861-70. See Appendix 1, deflated by Rousseau's WPI. 1871-1910. Feinstein 1972: T14-5.

nfi: 1831-60. Feinstein 1978, 69, deflated by Rousseau's WPI. 1861-70. Imlah 1958: 70-72 deflated by Rousseau's WPI. 1871-1910. NFI from Table 2.1 deflated by the implicit gdfi deflator of Tables 2.1 and 2.2

obca: 1831-70. Imlah 1958: 70-72. deflated by Rousseau's WPI. 1871-1910. OBCA from Table 2.1 deflated by the implicit deflator of gdfi of Tables 2.1 and 2.2.

npia: 1831-70. Imlah 1958: 70-72,96-97. 1871-1910. Feinstein 1972: T14-5.

gps, gs: GPS and GS of Table 2.1, deflated by Table 2.1 and 2.2's implicit gna deflator (GNA/gna).

Table 2.3

The Rate of Home Investment, Foreign Investment and Savings
in Current Prices, 1831-1910
(%)

Decade	GNA/Y	GDFI/Y	II/Y	NFI/Y	OBCA/Y	NPIA/Y	GPS/Y	GS/Y
				Great Britain				
1831-40	12.5	10.5	0.9	1.2	1.2	1.8	--	--
1841-50	13.3	10.8	1.1	1.4	1.2	1.9	--	--
1851-60	13.4	9.5	0.6	3.3	2.8	2.3	--	--
				United Kingdom				
1861-70	12.9	8.2	1.0	3.7	3.1	2.6	12.0	0.9
1871-80	15.2	9.8	1.4	4.1	3.9	4.2	14.3	0.9
1881-90	14.1	7.5	1.1	5.5	5.5	5.5	13.1	1.0
1891-1900	13.2	8.9	1.3	3.0	2.7	5.9	12.3	0.9
1901-10	14.2	9.1	0.5	4.7	4.5	6.3	13.6	0.6

Source: Table 2.1

percent with some fluctuation (table 2.3 and 2.4). By employing the numbers found in table 2.1, it is possible to calculate the proportion of overseas asset formation in national savings and investment (OBCA/GNA). In the 1830s and 1840s the OBCA averaged around 10 percent of gross national savings and investment. This proportion jumped to around 20 percent in the 1850s and then to 25 percent in the 1860s. From the 1870s to 1913 it averaged around one-third of gross savings and investment of the United Kingdom.

The effect of this break on the composition of British wealth was quite striking (table 2.5). If the proportion of net annual overseas asset formation in national savings and investment (OBCA/GNA) is relatively fixed over a long period of time, the proportion of overseas assets in total national wealth will eventually approach and hold that rate. Hence, it is likely that at the midcentury overseas assets were approximately 10 percent of national wealth. However, as just noted, OBCA/GNA began to rise in the 1850s, hitting a plateau of one-third from the 1870s to 1913 with some fluctuation. With some lag as expected, the proportion of overseas assets in national wealth also rose, reaching 30 percent just before World War I.

The facts seem quite clear; based on historical patterns British capital exports moved to unprecedented levels in the late nineteenth and early twentieth centuries. Measured in absolute value or relative to national product, accumulation, or wealth, the third quarter of the nineteenth century saw a break from a dawdling plateau of net capital export going back at least to the late eighteenth century. And, in the fourth quarter of the nineteenth century and the first decade of the twentieth century, capital export volumes and rates moved even higher.

As noted in chapter 1, France appeared as a capital exporter in the second third of the nineteenth century and Germany somewhat later in the 1880s. By the late nineteenth century the average rate of French capital export was 2 to 3 percent of national product; the German rate was somewhat less than 2 percent. Although little is known about the exact volumes of capital export from Belgium, the Netherlands, and Switzerland, there seems little doubt that these nations also became net capital ex-

Table 2.4

The Rate of Home Investment, Foreign Investment and Savings
in Constant Prices, 1831-1913
(%)

Decade	gna/y	gdfi/y	ii/y	nfi/y	obca/y	npia/y	gps/y	gs/y
				Great Britain				
1831-40	12.9	11.2	0.6	1.0	1.0	1.1	--	--
1841-50	13.6	11.7	0.7	1.2	1.0	1.3	--	--
1851-60	13.4	10.2	0.4	2.8	2.4	1.5	--	--
				United Kingdom				
1861-70	14.4	9.4	0.7	4.3	3.6	1.8	13.5	0.9
1871-80	15.7	10.3	1.0	4.3	4.1	3.0	14.8	0.9
1881-90	16.4	9.0	0.9	6.5	6.5	4.9	15.2	1.2
1891-1900	14.1	9.5	1.3	3.3	2.9	5.6	13.0	1.0
1901-10	15.4	9.9	0.5	5.1	4.9	5.9	14.8	0.6

Source: Table 2.2

Table 2.5

The Stock of Home and Overseas Wealth, 1815-1913

(1) Years	(2) GDK	(3) ANFI	(4) AG&S	(5) AOBCA	(6) W (2)+(3)	(7) ANFI/W (3)/(6)	(8) AOBCA/W (5)/(6)
				(current prices, £m.)			
1815	–	55	45	10	–	–	–
1830	–	171	60	111	–	–	–
1860	3380	470	100	370	3850	0.122	0.196
1870	3960	838	156	682	4798	0.175	0.142
1880	4750	1360	181	1179	6110	0.223	0.193
1890	5010	2109	188	1921	7119	0.296	0.270
1900	6650	2607	239	2368	9257	0.282	0.256
1910	7310	3582	270	3312	10892	0.329	0.304
1913	8500	4224	292	3932	12724	0.332	0.309

Abbreviations: GDK = gross domestic fixed capital stock at current replacement cost; ANFI = accumulated net foreign lending; AG&S = accumulated bullion; AOBCA = accumulated overall balance on current account (= accumulated net overseas asset holdings). Note: ANFI = AG&S + AOBCA.

Sources:

Col. (2). GDK. Feinstein 1972: T103-4.

Col. (3). ANFI. 1815: £10m. in net overseas assets Imlah 1958: 70 plus £45m. in bullion. 1830-1880: Accumulating annual NFI of Imlah on the 1815 stock. 1890-1913: Accumulating annual NFI of Feinstein 1972: T14-5, on the 1880 stock.

Col. (4). AG&S. 1815: An estimated based on Feinstein 1976: 67-8; the same figure of £45m. arises if one accepts Feinstein's firm figure for 1830 and decumulates with Imlah's 1958: 70 annual bullion data. 1830-1860: Feinstein 1976: 67-68. 1870-1913: Accumulating the annual bullion series of Imlah from the 1860 stock.

Col. (5). AOBCA. Col. (3) - Col. (4).

porters in the late nineteenth century (Woodruff 1966:150-51;155; Kuznets 1966; North 1962). It would thus appear that net capital exporting was a standard correlate of rapid nineteenth-century economic growth among the older economies of Europe. The rapid growers abroad such as the United States, Canada, Australia, and Argentina tended to be capital importers (Green and Urquhart 1976:244). However, these latter economies were regions of recent settlement, regions with no infrastructure investment and considerably higher rates of population growth than those of the European industrializers.

But even given this broader context, the volume and rate of British capital export in the late nineteenth century and early twentieth century is still quite exceptional. Indeed, in a sense an important concern of this study is to explain why the British rate so far exceeded the other European nations experiencing modern economic growth. Was it because Britons were much more involved in international trade, shipping, and overseas settlement than the other European industrializers and investment followed the British demand for overseas products? Certainly, the seventeenth- and eighteenth-century overseas investment evinced something like this pattern. Was it because greater participation in the international economy merely made Britons more aware of great opportunities abroad, regardless of the precise quantities of traded volumes or patterns of settlements? Or, perhaps the exceptional outflow of British savings betrayed something unique in the nature of the domestic British economy: low rates of return or biased and segmented capital markets? Clearly, the context of Britain's immense capital export in the late nineteenth and early twentieth centuries is not only Britain's own history with capital exporting but also its exceptional behavior in the broader framework of European and world modern economic growth.

LONG SWINGS, INVERSITY, AND THE RATE OF ACCUMULATION

Aggregate British overseas lending in the nineteenth and early twentieth centuries was quite volatile. From 1815 to 1860 or so this volatility took the form of repeating waves lasting between eight and eleven years. Starting sometime in the 1860s, however,

Table 2.6

Long Swing Dating

Phase	OBCA	New Issues
Trough	1862	–
Peak	1872	1872
Trough	1877	1877
Peak	1890	1889
Trough	1901	1901
Peak	1913	1913

Sources: OBCA. See Appendix 1.
         New Issues. Simon 1967: Table 1.

aggregate British overseas lending became subject to surges or swings of roughly double this duration. The new issue and OBCA data show close agreement on the dating of these long surges or swings (table 2.6). From 1815 to 1860 or so the range of OBCA from trough to peak of a typical cycle was perhaps zero to 3 percent of gross national product. In the period of long swings of 1860–1913, however, the typical trough-to-peak range was 6 to 7 percentage points of gross national product. Specifically, OBCA/Y went from troughs of 1.4 percent in 1862, 1.0 percent in 1877, and 0.7 percent in 1901, to peaks of 7.9 percent in 1872, 6.8 percent in 1890, and 8.8 percent in 1913 (see appendix 1).

Quite importantly, shortly after aggregate overseas investment moved into a pattern of long swings, aggregate domestic fixed capital formation also began to move in long swings. Equally important, the two aggregates moved inversely. This inverse long-swing motion is evident in their absolute values, but it is most striking in their ratios to gross national product shown in figure 2.2. Long swing troughs in the rate of gross domestic fixed capital formation occurred in 1869 (5.8 percent) and 1887 (5.8 percent), and peaks in 1876 (9.7 percent) and 1900 (10.3 percent). The turning points of domestic fixed investment and overseas investment were not perfectly matched; indeed, the peaks (and

Figure 2.2

U.K. RATES OF SAVING & INVESTMENT, 1856-1914

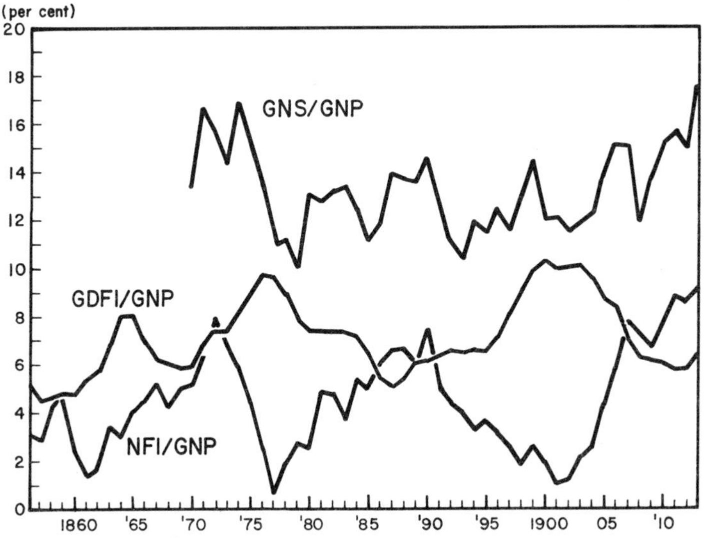

(per cent)

SOURCE: Appendix I.

troughs) in the rate of domestic fixed capital formation tended to lead the troughs (and peaks) of net overseas asset formation by one to three years. Nevertheless, in most years after 1870 the two series were moving in opposite directions; the simple correlation coefficient between the annual rates of overseas and home investment is -.77, 1870-1913. Clearly, the two aggregates were strikingly counterpoised.

The long swings in Britain's capital exports were positively correlated with long swings in British labor emigration; capital and labor inflows into the United States, Canada, Australia, and New Zealand; railway and urban residential capital formation in these overseas regions; and labor force formation rates in these regions.[15] There is also some evidence that, unlike the British case, long swings characterized the growth rate of national product in these regions of recent settlement. The U.S. experience with long swings in major components of gross national product stretches back into the second quarter of the nineteenth century, whereas in the other regions of recent settlement long swings started in the third quarter of the nineteenth century.

Table 2.7

Long Swing Expansions

A. Overseas Expansions

Phase	Year	NFI (£m.)	GNA' (£m.)	GNA (£m.)	NFI/Y	GNA'/Y	GNA/Y
T	1862	14	64	–	0.0158	0.0720	–
P	1872	97	188	198	0.0780	0.1511	0.1592
T	1877	10	130	140	0.0080	0.1039	0.1119
P	1890	107	196	211	0.0736	0.1347	0.1450
T	1901	19	216	241	0.0096	0.1086	0.1212
P	1913	235	394	440	0.0924	0.1550	0.1731

B. Home Expansions

Phase	Year	GDFI (£m.)	GNA' (£m.)	GNA (£m.)	GDFI/Y	GNA'/Y	GNA/Y
T	1869	59	110	(130)	0.0578	0.1078	0.1275
P	1876	124	155	170	0.0973	0.1217	0.1334
T	1887	68	156	186	0.0575	0.1164	0.1388
P	1900	199	233	233	0.1033	0.1210	0.1210

Source: Feinstein 1972: T8, T37.

An important issue of fact that follows from this international long-swing evidence is whether the British gross national savings rate was relatively fixed. Interest in this question stems from the possibility that the long-swing movements in either British home or overseas investment either caused or sharply emphasized the inverse long-swing motion of the other aggregate because of the constraint of a fixed British savings pool (Abramovitz 1968; B. Thomas 1954, 1972). Figure 2.2 displays the annual behavior of the gross national accumulation (savings and investment) rate, and table 2.7 presents data on the rates of net foreign lending, gross fixed domestic investment, and gross national accumulation during the three overseas and two domestic investment expansions, 1862–1913. As figure 2.2 illustrates, when both home and overseas investment was exceptionally high in the early 1910s, gross national accumulation was upward of 19 percent of gross national product. In between these two periods, the gross accumulation rate fluctuated in the range of 11 percent to 16 percent. Clearly, the rate of gross national savings was capable of wide fluctuation.

In pursuing the matter somewhat more closely, it is useful to ask whether the expansions in the net foreign lending rate or gross domestic fixed investment rate were accompanied by a fixed or expanding gross accumulation rate. The data of table 2.7 show that expansions of NFI/Y were not accompanied by a fixed GNA/Y. In the 1862–1872 and 1901–1913 expansions of NFI/Y, the savings rate (GNA/Y) moved up by roughly similar amounts as NFI/Y; in the 1877–1890 NFI/Y expansion, GNA/Y rose half as much as NFI/Y. Clearly, foreign investment was not bouncing against a fixed savings rate in its expansions, although there may have been some small constraining element in the expansion of the 1880s.

The long-swing expansions of domestic investment present a different story. In both domestic investment long-swing expansions, GNA/Y remained fairly fixed as GDFI/Y moved from trough to peak. Now, it is clear that the mere fact of a fixed savings rate during the periods of domestic investment expansion does not necessarily mean that it was this rate that caused the coinciding retreat of overseas investment. It is quite possible that overseas investment retreated for its own reasons. Pessimism with all foreign investment after the Baring Crisis of 1890 or an unusual drop in the profitability of major components of overseas investment are possible explanations.

Equally important, it should be asked why the savings rate seems to be proximally constraining in the expansions in the middle (1869–1876, 1877–1890, and 1887–1900) of the 1862–1913 period, regardless of the direction of investment, but not at the beginning or end. If the yield on Consols is assumed to act as the expected rate of return for the market as a whole, it is important that its movements trace a U shape from the 1870s to WW I, bottoming in the mid 1890s.

In any event, the evidence of figure 2.2 and table 2.7 suggests it would be foolish to assume that the savings rate was fixed over the full period, 1860–1913. Whether and to what degree NFI, GDFI, and GNA were behaviorally interdependent or ran lives of their own must be left to part III.

ACTIVISM AND CONTROL

It is generally held that in the nineteenth and early twentieth centuries the bulk of British overseas investment took the form of British purchases of portfolio capital. Furthermore, when Britons made direct investments, equity ownership was often held by a large number of private individuals rather than concentrated in the hands of a large British business. By mid-twentieth-century accounting definitions, overseas investment is termed *portfolio investment* when the assets purchased are either the debentures of governments or the equity and debentures of private enterprises in which Britons own less than a controlling share, say 30 percent, of the overseas enterprises equity. When Britons own a controlling share, say 30 percent or more, of the overseas enterprise's equity, the British holding of the latter's equity and debenture capital is termed *direct investment.*

The distinction between direct and portfolio investment typically suggests differences in the location of the initiator of the capital transfer, the activism of the asset owner, and the degree of control the owners are able to exert over the foreign borrower's managerial and financial decisions. *Portfolio investments* tend to be initiated by the host country, the asset owner is a relatively passive rentier investor, and the portfolio investor has a relatively small degree of control over the overseas borrower's operations. *Direct investments* are typically initiated by the capital exporter, the individual or corporate asset owner is an active entrepreneur-capitalist and, importantly, the direct investor has considerable control over the management and finances of the overseas operations. At present there do not exist data on the total of overseas portfolio versus direct investment by the United Kingdom in the late nineteenth and early twentieth centuries. However, a number of studies analyze important regional components, and these investigations permit reasonable inferences about the aggregate proportions of portfolio and direct investment.

Employing the modern definition of direct and portfolio investment with the 30 percent dividing line, Stone has detailed the composition of British investment in Latin America, 1865–1913 (I. Stone 1977). His data suggest that in 1865 78.8 percent of British investment in Latin America was portfolio and the percentage declined slowly but steadily to 53.7 percent in 1913 (1977:696). This decline was the result of two opposing trends. Latin American government issues fell from 76.4 percent to 37.8 percent of all British investment in Latin America, while corporate portfolio investment rose from 2.3 percent to 15.9 percent.

There is, however, some reason to doubt the usefulness of twentieth-century definitions in examing the nineteenth- and early twentiety-century experience. On the one hand, perhaps the most effective exertion of British control over its foreign borrowers in the late nineteenth century was the treatment accorded Argentinian borrowers subsequent to the Baring Crisis of late 1890. A large volume of Argentinian municipal debentures was in default and, until terms for the repayment of defaulted interest and principal were negotiated, municipal and many other Argentinian borrowers were frozen out of the London capital market through well-organized but nongovernmental pressures. Thus, the twentieth-century definitions of direct porfolio investment overlook the rare but sometimes surprising degree of private control exerted over overseas governmental borrowers by British *portfolio* investors.

On the other hand, the 30 percent rule for private enterprises misses the important fact that, in the nineteenth and early twentieth century, the British owners of the overseas enterprises equity and debenture shares were often quite different individuals or corporations (e.g., Bailey 1957–58). The typical overseas private enterprise receiving British funds was a railway or public utility company. It was rarely the case that the equity and/or debenture shares were closely held and thus, in turn, easily organized for joint pressure. Since it is quite uncertain whether the bond holders of an overseas enterprise with 30 percent or more British equity ownership had more control over their overseas debtors than if equity ownership was less than 30 percent, it seems appropriate to treat all debentures as portfolio investment. By recalculating Stone's data with all private enterprise debentures treated as portfolio investment, the percentage of portfolio investment in Britain's Latin American investments becomes 79.2 percent in 1865 and 71.7 percent in 1913.

The Canadian experience also suggests that the percentage of portfolio investments in British overseas lending was above the 70 percent mark. Paterson has generated an excellent series on British direct investments in Canada, 1890–1914. Extensive search in British and Canadian stock exchange and governmental records suggested that new direct investments, measured in terms of cash subscriptions, totaled $197.8 million across the twenty-five year period (Paterson 1976:26). These direct investments were unincorporated branches of British firms, or subsidiaries of British-owned companies, or Canadian companies owned by British residents. To discover the share of this direct investment in the total of direct and portfolio British investment in Canada, 1890–1914, requires data on the gross total inflow of British capital into Canada or gross British portfolio investment. The first figure is irretrievable from the sources of Canadian balance of payments data for this period. With regard to the total of portfolio investment in Canada, Simon catalogued the total of new equity and debenture issues raised on British stock exchanges for overseas purposes and the new equity issues of British companies clearly operating abroad, 1865–1913. According to Simon's data, the total of money calls on Canadian new issues raised in Britain was $1,581.6 million, 1890–1914 (1970:241). If the crude assumption is made that the latter sum is entirely portfolio in character, 89 percent of British investments in Canada, 1890–1914, were portfolio investments. This is obviously an overstatement because Paterson's data sources overlap with Simon's, and Paterson's direct investments should be subtracted from Simon's total to get the proper portfolio total. Paterson does not, however, believe the overlap is very important, for he is prepared to use Simon's figures as a proxy for new British portfolio investment in Canada throughout his monograph (Paterson 1976:9).

Importantly, Paterson does not use the 30 percent or more equity ownership rule to define automatically British direct investments in Canada. By employing this rule, much of Britain's investment in Canadian railway companies would be termed direct investment. Paterson argues, however, that the control of these railway companies rested with their Canadian managers; hence, he does not include the large British equity investment in Canadian railways in the direct investment total (1976:13–14). Stone applies, of course, the 30 percent or more rule to his Latin American data, and a high percentage of Britain's Argentinian railway investments, for example, are thus deemed direct investments. British owners seem, however, to have exerted much more control over their Argentinian railway investments than in the Canadian case (W. R. Wright 1974). Hence, the higher percentage of portfolio investment in the Canadian case represents a substantive, rather than merely a definitional, difference in the degree of activism and control.

To date there has been no careful sifting of the degree of portfolio versus direct investment in Europe, Asia, Australasia, and the United States. But it seems likely that the overwhelming portion of Britain's investments in these regions of the globe was portfolio in character. In Australia, about 70 percent of outstanding securities held by the British in 1870 and 1914 were issues of state or municipal governments (Hall 1963a:90). In the United States, almost two-thirds of British investment was in railroad companies, and most of this amount was in debentures (Simon 1970:242). The small amounts of U.S. railway equity held in Britain were very rarely a controlling share.[16] Since railway investment was a larger proportion of British investment in the United States than in Canada, it is likely that the share of portfolio investment in the United States was even larger than the 80 percent or more suggested in the Canadian case. Finally, a fairly high percentage of Britain's investment in Europe and India were either government securities or railway debentures.

Contrary to these cases, virtually all British investment in Ceylon was direct investment in tea plantations. Direct investments were also characteristic of British placements in many parts of Sub-Sahara Africa. As will be shown shortly, however, these regions were a rather minor portion of the total British investment abroad. Hence, the widely held belief that 80 percent or more of gross U.K. overseas investments in the nineteenth and early twentieth centuries were portfolio in character may be exaggerated but not by very much (Cottrell 1975:11).

The high involvement of portfolio investment in the nineteenth and early twentieth centuries is in sharp contrast to British overseas investment in the seventeenth and eighteenth centuries and the period since World War II. Before the nineteenth century and after 1945 most overseas investment took the form of direct investment in overseas structures, land, plant, equipment, and inventories by British individuals and businesses, many with substantial fixed and inventory investments in Britain. Indeed, net long-term British overseas investment abroad, 1960–1974, was virtually all direct investment. Why then was British overseas investment in the nineteenth and early twentieth centuries predominantly portfolio and, when direct, with British ownership so widely dispersed? The explanation probably lies in the nature and size of the real capital purchased with British funds.

INDUSTRY, ISSUERS, AND TIMING

Between 1865 and 1914, 69 percent of the new issues raised on British stock exchanges for overseas borrowers went into social-overhead capital formation (Simon 1967:40). This category of capital goods includes plant and equipment for railways, tramways, docks, telegraphs and telephones, and gas, electric, and water works. At least 41 percent of total new overseas issues went solely for railway plant and equipment. Of the 31 percent of new overseas issues not placed in social-overhead projects, extractive enterprise in agriculture and mining received 12 percent. Finance, land, real estate, and trading companies got 15 percent, the bulk of the finance, land, and real estate companies associated with either extractive enterprise or urban residential and social overhead projects. Very little of total new overseas issue, 4 percent, went into manufacturing. Importantly, the other major nineteenth-century capital exporters, France and Germany, followed the same pattern of heaviest involvement in social overhead capital projects, with minor investments in agriculture, mining, finance, etc. (Feis 1930:57–59, 78–80; Cameron 1963).

Social overhead projects are lumpy; that is, the initial size necessary to give service, let alone make a profit, is usually very large relative to the resources of either wealthy persons or businesses. Few individuals or businesses typically have the personal or corporate resources to fund social overhead projects, and for these few the risks of placing a large percentage of their wealth in one such investment could be quite large. Consequently, the typical borrower for social-overhead capital projects in modern times has been either a government or a large joint stock company.

British and continental governments had long raised large lumps of money for military purposes through public, often foreign, capital markets by breaking these lumps into small and transferable denominations. In the nineteenth century the involvement of many overseas and foreign governments in railway and other social-overhead projects was often the only way these regions could attract such masses of capital, locally or from abroad. Apparently, the organizing and taxing power of governments, backed by an often only recently acquired monopoly of violence, was necessary to impress the required mass of overseas lenders.

Joint stock organization and public issue of their equity and debt instruments first appeared in the early seventeenth century in Britain, at least in part as a *private* solution to the problem of the size and risk of certain projects and the resources of individual wealth holders. Large trading and colonizing enterprises, such as the British East India Company, with their lumpy capital needs for convoys of armed vessels, the large inventories of goods in transit, and warehouses, docks, warehouses, and plantations, were the first to use the joint stock form of organization. In the eighteenth century joint stock organization found domestic use in the period's canal and road building, and it was the only form of organization contemplated when the railroad first appeared in Britain in 1825.

In the mid-nineteenth century the principal overseas borrowers for railway and other social-overhead capital projects were either governments or joint stock enterprises whose dividends and interest payments were guaranteed by an overseas government. Across the late nineteenth and early twentieth centuries, however, the trend was toward placements in wholly private joint stock enterprises, probably reaching 50 percent of British social-overhead lending by 1914.[17]

What little is known about the evolution of government versus private involvement in particular overseas regions suggests that British perceptions of overseas law, order, and commercial justice were very important, there being some threshold level of political and economic development when private overseas borrowers would find British investors willing to fund their projects. This threshold seems to have been passed in the United States in the decade or so before the Civil War. In Argentina this point was passed only after the suppression of the Indians in the 1860s and 1870s.[18] Perhaps just as important, however, was the privately perceived expected rate of profit from the underlying economic activity. Simon suggested that "the rapid, although uneven development of [Latin America, Canada, other Empire areas] and the United States—reflected in rising populations, increased urbanization, and the expansion of markets for their primary products—opened up vast opportunities for private enterprise. . . . (1967:48). Given sufficiently high profits, and a modicum of law and order, a mixture of local and British entrepreneurship and capital was more and more willing to go it alone in large social-overhead capital projects.

Between 1865 and 1914 Simon reports that 34 percent of new overseas issues went to North America, 17 percent to South America, 14 percent to Asia, 13 percent to Europe, 11 percent to

Australasia, and 11 percent to Africa (1967:40). Simon's data are not broken down by colony and nation, but Feis' examination of the stock of outstanding British overseas issues in 1914 is grouped in this manner (1930:23). Feis found that the largest national or colonial receivers, computed at par value were the United States (20.0 percent), Canada and Newfoundland (13.7 percent), India and Ceylon (10.0 percent), South Africa (9.8 percent), Australia (9.4 percent), Argentina (8.5 percent), and Brazil (3.9 percent). Clearly, as Simon noted, the bulk of the 1865–1914 trans-European investment, 68 percent of £3530 million, went to regions of recent settlement, regions with a disproportionate demand for social-overhead and urban residential capital (Simon 1967:41).

Except for the United States, British investment to particular countries or colonies between 1865 and 1914 tended to occur for relatively short periods of time. Thus, the greater part of British investment in Australia occurred in the 1880s, in Canada after 1900, in South Africa in the early 1900s, and in Europe in the early 1870s and just before WW I. Hall attributed this spurt-like involvement of British capital to the flexibility of British investors, who shifted their horizons in the wake of the appearance of new opportunities (1963a:189). Unquestionably, British investors were quite flexible in this respect, but the nature of the opportunities was also important.

To some extent, the "one-shot" pattern of British overseas investment in Australia, Canada, and South Africa reflected the lumpiness of the social-overhead and urban development needs of these regions of recent settlement, their initially limited savings resources, and their immature capital markets. In a recently settled, small country it might well have been the case that a large backlog of massive social-overhead or urban development projects had to accumulate before their return was sufficiently great to draw attention to need for the special arrangements of either government enterprise or joint stock company formation. Going abroad for some of the entrepreneurship and capital might then be thought of as the cheapest means of arranging for these unwiedly projects. Having acquired a substantial proportion of the needed social-overhead capital with an initial spurt of home and overseas savings supplies, subsequent economic development either did not generate as many lumpy social-overhead projects or local savings and capital markets were now much more capable of handling the lumps that did appear. Some of these conditions also characterized the longer settled but economically backward regions of Eastern and Southern Europe, which received 75 percent of Britain's European investments.

The U.S. import of British capital was also variable, but it was continuous. Given the size and pace of the aggregate movements in the U.S. economy and its expansion into unsettled territory until the turn of the nineteenth century, the continuous flow of British capital is not surprising. The major use of British funds was either for lumpy social overhead capital projects in the newly settled regions or for purchasing the new issues of social-overhead enterprises in the older U.S. regions and thereby allowing Americans to purchase the frontier social-overhead issues.

From the perspective of the mid-twentieth century, when a substantial portion of overseas investment by the most developed capitalist economies is direct investment in manufacturing enterprise in other developed countries, it might be asked why so little British overseas lending in the nineteenth and early twentieth centuries went into manufacturing in the developed or under-developed regions of the globe. As noted earlier, Britain was not alone in this respect; for most of the years 1815–1914 German and French overseas lending funded social-overhead projects with minor involvements in agriculture, mining, finance, etc.

The structure of the nineteenth-century manufacturing enterprise and markets provides the simplest and most compelling explanation of this phenomenon. For the British manufacturer who might consider setting up a plant overseas, the most profitable, least risky places to locate manufacturing plants were, and still are, in regions with large markets and relatively high average incomes. In the early nineteenth century, Belgium, France, the Netherlands, Switzerland, and the United States would thus have been prime targets for British merchants or manufacturers strongly connected with cotton textiles, cotton textile machinery, iron refining, steam engines, and railway equipment and rails, that is, the sectors of the British economy where Britain had a substantial technological lead. By the middle of the nineteenth century inventions in steel refining and mechanization in other branches of the textile industry might be thought to lengthen the list for potential British direct investment abroad. However, given that the growth-inducing changes in class structure and extent of internal and external markets over the previous three or four centuries were phenomena affecting a number of Western European and North American regions, not solely British ones, the European and North American regions with large markets and relatively high incomes were very likely to have some manufacturing already present.

Indeed, in the early nineteenth century the high-income markets in Belgium, France, and the United States had established manufacturing sectors, albeit not as advanced in their technology as Great Britain (Landes 1969:124-52; Davis et al. 1972:419-21). Plans and craftsmen were smuggled out of Britain almost from the origins of the British Industrial Revolution in the late eighteenth century, but only a few firms in these overseas regions were close to the latest British developments. There were few legal monopolies in these regions; furthermore, there were no significant scale barriers in the sectors where British technology had taken a lead (Gatrell 1977; Davis 1957, 1958). The new and old products produced with the new technologies were quite undifferentiated, and there were few important patents that could not be finessed by slight changes or outright theft. Thus, competition was often quite sharp among local Belgian, French, and U.S. manufactureres, and any British importer who could leap the tariff walls (Mokyr 1976:26-81; Davis 1957, 1958; Davis et al. 1972:419-37; Davis and Stettler 1966). Given these conditions, what stands out as an explanation for the absence of large-scale British direct investment in overseas manufacturing is the inherent advantage of the local manufacturer. The basis of this advantage was intimate knowledge of local input and output markets, which could be costly to acquire.

A small amount of British manufacturing capital and entrepreneurship did migrate to Belgium, France, and the United States in the first half of the nineteenth century (Landes 1969:148-49; Henderson 1972:3rd ed.; Mokyr 1976:50; 76, 95; Rosenberg

1972:80). For the most the part it was not tightly linked to existing British manufacturing or merchandizing firms. Financially backed by personal contacts or their own resources, a few adventurous British entrepreneurs and craftsmen sought to take advantage of their superior technological knowledge and experience. These British-initiated firms appear to have had a sufficient technological lead to overcome any advantage of the more backward local firms for a while, but some local firms quickly adopted the new technologies. In the subsequent competition, the surviving British-initiated firms blended into the local economy, losing any contact with capital resident in Britain.

In the very late nineteenth century tariffs rose precipitously in nearly all regions of the globe with large markets and high incomes. Furthermore, products began to be differentiated and important patents were now enforced. At this point, direct overseas investment in manufacturing plants began to move in large quantities from British, French, German, and U.S. manufacturers toward each other's home markets, Canada, Australia, Austro-Hungary, Poland, and Russia (Coleman 1969; C. K. Hobson 1914:156–58; Wilkins 1970:70–112; Wilson 1968).

Portfolio participation in overseas manufacturing was also limited by the structure of the nineteenth-century industrial enterprise and markets. The typical manufacturing plant and firm was fairly small until late in the nineteenth century both in Britain and abroad. As in Britain, manufacturing capital needs in Belgium, France, and the United States were not large in the aggregate or lumpy in the individual case, relative to the resources of regional wealth in the nascent manufacturing districts. Nevertheless, extraentrepreneurial equity and debenture participation tended to be raised among local relatives, friends, and business associates, partly from desire and partly because of imperfections in local or national capital markets (Davis 1957, 1958). Up to the middle of the nineteenth century, outsiders, native or foreign, who wished to earn dividends or interest based on the new industries' profits had to migrate with their capital, as in the few British examples noted earlier. As manufacturing firm scale increased in the late nineteenth century, long-distance portfolio participation via organized capital markets and large investment banks appeared in the United Kingdom, Western Europe, and the United States. However, either high returns or information costs kept this long-distance participation regional or, at best national, up to 1914.

Ending our general description of British overseas investment in the nineteenth and early twentieth centuries with a discussion of segmented manufacturing markets is an appropriate entre to the subject of the next chapter, the question of whether segmented British capital markets helped to augment the flow of British capital abroad in the late nineteenth century. On the one hand, from the origins of the British Industrial Revolution in the late eighteenth century British industry was mainly funded locally. To an increasing extent short-term funds moved interregionally, but a good portion of industrial short-term funds and nearly all long-term funds were found, if not locally, within a shire or two. On the other hand, London's long-term capital market had developed an interest in the funding of overseas government and social-overhead projects, certainly from the beginning of the nineteenth century. Thus, as foreign investment began its dramatic increase in the third quarter of the nineteenth century, it occurred to some contemporaries, as well as to some later observers, that it was being fostered by some sort of market segmentation. Capital, it was said, moved in channels; regular patterns of information flow and trust tended to immobilize the placement of annual savings in well-trodden paths. Investors and financial intermediaries in London thus may have sent long-term funds abroad because their knowledge of long-term needs of British industry in the provinces was limited by institutional rigidities or investor biases.

PART II: MICRO PROCESSES

CHAPTER 3: **THE BRITISH CAPITAL MARKET, 1870-1913**

Like similar structures in other advanced economies of Western Europe and North America in the late nineteenth and early twentieth centuries, the organized institutions of the British capital market conducted two types of transactions. First, claims to ownership of domestic and overseas capital goods were traded in the equity market. Second, claims to future amounts of domestic and foreign monies were traded for current liquid assets in the debenture and preference securities market. Insofar as its operation facilitated the accumulation of capital goods by, on the one hand, making the traded assets more attractive than alternative forms of wealth through easier revision by exchange, and, on the other hand, providing a cheaper long-term financing service than available elsewhere, the capital market may be said to have aided in the efficient allocation of resources in the British economy. Through more precise knowledge of alternative allocations of financial resources, a relatively centralized market for trading assets from many sectors of the economy increases the opportunity for more efficient decisions by all borrowers and lenders, whether participants in the organized capital market or not.

Considerable controversy surrounds the role of the British capital market in the years between 1870 and 1913, and, while often not identified as such, in essence the central issue is the efficiency with which the market delivered its financial services. In large part, the heat of the debate derives from another, broader issue—the question of Britain's economic growth during this period. Britain is said to have faltered because, among other reasons, her capital market failed to effect a proper distribution of financial resources among the competing needs of her multiple activities at home and abroad.

Between 1870 and 1913 the nominal value of the stock of outstanding home and overseas long-term securities held in the United Kingdom increased by almost 350 percent (table 3.1). In the same period the proportion of nondomestic securities in-

Table 3.1

The Approximate Nominal Value of Outstanding Home and Overseas
Securities in the United Kingdom in 1870 and 1913

(£m.)

	1870	1913
DOMESTIC		
1. British Government Funds	880	1013
2. British Municipal Corporations	2	277
3. Home Railways	440	1330
4. Home Companies	101	1500 (±100)
Total Domestic	1423	4120 (±100)
NON-DOMESTIC		
5. Dominion, Provincial and Colonial Governments	30	676
6. Indian, Colonial and Foreign Municipal Corporations	–	153
7. Foreign Governments	400	297
8. Indian Railways	70	141
9. Dominion and Colonial Railways	20	306
10. American Railways	50	617
11. Foreign Railways	180	467
12. Non-Domestic Companies	93	1107
Total Domestic	843	3764
GRAND TOTAL	2266	7884 (±100)

Sources: These estimates are a reworking of Hall (1963a, 4, 16).
Relying on Parliamentary reports (Great Britain, 1914-16, Cmd. 8034,
i-xxi), Hall's 1870 estimate for Home Railways is increased to include
issues not known in London. Hall did not supply an estimate of American Railways for 1870; our estimate is a compromise among Adler
1970: 85-87, Carincross 1953: 183, and Jenks 1927: 413, 425-26. Using
Jenks (1927, 413, 425) Hall's estimate of Foreign Governents is reduced to amounts issued in London; Hall's total was based on amounts
issued world-wide. Finally, Hall's 1913 estimate of Home Companies
includes British-registered companies which operated abroad. A rough
attempt is made to exclude them from the present estimate. Companies
where there was no British production (e.g., coffee) were removed and
Feis 1930: 27 was employed to reduce the foreign component of certain
broader categories of securities (e.g., commercial and industrials).

creased from 37 percent to 48 percent. At the midpoint of the
nineteenth century the same statistic had stood at 25 percent (Jenks
1927:413). Having never before seen such a large proportion of a
nation's long-term assets committed abroad, contemporaries and
historians have, not surprisingly, speculated on the possibility of
bias in the workings of the British capital market. The same

sources, however, also reveal that long-term securities of domestic, nonrailway enterprises rose from around 4 percent of the total in 1870, to 19 percent in 1913. These, then, are the pivotal magnitudes. Did there exist a set of biases that restricted the flow of funds to domestic securities to a fivefold increase in their share of domestically held, long-term negotiable securities?

Two factors are given serious consideration as impediments to a more efficient allocation of the nation's financial resources. First, it is suggested that the facilities available to satisfy the expanding needs of domestic industry in Britain's largest center of financial activity, London, were quite slow in developing and grossly inadequate relative to the facilities available to governments and public utilities, home and foreign. Thus, Saville writes:

The increase in the size of the industrial unit, with its corresponding increased demand for capital, was met in part by the introduction of limited liability in the 1850s; but the development of the new institutional framework for long term investment was markedly slow. This tardiness in the emergence of new types of institutions in the English capital market was the product of many factors. . . .The first is the long establishment of the London capital market as the source of capital for overseas investors, and by the second half of the 19th century investment institutions of first class repute were concerned almost exclusively with the world demand for capital outside of the United Kingdom. . . . As the scale of capital requirements increased the individualistic traditions of self-financing no longer sufficed, but the absence of powerful . . . (domestic) . . . finance houses as well as what has been called the "entrepreneur" spirit in banking meant that the gap between individual resources, admittedly considerable, and the capital requirements of industry must have been growing before 1914 (1961:57).

That the costs of company promotion and expansion through public issues of securities were relatively high—particularly for small firms—is taken as a sign of this tardy and inadequate institutional development (Saville 1961:57; Cairncross 1953:101). International comparisons of facilities available in other advanced economies also raise a number of doubts about British methods (Landes 1969:349–50; Saville 1961:57).

Second, either British investors or inadequate financial developments are suspected of leading toward overcommitment of British wealth to certain types of safe assets, notably the large issues of governments, railways, and public utilities, home and overseas. In one version of this hypothesis British investors bear responsibility, manifesting an unusual preference for safe assets (Landes 1969:349–50). In a second variation the risk aversion of investors is taken for granted, and so responsibility for the overcommitment in safe assets rests with inadequate development of financial institutions that diversify risks into a financial package acceptable to at least some investors (Kennedy 1976). Such financial intermediaries might be deposit banks willing to lend both short and long, investment banking houses that would guide risky new enterprises through infancy, mutual funds or insurance companies with sufficient resources to bear high risks through efficient diversification, etc.

All of these views concerning the British capital market's performance draw the inference that overseas investment would have been somewhat smaller if funds had been better allocated in the late nineteenth and twentieth centuries. Hence, careful study of these ideas is an important task for understanding the fundamental causes of Britain's massive capital outflow during this period.

A. THE ORGANIZATION OF BRITISH CAPITAL MARKETS

In turning to the adequacy of British capital market services first, it is well to begin with the often-cited remarks of Henry Lowenfeld on the issuing services of London in the first decade of the twentieth century. Lowenfeld was a financial journalist who wrote several introductory volumes on financial and stock exchange affairs.

The cost of issue depends entirely upon the number of prospectuses sent out, the amount spent on advertising, the fees paid to the bank which receives the applications, to the brokers, solicitors and accountants whose names appear on the prospectus, and the cost of the underwriting fee. These expenses are very heavy in any case, and hardly ever amount to less than 2000 pounds, even on a modest issue. But as there are some firms of brokers and solicitors who consider themselves poorly remunerated by a fee of 1000 guineas for merely giving the promoters the right to print their name on a prospectus, their work and out-of-pocket expenses being paid extra, and as it is quite easy to spend 5000 pounds on advertising a prospectus, the cost of launching some issues very considerably exceeds the smallest sum which can be expressed in five figures. Whenever the issue is large this does matter, as even 25,000 pounds is only 2½% of 1,000,000 pounds; but on small issues 50,000 or 100,000 pounds the expense is proportionately burdensome (1909:174–75).

In sum, the charges for public flotation fall into four categories: fees for registration and other legal matters; fees for the various professionals and public figures required by law, custom, or necessity to attest to the issue's respectability; fees for increasing the public's awareness of the firm and its new issue; and lastly, fees to insure against failure, i.e., underwriting fees. The last three types of charges were directly related to the degree of risk and more importantly, the degree to which the amount of risk was uncertain. The higher the uncertainty, the more that had to be spent to overcome the public's ignorance or suspicion, to purchase reputable names, and to pay the underwriters.

The underwriter is paid a percentage which varies from 1% on the amount underwritten, up to 6% or even more in the case of issues of new companies which are speculative (Lowenfeld 1909:172).

Lowenfeld makes it quite clear that the unit costs of a large issue were lower than for a small one, but the reasons for this phenomenon are not immediately obvious. It may have been that issuing houses tended to more quickly reject large issues that they would not have rejected if the issue in question was somewhat smaller. In this case, the resulting price schedule for issuing service might still show falling unit costs as issue size rose, but the schedule would be misleading insofar as it was not pricing a homogeneous good. On the other hand, over the size range cited by Lowenfeld there was probably a vaguely defined level of advertising expenditure beyond which word-of-mouth and newspaper stories began to do an increasing part of the advertising job and thereby reduced the incremental advertising cost of attracting more buyers. Such external economies would be directly related to the breadth and depth of the demand for negotiable securities in London and the surrounding counties, as well as the size and vigor of London's financial press. Furthermore, the incremental research fee for a larger issue probably declined over the range of issue sizes mentioned by Lowenfeld. This, in turn, would cause the schedule of unit charges for underwriters and some of the other professional services to fall across issue size, again, given the size of demand. The view that Lowenfeld's data support the pressence of economies for larger issues, holding risk and uncertainty constant, seems to be confirmed on closer inspection of Lowenfeld's cost schedules. Importantly, the lowest unit costs for small and large issues are lower for large issues by 50 percent, if not more.

It follows from this analysis that there were probably sound technical reasons for specialization within the security-issuing industry. Instead of being the result of illogical habit or some ill-defined taste for domestic industrial affairs, the technology of issuing securities seems to explain the specialization of the City's first-class merchant banking houses in the business of floating the large issues of governments and railways, home and foreign. Why should a business, based on producing long runs of an item with the aforementioned economies, be particularly efficient at producing small batches of specialized items? Since a high proportion of the limited companies in need of the service of professional issuing houses were relatively untried enterprises, it is probable that there were even diseconomies in the joint production of small and large-size security issues. House stability was absolutely essential for effective public marketing of large issues. The first-class merchant bankers ignored small and medium-sized issues from overseas no less than they did domestic issues of the same size.

Very little is known about those who specialized in floating modest-sized issues. It is fairly certain that there were always individuals and firms engaged in arranging long-term financing for the relatively moderate needs of domestic firms, but their average business life was quite short. Between 1866 and 1883, 243 of the newly registered limited companies were interested in promoting domestic industrial and commercial enterprise; 45 percent were immediately abortive and 84 percent of the remaining public limiteds were dead within ten years.[1] The involvement of investment trusts in underwriting domestic industrial and commerical issues from the 1880s onward is well known, but it is likely that somewhat more informal and ephemeral underwriting facilities were usually the case for small-scale borrowers in London and elsewhere (Hall 1963a:78–83; Lavington 1921:208).

If little is directly known about the behavior of those engaged in domestic issuing activities, perhaps something can be inferred from other data. In concentrating on the facilities available in London, for the moment, it seems plausible to assume that, for firms of similar size, expected return, and uncertainty, the costs of London issue were higher for provincial firms than they were for firms from the London region. Familiar with local business through the newspapers, consumption, and work activities, the London investor was probably more easily, and therefore more cheaply, convinced of the worthiness of an investment in a local enterprise. This hypothesis helps to explain the fact that securities of London limiteds appear on the official list of the London Stock Exchange with a frequency that is well out of proportion to the region's share in the nation's industrial and commercial output or capital stock.

A second aspect of the funding of small and medium-sized issues in London is also explained by the hypothesized differential cost of issue for London and provincial firms. The first security issues of many provincial firms listed on the London exchange were not floated (publicly or privately) in London (Hall 1963a:28). Having raised their initial capital elsewhere, these companies acquired an official listing on the London exchange after doing business for a number of years. Subsequently, London issuing facilities were used to float supplemental amounts of equity and fixed-interest securities. If funding was unavailable elsewhere, London costs of flotation for a relatively moderate-sized issue of a *new* provincial venture could easily have been so high as either to constrain the firm's initial scale of operations or to abort the venture completely.

Most of the nation's industrial and commercial capital stock was located in the provinces, and for most of the period between 1870 and 1913 the vast majority of Britain's enterprises in these sectors had capital requirements below the level that Lowenfeld terms "moderate." It has been argued so far that location and moderate size of issue would lead to plausible differentials in the costs of issue through their effects on the costs of information. Thus, the question of rigidity or bias in the institutional arrangements of the British capital market becomes a matter of finding out whether institutional developments to minimize cost attributable to these and other "technical" factors were slow or inadequate and whether some form of imperfect competition was operating to significantly misdirect capital market behavior. It was just noted that London issue costs might have been sufficiently high to reduce initial scale or abort new provincial ventures. In fact, to view the costs of London issue as a matter of major importance for most provincial industrial and commercial firms is to misconstrue the locus of most of the nation's long-term external financing decisions in these sectors.

The vast majority of provincial public limiteds were floated locally, without use of the full complement of professional issuing services available in London. A frequent procedure was to place securities privately among the former partners, the directors (if the firm was already a limited), and wealthy friends and contacts. At a minimum the services of a local solicitor, banker, professional stock broker, or London company promoter would be purchased to handle the legal formalities and the cash transactions. If the new issue was large, or offered at a time when the local capital market was highly active, or floated for a new, relatively untried type of venture, their services would be further utilized to reach a wider group of local investors.

Importantly, competition was quite high among those performing these functions. One must not be misled by the frequently mentioned career of the London-based company promoter H. Osbourne O'Hagan (O'Hagan 1929). As with any new industry, in the case the promotion of domestic limited-liability companies, the returns to the highly responsive and innovative entrepreneur can be quite high. O'Hagan was often among the first to begin the conversion of an old industry to limited liability or to promote a new industry, but throughout his career from the 1870s to the 1920s he was invariably and quickly followed by a host of local solicitors, bankers, and professional stock brokers, as well as other London-based company promoters, all eager to reap the rumored high profits (O'Hagan 1929:1:150-51, 255-56). And, as might be expected, the competition and publicity rapidly lowered the cost of issuing services and raised the offer price of the new securities (1929:1:256-57). Nor should one place undue emphasis on the initiating role of London-based promoters. The Oldham cotton spinning limiteds were easily floated in the 1860s and 1870s by the local professionals mentioned earlier (Lavington 1921:208).

Integral to long-term external finance in the provinces was the availability and adaptability of the provincial stock exchanges and professional stock brokers. In 1873 eleven provincial towns, all major centers of the nation's industrial and commercial activity, had active stock exchanges, meeting several times weekly, if not daily (Great Britain 1878). By 1912 the number of towns with stock exchanges had nearly doubled, and it seems a fair guess that over the same period the growth in the number of formally associated brokers was almost as rapid as the growth in the London Stock Exchange membership (table 3.2).

Up to the 1870s provincial stock exchanges were primarily concerned with a trade in the securities of local railway and other social-overhead enterprises (see Killick and W. A. Thomas 1970:96-111). From the peaks of turnover in the late 1840s, provincial trading slackened fairly strongly in the late 1850s and 1860s. The depth of the London market and the relative advantage of the City's specialized services for large issues shifted the locus of ownership and trading to the metropolis and attracted the vendors of new public issue. As the conversion of British enterprise to limited liability accelerated in the late 1860s and 1870s, and more and more firms made immediate use of the new form of business organization, the character of the securities traded on the provincial stock exchanges changed accordingly. Killick and W. A. Thomas have recently argued that, first up to the home company boom of the 1890s the activity on the provincial stock exchanges remained fairly low and, second, brokers acted mainly as shunters of provincial securities to London (Killick and W. A. Thomas 1970:110). This latter point is quite important, for, combined with the fact that the nation's

Table 3.2

Great Britain's Stock Exchanges, 1873-1912

Provincial Stock Exchanges		1873-74	1881-82	1892-93	1902-03	1912-13
Aberdeen	F[a]	8	10	14	11	11
	M	-	-	(15)	(13)	(14)
Birmingham	F	14	12	15	27	36
	M	-	-	(22)	(46)	(61)
Bradford	M	-	-	-	12	8
	M	-	-	-	(17)	(12)
Bristol	F	20	12	18	20	20
	M	-	-	(26)	(29)	(30)
Cardiff	F	-	-	-	19	14
	M	-	-	-	(28)	(20)
Dundee	F	-	8	10	14	16
	M	-	-	(12)	(15)	(17)
Edinburgh	F	16	30	36	39	38
	M	-	-	(52)	(67)	(69)
Glasgow	F	30	81	92	123	147
	M	-	-	(142)	(207)	(260)
Greenock	F	-	-	6	6	6
	M	-	-	(10)	(13)	(11)
Halifax	F	-	-	-	10	5
	M	-	-	-	(12)	(8)
Huddersfield	F	-	-	-	6	9
	M	-	-	-	(9)	(15)
Hull	F	7	-	-	-	-
	M	-	-	-	-	-
Lancashire (Oldham)	F	-	-	-	-	-
	M	-	-	(35)	(26)	(27)
Leeds	F	12	8	8	8	15
	M	-	-	(13)	(17)	(31)
Liverpool	F	87	127	119	-	-
	M	-	-	(158)	(142)	(176)
Manchester	F	55	50	52	66	63
	M	-	-	(82)	(115)	(103)
Newcastle upon Tyne	F	4	7	8	11	15
	M	-	-	(10)	(14)	(22)
Nottingham	F	-	-	-	-	14
	M	-	-	-	-	(16)
Sheffield	F	18	18	15	16	16
	M	-	-	(26)	(40)	(40)
Southport	F	-	-	-	8	6
	M	-	-	-	(8)	(6)
Swansea	F	-	-	-	-	6
	M	-	-	-	-	(7)
Total Provincial	F	271	363	393[b]	396[c]	445[c]
	M	-	-	(603)	(818)	(945)

Table 3.2 (cont't)

		1873-74	1881-82	1892-93	1902-03	1912-13
London Stock	F	-	-	-	-	-
Exchange	M	(1500)	(2200)	(3377)	(4776)	(5040)

Notes:

[a]F = Firms, M = Members.

[b]The number of Oldham firms is unavailable and not included.

[c]The number of Oldham and Liverpool firms is unavailable and not included.

Source: Trade directories.

stock exchanges were in constant telegraphic contact by the late 1870s (Great Britain 1878:Q. 7894, 7907, 7952-54, 8141-61), it suggests the existence of a competitive national market in a large number of outstanding securities, as well as a fairly low transactions cost to surmount before interregional trade took place.

With regard to the first point of Killick and W. A. Thomas, that the total volume of business slackened in the late 1850s and 1860s is not necessarily a sign that local trading in non-social-overhead investments was also slack. First of all, it would be quite surprising if the new opportunities for non-social-overhead investment, made possible by the general limited-liability legislation of the late 1850s and early 1860s, were able to fill the place left by the very large trading volumes in railway securities. Second, it is highly probable that the bulk of the securities listed on the provincial stock exchanges from the 1870s to World War I were never traded in London. For each Oldham limited listed on both the Oldham and London exchanges in the late 1870s, there was another firm quoted in the Oldham lists that had yet to be quoted in London by 1913 (various Oldham newspapers and *The Investors Monthly Manual*). Similarly, most of the issues on the Birmingham exchange were never listed in London (Phillips 1887:309-11). Finally, O'Hagan leaves little doubt that private and public placement of new issues from local enterprises was a substantial part of the activity of all provincial brokers, including those who were members of the local stock exchanges (O'Hagan 1929:1:150-51, 255-56).

In any case, for most of the period, the majority of new and old provincial limiteds would never have thought of offering securities to investors in distant regions of the country. Local investors were automatically involved in any thoughts on the subject, their superior knowledge, interest, and loyalty simply assumed. For a new venture, short-term financing from local banks and merchants was probably far easier and cheaper if local men were known to be intimately involved in the affair. If one's credit was good enough, bank overdrafts and commercial credit notes were automatically renewed. Throughout the nineteenth century this was one of the most important methods of long-term external finance, though its importance for the larger industrial and commercial firms diminished with the development of local debenture markets in the 1880s (on debenture markets, see Jefferys 1938:249ff).

As evidenced by the large numbers of provincial businesses listed in *Burdett's* but not quoted in London, the expense of local provincial issue must have been fairly cheap. In any event, the cost of increasing investor awareness sufficiently to achieve a successful flotation was much less for most businesses than what London enterprises probably paid in London and usually less than what was necessary to convince more distant investors (Lavington 1921:208). In effect, the local brokers, solicitors, and bankers and the visiting London promoters were the professional issuing houses of the provinces. That the lawyers and bankers did not change their occupational designations while practicing a broker's or a promoters business or that the average cost of the less extensive issuing services in the provinces was lower than average London charges for similar firms should not have led Lavington, an early and careful researcher in this area, to ignore their essential, highly organized role in provincial financial affairs (see Anderson 1972, 1975).

On the whole, it was the leading firms that went limited and whose equity and debentures were traded on the local and, perhaps, the London exchange (for the generally leading position of the public limiteds in their respective industries, see Clapham 1968:2:138–42). Thus the liquidity of provincial investors was significantly enhanced; first, the volume of local assets with a regular market increased, and second, the assets were generally those of the leading local enterprises.

All the same, a number of provincial firms still found it necessary to turn to London's facilities for public issue and its market for outstanding issues for help with their financial needs. In the 1860s, 1870s and 1880s a number of industries, including cotton spinning, iron and steel, and some sections of the engineering sector, experienced several waves of conversions to limited liability. Concentrated in relatively few locations, local capital markets must have been severely strained by the size of the total demand on local resources. If conversion had proceeded slowly, local wealth might have been able to absorb the large number of new issues. The individual sizes of industrial equity and fixed-interest issues, calalogued in the annual volumes of *Burdett's* in the 1870s and 1880s but not mentioned in the new issues of *The Investor's Monthly Manual* or quoted on the official list of the London Stock Exchange, indicate that the provinces could absorb what London called a modest-sized issue under some circumstances. Perhaps it was here, during the conversion booms, that provincial brokers began to make their fees as shunters, unloading issues in London to help finance the next new issue in a provincial city.

Some iron and steel companies used the domestic issuing houses of London (e.g. Chadwicks) to market part of their initial equity issues, but this was unusual (Jeffreys 1938:295–98). As noted earlier, in these years and afterward, the new issue facilities of London were employed primarily for supplemental funding, usually subsequent to a period of London quotation of an outstanding issue of the given firm. With the London region somewhat more familiar with the securities of the firms, and perhaps other firms in the same industry as well, the cost of a supplemental issue in London was undoubtedly more favorable. At this point the aged provincial firm with "modest" borrowing needs probably paid issue costs not far from those paid by slightly younger London firms, and provincial firms with national reputations were probably able to place their securities privately or publicly on terms entirely comparable with London enterprise of similar size.

It was mentioned earlier that in the 1870s and 1880s the locus of individual demands on London by industrial and commercial firms was well within the size of issue that Lowenfeld termed "modest." The vast majority of individual issues from industrial and commerical long-term borrowers were significantly less than a million pounds per issue. In the mid-1880s, however, a new class of borrowers began to appear, floating issues of £0.5 to £2.0 million or larger. Firms in brewing, cotton textiles, chemicals, and iron and steel were most prominent among those forming the new class.

Starting with the flotations of Guinness and Ind Coope in 1886, the size of brewing firms expanded rapidly, largely the result of newly discovered economies of scale in distribution and a very high degree of competition in the industry (Mathias 1969:393ff). The movement reached a peak in the 1890s when Watney amalgamated with Combe & Reids, floating £15 million in equity and fixed-interest securities. In chemicals and cotton textiles, firms amalgamated in the 1890s for defensive purposes. Stiff competition in the face of unstable but secularly rising demand seems to have led to excess capacity, and the first task of the new, larger structures was to try to organize production and investment to eliminate this source of reduced profitability. In iron and steel, two factors were operating to encourage increases in the size of issues. Changing technology involved a fairly steady secular increase in the size of the efficient plant and, second, there seemed to have been sufficient savings in the combination of various stages of production to encourage vertical integration. From the mid-1890s to the turn of the century amalgamations to achieve the latter objective were quite widespread.

In the face of these enlarged demands, the evidence suggests that London responded fairly quickly. Investment trusts first became involved in underwriting industrial securities in the late 1880s, and it is certain they were involved in a number of amalgamation issues at the turn of the century (U.S. Securities and Exchange Commission 1939). Barings was involved in the Guinness issue of 1886, and leading joint-stock banks such as Westminster participated in other major issues of the period (Clapham 1968:3: 210). On the question of what these industrial and commercial giants paid for issuing services, relative to what was paid by the older large-scale borrowers, there is very little direct evidence. Insofar as yields on outstanding issues give some indication of the relative level of risk entering into issue costs, it seems likely that the relative costs of London's new issue facilities fell for large-scale domestic industrial borrowers starting in the mid-1880s. From that point to the outbreak of World War I, the gap closed between the yields on domestic industrial debentures on the one hand and home and overseas social-overhead investments on the other.[2] Since domestic railways and other social-overhead investments were probably far less risky than domestic industrial and commercial investments in this period, it is not surprising that yields on industrial issues did not fall below home social-overhead yields. Importantly, however, home industrial yields fell below the yields on a large proportion of overseas railway debentures in the 1890s and 1900s.

Britain was not, of course, alone among the advanced economies of the late nineteenth century that experienced a jump in the scale of industrial and commercial firm size. But the fact that Britain's giants were relatively modest by U.S. and German standards raises the question of whether Britain's financial institutions lacked something that inhibited the growth of firm size to the fullest extent (for a comparison of British and U.S. firm size, see Payne 1967:519-42).

L. Davis argues that rapidly growing advanced capitalist economies of the late nineteenth century were subject to three types of shock: growth that involved a shift in the location of industry, growth that involved significant shifts of resources to new industries, and, third, technological developments that involved large economies of scale (Davis 1966:255-72). With respect to attendant financial needs, the most important aspect of these shocks was their timing in relation to the currently available set of services for external finance. Davis concluded that Great Britain was much less subject to such shocks; there were few changes in the location of production, the older industries remained profitable and dominant, and substantial economies of scale were not found in the technologies profitable with Great Britain's natural resources.

Second, he found that British industry and commerce could rely on a much superior system for external financing, when and if shocks appeared. Regional banking facilities, mortgage markets, and commercial credit facilities were much older and better developed in Great Britain. It is well to point out again the important role of the automatically renewed short-term credit instrument among the methods available for long-term external financing.

Finally, as has been argued earlier, not only were the metropolitan and provincial capital markets older and more highly developed initially, but also they were capable of adapting fairly rapidly to changing circumstance. The American response to inadequacies in its financial structure was enlarged firm size, making possible internal financing through expanded net income. In sum, it appears it was the very adequacy of Britain's long-term external financing institutions for both modest and large-scale borrowers that helped to yield the relatively smaller scale of its enterprises, not the hypothesized rigidities (for a discussion of this point in the framework of European economic development, see Gerschenkron 1962:11-16).

B. THE FUNDING OF NEW ENTERPRISE

In setting aside the issue of funding the enlargement of British enterprise at the turn of the nineteenth century, there is also the question of whether Britain's financial institutions adequately funded new enterprise. Funding new enterprises was rarely an easy matter in the advanced capitalist countries during the nineteenth century. The issue is whether new enterprise in Britain met with greater difficulty then firms abroad did and, if so, why.

It has been argued that the British wealth portfolio was overcommitted to safe investments in government, railways, and public utilities, at home and abroad, because Britain lacked effective financial institutions for diversifying the high risks of new enterprise. Kennedy, for example, argues that the absence of large investment banks of the German variety was central to the British overcommitment to safe assets (Kennedy 1976). The large German banks were capable of nursing new enterprises with short- and long-term finance from bank resources, marketing services for issuing securities publically or privately, entrepreneurship, engineering advice, and many other services. During the early years of a new enterprise the German investment banks might hold a substantial equity position. However, the bank's reputation and equity position often made it possible to market some of the new firm's fixed-interest debt. By engaging in new projects in a number of industries and regions, as well as lending money short and long to older, established firms and governments, the German investment banks appear to have diversified some of the high risks of new enterprise for its own investors and depositors and for society, too.

Regardless of how well German industry was served by the big banks,[3] one must ask whether there was a strong, unfullfilled British need for these types of institutions before World War I. After all, the large German investment banking houses arose from a specific economic and institutional environment; the first German investment banking houses appeared under conditions of very poor capital markets and the need to fund the midcentury German railway expansion (Gerschenkron 1962; Cameron 1963, 1967). Britain's railways were funded through relatively direct sales of negotiable securities to the public either by private placement or public issue (Broadbridge 1970; Reed 1968, 1975; W. A. Thomas 1973). Most of the provincial stock exchanges had their origins in the railway construction booms of the 1830s and 1840s, and, of course, the facilities in London also expanded to accommodate the needs of the new transportation sector.

In the latter half of the nineteenth century many of Britain's newer industries, such as brewing, bicycles, telegraphs, and telephones, had relatively easy access to either local or London funding. A recent volume on British firms in international competition in both new and old product markets fails to raise long-term funding needs as a constraint on export expansion (Aldcroft 1968). Contrary to Kennedy's view that stock exchange speculation in certain high-flying overseas issues deflected attention from funding the new motor car industry after 1907, Saul's more comprehensive study finds that the principal constraint on meeting foreign competition at home and abroad was the inhibitions of British engineering practice (Saul 1962). Saul explicitly disavows capital as an important retarding factor.

In electricity, another new field sometimes suggested as growing too slowly, the principal problem appears to have been the anarchy of local regulation and unstandardized technical specifications in an industry whose technical characteristics begged for large local monopolies and national standardization as a basis for capturing the considerable economies of scale (Clapham 1968:3:135–38; Landes 1969:281–90). And another serious problem for the expansion of the electricity industry was that British cities were very efficiently served by gas. True, a big investment bank might have been an organizing agent for overcoming local regulation and the lack of standardization in new electrical generating and appliance equipment, but one wonders whether the real culprit is not free trade. As with automobiles, free trade permitted a much higher degree of competition in the early stages of the electrical generating and appliance equipment industry than took place in the highly protected American and German markets. In these countries, tariff-protected oligopolies or monopolies were the agents that forced standardization and dealt with recalcitrant local governments. One has to wonder whether a big British investment bank could have helped the problem of early French competition in motor cars or the anarchic local regulations and technical specifications in the electrical industry in the absence of tariff-induced and protected monopoly power.

Finally, there seems little reason to assume that the nonapperance of big investment banks in Britain was due to the supply-side blockage. The investment banking idea was a well-known European innovation by the mid-nineteenth century. Furthermore, Continental investment banks were quite willing to set up branches or new banks in other countries (Cameron 1963). Kennedy's research turned up several British attempts, albeit failing, to start investment banks in the 1860s and 1870s.

In sum, although new enterprise was never elastically funded, the question is whether long-term funding was a significant constraint for the growth of new enterprise of the period. The conclusion here is that the evidence is insufficient to prove the case. Thus, if funds flowed abroad it was not because new domestic industry was underfunded by institutional immaturity or inadequacy.

C. TESTING INVESTOR BIAS

Economic theory has long postulated the existence of a relationship between asset risk and return. The risk attaching to a particular asset may be viewed as the probability distributions of possible rewards accruing to the asset's owner at future points in time. Uncertainty refers to the degree of confidence the investor places in his perception of these distributions. The usual hypothesis is that, in the absence of barriers to competition in the capital market (including an unequal distribution of knowledge), differences between the returns to various assets depend on the relative degrees of risk and uncertainty associated with each asset. Recently, a fully articulated theory of the relationship between relative degree of risk and return has appeared (Lintner 1965a, 1965b; Sharpe 1964), an outgrowth of the mean-standard deviation models of portfolio choice first evolved by Markowitz 1959 and Tobin 1958. Importantly, the new model of capital asset pricing makes possible a test of the propositions that certain regional and scale-of-issue effects biased the allocations of financial resources passing through the British capital market. There are two hypotheses concerning the bias of the British capital market: British investors and capital market institutions, and particularly the issuing houses, were biased in favor of overseas assets; these same individuals and institutions were biased in favor of large borrowers. In both cases, given the high degree of competition in the market for outstanding securities, the implication of these hypotheses is that some factor or factors impinged on the British capital market's perception of risk and its effect on return.

This section is devoted to a test of the existence of such factors in the market for equity shares. While the equity market does not include the substantial amounts of government debt instruments found in the debenture market, it has the advantage of a much broader coverage in manufacturing and commerce than found in the debenture market. Furthermore, most hypotheses lump the behavior of the capital market toward government debt instruments with that of the railways, a sector well represented in the equity market. Finally, since the hypothesized investor biases and phobias are more likely to evince themselves in relation to assets with the highest levels of uncertainty, a test that concentrates on equity assets has implications about behavior toward less uncertain and risky types of assets. A test of bias performed with debenture data could not be said to carry over to equity behavior with as much strength.

Let us assume that (1) the British capital market consisted of risk averters who maximized their expected utility from end-of-period wealth, and (2) these investors made their optimal portfolio decisions solely on the basis of expected return and standard deviation of returns with the various available portfolios.[4] In other words, investors always chose the portfolio with a risk (standard deviation) for a given level of return, and, given the level of risk, they always chose the portfolio with the highest return. Further, let us assume that (3) all investors had similar decision horizons, (4) all investors had similar attitudes toward expected returns and their standard deviations, (5) the capital market was perfect in the sense that there were many buyers and sellers with the best information, and (6) investors could borrow and lend at the same rate of interest, having equal access to the same portfolio opportunities.

With these assumptions it is possible to build a pricing model for capital assets that gives the equilibrium relationship between risk and expected return. In this relationship the expected return on an asset is a linear function of the asset's risk vis-á-vis other assets and the return on a riskless asset. Thus,

$$E(R_j) = R_f + \lambda \; \text{Cov}(R_j, R_M) \tag{3.1}$$

where

$E(R_j) =$ the expected return on the jth equity instrument.

$R_f =$ the return to a riskless asset,

$\mathrm{Cov}(R_j, R_M) =$ the covariance of R_j, the return to the j th equity instrument, and R_M, the rate of return to the nation's portfolio of all assets (including, of course, the j th asset).

Another way of stating (3.1) is

$$\frac{E(R_j) - R_f}{\mathrm{Cov}(R_j, R_M)} = \lambda \qquad (3.2)$$

$E(R_j) - R_f$ is the return to the j th asset over and above the return to the riskless asset, that is, what is commonly called the "risk premium." $\mathrm{Cov}(R_j, R_M)$ is the asset risk variable in the Shapre-Lintner model. Risk on the individual asset is thus measured by its contribution to the risk of the national (or market) portfolio, or more simply, the asset's risk vis-á-vis other assets.

Equation 3.2 states that the relationship between an asset's expected return and its risk is proportional and the numerical value of the proportion is constant across all assets. It is implicit in assumption 2 that all assets were close substitutes, given expected return and risk. With numerous investors operating in many sectors of the capital market, differences in λ due to these two factors were probably reduced to a minimum through arbitrage.[5] However, if, for any reason, assets of differing region and scale of issue were construed to be somewhat differing commodities, λ need not be constant across all assets.

In order to test this hypothesis, two further assumptions must be made: (1) λ is not deterministic by stochastic, and (2) expectations were realized. The latter assumption is tantamount to assuming the default rate was roughly similar across region and scale of issue. In this regard, it is usually alleged that overseas securities had high default rates, with the implication that home investments were relatively free of such behavior. Shannon's work on the limited companies makes it quite clear that default was certainly not unknown to domestic enterprise, but precisely how much, relative to overseas rates, cannot be settled with available data.[6]

The statistical tests were carried out by fitting a least squares regression line to

$$\frac{(R_j - R_c)}{\mathrm{Cov}(R_j, r_m^i)} = a_1 + a_2 X + a_3 Sc + a \tag{3.3}$$

where

$R_j = R^{t-T}$, the compound annual rate of growth of equity wealth in the jth industry, invested at time t and sold at time T.

R_c = the compound annual rate of growth of wealth of a fixed sum placed in Consols at time t and sold at time T.

$\mathrm{Cov}(R_j, r_m^i)$ = the covariance over time from t to T of R_j and r_m^i a proxy for a national market rate of return,[7]

$X = (0$ if the jth industry was domestic, 1 if the jth industry was nondomestic),

$Sc = (0$ if the firms of the jth industry generally made issues of significantly less than a million pounds, 1 if the jth industry's issues were around a million pounds or more).

With regard to the direction of bias, if the capital market was biased in favor of nondomestic assets, a_2 should be negative in sign. This would mean that, in the act of bidding for nondomestic assets, the risk premium was bid down, relative to a unit of risk.

If the British capital market was biased in favor of large-scale issues, a_3 should have a negative sign. It is not clear, however, that all scale effects will be registered. If investors were biased toward large-scale issues because of a disproportionate belief in their marketability, the sign of a_3 could be negative for the same reasons presented above in connection with the bias for nondomestic issues—investors were willing to pay more per unit of risk and thus lowered the risk premium, $R_j - R_c$. On the other hand, if the scale effects were the result of economies of scale in the issuing procedures, the market price of the asset should not be affected. On the assumption that large and small borrowers' assets have the same level of risk (inclusive of marketability) and the same expected income stream per share, the issue price of the assets of the two borrowers should be the same if the issuing house has properly forecasted the effect of risk on each asset's price. In a competitive environment the large borrower would probably derive a part of the benefits from the lower cost of issue with the issuing house, at least in the short run, making somewhat higher profits. Obviously, once put out on the market, the costs of issue are irrelevant.

Equation 3.3 was estimated by using rate of return observations on thirty-five industrial groupings, 1870–1899, and thirty-seven industrial groupings, 1890–1913.[8] Two proxies for a market rate of return were tested: r_m^1, an equiproportionate weighting of all industrial groupings and r_m^2, employing the same groupings as r_m^1 but weighted according to a rough estimate of the market value of each industry's equity during the first decade of the twentieth century.[9]

In light of the changes in the scale of issue for industrial and commercial companies in the London capital market beginning in the mid-1880s, a different definition of scale of issue (Sc) was adopted for each regression. For the 1870–1889 test, only railway and social-overhead industries were treated as large-scale issuers (ScA). In the 1890–1913 regression, the textile, food, drink, chemical, and iron, coal, and steel industries were added (ScB).

The results of the regression tests may be found in table 3.3. On the whole they offer little encouragement for the scale-of-issue or regional-bias hypothesis. The R^2 values that measure the fit of the entire equation were uniformly terrible. With regard to the coefficients on individual variables, none pass t-test criteria. The usual upper bound for statistical significance is a probability level of 0.05, or, in terms of the t-test statistic given in table 3.3, a t value of about 2.04 or higher.[10]

Although none of the coefficients pass muster on t-test criteria, the signs of the coefficients are suggestive. The sign of the scale bias is uniformly negative, confirming the direction of bias, albeit

Table 3.3

U.K. Capital Market Biases: Regression Tests

Estimated equation:

$$(R_j - R_c)/Cov(R_j, r_m^i) = a_1 + a_2 X + a_3 Sc + e$$

Index of market returns Utilized	X	Coefficient t-values for ScA	ScB	R^2	# obs.
1870–1889:					
r_m^1	−.74	insig.		.02	37
r_m^2	−1.22	−.61		.05	37
1890–1913:					
r_m^1	1.68		−.46	.08	37
r_m^2	1.24		−.77	.10	37

weak, implied by the scale-of-issue hypothesis. Investors appear to have had a persistent but weak tendency to bid up the price of large-scale issues and thereby yield lower risk premiums per unit of risk.

In turning to the regional bias hypothesis, the sign on the regional variable's coefficient is negative in the 1870–1889 regression test but turns positive in the 1890–1913 test. British investors appear to have switched for a highly unstable and weak preference for nondomestic issues, 1870–1889, to a somewhat less unstable preference for domestic issues, 1890–1913. In the earlier period, investors showed a tendency to raise (lower) the risk premium on domestic (nondomestic) assets relative to a unit of domestic (nondomestic) risk. Later the market showed a disproportionate preference for domestic issues that led to a lower (high) price per unit of domestic (nondomestic) risk, a higher (lower) price on domestic (nondomestic) issues and a lower (higher) risk premium.

In conclusion, hypothesized scale-of-issue and regional biases in the British capital market do not appear to have significantly affected the long-run pricing of equity assets, 1870–1913. It would be misleading, however, to deny the presence of bias, even though the biases were not sufficiently stable to influence capital asset pricing in the long run. British investors evinced a weak and unstable preference for large and nondomestic issues in the 1870–1889 period. In the following twenty-four years, a somewhat less unstable bias for domestic issues appeared with the very weak bias for large issues continuing.[11]

D. SUMMARY

Between 1870 and 1913, limited liability became the major framework for private industrial and commercial enterprise in the United Kingdom.[12] In the process, something like £1400 million in domestic industrial and commercial securities were successfully issued, raising the share of such assets in the total of all long-term securities held in the United Kingdom from around 4 percent to 19 percent. The number of provincial brokers rose fourfold and the number in London increased by almost as much.[13] Rapid expansion of other occupations concerned with provincial and London services is also evident. Given the analysis of the technology of issuing services and the role of location, the rapid growth of specialized services in both the provinces and London does not seem to suggest institutional rigidity. Rather, it points toward an increased extent of market yielding a more nearly complete division of function. Direct evidence on increased liquidity and diminished relative costs of borrowing is slim, but the materials available are highly suggestive. Regular trading of a greatly enlarged proportion of Britain's industrial and commercial property could not help but increase liquidity,[14] especially in the provinces, if not lower the cost of borrowing.

Evidence has not been offered to substantiate the possible gains to Britain's productivity from the increase in the quantity and quality of information concerning her industrial and commercial sector, let alone the multiple overseas activities that sought and received funding from British wealth in this period. Nor has the question of externalities been raised.[15] A market that brings together private investors and borrowers will offer signals for the allocation of financial resources based on private, not social, rates of return. Any external economies or diseconomies from overseas railway investment, domestic and urban agglomerations, or overseas investment in the presence of domestic unemployment will not be fully registered, if at all. However, it does seem likely that two hypothesized biases that were alleged to have significantly altered the private signals of the market, regional and size of issue biases, were fairly weak in the long run.

CHAPTER 4: **MICRO PROCESSES Determinants of U.K. Annual** Investment in the United States and Other Regions

A. AGGREGATE AND MICRO PROCESSES: AN INTRODUCTION

As discussed in chapter 1 the writings of economists and economic historians afford four related explanations for the direction and magnitude of British overseas investment in the late nineteenth and early twentieth centuries. Three of these explanations argue that domestic British factors pushed the funds out of Britain. First, it is argued that various forms of institutional rigidity and investor bias led to underfunding of domestic industry and overfunding of overseas assets. Second, it is argued that domestic rates of return were either declining or unusually low and were thereby shifting investor attention to overseas projects, which were relatively more attractive. Third, it is suggested that Britons saved too much in the aggregate, the excess overspilling into overseas employments.

The fourth explanation differs from these first three in that it argues that an overseas factor was the dominant cause of the massive outflow; unusually high returns abroad pulled British savings to overseas assets. Institutional rigidity and investor bias were discussed in the previous chapter and it was concluded that insufficient evidence existed to treat these factors as major influences on the immense capital outflow. Discussion must now turn to testing the remaining three explanations—low domestic returns, excess domestic savings, and high overseas returns.

There are two levels at which these causal factors might manifest themselves. Examination of the aggregate movements of British savings, domestic investment, and net foreign lending can cast light on these determinants. As noted in chapter 2, domestic and overseas investments moved in inverse long swings of 15 to 24 years in length. By using models specifying the determinants of aggregate savings, domestic fixed investment, and net foreign lending, several methods are available to test the importance of the three hypothesized causes of the massive outflow.

However, differences across overseas regions and sectors in the timing and extent of their use of British savings strongly suggest that a diverse and changing set of British savers, British investment opportunities, and overseas borrowers influenced the aggregate flow of British funds abroad. As many authors have noted, long swings do not manifest themselves most sharply in national aggregative data. Their strongest manifestation is seen in railway investment, urban residential investment, urban utility investment, and internal and external population migration in Britain and movement to each of the regions of recent settlement, Argentina, Australia, Canada, New Zealand, and the United States.[1] Data on the net international capital movements and new long-term overseas issues raised in Britain make it quite clear that the timing of British lending to specific overseas regions did not always closely adhere to the long-swing pattern shown by the aggregate (Bloomfield 1968; Simon 1967). U.S. and Argentinian capital imports show substantial involvement in a long-swing pattern and fairly close timing with aggregate British capital exports. However, the strength of the surges in capital imports into Australia in the 1880s, Canada in the decade before World War I, Europe in the early 1870s and just before World War I, and South Africa at the turn of the nineteenth century suggests that movements in capital imports were not a necessary concomitant of long swings in these regions' railway and urban residential sectors. Indeed, as noted in chapter 2, capital imports into these regions were perhaps one big shot, rather than repeated long swings. Finally, each overseas region raised money abroad for different purposes at different times and with a shifting mix of government versus private enterprise (Simon 1967, 1970; I. Stone 1968, 1977). This reduces the chances of isolating the precise causal mechanisms of the outflow in the aggregate British savings and investment data, let alone of beginning to weigh the importance of the various determinants. Indeed, to date, econometric testing of the determinants of aggregate British net foreign lending has been quite unsuccessful.[2]

Of course, the aggregate savings desires of British households and firms, and the extent of profitable opportunities home and overseas, were not unlimited. A nation's income and its distribution, wealth and its distribution, consumption desires, technologies, and industrial organization place constraints on the pace of accumulation. Hence, to dispense with an aggregate analysis is to evade an important part of the economic reality. Nevertheless, the diversity hidden behind the aggregates warrants considerable discussion before an attempt to analyze aggregate behavior.

Most economic histories of British lending in the late nineteenth and early twentieth centuries have taken a disaggregated approach, typically focusing on the borrowing of one overseas region.[3] The advantages of disaggregation are presumably that if the market for a particular overseas asset is sufficiently well defined, the stable behavior of the particular lenders and borrowers will have a good chance of revealing itself in the quantitative and qualitative data. Data limitations often mean the smallest unit of observation is a large political unit such as a colony or nation. However, there are also sound economic and historical reasons for this level of aggregation. First, it was often the case that British investment in a colony or nation was predominantly in one sector, for example, mining in South Africa or railways in the United States and Argentina. Just as often, even though British investment went to several sectors, the opportunities in these sectors were strongly linked. The fundamental cause of the region's attraction to British capitalists was often relatively unsettled and highly productive lands. The returns to land, labor, and capital excited agricultural expansion and, in the process, raised the returns to all sorts of social-overhead and residential capital in the immediate surroundings, as well as the avenues of transport and communication to distant markets. British lenders perceived these links and often acted on them; failure of one sector in an overseas region tended to turn British investment elsewhere. Finally, although the sectoral and government-private mix of British investment in each overseas region varied across time, these shifts were less pronounced than differences across countries (Simon 1967; I. Stone 1968, 1977). In sum, aggregation to the level of colonial or national economic activity can be plausibly supported, even if it bears continual attention.

It is taken for granted in these disaggregated studies that *ex ante* rates of return, net of risk, were relatively higher abroad than at home in the United Kingdom. Examination of this assumption, as well as a host of other issues connected with rates of return on financial capital, is reserved for chapters 5 and 6. To the extent that *realized* returns are any indication of *expected* returns, the evidence presented in chapter 5 suggests that the assumption is correct in the aggregate and for all tested sectors, gross and net of risk premiums. Apart from the average value of expected returns, the new markets, new technologies, and altered national economies also afforded new opportunities for European portfolio diversification.

But once the grounds for the dominant direction of Britain's international capital flow have been indicated, the problem remains of how investors in the United Kingdom and overseas responded to the opportunities created by the gap in risk-adjusted rates of return. Did U.K. or overseas participants dominate the play of the market and in what manner? One possibility is that overseas borrowers were eager to raise funds in Britain, the timing of their needs determining the action of the U.K. capital market for financing instruments. In the extreme, there might be evidence of an overseas-induced glut of securities. Another possibility is that U.K. wealth holders were eager to hold these relatively high-return securities. Finally, it might be the case that neither overseas nor U.K. participants showed any special eagerness but that the speed of overseas capital formation or the rapid accumulation of wealth in the United Kingdom dominated the market. Again, the question is, given a disequilibrating event in risk-adjusted rates of return that created a gap between overseas and home returns, who dominated the market and in what manner?

The problem readily lends itself to econometric testing by use of a reduced-form approach.[4] A specific set of independent variables reflecting U.K. and overseas "opportunities" is judged to be involved in determining the variations in the flow of funds to an overseas region. This set of independent variables is then regressed on a measure of the flow of capital to the given region, and the balance of U.K. versus overseas influence is determined by the size of the increment to the multiple correlation coefficient.

In this literature no attempt is generally made to determine a detailed structure of the economic processes guiding the transfer of capital. Thus, it is never clear whether the statistical contribution of a particular variable is due to the responsiveness of the capital flow to a given (percentage) increase of an independent variable (that is, its elasticity) or to the relative size of the independent variable's movements. For example, assume that the supply of assets from a particular overseas country is infinitely elastic and that the U.K. demand for this country's assets responds to movements in U.K. national wealth, along with several other variables. If the demand elasticity with respect to wealth is relatively high, this may signal the relative desirability of the overseas country's assets; if the growth of the wealth variable itself is relatively rapid, this is an indication of the extent of U.K. thrift with respect to all assets. Furthermore, little attention has been paid to the possibility that there were important changes in the underlying economic structure guiding the overseas region's capital imports. New industrial sectors and new financing arrangements may rise to prominence, possibly altering the structure of supply-and-demand relations for the overseas region's assets abroad. Even within a sector, factors such as a government guarantee or land grants may change the relative quality of a sector's securities, again altering the underlying economic structure guiding the market for a region's assets abroad.

This chapter develops a model of the structure of the export of U.K. funds, 1870–1913, encompassing both demand and supply behavior (section B). Using data (section C) on the transfer of capital from the United Kingdom to the United States, the model's structural parameters, the elasticities, are statistically estimated and discussed (section D). The choice of investigating the transfer to the United States is dictated, to some extent, by availability of data, but the pattern of U.S. investment bears special interest because it was the United Kingdom's largest investment in a single overseas nation or colony. In 1914, U.S. assets were a fifth of total U.K. overseas holdings (Feis 1930:23). Furthermore, the relative riskiness and other characteristics of the United Kingdom's American holdings suggest it may have implications for the pattern of investment in other, noncolonial areas.[5]

The estimated structural equations are then solved for the

"reduced-form" equation in the capital transfer variable, and the question of which participants most strongly influenced the marketing of these overseas assets and in what manner is studied by examining the contribution of the movements in the exogenous variables and the estimated elasticities (section E). These U.S. results are then compared with the findings of studies of other regions of recent settlement (section F), and the chapter concludes with a brief summary (section G).

This chapter does not examine the "push" versus "pull" problem as it was defined in chapter 1 or the beginning of this chapter. It assumes that either a push or pull in risk-adjusted returns created the grounds for the movement of funds from the United Kingdom to a particular region's assets. What is addressed in this chapter is how overseas borrowers and U.K. lenders reacted to the opportunities created by the push or pull and with what force. As in the case of the investigation of the microeconomics of U.K. capital market institutions in the previous chapter, the current investigation of the microeconomies of the U.K. market for a single overseas region's assets forms a fundamental building block of the international process. The justification of this approach is that the behavior in a single, carefully delimited arena forms the best starting point for understanding the complexities of overseas investment in this period. In chapters 5 and 6 the behavior of many markets is investigated through the study of realized return and risk on all U.K. home and overseas assets, empirically demonstrating the gap in risk-adjusted returns assumed in this chapter. Then, in part III analysis moves to the aggregate level, examining aggregate U.K. savings behavior and its interaction with investment demands at home and abroad.

B. MODELING THE MICRO PROCESSES

Most U.K. overseas investment took the form of portfolio, rather than direct investment (see chapter 2). It therefore seems reasonable to examine the role of U.K. lenders and overseas borrowers in the context of those forces that influenced the demand and supply for negotiable overseas assets offered and held in the United Kingdom.[6]

Recent work in the theory of the demand for financial assets begins by stressing that each asset or group of assets had distinct return and risk characteristics (see, e.g., Sharpe 1970). Demand behavior focuses on obtaining desired amounts of those assets that provide the individual's (or institution's) choices of return and risk characteristics as constrained by the individual's (or institution's) total wealth. For any given asset or group of assets the dependent variable in the individual's demand relation is thus taken to be the desired ratio of the stock of the asset or group of assets to the stock of the individual's total wealth.

If the ratio demand relation holds, the elasticity of the desired stock of the given asset with respect to wealth should be approximately unity. The demand elasticity with respect to wealth could, however, be different from unity and statistically stable if the average level of wealth, the distribution of wealth, or the underlying structure of return-risk tastes change so as to disproportionately favor or disfavor the assumed stable return-risk characteristics of the given asset or group of assets.

The use of a U.K. wealth concept that incorporates both domestic and nondomestic assets represents a departure from previous studies. In these studies U.K. forces included the domestic component of U.K. wealth only, implicitly ignoring the effects of wealth accumulated in overseas assets. Such an approach misrepresents what most economists would deem to be the appropriate behavioral relationship guiding the demand for a particular asset or group of assets, substituting a portion of the relevant individuals' wealth for their total wealth in the demand relation. It also misrepresents the actual behavior of U.K. investors. Clearly, the facility with which U.K. investors moved around the globe suggests that a high return for given risk was sought anywhere, at home or abroad. Therefore, if U.K. participation is taken to mean U.K. *controlled and initiated* forces guiding the urge to invest in a particular region, a geographically all-encompassing concept of wealth must be employed to capture the effects of the increasing and changing needs of British capitalists in pursuit of the best combinations of risk and return for their portfolios. A large but partial component of that accumulated wealth is insufficient.[7]

While some asset demand theories assume a homogeneity of all wealth holders' decision horizons and their views on expected return and risk, it is probably most realistic to stress differences in portfolio demand behavior that are based on the size of an individual's wealth (Arrow 1971:ch. 3). Thus, when individual demands are aggregated into a national demand function, the relevant wealth variable should be something approximating the total wealth of those of similar outlook. To be more specific, it is highly likely that the wealth position of those U.K. citizens who owned post office savings accounts had little to do with the demand for risky assets, such as a U.S. bond or equity instrument. Thus, some attempt should be made to estimate and employ a concept of wealth, at least as far as U.S. assets are concerned, that reflects the accumulations of those potentially interested in risky assets.

The other two prominent variables influencing the demand for the stock of a particular asset are the asset's own expected yield and the expected yield on alternative assets. The introduction of separate measures of risk and return in the demand relation would be of considerable interest, but a wide-ranging search for a time series risk variable proved a total failure.[8] If yields are dominated by a positive correlation with movements in pure return, as is generally assumed, the signs of the own- and cross-elasticities should be positive and negative, respectively.

Although there are no historical hypotheses on the numerical value of the own-return elasticity, the cross-elasticity has been the subject of a long-standing debate on the substitutability of home for foreign investment (see Kindleberger 1964:61–67 for an excellent summary of the debate). If the demand-side market segmentation implied by the 1931 MacMillan Report (the so-called MacMillan Gap) holds true, the cross-elasticity of British holdings of a given overseas country's assets with respect to domestic British returns is likely to be low and relatively unchanging (Great Britain 1931:171). In chapter 3 it was suggested that the isolation of the massive London capital market from provincial affairs was not the result of rigidity of London's capital market facilities, of the unwillingness of domestic industrial borrowers to offer debt instruments of the type most desired by the new "trustee" investor, or of a bias of U.K. asset owners for overseas assets. Rather, the isolation stemmed from the ability of provincial capital markets and wealth to satisfy home industry's then generally small-scale needs cheaply and flexibly. As the scale of domestic industry and commerce rose in the latter half of the period, however, the wealth and facilities of the London capital market soon became seriously involved in the long-term funding of domestic industry. The implication of these findings for the British demand function for a given overseas country's assets is that, while the cross-elasticity with respect to home returns might have been low in absolute value initially, it should have risen over the period.

By allowing for the possibility that the elasticity of the demand for overseas assets with respect to wealth might be other than unity (although positive) and by introducing notation that anticipates our interest in the capital transfer to the United States, the U.K. demand relation may be written either as:

$$A^D / W = f(\overset{+}{W}, \overset{-}{r^{UK}}, \overset{+}{r^A}), \tag{4.1}$$

or

$$A^D = g(\overset{+}{W}, \overset{-}{r^{UK}}, \overset{+}{r^A}), \tag{4.2}$$

where A^D = the U.K. demand for the stock of U.S. assets; W = the stock of wealth of U.K. investors potentially interested in risky overseas assets; r^A = the yield on U.S. assets; and r^{UK} = the yield offered on alternative assets. The signs above the variables indicate the expected direction of the relationship with A^D.

The principal supplier of U.S. assets to the U.K. capital market during the years 1870 to 1913 was the U.S. railway industry. U.S. government securities were an important element in the U.S. component of U.K. portfolios at the beginning of the period, but by 1880 U.S. railway securities were, overwhelmingly, the dominant element in U.K. holdings of U.S. assets. It therefore seems reasonable to assume that conditions relating to U.S. railway investment and finance were the central determinants of the supply of U.S. assets offered in the U.K.

By proceeding on this assumption, two aspects of U.S. railway development further simplify the task of specifying the supply side of the trans-Atlantic capital flow. First, retained earnings were, on average, a fairly small source of funds for U.S. railway investment expenditure until the years just before 1913. According to Ulmer, during the years 1880–1890, 1893–1907, and 1907–1916, retained earnings plus depreciation reserves represented 2.4 percent, 9.5 percent, rising to 42.9 percent, respectively, of the sources of railway investment expenditure (Ulmer 1960:502). Thus, for all but the last seven years of the period 1870–1913, it seems safe to treat corporate savings as a minor influence on external financing decisions.

The second simplification derives from the research of Kmenta and Williamson (1966), and Neal (1969) on the demand for U.S. railway investment goods. While these authors differ substantially on a number of issues, one similarity in their conclusions is that the demand for U.S. railway investment goods in the late nineteenth and early twentieth centuries was not related contemporaneously to the yield of U.S. railway equity or bonds. Lagged values of these yields were related to the current demand for railway investment goods but not their current values. This suggests that the determinants of U.S. railway investment goods demand occurred prior to the period in which financial quantities and prices were determined in the trans-Atlantic asset market.[9] Hence, the desired level of railway investment expenditures may be taken as an approximately exogenous determinant of the trans-Atlantic capital flow, and a separate U.S. railway investment demand relation need not be estimated as part of the economic relationships that simultaneously interacted to determine that flow.

Thus, in setting aside the specification of a corporate savings and an investment goods demand relation, the task of modeling the supply side of our model reduces to specifying the determinants of the supply of financial assets and the degree to which the asset demands of U.S. investors conditioned the links between the U.S. railway companies and the U.K. capital market. On the tentative assumption that the U.K. and U.S. capital markets were tied closely by arbitrage,[10] two behavioral relationships command our attention: first, the relationship that guided the U.S. railway companies' total offerings of long-term securities and, second, the relationship that guided the U.S. demand for these assets.

With some oversimplification, the relationship guiding the total amounts of long-term securities offered by U.S. railway companies may be written as

$$dX = h(\overset{+}{IUSR}, \overset{-}{r^A}), \qquad (4.3)$$

where $dX = X_t - X_{t-1}$ = the net annual issue of long-term railway debt instruments at time t; $IUSR$ = the desired amount of railway investment expenditure; and r^A = the yield on U.S. railway financial assets. The role of the desired amount of U.S. railway investment expenditure in determining the amount of railway securities issued is obvious. A combination of relatively limited profits and owner interest dictated a heavy reliance on external funding that, in turn, suggests that expected investment expenditures should be a very important and stable factor in accounting for variations in the long-term security offerings of American railway industry; r^A is present to capture the role of the cost of finance.

The U.S. demand for long-term railway securities can be characterized by a portfolio demand relation analogous to equation 2:

$$Z^D = j(\overset{+}{T}, \overset{-}{r^{US}}, \overset{+}{r^A}) \qquad (4.4)$$

where Z^D = the U.S. demand for the stock of U.S. railway debt; T = the stock of wealth of U.S. investors interested in risky assets; r^{US} = the yield on alternative U.S. assets; and r^A = the yield on U.S. railway assets. The signs above the variables indicate the expected direction of the relationship.[11]

A model of the trans-Atlantic capital migration is now possible, consisting of a U.K. demand relation, equation 4.2, a trans-Atlantic supply relation (which combines the behavioral patterns underlying equations 4.3 and 4.4), and an equilibrium condition that assumes the trans-Atlantic supply of securities was equal to the U.K. demand. Unfortunately, a problem immediately arises from the fact that the asset supply behavior underlying equation 4.3 is formulated in terms of the net change in the outstanding stock of financing instruments, that is, in terms of flows, while the portfolio demand relations are formulated in terms of outstanding stocks. This problem is further complicated by the fact that careful estimates of the total outstanding debt of the U.S. railways, X_t, are not available at present. Thus, either the demand relationships must be rewritten in terms of flows or the trans-Atlantic supply relation in terms of stocks.

Clearly, the latter does less violence to underlying behavioral patterns. Portfolio theory is explicitly formulated to incorporate behavior toward the stock of outstanding debt and its current increment. In a fairly stable institutional environment, it is plausible to have the desired total stock of outstanding long-term debt roughly proportional to the nominal value of the desired tangible capital stock. To the extent that the average contributions of retained earnings and short-term debt markedly rise or fall on trend, this rough proportionality of the stock of debt and tangible capital stock will not hold. However, given the trend stability suggested by Ulmer's data (except for the years 1907–1913), a rough integration of equation 4.3 seems a reasonable simplification. Rewriting 4.3 in terms of stocks, we get:

$$X_t^S = g(\overset{+}{K}, \overset{-}{r^A}), \qquad (4.5)$$

where K = the desired nominal stock of U.S. railway tangible capital. Then, by subtracting (4.4) from (4.5), the excess supply relationship emerges as:

$$A_t^S = X_t^S - Z_t^D = g(K, r^A) - j(T, r^{US}, r^A)$$

$$= k(\overset{+}{K}, \overset{-}{T}, \overset{+}{r^{US}}, \overset{-}{r^A}), \qquad (4.6)$$

where the signs above the variables again denote the expected direction of the relationship. Note that, with U.S. excess supply conditions now expressed in terms of A, the coefficients on K, T, r^{US} and r^A may reflect the fact that the British purchased more bonds relative to common stocks than were issued by the U.S. railway companies. If so, the estimated coefficients of the excess supply equation should capture U.S. demand and supply conditions for this mix of assets and not the spectrum of risk and return embodied in the mix offered by the U.S. railway companies. Note also that, while T and r^{US} can be reasonably identified as measures of the influence of U.S. demand conditions and K as a measure of U.S. supply conditions, r^A is an amalgam. In the trans-Atlantic, excess supply relation, r^A is an index of both the cost of external financing to U.S. railway companies and the gains to U.S. assets demanders. For example, if r^A rises, this will tend to cause a reduction in all external financing and a rise in U.S. demand for these assets, each factor tending in turn to reduce U.K. placements of U.S. railway assets.

With little loss in generality, it is both mathematically and statistically useful to write the specific mathematical form of the demand and excess supply functions, the structural relations, in multiplicative form. Let

$$A^D = c_1 W^{a_1} r_{UK}^{a_2} r_A^e \tag{4.7}$$

and

$$A^S = c_2 K^{b_1} r_{US}^{b_2} T^{b_3} r_A^{-g} \tag{4.8}$$

where A^D, A^S, W, T, K, r_A, r_{US}, and r_{UK} are defined above; e, a_1, and a_2 = the elasticities of demand with respect to the own-interest rate, U.K. wealth, and interest rates on alternative assets obtainable in the United Kingdom, respectively; g, b_1, b_2, and b_3 = the elasticities of supply with respect to the own-interest rate, U.S. railway tangible capital stock, alternative yields obtainable in the United States, and U.S. wealth, respectively; and c_1 and c_2 are constants. By assuming a process of market equilibration,

$$A^D = A^S \tag{4.9}$$

and letting D and S stand for the effect of the demand and supply shift variables, that is,

$$D = C_1 W^{a_1} r_{UK}^{a_2} \tag{4.10}$$

and

$$S = c_2 K^{b_1} r_{US}^{b_2} T^{b_3}, \tag{4.11}$$

the equilibrium capital transfer and its interest rate are given by solving equations 4.4, 4.5, and 4.6 for A and r_A, that is

$$A = D^{g/(g+e)} S^{e(g+e)} \tag{4.12}$$

and

$$r_A = (S/D)^{1/(g+e)}. \tag{4.13}$$

These latter two equations are the reduced forms.

Since our interest concerns the behavior of A, the stock of U.S. assets held in the U.K., the important relation is the reduced form equation 4.12 and its rate-of-growth transformation,

$$\overset{o}{A} = (g/(g+e))\overset{o}{D} + (e/(g+e))\overset{o}{S}, \tag{4.14}$$

where

$$\dot{D} = a_1 \dot{W} + a_2 \dot{r}_{UK}$$

$$\dot{S} = b_1 \dot{K} + b_2 \dot{r}_{US} + b_3 \dot{T}$$

(a dot above a variable denotes a rate of growth). The total effect of U.S. participants on the growth of U.K. holdings of U.S. securities, $\dot{A}$, is represented by $(e/(g+e))\dot{S}$, where $\dot{S}$ is the rate of growth of the combined effects of K, T, and r_{US} (the three exogenous trans-Atlantic supply shift variables) and $e/(g+e)$ registers the effect of the relative disparity in the size of the own-interest demand elasticity.[12] Analogously, the effect of U.K. participation would be the immense accumulation of U.K. wealth searching for new opportunities at home and abroad ($W1$

or $W2$), and the return on alternative non-U.S. assets (r_{UK}). Formally, the total effect of U.K. participants on the growth of A is represented by $(g/(g + e))\dot{D}$, where D is the rate of growth of the combined effects of $\dot{W}$ and r_{UK} (the two exogenous U.K demand shift variables) and $g/(g + e)$, which captures the effects of the relative disparity in the size of the own-interest, trans-Atlantic, supply elasticity.

The numerical values of the structural parameters, e, a_1, a_2, g, b_1, b_2, and b_3, are likely to change over long periods of time. The demand elasticities may change owing to shifts in the average level of wealth, the distribution of wealth, return-risk tastes, and the asset's return-risk characteristics. For example, although the U.K. demand elasticities with respect to own-interest (e) and alternative rates of return ($a2$) may be relatively low within certain periods, indicating some form of market segmentation, a slow but ultimately substantial secular change in an asset's return-risk characteristics may still affect the transfer through a shift in the demand elasticity with respect to wealth. The elasticities in the excess supply relation may also shift, the result of changes in the size and structure of U.S. wealth or improved U.S. capital markets. Over periods as long as twenty years these elasticities may remain fairly constant; historically, the level and distribution of wealth, return-risk tastes, the return-risk characteristics of assets, and the comparative advantage of capital markets change very little from year to year. However, when the period of observation for two rapidly developing economies is forty-four years, the constancy of these elasticities bears testing.

C. THE DATA SET.

In turning to the data required to estimate our model, the estimator of the stock of U.S. assets held in the U.K. (A) is a cumulation of Simon's time series of the flow of money calls on sales of U.S. portfolio assets through London Stock Exchange.[13] As has been noted by Simon and Hall, a more accurate estimator of net U.K. holdings would also reflect movements in outstanding securities, redemptions, purchases of new issues first offered in New York or continental European exchanges, and the movements of those elements in the short-term accounts that through stable increase acted like long-term assets (e.g., deposits raised in Britain by banks operating abroad) (Simon 1967:53; Hall 1968:13, 36). It is probable, however, that movements in money calls on the London new issue market reflected the missing elements in the correct total in most years and that the errors in the other years would be largely random. If, for example, outstanding securities were moving from British to U.S. portfolios because the British were selling and Americans were buying, it would be expected that the quantity of new issues offered in London would also slow down. Similarly, the new issue market must have been affected by movements in redemptions, purchases on overseas exchanges, and the generally stable deposits of banks operating abroad. In other words, the fact that London was a very active and highly competitive market strongly suggests that movements of securities in the new issue market, overwhelmingly the most important element in any correct total of U.K. holdings, are a good proxy for the movement, timing and, to a lesser extent, the amplitude of the correct net holdings total.

Two estimates of U.K. wealth, W, were prepared for the U.K. asset demand function. The first, $W1$, starts with an estimate of the stock of U.K. reproducible capital in 1870 and proceeds to 1913 by cumulating net domestic fixed investment and net foreign lending.[14] The second estimate of U.K. wealth, $W2$, attempts to approximate more closely the wealth of those investors specifically interested in acquiring risky assets. $W2$ is thus the sum of outstanding commercial bank loans, the stock of foreign portfolio investments, and the stock of domestic portfolio investments.[15] The length of the $W2$ series limits any test of the differential behavior of the owners of wealth to the period 1895–1913.[16] T, the wealth of U.S. investors, is approximately by Kuznets' series on the U.S. tangible capital stock.[17]

The proxy for the expected level of the U.S. railway tangible capital stock, K_{US}, is the actual nominal stock of railway tangible capital (Ulmer 1960:256–57, col. 1). While this substitution might be quite inappropriate if one were examining the relationship between the desired stock or flow of investment expenditures (or their determinants) and domestic U.S. security issues, several factors suggest that the actual level of K_{US}, current or lagged, may bear as much information for the *non-U.S. lender* as lagged profits or other determinants of desired investment expenditures. Movements in U.K. holdings tended to lag behind U.S. issues by one or two years, probably owing to transactions costs and the interests of U.S. asset owners.[18] In a sense, therefore, non-U.S. borrowers had the benefit of concrete information of future investment prospects because the actual capital expenditures taking place gave powerful testimony to the strength of the profit expectations of the U.S. railway companies. Finally, the substitution of variables that could be reasonably said to determine the desired stock leads to difficult multicollinearity problems, and these problems are avoided by using K_{US}.

With regard to the rental rates of the various assets, r_A is estimated by the yield on first-class U.S. railway bonds listed in London, r_{US} is the yield on U.S. industrial equity, and r_{UK} is the yield on first-class U.K. railway bonds listed in London.[19] Other yields series, such as U.K. industrials, Latin American railway bonds, and Australian government bonds, were also introduced into the U.K. demand relation regressions to try to pick up the effects of a broader range of alternative investments, but severe problems of multicollinearity again appeared. A principal components analysis reveals that movements in the yield on U.K. railway bonds provides an excellent proxy for movements in both domestic and colonial yields and a fair one for Latin American yields.[20]

D. ESTIMATING THE U.S. MODEL

In order to use linear regression methods, equations 4.7 and 4.8, the structural demand and excess supply relations must be expressed in logarithmic form. Let the prefix "L" indicate the log transformation; equations 4.7 and 4.8 thus become:

$$LA^D = c_1 + a_1 LW + a_2 Lr_{UK} + e Lr_A \qquad (4.15)$$

and

$$LA^S = c_2 + b_1 LK + b_2 Lr_{US} + b_3 LT + g Lr_A. \qquad (4.16)$$

Both 4.15 and 4.16 overidentified, and it is appropriate, therefore, to employ some method of structural estimation. The principal method of estimation adopted for this study was two-stage least squares with r_A and A as the jointly dependent, endogeneous variables with W, r_{UK}, K, r_{US}, and T as their exogenous determinants.

Early econometric testing established that the basic model was quite robust. Attention then focused on testing for shifts in the structural parameters of the demand and excess supply equations and on specifying their respective lag structures. Chow tests suggested that, regardless of any tentatively assumed lag structures, the structural parameters were not constant throughout the years 1874–1913. Further experiment extablished that the structural parameter estimates were fairly stable within the subperiods 1874–1894 and 1895–1913; this periodization has been adopted for the remainder of the study .

Portfolio theory implies that the manner in which capital market behavior adjusts through time is best described by the stock adjustment model of lagged behavior. In brief, the right-hand variables of 4.15 and 4.16 are said to determine the desired stock of assets to be held or offered, but the annual adjustment to the desired stock is only partial. By following the usual procedure for estimating the parameters of a stock adjustment model, the lagged endogenous variable, LA_{t-1}, was added to equations 4.15 and 4.16 for each of the subperiods 1874–1894 and 1895–1913.[21] T-tests established that the regression coefficients of LA_{t-1} were statistically significant and thus the stock adjustment hypothesis of lagged behavior could not be rejected.[22] Unfortunately, the addition of LA_{t-1} to the demand and excess supply relations introduces the problem of multicollinearity into the demand relation for 1874–1894 and the excess supply relation for 1895–1913 to a degree that cannot be ignored. A commonly accepted method for dealing with this problem is to drop one of the collinear right-hand variables. Rather than drop an element of the basic behavioral structure, LA_{t-1} was eliminated from these two equations.[23]

Table 4.1 presents the parameters of the demand and excess supply equations for 1874–1894 and 1895–1913 estimated by two-stage least squares regression. The r^2 statistics are quite good

Table 4.1

The Demand and Supply of U.S. Portfolio Assets Held in the U.K., 1874-1913[a]

	c	LW1	LW2	Lr^{UK}	LK	LT_{t-1}	Lr^{US}_{t-2}	Lr^A	LA_{t-1}	r^2	dw	rho
I 1874-1894												
1 LA^D	-13.2015 (3.74)	2.3023 (6.67)						.4216 (1.20)		.99	1.34	.59
2 LA^S	.9788 (.72)			-.0876 (.30)	.0911 (1.25)	-.0202 (.08)	-.0904 (2.01)	-.1815 (.86)	.8582 (3.42)	.99	2.02	-.16
II 1895-1913												
3 LA^D	-3.886 (2.10)	.8062 (2.27)		-.1087 (.75)				.1739 (2.69)	.5628 (3.00)	.99	2.03	–
4 LA^D	-4.658 (1.68)		1.041 (1.69)	-.1853 (.92)				.3742 (1.95)	.3998 (1.12)	.99	1.98	–
5[b] LA^S	2.6202 (1.00)				1.0197 (1.54)	-.2733 (.40)	.1274 (.78)	-.5957 (1.81)		.97	.57	.22

[a] The bracketed terms values of the t-statistic. For sample sizes of around 20, t = 2.09 at the .05 level, 2.85 at the .01 level. With 2-stage least squares estimators these statistics are only asymptotically correct, i.e., in large samples. Furthermore, there is undoubtedly multicollinearity present which commonly leads to underestimation of their true value.

[b] Equation (5) was estimated using LW2 as the exogenous instrument for U.K. wealth. A separate supply equation employing W1, complementary to Equation (3)'s demand curve could not be estimated. Extreme multicollinearity during the first stage of estimation seems to have resulted in intractable computational difficulties.

Data Source: See text Section C and notes.

given our use of structural estimation methods.[24] If ordinary least squares methods are employed to estimate the equations comprising table 4.1, the resulting r^2 statistics are equally good. The low t-statistics are largely due to the irreducible residue of the multicollinearity problem. The lags on T and r^{US} follow from the crude findings that movements in U.K. holdings of U.S. assets tended to lag one year behind movements in U.S. holdings of U.S. railway securities. If U.K. holdings lagged U.S. holdings by one year, it seemed plausible that the exogenous determinants of the U.S. demand for U.S. railway securities would evince a similar lead-lag pattern. Experiment rapidly revealed that a one-year lag on LT and a two-year lag on Lr^{US} was the best pairing.

In turning to the various structures presented in table 4.1, it seems clear that the U.K. demand for U.S. assets was related to the needs and views of U.K. investors who were interested in risky assets. This finding is indicated by the improved properties of the U.K. demand relation for 1895–1913 when use is made of $W2$ (the variable representing the amount of wealth commanded by this type of investor). While the coefficient on the wealth variable is not strongly affected by the substitution of $LW2$ of $LW1$, the coefficient on Lr^A increases significantly. This is precisely the direction one might anticipate if the behavior of risk-oriented investors influenced the U.K.'s demand for U.S. assets. The increase in the own-elasticity directly implies a greater sensitivity to the return on U.S. assets.

The Chow test for structural shift noted earlier suggested that some of the parameters of the demand and supply relations had shifted across the period 1874–1913. It will also be remembered that the coefficients of equations 1 and 5 of table 4.1 are approximations of their long-run values. In order to make consistent comparisons, the coefficients on the lagged endogenous variable must be employed to extract the long-run coefficients in equations 2, 3, and 4 of table 4.1. By multiplying the estimated coefficients of these three latter equations by $1/(1-p)$, where p is the coefficient on LA_{t-1}, in the given equation, the following equations group all five estimates of the long-run asset demand and excess supply behavioral structure.

1874–1894

$$LA^D = -13.20 + .42Lr^A - .09Lr^{UK} + 2.30LW1 \qquad (4.17)$$

$$LA^S = 6.90 - 1.28Lr^A - .64Lr^{US}_{t-2} - .14LT_{t-1} + .64LK \qquad (4.18)$$

1895–1913

$$LA^D = 8.89 + .40LR^A - .25Lr^{UK} + 1.84LW1 \qquad (4.19)$$

$$LA^D = 7.76 + .62Lr^A - .31Lr^{UK} + 1.73LW2 \qquad (4.20)$$

$$LA^S = 2.62 - .60Lr^A + .13Lr^{US}_{t-2} - .27LT_{t-1} + 1.02LK \qquad (4.21)$$

E. THE DETERMINANTS OF U.K. INVESTMENT IN THE UNITED STATES

The structure of U.K. market for U.S. portfolio assets just specified permits a detailed examination of which participants most strongly influenced the transfer of capital to the United States and in what manner. As noted earlier, it is assumed that either unusually high returns to U.S. assets or unusually low returns to U.K. assets created a gap in *ex ante* risk-adjusted returns. The problem here investigated is with what force and in what manner long-term lenders and borrowers in the United Kingdom and the United States responded to the opportunities created by this gap. The response could manifest itself in several forms. U.S. asset suppliers might flood the U.K. market with new securities every time a new U.S. project was organized. The manifestation of this tendency might be a very high asset supply elasticity for the variable K, b_1. U.K. asset demanders might fall over themselves trying to build up holdings of these new assets. This might manifest itself in the U.K. demand functions as a very large wealth elasticity, a_1. Alternatively, the various elasticities might be quite "normal" and the determining elements in the market might be the rapidity of U.S. railway capital formation (a relatively high K growth rate) or the drive of U.K. thrift (a relatively high W growth rate).

The framework for investigating these issues is equation 4.14:

$$A = (g/(g + e))\dot{D} + (e/(g + e))\dot{S},$$

As noted earlier, the total effect of U.S. participants in the growth of U.K. holdings of U.S. securities, $\dot{A}$, is represented by $(e/(g + e))\dot{S}$, where $\dot{S}$ is the rate growth of the elasticity-weighted effects of $\dot{K}$, $\dot{T}$, and $\dot{r}^{US}$ (the three exogenous U.S. excess supply shift variables) and $e/(g + e)$ registers the effect of the relative disparity in the size of the own-interest demand elasticity. The total effect of U.K. participation is represented by $(g/(g + e))D$, where D is the

Table 4.2

A Ranking of the Anticipated Return on U.K. Held Debenture
Capital, 1870-1913

Yield	1870-79 Dom	1870-79 Nondom	1880-89 Dom	1880-89 Nondom	1890-93 Dom	1890-93 Nondom	1900-13 Dom	1900-13 Nondom
2.50					Cons			
2.75								
3.00			Cons		Corp Rwy	Rents InRwy	Cons	Rents
3.25	Cons				SO			
3.50			Corp Rwy			C&PG	Corp Rwy SO	WERwy
3.75			SO	Rents InRwy	I&C	CnRwy WERwy		C&PG InRwy CnRwy USRwy
4.00	Corp Rwy			C&PG		CCorp		LARwy
4.25		InRwy		CCorp CnRwy WERwy		USRwy LARwy	I&C	CCorp
4.50	C&PG			LARwy		OSO		OSO
4.75		Rents		USRwy OSO				
5.00		CCorp						
5.25		WERwy		EERwy				
5.50		EERwy LARwy						
5.75		OSO						
6.00		CnRwy						
6.25								
6.50		USRwy						

Table 4.2 (con't)

Abbreviations:

C&PG	Colonial & Provincial Governments
CCorp	Colonial Corporations
CnRwy	Canadian Railways
Cons	Consols
Corp	Domestic Corporations
EERwy	Eastern European Railways
I&C	Industry & Commerce Co's
InRwy	Indian Railways
LARwy	Latin American Railways
OSO	Overseas Social Overhead Co's
Rents	French Rentes
Rwy	Domestic Railways
SO	Domestic Social Overhead Co's
USRwy	United States Railways
WERwy	Western European Railways

Source: Edelstein 1970: Appendix A

rate of growth of the elasticity-weighted effects of W and $\dot{r}^{UK}$ (the two exogenous U.K. demand shift variables) and $g/(g + e)$ captures the effect of the relative disparity of the own-interest excess supply elasticity. Table 4.2 presents the long-run elasticities of equations 4.17 to 4.21, the rates of growth of the exogeneous U.K. demand and U.S. excess supply variables, and the rates of growth for the weighted sums of the demand and excess supply shift variables, $\dot{D}$ and $\dot{S}$, calculated from equation 4.14.

Broadly speaking, the conclusion of these calculations is that U.K. participation was the dominant influence within the economic environment of the 1875–1894 period and, by a much smaller margin, the dominant influence within the economic environment of the 1895–1913 period.

1874–1894   During the 1874–1894 period the preeminence of U.K. involvement seems largely due to the very high U.K. demand elasticity with respect to wealth, a_1. The effect of the downward movement of alternative U.K. and colonial asset returns on U.K. demand behavior was nullified by the low cross-elasticity, a_2. On the excess supply-side, the disparity in the opposing movements of T and r^{US} was effectively offset by a roughly equal but reverse disparity in the size of their respective elasticities.[25] U.S. demand forces apparently were a weak influence in the market for U.S.

securities in London, 1874–1894. With regard to U.S. supply forces, the size of b_1 suggests that there was little tendency for the U.S. railway companies to flood the United Kingdom with U.S. railway securities with each new railway project. The value of b_1 indicates that, for every 1.0 percent increase in the U.S. railway capital stock, there was a 0.64 percent increase in U.K. holdings of U.S. railway securities. If there had been some tendency to flood the U.K. market, this elasticity should have been significantly greater than 1.0 and thereby would have suggested a disproportionate use of the U.K. market. Since British wealth ($\dot{W}$) and the desired U.S. railway tangible capital stock ($\dot{K}$) expanded at roughly the same rate and the growth rate of K was clearly not as rapid as total U.S. wealth, the fact that a_1 was almost four times the size of b_1 becomes the critical element in the dominance of U.K. demand forces.

Given the U.K.'s increasing stock of wealth and the fact that U.S. railway equity and bonds were probably riskier than the domestic and colonial government and railway securities that constituted half of the U.K. negotiable portfolio investment, the large size of a_1 could reflect both an increased desire for risky, high-return assets and an absence of other sources to satisfy the demand for this type of asset. On the first point, all that can be said is that increasing wealth is generally believed to lead to more than proportionate increases in risky holdings. Empirical testing is impossible without either random sampling of national wealth holdings or a very nearly complete breakdown of the national portfolio over several decades, neither of which is currently available. On the second point, the massive injections of new securities from the new U.K. railway sector were largely over by 1870 as the system closed in on its market limits. Furthermore, in the period 1872–1894 the limited external financing needs of domestic U.K. industry were still satisfied, for the most part, by provincial capital markets and wealth. Finally, offerings of other large midcentury suppliers of readily negotiable high return-risk assets such as the Indian and European railway systems had slowed substantially owing either to completion of their initial networks or the development of larger and more sophisticated local capital markets. Thus, it would appear that the United

States, among other overseas regions, was the beneficiary of some combination of enlarged preferences for risky assets and relatively sparse sources of such assets originating elsewhere.

Note that the dominance of U.K. participants in the years 1874–1894 appears to be further augmented by the fact that own-interest elasticity, g, of the trans-Atlantic supply curve was twice the magnitude of the own-interest elasticity, s, of the U.K. demand relation. The exact role of these own-interest elasticities, however, is probably overstated by the estimated parameters used in table 4.2's calculations. The comparison of the two wealth concepts in the U.K. demand relation for the 1895–1913 period (see table 4.1) suggests that the use of W 1 in estimating the 1874–1894 demand relation probably biased the size of a downward. In this case, g and e were probably much closer in actual size during the 1874–1894 period, and, hence, the actual importance of their disparity in the balance of U.K. versus U.S. influence was fairly minor.

1895–1913 In the period from 1895 to 1913, U.K. and U.S. involvement was roughly balanced in their influence on the growth of A. U.K. influences remained stronger, but only by a small margin. Relative to the previous period, U.K. demand pressures fell and U.S. excess supply forces rose.

Structural changes seem to have been the major factor slowing U.K. demand forces. The wealth (a_1) and own-return (e) elasticities fell from their 1874–1894 levels and the cross-elasticity (a_2) rose. The explanation for these movements seems to hinge on the changing relative quality of U.S. railway assets. Between 1895 and 1913 the yield on U.K. railway bonds rose 2.38 percent per annum while U.S. railway bond yields in London fell by 1.92 percent per annum. In the light of the increased maturity of U.S. capital market and the growing power and diversity of U.S. industrial structure during this period, it seems fairly reasonable to attribute at least some of this relative decline in the U.S. yields to declining risk premiums.[26] Given the accompanying massive accumulation of U.S. tangible railway capital, this relative decline may also reflect a lowered risk-adjusted return. Shifts in the demand elasticities were probably influenced by changes in the pace and character of capital formation in the U.K. as well.

Whereas from 1872 to 1894 the rates of growth of the U.K. gross and net nonresidential real tangible capital stock were 1.41 percent and 0.85 percent per annum, from 1895 to 1913 they were 1.91 percent and 1.75 percent per annum (Feinstein 1972:T96, T103). If the financing modes of the 1870s and 1880s had merely continued into the 1890s and 1900s, the augmented pace of tangible capital formation probably would have led to increased

Table 4.3

Elasticities and Average Annual Rates of Growth
of the Variables

	1874-1894	1895-1913		
Elasticity		Value		
e	.42	.40		.62
a_1	2.30	1.84		1.73
a_2	-.09	-.25		-.31
g	-1.28		-.00	
b	.64		1.02	
b_1	-.64		.13	
b_2	-.14		-.27	
$g/(g+e)$	.75	.60		.49
$e/(g+e)$	.25	.40		.51
Variable		Rate of Growth		
W1	1.87	2.20		
W2				2.38
r_{UK}	-1.65		2.38	
K_{US}	1.94		4.21	
$r_{US,t-2}$	-.85		-1.48	
T_{t-1}	4.64		4.15	
D	4.45	3.45		3.38
$\dot{S}$	1.84		2.98	
$(g/(g+e))\dot{D}$	3.34	2.07		1.66
$(e/(e+g))\dot{S}$	.29	1.19		1.52
$\dot{r}_A$	-1.95	-.47		-.33
$\dot{A}$	3.61	3.26		3.13

Sources: Elasticity values: calculated from table 1; see accompanying text. Rates of growth: the rates of growth of W1, W2, r_{UK}, K_{t-2}, r_{US}, and T were estimated from regressions of their logarithms on time. See text Section C for data sources. The rates of growth of A, D, and S are calculated from Equation (14). The rates of growth of r_A are calculated from the rate-of-growth transformation of Equation (13). It is interesting to note that the actual annual rates of growth of A, derived in the same manner as W1, W2, etc., are 3.55 for 1874-1894, and 3.17 for 1895-1913, and those for r_A over the same periods are -1.92 and -.15.

offerings of domestic long-term debt instruments for that reason alone. But, as noted earlier, the late 1880s and 1890s saw the appearance and spread of large-scale U.K. industrial and commercial corporate enterprises (see chapter 3 and Payne 1967:519–42). From their beginnings these U.K. corporations relied more heavily on external long-term financing than the smaller scale firms of the previous decades.[27] Most important, their debt instruments appear to have been quite comparable with U.S. assets in their expected return-risk characteristics, as do alternative overseas securities such as colonial corporation debentures, overseas urban utility companies, and Canadian railways (table 4.3).[28]

Regardless of the precise sources of the relative decline in U.S. railway yields, it is probable that the effect of the decline was to reduce the degree of demand-side market segmentation. This had been fostered initially by what must almost certainly have been a very strong differential in the U.S. railway assets' relative return-risk characteristics. The high and declining elasticity of the wealth variable is strong testimony for this point. Perhaps the best support of demand-side market segmentation during the early years and its subsequent diminution is the extremely low, but rising, cross-elasticity of demand with respect to home and colonial asset returns. This mode of behavior could occur only if U.S. assets were initially considered to be substantially unlike, and therefore unrelated to the decision to purchase, alternative home and colonial assets, and if the degree of such isolation diminished as the period progressed.

In brief, it appears that the fall in the U.K. wealth elasticity (a_1) and the rise in the U.K. cross-elasticity (a_2), 1895–1913, were due to the relatively less favorable return-risk characteristics of U.S. portfolio assets. A quick calculation assuming the 1874–1894 elasticities as weights for the 1895–1913 growth rates of W and r^{UK} would show that, if the 1874–1894 structure had continued into the years 1895–1913, U.K. demand forces would have increased their pressure in the market for U.S. assets. The conclusion must therefore be that structural change was the main contributor to the lowered influence of U.K. demand forces in the 1895–1913 period.

The augmented strength of U.S. influence, 1895–1913, was largely due to the jump in the growth rate of the nominal value of the American railroad capital stock. From a rate of growth of 1.94 percent per annum in 1874–1894, K_{US} surged to 4.21 percent per annum, 1895–1913. The pace of real U.S. railway capital accumulation slowed somewhat across these two periods, and hence, the rapid rise in the price of railway capital goods was the crucial influence in K_{US}'s augmented growth rate (Ulmer 1960:256–57).

A further factor enhancing the strength of American forces in the trans-Atlantic capital flow is the fact that b_1 rose by about 35 percent; that is, America tended to supply larger amounts of securities to the U.K. market for a given change in the desired stock of railway capital. The reasons for this shift are not readily apparent. Following considerable financial distress in the 1893–96 depression, the financial structures of many U.S. railway companies were radically reorganized and many companies disappeared through consolidation (Neal 1969:126–27). By 1902, "morganization" had resulted in a much more concentrated industry with 70 percent of the U.S. trackage controlled by eight great railway systems and a shift of external financing arrangements into the hands of a few elite Wall Street firms. In the process the U.S. railway system regained financial health and profitability and moved into a fairly strong investment boom.

It might thus be hypothesized that the high propensity to market securities in the United Kingdom in the years 1895–1913 occurred because either the reorganized railway companies were able to make more rational use of the U.K. market or the elite Wall Street firms that now dominated the external financing arrangements of the U.S. railway companies had better U.K. connections, on average, than the set of financial agents in the 1874–1894 period. There is some evidence that the latter hypothesis may have some merit. However, a more plausible hypothesis rests on the contemporary appearance of new competition for railway securities in the U.S. market for medium-risk securities and conservative investors. Starting in the early 1890s U.S. industry also went through a rapid and widespread concentrating movement. The new industrial giants issued equity and preferred stock in roughly equal amounts with debentures taking a very minor role. The preferred stock quickly found a market with conservative U.S. investors when industrial preferreds weathered the 1893–96 depression much better than comparable railroad securities (Navin and Sears 1955:122, 137). It thus seems very likely that the propensity of U.S. railway companies to fund in Britain rose in the 1894–1913 period because the new U.S. industrial preferreds offered strong competition in a corner of the U.S. capital market previously dominated by railway preferreds and debentures.

Indeed, the vigor of U.S. railway financing needs and the enlarged propensity to market in London might have led to a dominance of U.S. influences in the trans-Atlantic capital market if U.S. asset demands had not also changed. From acting as a proxy for the U.S. opportunity costs for U.K. financing, r^{US} appears to have shifted to a role as an index of alternative opportunities for U.S. investors. This shift is indicated by the change in b_2's sign from negative to positive. The increased force of U.S. demand conditions is also reflected in the rise of b_3, the U.S. wealth elasticity. These shifts clearly suggest that some U.S. investors, perhaps the rising U.S. insurance giants and banking trust departments, had increased their sensitivity to the yields on the type of securities favored in the United Kingdom and the various U.S. portfolio alternatives.

Nevertheless, the net influence of U.S. railway financing needs and U.S. asset demand forces was a doubling in the thrust of U.S. forces in the trans-Atlantic capital market, 1895–1913, from their level during the previous twenty years. Since there was little disparity in e and g, the own-interest demand and supply elasticities in the early twentieth century (table 4.2, col. 3), the shift indices, $\dot{S}$ and D, are again the key factors in judging the relative influence of U.K. and U.S. influence and involvement. Because these indices are nearly equal, it must be concluded that these two sets of forces were fairly even during the last two decades of the Pax Britannica.[29]

F. COMPARISONS WITH OTHER REGIONS OF RECENT SETTLEMENT

The question that immediately arises is how general the U.S. case is. Fortunately, there are a number of econometric studies of British investment in Argentina, Australia, and Canada in the late nineteenth and early twentieth centuries. However, they involve differences of method that limit the range of comparison. First, these studies rely on a reduced-form estimation approach instead of our structural approach, and, second, they focus on the annual flow of funds from the United Kingdom rather than the accumulating stock of overseas assets. A reduced-form approach in the U.S. case would have involved econometric estimation of equation 4.14, the equation that is the mathematical solution of the structural demand (4.7) and supply (4.8) equations for the equilibrium value of A. Beta coefficients can be employed to assess the contribution of individual variables in the reduced-form approach. Given the same exogenous supply and demand variables, beta coefficients will ordinarily provide the same answers as our S and D indices for the purpose of judging U.K. versus overseas market influence and involvement. (As noted in section A of this chapter, what is generally lost in the reduced-form approach is the knowledge of whether it is a variable's elasticity or its movement that is affecting the rate of capital export).

As regards the stock-versus-flow difference, in separate studies Bloomfield and Williamson investigated the flow of British funds to the United States; beta coefficients calculated from their results show the same dominance of U.K. participants as was found in our study of stocks.[30] Thus, although there are differences of method, on the central question of whether U.K. or overseas participants dominated the market for the given overseas regions' assets in the United Kingdom, some fruitful comparison is possible. Note, it is again the implicit assumption that a gap existed between U.K. and overseas *ex ante*, risk-adjusted returns, dictating the direction of international capital movements from the United Kingdom to overseas points. The issue under investigation is which participants, United Kingdom or overseas, dominated the market reaction to this opportunity.

Argentina Between 1870 and 1913 Argentina raised £346.3 million through new issues in the United Kingdom, approximately 8 percent of total new overseas issues placed in the U.K. during these years (I. Stone 1972:546; Simon 1967:52–53). The timing of these new issues from Argentina involved at least two long swings, peaks occurring in 1889 and 1909 and troughs in 1879 and 1894. With a very limited set of variables at his command, Ford investigated the balance of U.K. versus overseas involvement in Britain's long-term investments in Argentina from the mid-1880s to World War I (Ford 1971). The following Ford equations had the best R^2s and Durbin-Watson statistics: t-statistics (bracketed) and beta coefficients (underlined) have been added, calculated from Ford's data set[31]:

1886-1913

$$A_t = -12.290 + 3.616P_{t-1} + .080F_t \qquad R^2 = 0.660$$
$$\quad (4.70) \qquad (4.42) \qquad (4.00) \qquad d.w. = 1.510 \qquad (4.23)$$
$$\qquad\qquad \underline{.532} \qquad \underline{.469}$$

$$A_t = -8.131 + 3.997P_{t-1} + .074F_t - .056I_t \qquad R^2 = 0.824$$
$$\quad (3.04) \qquad (5.87) \qquad (4.35) \quad (2.95) \qquad d.w. = 2.156 \qquad (4.24)$$
$$\qquad\qquad \underline{.588} \qquad \underline{.433} \quad \underline{3.07}$$

1887-1912

$$A_t = -12.243 + 3.223P_{t-2} + .098F_t \qquad R^2 = 0.788$$
$$\quad (4.93) \qquad (3.69) \qquad (3.92) \qquad d.w. = 1.621 \qquad (4.25)$$
$$\qquad\qquad \underline{.475} \qquad \underline{.500}$$

$$A_t = -9.685 + 3.273P_{t-2} + .095F_t - .027I_t \qquad R^2 = 0.803$$
$$\quad (3.04) \qquad (3.79) \qquad (3.76) \quad (1.23) \qquad d.w. = 1.727 \qquad (4.26)$$
$$\qquad\qquad \underline{4.82} \qquad \underline{.480} \quad \underline{.141}$$

where A_t = the annual flow of net issues to Argentina (m.),
P_t = Argentina railway profits as a percentage of capital employed (%),
F_t = total new overseas issues placed in the U.K. minus A_t (m.),
I_t = net domestic fixed investment in the U.K. (m.).

Ford viewed P and I as measures of Argentinian and British prospects, respectively. With regard to F, Ford suggested that British investors probably found Argentine investments appealing, depending on the state of the entire overseas new issues market. Disastrous circumstances elsewhere overseas would also affect the climate for Argentine new issues. However, Ford acknowledged that F would incorporate "some influence of . . . British domestic prospects since, when the trend of British overseas investment was high, home investment was low and *vice versa* (Ford 1971:655)." Ford concluded that his "results do not provide much support for the hypothesis that the ". . . variation . . ." of British domestic prospects (as reflected in the behavior of domestic investment) directly influenced Argentinian new issues. However, it might be mistaken to dismiss it entirely since . . . British overseas new issues were implicitly linked with the state of British home prospects, as well as overseas prospects, and the variable F might pick up both influences (Ford 1971:656)."

Ford's caveat takes on new importance when seen in the light of our U.S. results. U.S. new issues were 21 percent of total new overseas issues, 1886–1913, at least double the size of the Argentinian capital import from the United Kingdom over the same years. The American new issues are thus a quarter of Ford's F variable. With a much more complete set of data we have concluded that Britain's investment in the United States was dominated by U.K. participation though decreasingly so toward World War I. Thus, Ford's caveat is confirmed to some degree. As will shortly be shown, the Canadian and Australian econometric evidence also confirm the caveat and thus suggest that domestic U.K. factors were far more powerful in the Argentinian case than Ford's evidence suggests at first glance. Furthermore, given the beta coefficients of Ford's equations, it is possible that the U.K. variables were the stronger factor, albeit by a slim margin.

Australia Between 1870 and 1913 Australian new issues absorbed by the United Kingdom amounted to some £325 million, approximately 8 percent of total new overseas issues absorbed in the U.K. during these years (Hall 1963:206; Simon 1967:52–53). The timing of Britain's investment in Australia involves a long and strong rise starting in the 1860s, gathering speed in the late

1870s, a sharp fall off in the early 1890s, a brief return in the late 1890s, and then virtual cessation of long-term borrowing until just before World War I (Hall 1963a:206; Butlin 1962:444). In a study developing the fundamental data of Australian accumulation and total product in the late nineteenth century, Butlin argued that "Britain had an important role in sustaining general expansion. But specifically, the critical decisions in capital formation and in the orientation of the economy were taken in Australia, by Australians and the light of Australian criteria (1964:5; see also 31, 337)." A somewhat different tack is taken by Hall in his study focusing on the London capital market and Australian borrowing, 1870–1913. According to Hall,

it is wrong to discuss the story of British capital inflow simply in terms of the initiative of Australian borrowers and conversely to regard the activity of British investors as passive . . . the passiveness implied by saying "yes" to an inveterate borrower must sooner or later be converted into a positive "no." That "no" was said in the early 1890s and even, perhaps, in the more important sense of "no greater rate" in the middle 1880s, is not the crucial point. What is crucial is that the very fact of British capital inflow helped to shape the conditions under which Australian entrepreneurs excerise their initiative on any one set of participants. The only fruitful way to view the process of British capital inflow into Australian is to regard it as one of interaction between condition in Australian and in Britain (1963a:199).

Bloomfield has made some simple regression tests of the determinants of net capital imports into Australia, 1870–1913 (1968:37–38). The following equations were Bloomfield's best; the beta coefficients (underlined) have been added based on Bloomfield's data set:

1870–1913

$$AUC = 1.591 - 1.036GBCF + 2.295AUR - .185UCR$$

$$\quad\quad\quad\quad (5.02) \quad\quad\quad (7124) \quad\quad\quad (7.36)$$

$$\quad\quad\quad\quad \underline{0.396} \quad\quad\quad \underline{0.728} \quad\quad\quad \underline{0.719}$$

$$R^2 = 0.687$$
$$d.w. = 1.505 \quad (4.27)$$

$$AUC = 1.701 - .114\,TS - A + 2.421\,AUR$$
$$\quad\quad\quad\quad (6.40) \quad\quad\quad (5.81)$$
$$\quad\quad\quad\quad \underline{0.903} \quad\quad\quad \underline{0.888}$$

$$R^2 = 0.737$$
$$d.w. = 2.004 \quad (4.28)$$

where AUC = Australian net capital imports,

$\quad\quad GBCF$ = U.K. gross domestic fixed-capital formation,

$\quad\quad UCR$ = the sum of net railway investment in the United States and Canada,

$\quad TS - A$ = British total savings minus AUC,

$\quad\quad AUR$ = Australian Net railway investment.

Simply stated, neither of these equations supports Butlin's contention that Australian conditions dominated the course of British investment in Australia. Equation 4.27 suggests that, although Australian prospects were important (AUR), circumstances in Britain $(GBCF)$ and elsewhere (UCR) found an equally important counterpoint. Equation 4.28 represents Bloomfield's supposition that the appropriate British push variable was total U.K. savings rather than merely that part employed for domestic investment. This supposition is analogous to our earlier point that the appropriate constraint on the British demand for U.S. assets was some index of total U.K. wealth ($W1$ or $W2$). Bloomfield is, of course, dealing with changes in U.K. wealth (TS) and the net additions to Britain's holdings of Australian assets (AUC). Unfortunately, Bloomfield's equation 4.28 lacks many of the variables suggested by economic theory. Nevertheless, equation 4.28 contains two variables that in stock form were among the most powerful in our U.S. model, and, truncated as it is, it does yield a better statistical fit than the alternative model (4.27). If it is then accepted that equation 4.28 approximates a superior model and fit, it follows from the equation's beta coefficients that U.K. participants dominated the export of British capital to Australia. Needless to say, the margin of error in the beta coefficients is sufficiently large so that it would be safer to conclude that U.K. and Australian participation and influence roughly balanced in the Australian case and thus confirm Hall.

Canada Britain's investment in new long-term Canadian issues totaled £364.6 million, 1870–1913, approximately 9.7 percent of total overseas new issues taken up by the United Kingdom during these years (Simon 1970:241; 1967:52–53). The time shape of Britain's investment in Canada suggests the possibility of three long swings with peaks in 1874, 1888, 1913, and troughs in 1880 and 1895–96. However, the rise after 1907 is so strong relative to previous experience that it is at least as fruitful to think of the Canadian import of capital from Britain as another example of the "one-shot" pattern. Some 54 percent of Britain's new issue investment in Canada, 1870–1913, occurred in the seven years 1908–1913. Bloomfield ran a number of tests to examine the influence of U.K. versus Canadian participation in the U.K. market for Canadian assets over the year 1870–1913.

A simple univariate regression between Canadian net capital imports and Canadian net railway investment gave a very high coefficient of determination. Adding in British gross domestic fixed-capital formation and the sum of new railway investment in the U.S. and Australia as explanatory variables scarcely altered the coefficient of determination but yielded coefficients for these two variables with t-ratios well below two (1968:37)

He also tried formulations similar to equation 4.28 above, but these too failed their *t*-tests. His conclusion was the Canadian net capital imports were solely determined by Canadian conditions.

One problem with Bloomfield's analysis is that, unlike the Argentinian and Australian cases, Canada received a significant amount of capital from a non-U.K. source, the United States. Importantly, this flow of funds from the United States is part of Bloomfield's net capital import variable. A better test of the interaction of British versus Canadian market involvement should focus on the behavior of Canadian new issues placed in the United Kingdom, a series developed by Simon after Bloomfield's investigations. This is precisely what Paterson has done, albeit only for the years 1890–1913: (Paterson 1976:35)

1890–1913

$$S = 27.897 + .011D_t - 3.219I_t^{GB} + .905T \qquad R^2 = 0.829$$
$$\quad (1.11) \qquad (2.65) \qquad (1.82) \qquad d.w. = 1.137 \qquad (4.29)$$

where S = Canadian new issues placed in the United Kingdom
D = aggregate Canadian dividend payments
I^{GB} = gross domestic capital formation in the United Kingdom
T = time.

Owing to some computational difficulties it was impossible to produce beta coefficients, but the t-statistics (the bracketed items) offer a good index of the betas.

By setting aside the T variable for the moment, it appears that British forces were more powerful than Canadian forces in Paterson's equation. Interpreting the meaning of the T variable is crucial, however. Since Canadian and U.K. wealth variables were missing from this equation, T may be a proxy for the gradual accumulation of wealth in Canada and the United Kingdom. However, since net capital imports were a large proportion of Canada's gross savings during these years (Green and Urquhart 1976:241, 244), T is more likely to be a proxy for Britain's savings behavior than Canada's. Hence the Paterson equation leaves the distinct impression that U.K. influence and participation were very important to the transfer of Britain's savings to Canada and quite possibly the dominant force.

Tentative Inferences   From the point of view of the theory presented in section C, none of the regression tests of the Canadian, Argentinian, or Australian experiences is satisfactory. Nearly all equations ignore the dynamics of savings in the United Kingdom and the receiving country. Owing to data limitations, rate of return variables are missing. Thus, at best, these tests of balance of U.K. versus overseas influence and participation in these regions are rough. Still, with an eye to the missing variables, analysis of these regression equations points to one strong conclusion; it would be foolish to assume the markets for the assets of these regions of recent settlement was dominated solely by forces in these regions. Although the regression models are insufficient to carefully detail the specific workings of the markets for Argentine, Australian, and Canadian long-term assets in Britain, the econometric tests point toward a balance of U.K. and overseas influences. In some tests, British forces were slightly more important, but this may be forcing the evidence. More careful specification and surer judgement must await more and better data.

G. SUMMARY

In brief, an assumed gap in the *ex ante* risk-adjusted returns between U.S. and U.K. assets seems to have been most prominently played out through the actions of U.K. assets buyers in the years 1874–1894. This early domination of U.K. demand forces in the U.K. market for U.S. assets appears to have been the result of the high-return–medium-risk characteristics of U.S. railway assets, the relative dearth of similar assets from the United Kingdom and elsewhere, and perhaps a heightened U.K. desire for relatively risky, publically traded portfolio assets among conservative investors as U.K. wealth increased. Certainly, there is no indication of any propensity for U.S. railway companies to flood the United Kingdom with their financing instruments. It is well to remember that during these years the organized capital markets of the United States funded the majority of the enlarging U.S. railway system.

In the 1894–1913 period the assumed *ex ante* risk-adjusted gap and its opportunities were played out in a somewhat different manner. On the other hand, either because their risk or risk-adjusted return fell, U.S. railway assets seemed somewhat less, though still quite strongly, attractive to conservative U.K. wealth holders. On the other hand, the pressure of augmented U.S. railway financing needs and competition with new U.S. industrial securities in the U.S. market for conservative investors raised the pressure of U.S. railway companies to acquire funds in the United Kingdom.

Data and modeling limitations prevent detailed comparison of these findings on the market for U.S. assets in the United Kingdom with British investment in other regions. However, rough comparison is possible with studies of the Argentinian,

Australian, and Canadian cases. A review of these studies suggests that net asset supply forces from abroad certainly did not dominate the flow of British savings to these regions. Indeed, the crude evidence best supports the view that forces in these three regions and in Britain were roughly balanced in determining the size and pace of British investment in each region. In the Argentinian, Australian, and Candian cases, the assumed *ex ante* gap in risk-adjusted returns was seized by U.K. lenders and overseas borrowers in a fairly balanced fashion; in the U.S. case, for a substantial part of the years 1870–1913 the drive of U.K. asset buyers seems to have been dominant. This raises the distinct possibility that the *ex ante* gap in risk-adjusted returns was somewhat stronger in the U.S. case. In the next chapters evidence on *ex poste* returns and risk will be investigated that should have some bearing on this issue.

CHAPTER 5: PRIVATE REALIZED RATES OF RETURN ON HOME AND OVERSEAS INVESTMENT OVER THE LONG TERM

Were private rates of return on the United Kingdom's overseas assets higher than those prevailing on domestic assets during the years 1870–1913? Was the gap widening between home and overseas return? Did home and overseas rates of return move in inverse cycles of 15 to 25 years' duration? The answers to these questions have played an important role in the historiography of late-nineteenth-century U.K. imperialism on the one hand and U.K. overseas investment behavior between 1870 and 1913 on the other.

Fundamental to many models of late-nineteenth-century imperialism are the assumptions that, first, the level of overseas asset returns was substantially higher than that prevailing at home, and second, the difference between overseas and home returns was increasing.[1] Furthermore, it is often assumed that domestic rates of return were declining secularly and, if not actually declining, would have been doing so in the absence of the foreign sources to absorb the amount of savings generated; the analogous long-run tendency for overseas rates of return was either much weaker or had yet to appear. Given the increasing relative profitability of trade and investment opportunities abroad, it has often been suggested that formal acquisition of colonies was necessary because the U.K.'s American and European competitors were increasingly protectionist at home and were intensifying the competitive struggles for goods markets and investment opportunities in Africa, Asia, and Latin America. Formal rule was strategically useful to protect previous investment and markets and to ensure access to at least some profitable opportunities abroad in the foreseeable future.

Although risk minimization may have been part of the U.K. investor's motivation for acquiring overseas investments,[2] most views of U.K. home and overseas investment behavior assume that a relatively higher level of overseas returns was the primary motive. In chapter 3 it was assumed that *ex ante* rates of return, net of risk, were higher abroad. Expected returns on debenture securities were then employed to explore the relationship between the pace of return and U.K. investment in the United States. Other studies of the growth of U.K. capital exports have utilized output and investment variables as rate-of-return proxies, implicitly indulging in the same assumption (B. Thomas 1972; Richardson 1972). As these rate-of-return proxies often manifest long swings of 15 to 25 years' duration, domestic and overseas rates of return are implicitly assumed to display a similar cyclical pattern. The importance of these assumptions on the level, direction, and timing of rates of return for the understanding of late-Victorian and Edwardian imperialism and investment behavior provides ample justification for an empirical investigation.

Chapters 5 and 6 undertake to examine realized, price-deflated rates of return on U.K. financial capital from 1870 to 1913, employing new data on 566 first- and second-class equity, preference, and debenture securities. A realized rate of return measure has the valuable property of incorporating both dividend (or interest) payments and net capital gains. The research reported here is distinguishable from the few previous empirical studies of these matters in that the new data span the entire period and incorporate a substantially wider range of industries, regions, and asset types.[3] The primary questions addressed are the following: (1) Did a significant differential exist between realized, price-deflated returns to U.K. holdings of home and overseas assets over the years 1870–1913 or any significant subperiod? (2) How much of any gap between home and overseas returns can be attributed to long-term risk factors? (3) Did realized rates of return to domestic assets manifest a significant downward trend between 1870 and 1913 or any lengthy subperiod? (4) Did rates of return to U.K. holdings at home and abroad evince regular cycles and, if so, of what duration? In the first section of this chapter the rate-of-return estimator, the data base, and the aggregation procedures are described. Succeeding sections of this chapter and chapter 6 address themselves to the questions just raised. A full summary of the principal findings is presented at the conclusion of chapter 6.

A. ESTIMATOR, DATA BASE, AND AGGREGATION

As Stigler notes in a much-quoted passage from his study of U.S. industrial rates of return, there is no more important proposition in economic theory than that under competition the rate of return on investment tends toward equality (1963:54). The mobility of capital under competitive conditions should ensure that highly profitable activities will draw forth new funds and capital equipment either from existing enterprises or through entry of new entrepreneurs and lenders. In a world in which the future is perfectly anticipated, and funds and capital goods are elastically supplied, every opportunity for profit or loss would be acted upon quickly. Rates of return on financial and real capital would differ only insofar as there were differences due to risk. In such a world, the major impact of new or disappearing opportunities for profit would be variations in rates of investment and a shifting portfolio of financial and real capital.

Indeed, the principal evidence to date suggesting that overseas assets manifested better return or risk characteristics than domestic U.K. assets is the massive shift in the U.K. portfolio of financial and real capital that occurred between 1870 and 1913. A rough calculation of the nominal value of outstanding home and overseas long-term negotiable securities indicates that, whereas overseas accumulations were around 33 percent of such assets in 1870, their share rose to 45 percent in 1913 (see table 3.1). Feinstein's estimates suggest that, whereas overseas accumulations were around 14 percent of the reproducible capital stock in 1870, by 1913 the share of overseas accumulations had risen to around 31 percent (see table 2.5).

Entrepreneurs and lenders do not, however, perfectly anticipate new or disappearing opportunities. New capital equipment is not always rapidly supplied. Financial intermediaries and lenders may hesitate to supply new funds because of poor information[4] or biases toward certain types of issues. Facilities for diversifying the new risks may be initially inadequate or biased. In fact, hypotheses suggesting that nineteenth-century U.K. investors and financial intermediaries were biased either for or against overseas investments are a prominent feature of nineteenth-century U.K. capital market affairs. Chapter 3 suggested that the United Kingdom's stock exchanges were substantially unbiased in the long run as between home and overseas assets, but clearly there were periods when the trials of learning or bandwagon effects led to biased pricing of both home and overseas segments of the capital market.[5]

Many of these impediments to the mobility of capital can be mitigated or eliminated, but such a process involves years, not days or months (Stigler 1963:54–72). Hence, over a period of years, as long as the economic system is not continually shocked by new economic opportunities or noneconomic phenomena, one should expect to find returns to firms, industries, and regions manifesting some tendency toward equalization, apart from risk differentials. Indeed, long-term averages of rates of return may permit an examination of return differentials due to underlying risk conditions. Still, in the annual evidence, there will be plenty of opportunity to observe the disequilibria generated by the appearance and disappearance of profitable opportunities, and these opportunities will thereby allow an examination of just those tendencies that have heretofore been largely assumed to characterize late-nineteenth- and early-twentieth-century U.K. rates of return.

The estimation of rates of return, however, is subject to a number of theoretical and measurement problems. The investigator is immediately confronted by the choice of studying rates of return to real capital or financial capital.[6] The procedure adopted here is to examine rates of return on financial capital, the titles or liens on an enterprise's stream of earnings. The main advantage of this method is that the capital market's evaluation of a firm is appropriately focused on its future income and risk. Data considerations also play a role in this choice. Nineteenth-century accounting methods make a large-scale study of real returns quite difficult, whereas stock exchange records, fortunately, are quite accessible. Finally, any study of rates of return to real capital runs into a problem of comparability in incorporating the United Kingdom's immense overseas wealth; the overwhelming majority of overseas wealth was portfolio capital.

A study of returns to financial capital should optimally involve analysis of both failures and successes. The data base therefore must incorporate either every asset ever offered or a large random sample of this population. In either case the task is too vast if an attempt is made to include the experience of the multitude of ventures in which U.K. funds participated. One alternative, the method pursued here, is to examine the return history of publicly traded, first- and second-class, equity, preference, and debenture instruments from a wide variety of industries and countries. Accessibility of dividend, interest, and asset price data dictates that the study concentrate on publicly traded securities. The choice to restrict attention to first- and second-class investments is dictated by a combination of time and the poor quality of stock exchange information on third-class and disappeared listings. Although many issues disappeared from the stock exchange's lists because of company failure, many left for other reasons. Companies removed themselves from the lists to organize themselves on a more restricted basis. Others disappeared under the threat of failure but ultimately regained profitability. Stock exchange records rarely mention third-class investments that disappeared from the lists, let alone specify the reasons for the disappearance in appropriate detail.

The sampling obtained for the first- and second-class subpopulation is fairly large, and hence, their indices of return are, at a minimum, accurate indicators of the level and timing of the United Kingdom's best home and overseas holdings. Of course, because these data represent only a portion of the full spectrum of portfolio investments, any inference concerning the *level* of returns for all enterprises must be treated carefully. This liability is explicitly recognized in the discussion of the average level of home and overseas returns in the next section, where several tests are performed to assess the validity of inferring global averages from our limited sample.

With regard to the generality of the *timing* and *direction* of our indices movements, recent studies of capital market behavior suggest that first- and second-class returns are fairly good estimators for the full spectrum's movements (Brealey 1969:55–64, 104–7). An important reason for this finding is the interaction of all parts of the spectrum. In the nineteenth century, many wealth holders owned assets in both the best and worst parts of the national portfolio. It is plausible to assume that they allocated their funds according to their relative profitabilities and risks and, hence, provided a strong equilibrating force. Perhaps a stronger equilibrating force was the presence of publicly traded companies in nearly all U.K. industrial sectors by the end of the nineteenth century.

In the selection and composition of the portfolio instruments, the greatest problem is the search for an operational definition of first- and second-class securities.[7] Because there were no regular market-rating services during the years 1870–1913, four minimal criteria are used to define the relevant population. Briefly, these are the following: (1) An acceptable equity share either paid dividends regularly or manifested dividend behavior similar to that of the securities of leading companies in the same industrial grouping; (2) an acceptable preference or debenture share paid dividends or interest without interruption; (3) either securities with long periods of heavy price discount for reasons other than dividend nonpayment are completely excluded or the affected portion of the securities' yield history is eliminated; and (4) acceptable securities had to be quoted continuously for a significant portion of the period or their term to maturity. The field is narrowed further through the use of contemporary evidence, secondary sources, and scaling procedures. A listing of the equity, preference, and debenture shares selected for inclusion is presented in tables 5.1 and 5.2, grouped according to the regional and industrial categories that form the basis of the regional and industrial rate of return indices. Although several equity indices are based on very small sample sizes, additional shares fulfilling the selection criteria do not appear to be available after extensive search. With regard to the debenture indices, the limited sample sizes may be safely ignored because in all cases these indices group the issues of government units that offered only a few debenture series at one time.[8]

The Investors Monthly Manual is the principal source of price, dividend, and interest information. Provincial newspapers provided the earliest price and dividend information for the Oldham cotton-spinning firms and several other home equity groupings.

Table 5.1

The Time Composition of the Equity Data Base

	1870	1880	1890	1900	1910	1913
A. Domestic Securities						
1. Railways (19)[a]	16	16	16	15	15	15
2. Finance						
a. Banks (19)	16	18	17	16	15	14
b. Insurance (14)	12	14	14	14	13	12
3. Light industry & commerce						
a. All textiles (14)	3	6	6	11	13	14
b. Oldham cotton spinners (11)	-	10	8	11	11	11
c. Food (9)	-	-	3	6	8	8
d. Drink (7)	1	1	4	6	6	6
e. Retail stores (5)	-	-	-	4	5	5
4. Heavy industry						
a. Iron, coal, steel, & heavy fabrication (25)	8	13	15	21	25	25
b. Mechanical equipment (14)	6	8	9	11	10	11
c. Electrical equipment (3)	1	1	1	3	3	3
d. Building & construction materials (4)	-	2	3	2	3	3
e. Chemicals	2	2	5	4	6	6
5. Social overhead						
a. Electricity (3)	-	-	1	2	3	3
b. Gas (5)	3	5	5	5	5	5
c. Water (7)	6	7	7	7	-	-
d. Canals and docks (8)	5	7	7	6	4	4
e. Shipping	8	8	10	10	8	7
f. Telephone & telegraph (4)	1	2	2	3	2	1
g. Tramways & omnibuses (3)	1	3	3	2	2	1
Subtotal	89	123	136	159	157	154
B. Nondomestic securities						
1. Railways						
a. India (11)	6	7	7	8	8	8
b. Western Europe (11)	9	11	9	6	4	2
c. Eastern Europe (4)	2	3	4	2	2	2
d. United States (10)	3	4	6	9	9	9
e. Latin America (11)	6	7	8	9	9	9
2. Banks						
a. Asia & Australasia (13)	12	13	12	7	7	7
b. South Africa (1)	1	1	1	1	1	1
c. Canada (1)	1	1	1	1	1	1
d. Eastern Mediterranean (4)	4	4	4	4	4	4
e. Latin America (3)	2	2	2	3	3	3

Table 5.1 (con't)

	1870	1880	1890	1900	1910	1913
3. Social overhead: Industrial groupings						
a. Electricity (6)	-	-	-	-	6	5
b. Gas (14)	6	10	10	11	11	10
c. Telegraph & telephone						
(15)	-	10	13	12	13	13
d. Tramways (10)	1	4	7	5	6	4
4. Social overhead: Regional groupings^b						
a. India and China (8)	3	4	6	6	8	8
b. Western Europe (10)	2	6	8	8	8	7
c. North America (5)	-	2	2	2	4	4
d. Latin America (19)	3	11	12	10	13	11
5. Tea & coffee (16)	2	5	7	15	14	14
Subtotal (130)	55	82	91	93	98	92
Grand Total Equity Securities (326)	144	205	227	252	235	246

Source: Edelstein 1970: Appendix II.

^{a}The figures in parentheses represent the total number of securities used.

^{b}The securities in the Social Overhead: Regional Groupings category are not included in the subtotals for nondomestic equities or the grand total for equity instruments. To include them would involve double counting the securities already enumerated in the Social Overhead: Industrial Grouping category.

The estimator of annual returns adopted for this study is characterized by three important properties. First, unlike many measures of return found in the financial press, it incorporates capital gains and losses. Second, the estimator of return is deflated by the rate of increase or decrease of consumer prices. Third, the estimator implicitly assumes that the typical investor practices a simple, but not altogether realistic, type of holding behavior and portfolio construction.[9] Let

P_{ijkt} = the latest sterling price of the ith security of the jth type in the kth sector, recorded in the last week of December of the tth year and printed in *The Investors Monthly Manual.*

D_{ijkt} = the sterling cash dividend or interest payment on the ith security, etc., between the last week of December of the $(t-1)^{th}$ year and the last week of December of the tth year;

I_t = the consumer price index for the tth year,

Table 5.2

The Time Composition of the Preference and Debenture Data Base

	1870	1880	1890	1900	1910	1913
I. Preference shares						
A. Domestic						
1. Railways (17)[a]	4	7	7	7	7	7
2. Manufacturing & commerce (16)	1	1	2	9	16	14
Total preference (33)	5	8	9	16	23	21
II. Debenture shares						
A. Domestic						
1. Consols (3)	1	1	1	1	1	1
2. Municipals (45)	4	10	25	37,	38	36
3. Railways (31)	15	21	20	15	15	15
4. Social overhead (26)		3	12	17	14	14
5. Manufacturing & commerce (40)	—	—	4	27	39	36
Subtotal (145)	20	35	62	97	107	102
B. Nondomestic						
1. French rentes (1)	1	1	1	1	1	1
2. Colonial & provincial governments (52)	12	21	31	42	35	34
a. Australia (21)	4	9	14	17	13	13
b. Canada (10)	2	4	6	8	6	6
c. India (6)	2	2	3	4	4	4
d. Jamaica (1)				1	1	1
e. New Zealand (4)	2	2	3	4	3	2
f. South Africa (10)	2	4	5	8	8	8
3. Colonial municipals (23)		7	13	19	17	16
4. Indian railways (10)	1	4	4	5	9	9
5. Canadian railways (7)		3	5	7	5	4
6. W. European railways (15)	8	12	12	9	8	6
7. E. European railways (8)	6	8	4	2	2	2
8. U.S. railways (51)	1	14	30	38	28	26
9. Latin American railways (16)	1	3	5	12	12	11
a. Argentine railways (9)		1	1	6	6	5
b. Brazilian railways (2)		1	2	2	2	2
10. Social overhead (24)	—	2	7	9	15	14
Subtotal	30	75	112	144	132	122
Total debentures	50	110	174	241	239	224

Source: Edelstein 1970: Appendix II, pp. 262-274.

[a]The figures in parentheses are the total number of securities in the data base, 1870-1913.

where

$i = 1, \ldots, m$, securities,

$j = 1$ (equity), 2 (preference), 3 (debentures),

$k = 1, \ldots, n$, sectors (i.e., industrial sectors, governmental units),

and

t = the calendar year.

The estimator of annual, realized, price-deflated returns to the ith security is

$$r_{ijkt} = \frac{(P_{ijkt} + D_{ijkt})/I_t}{(P_{ijkt,t-1})/I_{t-1}} \tag{5.1}$$

As defined, r_{ijkt} measures the real wealth accumulation deriving from net capital gains and dividend (or interest) income on a single security realized over a 1-year period. It quantifies the net relative increase of cash plus dividends (or interest) accruing to an investor who purchases an equity, preference, or debenture share for 1 pound sterling in December of the previous year and sells it in December of the current year.[10]

The index of annual return to the jth type of security in the kth sector (e.g., all equity in U.K. railways) is

$$r_{jkt} = \frac{\sum\limits_{}^{m}(1 + r_{ijkt})}{m} - 1 \tag{5.2}$$

This index of sectoral returns has the property that each security carries an equal weight. In effect, it is assumed that the investor has purchased a portfolio of, for example, U.K. railway equity, consisting of equal amounts of each railway company's shares. A better method of indexing sectoral returns would involve weighting each security's return by the market value of its outstanding stock. Unfortunately, for individual issues the quality of the published data on the number of outstanding shares is far worse than their price and dividend information.[11] Although these errors might cancel out in summing over all issues in the market, when a small number of first- and second-class securities of a given sector are involved, employing these inferior data as weights might be quite dangerous.

The estimator of sectoral performance over a period of years (from t to T) is a geometric average of the r_{jkt}, i.e.,

$$R_{jk}^{t,T} = \prod_{i}^{n} (1 + r_{jkt})^{1/(T-t-1)} - 1. \tag{5.3}$$

This index of long-term sectoral performance is the compound annual growth rate of wealth, held for $(T - t + 1)$ years, with the dividends (or interest) reinvested along with the appreciating or depreciating principal. It thus assumes that capitalists do not consume any of their accumulated wealth during the holding period.

The principal hypotheses concerning the return on U.K. investments, 1870–1913, are framed in terms of broad national or supranational aggregates. For example, it is often suggested that overseas returns were higher than domestic returns. Several methods of aggregation to national and supranational levels are available, no one of which is entirely satisfactory.[12] The method adopted here is to weight the sectoral indices, the r_{jkt}, by their shares in the national portfolio in 1913. This method assumes that the r_{jkt} are good indicators of the return to their respective industrial and governmental units, at least relative to each other. Of course, given that the data base consists of first- and second-class securities, there is an inherent upward bias in the estimated level of each sector's return. Now the upward bias also inheres in the national and supranational indices. As noted earlier, the degree of distortion is discussed when the data on the level of realized returns are presented.[13]

The annual price deflator is taken from Phelps Brown's reexamination of nineteenth- and twentieth-century real wages.[14] This price index is probably more accurate in its depiction of the direction and magnitude of long-term, rather than short-term, price movements.

B. AVERAGE REALIZED RATES OF RETURN, 1870–1913

Estimates of the realized, price-deflated return, 1870–1913, to first- and second-class equity, preference, and debenture shares from a variety of industrial and governmental units are presented in tables 5.3 and 5.4. The estimator of return is the geometric mean of annual increments to wealth defined in equation 5.3.

Before considering the issue of home versus foreign returns, it is important to note that the rank order of returns to the three types of securities—equity, preference, and debenture—roughly conforms to commonly held concepts of their relative risk. Within a given region, equity returns generally exceeded preference returns and, in turn, preference returns generally exceeded debenture returns. Thus, for example, between 1870 and 1913, U.K. manufacturing and commercial equity returns fell roughly in the range 6.00 percent to 9.00 percent per annum, preference returns averaged 5.34 percent per annum, and over a somewhat shorter period (dictated by data limitations), 1888–1913, debentures averaged 4.00 percent per annum. To take another example, from 1870 to 1913 the average return to Latin American railway equity was 8.41 percent per annum. Over the same period, Latin American railway debenture returns average 5.30 percent per annum. The one striking exception to this finding occurred in the U.K. railway sector. Although average U.K. railway equity and preference returns exceeded U.K. debenture returns, equity returns do not appear to have exceeded preference returns.

With regard to the hierarchy of first- and second-class returns by region it seems to be the general rule that, when instruments of a given sector and type (e.g., railway equity) were represented in both the home and overseas portfolios, overseas returns exceeded home returns. With few exceptions, the realized returns to the debentures of overseas governments, municipalities, railways, and social-overhead enterprises surpassed their domestic counterparts. For example, Canadian, Argentinian, Brazilian, Western European, Eastern European, and United States railway debenture returns surpassed those of the United Kingdom. A similar rule appears to hold for the equity instruments of home and overseas railway, banking, and social-overhead enterprises.

There are three exceptions to this general rule, home tramway

Table 5.3

Ranking of Realized Returns on U.K. Equity by Industry and Region,
Geometric Means, 1870-1913

	Domestic	Nondomestic
2.00-2.99	Electricity (2.10) Canals and docks (2.40)	Eastern European railways (2.58)
3.00-3.99		
4.00-4.99	Railways (4.33)	Indian railways (4.97)
5.00-5.99	Shipping (5.13)	
6.00-6.99	Banking (6.31) Telegram and telephone (6.46) Electrical equipment (6.55) Gas (6.69) Water (6.81)[b] Oldham cotton spinners (6.92)[c]	Canadian banking (6.07) Western European railways (6.31) Tramways (6.51) North American social overhead (6.55)[a]
7.00-7.99	All textiles (7.29) Bldg. and construction materials (7.51)[d] Drink (7.54)	Eastern Mediterranean banking (7.11) Gas (7.42) Indian social overhead (7.48) Asian and Australasian banking (7.50)
8:00-8.99	Insurance (8.17) Iron, steel, coal, and heavy fabrication (8.17) Tramways and omnibuses (8.95) Chemicals (8.99)	Western European social over- head (8.01) Latin American social overhead (8.41) United States railways (8.41) Electricity (8.42)[h] Latin American railways (8.43) Telegraph and telephone (8.93)[e]
9.00-9.99	Retail stores (9.33)[f] Mechanical equipment (9.93)	Tea and coffee (9.34)
10.00-10.99		South African banking (10.53)
11.00-11.99		Latin American banking (11.32)
12.00-12.99		
13.00-	Food (13.01)[g]	

Table 5.3 (con't)

Data Source: Edelstein 1970: 275-291.
  [a]1890-1913
  [b]1870-1903
  [c]1875-1913
  [d]1876-1913
  [e]1871-1913
  [f]1982-1931
  [g]1880-1913
  [h]1901-1913

equity, Eastern European railway equity, and Indian railway debentures. An examination of table 5.3 suggests that Eastern European railway equity and home tramway equity had usually low and high returns, respectively, for their sectors and security types. Their failure to conform suggests that these two groupings were subject, respectively, to substantial unexpected failure and success. The fact that the return to Indian railway debentures (table 5.4) fell short of the return to U.K. railway debentures probably reflects the Indian government's guarantees. Despite similar guarantees on Indian railway equity, however, Indian railway equity returns were greater than U.K. railway equity returns. Like the curiosum of U.K. railway equity returns falling short of U.K. railway preference returns, this result warrants further discussion.

Even though overseas returns tended to exceed domestic returns when securities of a given sector and type appeared in both the home and overseas portfolios, a number of home manufacturing and commercial groupings generated equity returns in the same range as the highest nondomestic equity groupings. Furthermore, domestic manufacturing and commercial preference shares earned returns well within the range of the most remunerative overseas debenture groupings. Domestic manufacturing and commercial debentures seem, however, to have earned returns well below the highest overseas debenture returns.

By basing inferences on the hierarchy of first- and second-class returns, it would therefore appear that although overseas returns in the aggregate might have been higher than the aggregate return

Table 5.4

Ranking of Realized Returns on U.K. Preference and Debenture Shares
by Industry and Region, Geometric Means, 1870-1913

	Domestic	Nondomestic
2.50-2.99	Consols (2.59)	Indian governments (2.99)
3.00-3.49	Social overhead[a] (3.47)[d] Municipals (3.49	Jamaican governments (3.35)[e]
3.50-3.99	Railways (3.74)	Indian railways (3.65)
4.00-4.49	Manufacturing and commerce (4.00)[f]	Colonial and provincial governments[b](4.14) Australian governments (4.18) Canadian governments (4.18) French rentes (4.26) New Zealand governments (4.49) South African governments (4.49)
4.50-4.99	Railway preference (4.52)	Colonial municipals (4.85)[g] Canadian railways (4.99)
5.00-5.49	Manufacturing and commerce preference (5.34)	Brazilian railways (5.10)[h] Argentine railways (5.13)[i] Western European railways (5.28) Overseas social overhead[a] (5.31) Eastern European railways (5.33) Latin American railways[c] (5.33)
5.50-		U.S. railways (6.03)

Data Source: Materials described in Edelstein 1970: 238-274
Note: Unless otherwise noted, the indices are debenture share returns.

[a]Social overhead includes canals, docks, electricity, gas, telephone, telegraph, tramway, and waterworks companies.

[b]Includes the colonial and provincial governments of Australia, Candada, India, Jamaica, New Zealand, and South Africa.

[c]Includes the Brazilian and Argentinian railways separately presented in the table, plus Chilean and Mexican debenture shares.

[d]1878-1913.

[e]1893-1913.

[f]1888-1913.

[g]1874-1913.

[h]1876-1913.

[i]1873-1913.

Table 5.5

Realized Rates of Return, Aggregate Indices, Geometric Means,
1870-1913

	Equity Shares	Preference shares	Debenture shares	All shares[a] A	B
Domestic					
Gm	6.37	4.84	3.21	4.41	4.60
Am	6.61	4.23	3.35	4.58	4.52
Asd	7.29	3.06	2.34	3.79	3.55
Nondomestic					
Gm	8.28		4.92	5.72	
Am	8.66		4.94	5.81	
Asd	9.25		2.35	3.56	
Market					
Gm	6.96		4.12	4.92	4.90
Am	7.33		4.17	5.15	5.06
Asd	6.71		2.14	3.26	3.15

Data Source: Edelstein 1977: 326-7.
Note: , Gm, geometric mean; Am, arithmetic mean; Asd, arithmetic
standard deviation.

[a]The "A" estimate excludes domestic preference returns; the "B"
estimate includes domestic preference returns.

at home across the full period under study, the gap might not have
been very large. To examine this issue more closely, however, the
returns to the various types of securities and sectors must be
aggregated into home and overseas indices. Table 5.5 presents the
geometric mean, arithmetic mean, and arithmetic standard deviation of these aggregate indices where, as noted earlier, the weights
are the 1913 shares of the groupings in the U.K. portfolio found in
tables 5.3 and 5.4.

According to the results presented in table 5.5, domestic
securities had a geometric mean return of 4.60 percent per annum,
1870-1913, while overseas assets showed a geometric mean return
of 5.72 percent per annum. This result affirms the assumption of
most historians of the late nineteenth and early twentieth
centuries; indeed, if anything, this result underestimates the gap
that has been widely assumed heretofore. It is, of course, quite
possible that the gap was far greater during certain subperiods
between 1870 and 1913. This hypothesis is addressed in chapter 6.

For the moment, however, it is quite important to examine carefully any possibility that the gap for the period as a whole has been overestimated.

The possibility that table 5.5's results have overestimated the gap between overseas and home returns, 1870–1913, has two aspects to it. First, does table 5.5's estimate of the gap have errors that bias the gap between first- and second-class overseas and home returns upward? Two sectors are missing from table 5.5's calculations: overseas extractive and industrial issues (mainly equity shares) and foreign government debentures. Second, does table 5.5's estimate of the gap for first- and second-class returns present a false impression for the return to all classes of home and overseas assets? The largest potential source of error here is the role of home versus overseas default and insolvency. These two issues will now be discussed in turn.

Since the major omitted sectors from table 5.5 are overseas sectors, a test of the possibility that the omission of these sectors has led to an overestimate of the overseas–home gap for first- and second-class returns reduces to a question of whether first- and second-class overseas returns have been overestimated. The plausibility of this proposition can be judged with a simple calculation involving known quantities and some reasonable assumptions. Let OV equal the return to the overseas sectors included in table 5.5 XM the return to overseas extractive and manufacturing assets, and FG the return to foreign governmental debentures. Further, let a, b, and c be their respective shares in the total first- and second-class overseas portfolio, and Z be the return to the latter portfolio, Mathematically,

$$Z = a(OV) + b(XM) + c(FG) \tag{5.4}$$

Estimates of the shares of the included and omitted sectors in the total overseas portfolio, a, b, and c, are approximately known.[15] From table 5.5 it is known that the value of OV was 5.72 percent per annum, 1870–1913. A plausible *lower*-bound estimate of the return to first- and second-class overseas extractive and manufacturing securities may be derived from Frankel's study of the return to South African gold mining, i.e., 5.2 percent per annum,

1870-1913.[16] This leaves two unknowns in equation 5.4, Z and FG. Fortunately, the question at issue allows us to make an assumption about the value of Z and test its plausibility by the mathematically implied value of FG.

Contrary to the evidence of table 5.5, let us assume that overseas returns were equal to home returns, that is, Z was equal to 4.60 percent annum, 1870-1913. Substituting this value into equation 5.4 with the other known quantities yields the implication that the return to first- and second-class foreign government debentures was −2.00 percent per annum. Needless to say, this is a highly unlikely possibility for a capital market of London's maturity. During the 1870s when gross nominal defaults of Latin American and Middle Eastern governments were perhaps £60 million, Cairncross reports that all, not just first- and second-class, foreign government debentures had an average realized return of 4.14 percent (1953:228-29). In sum, the assumption that overseas returns were equal to, instead of greater than, home returns ultimately implies a quite implausible estimate of first- and second-class foreign government returns. The combined return to the omitted sectors must have been greater than the plausible lower bound estimate for overseas extractive and manufacturing returns and the implausible foreign government return. Therefore, it is unlikely that direct estimates of the omitted sector's return would seriously lessen the gap between overseas and home returns given in table 5.5. Indeed, such direct estimates would very likely enlarge it.

If table 5.5's estimates do not exaggerate the gap between overseas and home returns to first- and second-class placements (and they probably understate it), do these estimates overstate the gap between all classes of overseas and home returns? As noted earlier, the largest potential source of error affecting this inference involves the role of home versus overseas defaults and insolvencies. If the rate of net default and insolvency was higher abroad than at home, it is possible that the realized return to all classes of securities was greater at home than abroad! Data limitations make precise measurement of the net default and insolvency losses very difficult, but a rough calculation suggests that overseas default and insolvency have been greatly overestimated heretofore.

Macgregor estimates that the rate of net insolvency loss on the paid-up capital of U.K.-registered, nonrailway companies, 1893–1902, was roughly 2.7 percent per annum (1929:500–501). This rate is probably lower than the actual rate that prevailed in the 1870s, given the newness of general limited liability and the high proportion of young companies in the early lists. Let us assume, however, that this rate applies across the entire period, 1870–1913. Employing Board of Trade and Stock Exchange records to estimate that annual amount of paid-up capital in domestic, nonrailway companies, Macgregor's insolvency rate implies that around £1 billion was lost, 1870–1913, through the failure of these types of enterprises.[17] Since the United Kingdom's national government, local governments, and railway companies did not default or become insolvent during these years, this sum of £1 billion represents the net loss to U.K. investors on outstanding domestic portfolio investment.[18]

Domestic portfolio capital fell from around 67 percent of U.K.-held, long-term negotiable capital in 1870 to around 55 percent in 1913 (calculated from table 3.1). On the assumption that the average was 61 percent, 1870–1913, net losses from overseas investment would have to have been £640 million if overseas and domestic holdings were equally risky.[19] Thus, the question of whether overseas asset failure so exceeded home failure as to suggest that total home returns exceeded those abroad boils down to whether overseas default and insolvency exceeded or fell short of £640 million and by how much.

For the moment, assume that the rate of net insolvency for overseas companies was the same as for domestic companies. By employing Board of Trade and Stock Exchange data to estimate the paid-up capital in overseas companies, it appears that approximately £450 million was lost on these issues.[20] Turning to the losses on overseas government issues, Cairncross estimates that the gross nominal value of overseas government defaults in the 1870s was around £60 million (1953:228–29). The records of the Corporation of Foreign Bondholders reveal that at least 50 percent of this was recovered. From 1880 to 1913 the worst defaults occurred in the early 1890s when various Argentinian government bodies defaulted on around £40 million of debentures. However, virtually all of this amount was recovered by the mid-1900s. Thus,

£50 million appears to be a plausible *upper* bound estimate of the net losses from overseas government defaults, 1870–1913.

The total net losses from overseas government default and company insolvency therefore appear to have been around £500 million, given the assumption of equal home and overseas company insolvency rates.[21] This sum is well short of the amount, £640 million, that would imply domestic and overseas investments were equally exposed to default and insolvency. Of course, the rate of net insolvency on overseas companies was probably somewhat higher than 2.7 percent. Overseas company investment contained a higher proportion of mining and other relatively risky enterprise than domestic company investment. However, even if overseas company insolvency was a third greater than the Macgregor estimate implies, domestic and overseas investments would still have been approximately equal in their default and insolvency exposure.

In summary, the conclusion that first- and second-class overseas-realized returns exceeded home-realized returns appears to stand. Indeed, an experiment testing the probable effect of some omitted segments of the first- and second-class portfolios strengthens this conclusion. A reasonable inference from these data on first- and second-class issues might be that overseas-realized returns exceeded those at home for all classes of securities. A second experiment tested whether overseas default and insolvency were such as to reverse this inference. Given currently available evidence, this experiment cannot be claimed as a conclusive test. However, it leaves the distinct impression that if, in fact, the rate of overseas default and insolvency was greater than the domestic rate, it was not so much greater that it would reverse the hypothesis that total overseas returns exceeded those at home.

C. THE ROLE OF RISK

Given that overseas returns appear to have exceeded home returns between 1870 and 1913, the question immediately arises about what systematic factors, if any, helped to generate the gap. The gap may represent a reward to investors for their correct *ex ante* perceptions that overseas investments were somewhat riskier than home investments. The gap could reflect a systematic tendency for overseas regions to generate greater amounts of profitable innovations and new market opportunities. The larger amounts of innovation and opportunity overseas could have created stronger, periodic disequilibria abroad. New financing and capital goods would probably move to reduce the disequilibrium rate of return differentials, but the rents generated during the disequilibrium would leave their mark on our long-term realized-return averages. The gap could also be the result of a persistent tendency for overseas areas to generate stronger monopoly rents. The purpose of this section is to examine whether the gap arose from the rewards for having borne greater risks or from the existence of higher "risk-adjusted" returns. Resolving the question of whether the latter were due to greater amounts of new opportunities or monopoly power must be reserved for another study.

Examing whether the gap between overseas and home returns represents a reward for having borne higher risks or the existence of higher, "risk-adjusted" returns is a hazardous issue. Although economic theory offers a reasonably articulated theory of the *ex ante* relationship of return and risk, the relationship between *ex post* measures of return and risk may only crudely reflect the *ex ante* relationship.[22] However, let us assume, as do many studies of recent capital market behavior, that the measure of *ex ante* risk suggested by Sharpe and Lintner, the covariance of a security's (or a portfolio's) return and the market rate of return, affords the best, albeit quite crude, measure of the level of *ex ante* risk for groupings such as those found in tables 5.3 and 5.4.[23] Since the Sharpe-Lintner model suggests a linear relationship between return and risk, it follows that the residuals from a linear regression of *ex post* (i.e., realized) returns on the Sharpe-Lintner measure of *ex ante* risk roughly indicates the portion of a grouping's return that was not due to the rewards of risk bearing.[24] Thus, the distribution of these residuals is literally the unusual winners and losers, given investor anticipations of risk.

Early statistical tests of the hypothesized Sharpe-Lintner model of risk and return revealed that the residuals of the debenture and preference groupings, regardless of location, were significantly lower than the residuals from the equity groupings. To test this hypothesis, a dummy variable, D, was created that took the value of zero if the observation was an equity grouping one if it was a preference or debenture grouping. Added to the simple risk-return regression equation, D yielded a statistically significant negative coefficient. The most plausible interpretation of this result is that the Sharpe-Lintner measure of risk is an imperfect index of risk across asset types, at least as the variables are measured here. One possibility might be that our indices of equity and debenture realized returns are not strictly comparable for measuring a uniform price of risk because they somehow fail to incorporate the different average maturities of these security types. Equity shares are implicity perpetuities, whereas debentures often have long but finite terms to maturity. Accordingly, the statistically significant coefficient on D represents a part of a security's risk that is incompletely captured by the covariance measure of risk.

The estimated parameters of this augmented risk-return relationship are presented at the top of table 5.6. They are derived from a linear, least squares regression of R_{jk} (the arithmetic mean return to the groupings of tables 5.3 and 5.4) on $Cov(R_{jk}, R_m)$(the Sharpe-Lintner measure of risk) and D (the dummy variable for security type).[25]

This equation purports to incorporate all variation in realized returns due to risk. Hence, the difference between the actual realized return of a security grouping and the one predicted by table 5.6's equation, the residual error in a statistical sense, is the part of the grouping's return which cannot be predicted by risk factors, that is, its non-risk element. To be precise, an index of risk-adjusted return $(IRAR_{jk})$ may be calculated by substituting the actual values of the three regression variables into the following equation:

$$IRAR_{jk} = R_{jk} - (6.38 + 1012.64\ Cov(R_{jk,}\ R_m) - 2.61D) \quad (5.5)$$

The values of $IRAR_{jk}$ are the basis of table 5.6's rank order of risk-adjusted returns.

Before turning to the broader patterns of "risk-adjusted" return revealed by table 5.6, it is interesting to use this new evidence to

Table 5.6

Index of "Risk-Adjusted," Realized Rates of Return, 1870-1913; Residuals from the Regression

$$R_{jk} = 6.36 + 1012.64 \text{ Cov}(R_{jk}, R_m) - 2.61D, \quad r^2 = 0.63^a$$
$$\phantom{R_{jk} = }\;(6.9)\quad\;(2.0)\qquad\qquad\qquad\qquad\;(3.4)$$

	Domestic[b]	Nondomestic[b]
>1.90	Tramways and omnibuses (4.75)[b] Mechanical equipment (3.04)	Latin American banking (3.69) Tea and coffee (2.66) United States railways (2.18) South African banking (1.95)
0.95-1.89	Iron, coal, steel and heavy fabrication (1.04)	United States railways (1.86) Latin American railways (1.19) Western European railways (1.14) Telegraph and telephone (0.97)
0.0-0.94	Drink (0.92) Manufacturing and commerce preference (0.89) Electrical equipment (0.60) Insurance (0.47) Chemicals (0.39) All textiles (0.23)	Eastern European railways (0.90) Latin American social overhead (0.85) Asian and Australasian banking (0.64) Tramways (0.61) New Zealand governments (0.34) Eastern Mediterranean banking (0.25) French rentes (0.18) Indian social overhead (0.04)
0.94-0.0	Railway preference (-0.36) Municipals (-0.76) Railways (-0.88)	South African governments (-0.02) Western European social overhead (-0.10) Latin American railways (-0.10) Canadian governments (-0.12) Australian governments (-0.13) Colonial and provincial governments (-0.20) Gas (-0.71) North American social overhead (-0.77) Indian railways (-0.91) Western European railways (-0.92)

Table 5.6 (con't)

-1.89 - -0.95	Telegraph and telephone (-1.00)	Canadian banking (-0.99)
	Banking (-1.10)	Indian governments (-1.35)
	Gas (-1.28)	
	Consols (-1.74)	
	Shipping (-1.89)	
<1.90	Railways (-4.00)	Indian railways (-2.33)
	Canals and locks (-5.41)	Eastern European railways (-4.67)

[a] R_{jk} is the arithmetic mean, realized rate of return, 1870/71-1913, and Cov is the covariance of the R_{jk} and the market-realized return, 1870/71-1913.

[b] Underlined groupings are equity groupings.

reexamine the various curiosa of tables 5.3 and 5.4. The evidence of tables 5.3 and 5.4 suggests that the realized return to U.K. railway equity was lower than the realized return to U.K. railway preference shares. It was noted that this ordering ran strongly counter to commonly held conceptions of the relative risk of these two types of assets and therefore their expected rewards for risk bearing. The results of table 5.6 suggest that U.K. railway equity received much lower risk-adjusted returns than U.K. railway preference shares, the difference being large enough in fact to swamp any reward for their larger risk.[26] It would thus appear that the textbook view of the late-nineteenth- and early-twentieth-century British railway system as suffering from high competition both internally and with the coastal trade, government regulation of prices, and technological backwardness is correct, the industry's equity instruments, by virtue of their differential exposure to unforeseen events, absorbing the brunt of these forces (Ashworth 1960:118–126; Kindleberger 1964:141–45).

The evidence of table 5.6 also provides an interesting insight into the role of the Indian government's dividend and interest guarantees as they affected the performance of Indian versus U.K. railway issues. Table 5.4 suggests that Indian railway debentures were the only overseas railway debenture grouping whose realized return fell short of U.K. debenture returns. According to table 5.6, Indian and U.K. railway debentures derived roughly the same risk-adjusted return. Hence, it would appear that the Indian government's guarantees did, in fact, work to reduce the level of risk, and therefore the risk premium paid for Indian railway debentures. It will be remembered, however, that Indian railway equity earned a higher realized return than U.K. railway equity, an ordering that defies what might be expected to follow from the Indian government's guarantees on equity dividends. On the basis of the Sharpe-Lintner risk measure, table 5.6's regression equation suggests that the indices of the risk premiums of U.K. and Indian railway equity were 2.30 percent and 0.53 percent, respectively. However, the unexpectedly low risk-adjusted return to U.K. railway equity overwhelmed the ordering that would have been consistent with the presumed effects of the Indian government's guarantees.

The two remaining curiosa of tables 5.3 and 5.4 concern U.K. tramway and Eastern European railway equity. An examination of the timing of realized returns to U.K. tramway and omnibus enterprise makes it clear that the bulk of the extraordinary returns to this sector occurred in the early twentieth century, coinciding with the period of widespread municipalization of this sector. Table 5.6 suggests that this sector drew a very high risk-adjusted return from 1870 to 1913. Since the rate of dividend payment did not increase in the early twentieth century, it seems reasonable to infer that the circumstances of municipalization led to state purchase at prices well in excess of those reflecting the sector's long-run risk characteristics as private enterprises. In turning to Eastern European railway equity, Table 5.6's evidence indicates that this grouping earned some of the lowest risk-adjusted returns in the British portfolio. This result reflects what was well known at the time, that is, that the Russian railways, which comprise the bulk of this grouping, were not generating very high profits. The Russians were also, of course, aware of this and relied heavily upon government or government-guaranteed debentures to acquire foreign long-term finance. The risk-adjusted return on Eastern European railway debentures, according to table 5.6's evidence, did substantially better than Russian equity issues.

Among the broader patterns suggested by table 5.6, four aspects of the nondomestic orderings are important. First, groupings closely associated with primary product enterprise earned some of the highest risk-adjusted returns; these were tea and coffee, Latin American banking, and South African banking. Second, overseas banking generally did well, relative to U.K. banking, adding new evidence to chapter 3's hypothesis that, if there was an expansion of U.K. resources in overseas financial intermediation, it was based on its profitability, rather than on rigidity or prejudice in the City's institutions or personnel. Third, on the assumption that the variable D adjusts for either the imperfection of the Sharpe-Lintner measure or risk or British investor desires for "safe" types of assets, the railway debenture assets of the United States, Western Europe, and Latin America delivered rather high risk-adjusted returns. Fourth, both the equity and debenture assets of U.S. railway companies offered very high risk-adjusted returns, confirming the special desirability of U.S. assets that was assumed in chapter 4. A sixth of Britain's overseas holdings in 1913 were placed in U.S. securities, more than in any other nation or colony, and table 5.6's results suggest a simple but powerful element in the explanation.

On the domestic side, the equity of the mechanical equipment sector appears to have delivered the highest risk-adjusted returns among the U.K. industrial groupings sampled. Half of the equity instruments in this grouping are from railway equipment firms for which the overseas railway companies, which themselves did well, were quite important markets. The high ranking of the mechanical equipment grouping and the iron, steel, coal, and heavy fabrication grouping is somewhat surprising, however, given the "climacteric" that British industry is often hypothesized to have been undergoing during these years. Of course, this hypothesis has never been localized to old versus new or heavy versus light industry, but until recently these two sectors have been thought to be among the technological laggards.[27] In any event, table 5.6's evidence suggests that these sectors were not unprofitable financial investments, regardless of whether they were technologically senile or not.

Finally, it is time to take up the central issue of how much of the gap between overseas and home realized returns is explained by risk vs. non-risk elements. The rank order of home and overseas risk-adjusted returns of table 5.6 suggests a tendency for overseas risk-adjusted returns to exceed those at home. A better method for testing this issue is available through combining the risk-return equation of table 5.6 and the data on aggregate home and overseas returns underlying table 5.5. In table 5.6 the actual values for each security grouping's R_{jk}, $Cov(R_{jk}, R_m)$ and D (the dummy variable for type of security) were substituted into the risk-return regression equation of table 5.6 and the residual was taken to be the portion of the actual return not predicted by risk factors, that is, the index of risk-adjusted returns specified in equation 5.5. If table 5.6's equation is acceptable as a rough description of the relationship between risk and return, then the data on the various aggregate home and overseas return indices can be substituted into the equation to produce indices of risk-adjusted returns for these aggregate home and overseas indices. For the aggregate home and overseas equity, preference and debenture groupings of table 5.5, it merely needs substituting their R_j, $Cov(R_j, R_m)$, and D into equation 5.5 where D takes the value of zero if the aggregate index is composed of equity shares and one if it is preference or debenture shares. For example, the index of risk-adjusted returns for domestic equity is derived from table 5.7's first five columns of data as follows:

$$IRAR = 6.61 - (6.36 + 1012.64(.001952) - 2.61(0.0))$$

$$= 6.61 - (6.36 + 1.98)$$

$$= -1.73.$$

For the aggregate home and overseas indices of table 5.5 that include all types of securities, D takes the value of the share of debentures and preference shares in the aggregate home and overseas return indices.[28]

From these calculations it appears that, although overseas returns manifested a slightly lower level of risk, the index of the risk-adjusted return of overseas assets was substantially higher than that on home assets.[29] The index of risk premium on home assets was −0.75 percent, whereas the risk premium on non-domestic assets was lower at −1.04 percent. This difference is due to the slightly lower covariance of overseas assets with the market rate of return and a slightly higher proportion of the overseas portfolio placed in fixed-interest assets.[30] However, this difference due to risk is so small and the calculation so rough that not too much weight should be placed on the risk differential. On the other hand, the risk-adjusted return on overseas assets is 0.49 percent and, on home assets, −1.09 percent, a difference amounting to 1.58 percentage points and too large to assign merely to random error.

In short, overseas returns tended to exceed home returns over the years 1870–1913, and the results of this section's experiments indicate that the major reason for this differential was not the long-term *ex ante* risk characteristics of these two elements of the national portfolio. What, then, is the explanation of the differential in risk-adjusted returns? One plausible hypothesis is that our measure of risk is inadequate insofar as it implicitly assumes U.K. investors were indifferent to the location of their wealth

Table 5.7

An Index of "Risk-Adjusted," Realized Returns, Aggregate Indices, 1870-1913

	Actual return (1)	SD (2)	Corr. (3)	Cov. (4)	D (5)	Index of "risk premium" (6)	Index of "risk-adjusted" return (7)
A. Domestic							
1. Equity	6.61	7.29	0.8501	0.001952	0.000	1.98	-1.73
2. Preference	4.23	3.06	0.7401	0.000713	1.000	-1.89	-0.24
3. Debenture	3.35	2.34	0.7740	0.000571	1.000	-2.03	-0.98
Total	4.52	3.55	0.9201	0.001029	0.685	-0.75	-1.09
B. Nondomestic							
1. Equity	8.66	9.25	0.6986	0.002036	0.000	2.06	0.24
2. Debenture	4.94	2.35	0.8267	0.000512	1.000	-1.99	0.57
Total	5.81	3.56	0.8414	0.000944	0.766	-1.04	0.49

Note: Column (1) The arithmetic mean return from table 5.3; (2) the standard deviation from table 5.5; (3) the partial correlation coefficient of the aggregate index and the market rate of return; (4) the covariance of the aggregate index and the market rate of return, equal to the product of their correlation coefficient and their standard deviation; (5) the proportion of the aggregate index in preference and debenture shares; (6) 1012.64 x Col. (4) - 2.61 x Col. (5); see text; (7) Col. (1) -[6.36 + 1012.64 x Col. (4) - 2.61 x Col. (5)]: see table 5.6.

holdings. U.K. investors may well have preferred home assets, on average, 1870–1913, as Ricardo predicated:

Experience . . . shows, that the fancied or real insecurity of capital, when not under the immediate control of its owner, together with the natural disinclination which every man has to quit the country of his birth and connections, and intrust himself with all his habits fixed, to a strange government and new laws, checks the emigration of capital. These feelings induce most men of property to be satisfied with a low rate of profits in their own country, rather than seek a more advantageous employment of their wealth in foreign nations (1818:155)

In effect, Ricardo seems to argue that U.K. investors demanded and received on average a lump-sum premium for placing their funds abroad, regardless of the covariance characterisitcs of these overseas assets. In reply to this hypothesis it might be argued that by 1870–1913 U.K. investors had a good deal of experience with economic and political conditions in many parts of Europe, North and South America, and elsewhere, and therefore such matters as the special difficulties of recovery of funds subsequent to default or bankruptcy would be incorporated in the volatility of the capital value of overseas assets.

A second plausible hypothesis is that U.K. investors were indifferent to the location of their wealth holdings but that the overseas regions had a tendency to generate greater amounts of profitable innovations and new market opportunities, periodically fostering greater disequilibria, which in turn left their mark on their realized returns. A third possibility is that overseas areas evinced a tendency to generate more circumstances involving imperfect competition and, possibly, greater monopoly rents.

Of course, elements of each hypothesis could be responsible for the risk-adjusted gap, one hypothesis dominating the others in certain periods and regions. Needless to say, empirical testing would be difficult. Ricardo's hypothesis would appear the most plausible in the case of investments in an overseas region with a relatively untried legal system. It would be this author's guess, however, that the returns and risks of innovations and other new opportunities in the United States, for example, periodically falsified the U.K. investor's anticipations.

CHAPTER 6: TRENDS AND CYCLES IN PRIVATE REALIZED RATES OF RETURN

A. TRENDS: DECLINING RETURNS?

If the average price-deflated, realized rates of return to overseas financial assets from 1870 to 1913 were higher than those at home owing largely to unexpected opportunities, what was the time shape of home and overseas returns and their differential? Interest in answering this question stems from several sources. Rates of return to financial assets can be both a symptom and a cause of the accumulation of wealth. In chapter 5 their role as a symptom has been stressed because our indices are literally measures of realized, not expected, rates of return. Of course, realized returns are an important influence on expected returns, but they are not the only influence. From this perspective, if realized home returns or overseas returns, or both, were subject to a secular drift, this may be a symptom, and to some degree a cause, of capitalist choices between the accumulation of wealth and consuming goods. Independently, the time path of the differential between home and overseas returns has interest because it is symptom, and to some degree a cause, of the allocation of wealth between home and overseas assets. Furthermore, the time path of the differential may have some influence on the timing of political, as well as economic, expansion abroad. In this section, annual realized returns to home and overseas assets are examined to test for the presence of a secular trend. The gap between home and overseas returns is also examined. Here the issue is whether the gap was fairly constant, slowly drifting wider or closer, or shaped by alternating periods of home and overseas dominance.

To assess whether realized returns to home and overseas portfolio assets were subject to secular drift, in which direction, and at what rate, the logarithms of their annual values were regressed on time (T) and time squared (T^2). Table 6.1 presents these regression equations and their associated statistics. Equation 6.1.7 clearly reveals that home returns had a slow but strong downward trend. The sign on b_1, the regression coefficient of T, is

141

Table 6.1

Trends in Aggregate Realized Rates of Return, 1870-1913

$$Log(r_{jk}) = b_1 + b_2T + b_3T^2$$

	b_1	b_2	b_3	r^2
A. Domestic				
6.1.1 Equity	0.1068	-0.0021		0.19
	(5.7)	(2.8)		
6.1.2 Equity	0.1223	-0.0043	0.000051	
	(4.5)	(1.5)	(0.8)	
6.1.3 Preference	0.0802	-0.0015		0.36
	(9.2)	(4.2)		
6.1.4 Preference	0.0914	-0.0013	0.000037	0.40
	(7.2)	(2.3)	(1.2)	
6.1.5 Debenture	0.0486	-0.0007		0.24
	(7.7)	(2.9)		
6.1.6 Debenture	0.0423	0.0002	-0.000021	0.29
	(4.6)	(0.2)	(0.9)	
6.1.7 Total	0.0731	-0.0013		0.28
	(7.9)	(3.5)		
6.1.8 Total	0.0770	-0.0019	0.000013	0.31
	(5.7)	(1.3)	(0.4)	
B. Nondomestic				
6.1.9 Equity	0.1043	-0.0011		0.07
	(4.2)	(1.1)		
6.1.10 Equity	0.0908	0.0008	-0.000045	0.09
	(2.5)	(0.2)	(0.5)	
6.1.11 Debenture	0.0693	-0.0010		0.44
	(12.0)	(4.4)		
6.1.12 Debenture	0.0651	-0.0004	-0.000014	0.49
	(8.0)	(0.5)	(0.8)	
6.1.13 Total	0.0782	-0.0010		0.25
	(8.5)	(2.8)		
6.1.14 Total	0.0719	-0.0001	-0.000021	0.30
	(5.3)	(0.1)	(0.6)	
C. Market				
6.1.15 Total	0.0753	-0.0012		0.33
	(9.5)	(3.8)		
6.1.16 Total	0.0749	-0.0011	-0.000001	0.37
	(6.4)	(0.9)	(0.1)	

Data Source: Edelstein 1977: 326-27.
Note: The bracketed figures are t ratios. With 44 observations, the t ratio
    for the 0.05 significance level is approximately 1.7.

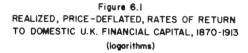

Figure 6.1
REALIZED, PRICE-DEFLATED, RATES OF RETURN
TO DOMESTIC U.K. FINANCIAL CAPITAL, 1870-1913
(logarithms)

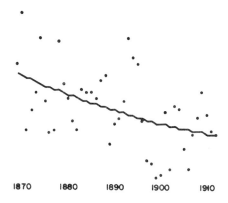

negative. The t ratio of b_1 is 3.5, and hence, the null hypothesis that domestic returns were trendless (i.e., $b = 0$) can be rejected with a very low probability of error. Equation 6.1.8, which adds the T^2 term, suggests that the downward trend of home returns may have moderated in the latter part of the period, but figure 6.1, which depicts the actual values of the logarithm of home portfolio and equation 6.1.8's regression line, indicates that this moderation was a very minor influence on the time shape of home returns.

Among domestic security types, equity and preference returns showed the strongest downward movement, a moderating trend appearing after the turn of the nineteenth century. The trend in debenture returns was fairly level until the early 1880s, when they, too, turned downward. Thus, if the downward trend of total home returns moderated after the turn of the nineteenth century, the movements in equity and preference returns appear responsible.

Importantly, price-deflated, realized rates of return to British-held overseas assets also manifested a downward secular trend, as witnessed by equation 6.1.13 in table 6.1. Again the sign on b_1 is negative and the t ratio gives strong assurance that this fact is statistically significant. Unlike the trends among domestic security types, however, equations 6.1.9–12 in table 6.1 indicate that overseas equity and debenture returns demonstrated quite similar, downward secular movements.

In sum, both domestic and overseas returns were subject to secular decline between 1870 and 1913. Since U.K. overseas investments were small relative to the total of world savings, it might be thought that U.K. holdings of home and overseas assets were subject to declining returns for largely independent reasons. This hypothesis, however, has several weaknesses. First, it assumes that the assets Britain bought abroad were closely linked by good capital markets with the remainder of overseas assets. This may be the case for North America and Australasia but is far less true for South America, Africa, and Asia. Second, although U.K. savings flowing abroad were small relative to total overseas accumulations, British overseas investments often concentrated in a few regions. As a result it is likely that British overseas placements were an important determinant of the pace of accumulation for long periods in these localities and, in all probability, of their rates of return as well. It therefore seems likely that the joint secular decline of returns to domestic and overseas assets held by U.K. investors was the product of both interdependent and independent forces. A more thorough discussion of these issues awaits rate-of-return studies that focus on the full spectrum of assets in several overseas regions.

To find that home and overseas rates of return were both falling, 1870–1913, is not to say that they were falling at the same secular pace or during the same years. To examine these issues, the time path of the gap between overseas and home returns must be studied. It is useful to distinguish two archetypal patterns before examining the data. The gap could be relatively constant or slowly changing in its year-to-year movements. Given the volatility of annual home and overseas returns, the latter type of movement in their gap would involve a close positive correlation between annual home and overseas returns. Alternatively, the gap could be subject to strong cycles, the proximal result of strong negative correlation between home and overseas returns. In the latter case, the cycling of the gap would produce periods of dominance of both overseas and home rates of return. However, to produce the 1870–1913 average edge of overseas returns over home returns, the overseas periods of dominance would have to be either longer or stronger. Importantly, if the gap was relatively constant or slowly changing, the hypothesis that a large portion of the average difference between overseas and home returns was due to unanticipated events would not have much plausibility. A relatively constant or slowly changing gap would imply a disequilibrium lasting 44 years, a possible but improbable event. The kind of unanticipated profits and disequilibria that are likely to have affected our aggregate indices are generally thought either to appear randomly or to cluster periodically.

A comparison of equations 6.1.7 and 6.1.13 in table 6.1 suggests that the simple linear trend of overseas returns fell somewhat more slowly than domestic returns. The difference between their respective estimates of b_1, the geometric rate of decline, however, is not statistically significant. There is somewhat stronger evidence for a significant secular divergence in their long-run movements when the possibility of a nonlinear trend is introduced in equations 6.1.8 and 6.1.14 in table 6.1. At this point, however, it seems best to examine the difference between home and overseas returns directly.

In figure 6.2 the actual values of the absolute difference between

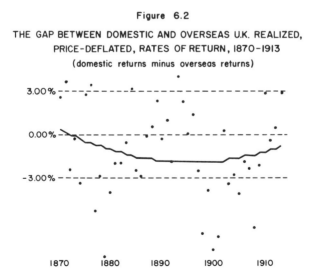

Figure 6.2

THE GAP BETWEEN DOMESTIC AND OVERSEAS U.K. REALIZED,
PRICE-DEFLATED, RATES OF RETURN, 1870-1913

(domestic returns minus overseas returns)

annual home (HR) and overseas (OR) returns are plotted along
with the regression line,

$$(HR - OR) = 0.0050 - 0.0013T + 0.000035T^2, r^2 = 0.04 \qquad (6.1)$$
$$(0.3) \qquad (1.1) \qquad (1.0)$$

The scatter of actual values of the gap and the regression line
depict overseas returns as tending to exceed home returns in the
last quarter of the nineteenth century but for these two series to
converge after the turn of the century. Nevertheless, the low values
of the t ratios and r^2 statistic suggest these secular movements in
the gap were only weak tendencies.

B. LONG SWINGS, INVERSITY AND DISEQUILIBRIUM

One distinct impression given in figure 6.2 is that the most
important force determining the time shape of the gap between
home- and overseas-realized rates of return was not a 44-year
secular configuration but long cycles about 20 years in length.
Figure 6.3 plots the indices of annual home- and overseas-realized
returns with the periods of home and overseas dominance

Figure 6.3

REALIZED RATES OF RETURN TO HOME AND OVERSEAS
LONG TERM SECURITIES, PRICE DEFLATED, 1870-1913

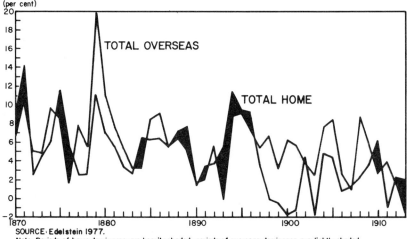

SOURCE: Edelstein 1977.
Note: Periods of home dominance are heavily shaded; periods of overseas dominance are lightly shaded.

separately identified. The graph suggests the following periodization of home and overseas domination[1]:

> 1870–1876, home (weak)
> 1877–86, overseas
> 1887–96, home
> 1897–1909, overseas
> 1910–13, home.

Detrended and smoothed with a 7-year moving average, the long
swings in domestic returns peak in 1871, 1895, and 1911 with
troughs in 1878 and 1900; in overseas returns, the peaks occur in
1879 and 1905 with the troughs in 1874, 1891, and (1913).[2]

In chapter 5 it was suggested that overseas returns, 1870–1913,
exceeded home returns on the average. How does this finding
evidence itself in the long-swing movements? To aid in ad-
dressing this question, the geometric mean return of the various
aggregate indices during the alternating periods of home and
overseas dominance are presented in table 6.2. According to table
6.2, row C.3, the absolute value of the difference between home
and overseas returns was smaller during the 1870–76, 1887–96, and
1910–13 periods of home dominance than the 1877–86 and 1897–
1909 periods of overseas dominance. The greater strength of the
periods of overseas dominance thus accounts for the average
divergence between overseas and home returns, 1870–1913. Furthermore, since the 1897–1909 period of overseas dominance was
both the longest period of overseas or home dominance and,
according to table 6.2, the strongest in the absolute size of the gap,
it is clear why the secular path of the gap appears as U-shaped in
figure 6.2. However, the prominent and statistically significant
long swings of figure 6.3 clearly demonstrate that figure 6.2's
weak, nonlinear trend is an inadequate focus for analyzing the
time shape of home versus overseas returns.

For most students of the 1870–1913 period, it should not be
surprising that realized rates of return to home and overseas
portfolio investment were subject to inversely timed long cycles.
Since the pioneering work of Cairncross, it has been widely
accepted that U.K. home and overseas investment flows moved in
inverse cycles of 15 to 25 years in length.[3] The precise mechanisms
behind these long cycles in investment flows remain subject to

Table 6.2

Realized Rates of Return, Aggregate Indices, Selected Subperiods, Geometric Means, 1870-1913

	1870-1876	1877-1886	1887-1896	1897-1909	1910-1913
A. Domestic					
1. Equity	11.94	7.19	8.93	.92	6.44
2. Preference	9.08	5.70	6.10	1.85	3.25
3. Debentures	4.36	4.12	4.92	1.40	1.84
4. Total	7.62	5.37	6.42	1.35	3.60
B. Nondomestic					
1. Equity	7.34	13.27	5.34	9.54	1.37
2. Debentures	6.29	6.40	5.16	3.82	1.90
3. Total	6.60	8.06	5.23	5.20	1.79
C. Nondomestic minus domestic					
1. Equity	-4.60	6.08	-3.59	8.62	-5.27
2. Debentures	1.93	2.28	0.24	2.42	0.06
3. Total	-1.02	2.69	-1.19	3.85	-1.81
D. Market	7.72	6.51	5.92	2.97	2.84

Data Source: Edelstein 1977: 326-27

debate, however. Some investigators see the long swings in national investment flows based on a complex interaction between economic and demographic factors. Others emphasize the technical and financial foundations for the long gestation period of transportation and other social-overhead investment, the elements of national investment that most prominently display the long cycles. With regard to the inversion of British home and overseas investment flows, some argue that the alternation of home and overseas investment was largely regulated by the strength of long-swing forces in the domestic British economy; others view the inverse motion as foisted on the British by the long-swing timing of the United States' immense demands for capital and labor. These issues cannot be settled here, but it may be useful to suggest briefly some plausible reasons why realized rates of return to aggregate U.K. home and overseas investment might reflect the long-swing pattern in investment flows.[4]

First, and perhaps most important, it is likely that realized returns to portfolio capital rose because of the appearance of unanticipated opportunities and the various disequilibria generated by lags in the supply of labor, finance, and capital equipment attempting to take advantage of these opportunities. For example, in the case of railroad investment it is doubtful whether the profits from economics of scale or the ownership of adjacent land were ever fully anticipated. Given the lumpiness of the railroad, public utility, and residential investment projects that most clearly manifested the long cycles, the lags between the recognition of new profit sources and new output could be quite long. Consequently, the unanticipated returns to the existing capital in these sectors could be quite high, albeit temporary. Long swings in unanticipated gains and losses probably also characterized non-social-overhead portfolio capital. A key aspect of the long cycle was that high returns to labor and capital in the first years of the expansion fostered interregional and international labor and capital movements that, in turn, helped to carry the expansion further. Non-social-overhead, as well as social-overhead, investments probably received unanticipated gains and losses from these interactions.

Second, it is likely that long swings in the degree of objective risk attended the periodic long swings in home and overseas investment and, consequently, in the rewards for bearing this risk. The first projects undertaken during the expansion phase of a long swing were probably the least risky for a given return. As the long-swing expansion proceeded, projects would draw increased attention. On average, then, one would expect long swings in the gap between home- and overseas-realized returns because of the long-swing rhythm of investment risk.

A third source of long swings in unanticipated realized returns might be inadequate knowledge of the long cycle itself. For example, if anticipations with respect to U.S. social-overhead profits, 1870–1913, were built around the 4-year trade cycle, both unexpected gains and losses to portfolio investment would accrue because some trade cycles were relatively strong or weak depending on which phase of the U.S. long swing was operative.

C. OTHER CYCLES

As one might thus expect, the industries and regions that generated the highest realized rates of return varied with each long swing. It is also the case that many industries and regions did not closely follow the alternating long-swing pattern found in the aggregate home- and overseas-realized return indices. The purpose of this section is to show some of the diversity that lies behind the movements of these broad aggregates. Discussion first focuses on the industrial and regional diversity within the long-swing aggregate pattern and then turns to a brief examination of other patterns of industrial and regional covariation. To aid in the discussion of the first topic, table 6.3 presents the geometric mean return for each of the 64 industrial and regional indices in the five periods of alternating home and overseas dominance. It will be remembered that home returns were dominant in the years 1870–76, 1887–96, and 1900–1913, with overseas returns dominant in the years 1887–86 and 1897–1909.

During the 1870–76 period, holdings in the relatively new domestic industries of chemicals, drink and of tramways and omnibuses seem to have paid the highest returns, but other domestic industries, including railways, banking and insurance, and iron, coal, steel, etc., also did very well. As noted earlier, this is a period when home returns were only weakly dominant. The principal overseas challengers were Indian, South African, Chinese, and Australasian holdings. Importantly, these sectors do not manifest a long-swing trough in the early 1870s, as do most overseas indices.

During the first period of overseas dominance, 1877–86, Latin American equity holdings were exceptional in their realized returns. In banking, railways, and social-overhead equity placements, Latin American realized returns led all other regions. Among debenture placements, Canadian, Eastern European, U.S., and Latin American railway debentures were the leaders. Significantly, these debentures did quite well relative to overseas equity holdings during these years of general price deflation.

In the second period of home dominance, 1887–96, light industry clearly offered the highest realized returns, although several heavy industries, iron, coal, steel, etc., mechanical equipment, and chemicals, were not far behind. Among domestic social-overhead placements, only the returns to the relatively new telegraph sector ranked with the other domestic leaders.

The longest and strongest period of dominance for either home or overseas returns was the second period of overseas dominance, 1897–1909. Latin American equity and debentures from all sectors did quite well. However, both equity and debenture returns were led by U.S. railway instruments. Indeed, the continued relative strength of U.S. and Latin American returns during the last years of this period appear to be one determinant of the exceptional dominance of overseas returns in this period. Latin American returns peaked with most other overseas regions in 1905 but did not fall off very rapidly. The U.S. returns peaked in 1900, much earlier than most other overseas regions, and then turned down sharply. After 1905, however, when most overseas returns were falling, U.S. returns were on the rise again.

A more important determinant of the exceptional dominance of overseas returns in the 1897–1909 period appears to be the unusual weakness of home returns. Whereas in the previous period of overseas dominance, 1877–86, a large number of home industries still maintained strong returns, especially such new industries as drink and electrical equipment, this was not the case in the 1897–1909 period. Realized returns to the newer light and heavy industries were in a sharp slump. The only domestic equities that did even moderately well were iron, coal, steel, etc., shares, apparently responding to augmented armaments demands and the strong overseas market for British coal. Indeed, negative returns were quite widespread among domestic railway and social-overhead equity shares.

If inordinately weak in the years 1897–1909, home returns did return to dominance, 1910–13. Light industry again offered the best returns, with only shipping, of the remaining domestic equity vectors, rivaling its leadership. Domestic, as well as overseas, debentures, did very poorly during this short period, owing in part to the slow inflation that eroded the real value of fixed-interest payments.

Strikingly, tea and coffee equity shares never followed the long-swing pattern of other overseas holdings. Instead, their realized returns followed the long-swing movements of domestic returns. Although more detailed research seems warranted, one plausible hypothesis is that the pace of British tea and coffee consumption was similar to that of Britain's light manufactures and thus generated the similarity in the timing of their returns.

Another aspect of the timing of British consumer goods returns also calls for special comment. The surging performance of the U.K. cotton textile industry prior to World War I is often examined very closely for signs of incipient overcapacity, in large part owing to the post-World War I difficulties with this problem. It is often assumed that too much capacity was created in an overoptimistic response to strong pre-World War I sales to the older colonial possessions. The evidence of table 6.3 suggest, however, that, if the return to Oldham Cotton Spinning shares is indicative of the performance of the entire cotton textile sector, its return in the pre-World War I years was part of the broadly superior performance of light British industries. Thus, rather than emphasize the export market in the expansion of the cotton textile industry in the early twentieth century, it may be useful to give some attention to the influence of the home market.

Although the long-swing motion of the individual industrial and regional indices captures a significant characteristic of their

Table 6.3

Realized Rates of Return, by Industry and Region,
Long Swing Highs and Lows, 1870-1913

	1870-76	1877-86	1887-96	1897-09	1910-13
Domestic Equity					
Railways	11.19	5.19	6.87	-0.83	1.51
Banks	10.75	7.00	7.85	4.46	-0.56
Insurance	13.50	10.44	8.73	3.52	7.54
All textiles	10.86	6.79	11.13	2.96	7.30
Oldham cotton spinners		7.18	-0.94	4.01	9.35
Food			24.63	0.80	10.59
Drink	18.28	12.59	13.33	-7.33	15.47
Retail stores				2.45	5.55
Iron, coal, etc.	11.07	3.82	10.79	9.64	3.21
Mechanical equipment	10.43	5.61	17.32	7.71	9.49
Electrical equipment	-1.32	18.98	4.44	4.73	2.90
Blgd. and constr. material		10.50	9.66	4.01	7.10
Chemicals	19.05	6.79	12.83	4.24	4.15
Electricity				-1.33	7.92
Gas	11.12	9.81	8.62	2.07	2.13
Water	7.94	9.68	6.54		
Canals and docks	8.17	5.30	4.72	-2.97	-2.30
Shipping	6.56	3.52	5.75	2.68	13.55
Telephone and telegraph	2.37	10.73	10.43	3.84	2.29
Tramways and omnibuses	13.78	13.79	4.43	-2.70	3.82
Nondomestic equity					
Indian railways	5.46	8.22	6.46	1.48	3.94
W. European railways	8.39	10.27	7.97	3.17	-0.59
E. European railways	-3.82	8.19	6.41	0.61	-2.35
U.S. railways	8.12	11.47	1.06	16.52	-4.28
Latin American railways	5.74	18.72	3.81	8.14	1.60
Asian and Australasian bnkg.	10.06	8.05	4.48	9.76	2.21
Canadian banking	9.79	8.15	3.32	5.94	2.10
South African banking	25.65	12.27	10.45	5.12	0.15
E. Mediterranean banking	1.54	13.25	6.00	8.49	0.67
Latin American banking	10.89	18.80	11.04	8.67	3.63
Electricity					8.16
Gas	12.21	12.38	6.35	3.57	2.61
Telegraph and telephone		8.94	10.89	7.70	8.57
Tramways	-7.49	15.23	5.45	10.61	1.58
Western European soc. ov.	7.34	13.18	10.17	4.30	3.56
North American soc. ov.		4.85	10.74	7.06	3.16
Latin American soc. ov.	5.03	13.59	6.27	8.76	6.02
Indian and Chinese soc. ov.	9.24	8.21	7.33	6.51	5.18
Tea and coffee	22.03	3.04	11.61	3.66	18.28

Table 6.3 (con't)

	1870-76	1877-86	1887-96	1897-09	1910-13
Domestic preference					
Railways	8.76	5.46	6.18	1.02	1.99
Manufacturing and commerce	9.38	6.09	5.93	3.12	5.21
Domestic debentures					
Consols	3.59	3.76	4.13	0.93	-0.37
Municipals	4.69	4.86	5.31	1.77	1.32
Railways	6.01	5.09	5.95	0.64	1.25
Social overhead				1.55	2.05
Manufacturing and commerce				3.31	3.43
Nondomestic debentures					
French rentes	4.79	5.41	5.55	2.73	2.34
Colonial and provincial gov'ts	6.08	4.72	4.95	2.78	1.77
Australia	6.41	4.63	4.59	2.94	2.20
Canada	6.43	5.17	4.26	2.96	1.64
India	4.07	3.26	5.28	1.64	-0.42
Jamaica				2.36	2.32
New Zealand	6.22	5.07	5.34	3.13	2.23
South Africa	6.60	4.99	5.83	2.74	2.04
Colonial municipals		6.11	6.34	3.80	2.43
Indian railways	4.63	4.70	6.01	0.74	2.36
Canadia railways		9.40	4.92	4.09	1.83
W. European railways	6.96	6.63	5.03	4.72	1.56
E. European railways	4.85	8.53	6.15	3.45	2.30
U.S. railways	7.84	7.69	4.63	6.13	2.08
Latin American railways	5.96	7.04	6.77	4.09	1.73
Argentine railways		7.07	6.53	3.33	1.34
Brazilian railways		6.39	5.28	5.11	3.41
Social overhead			5.20	3.70	2.55

Source: Edelstein 1970: 275-291.

behavior between 1870 and 1913, a closer look at table 6.3 indicates the possiblity that other patterns of covariation were also important. However, using graphs to try to understand the interactions of 64 indices moving through time would be extremely difficult; the eye might easily become lost in a maze of detail. To surmount this problem, a principal-components analysis was applied to the annual observations of those individual industrial and regional indices that spanned the entire period (table 6.4).[5]

The most striking fact that emerges from the principal-components analysis is the heterogeneity of the timing of home and overseas industrial and regional returns.[6] It takes six components to account for 60.9 percent of the total variance of the 46 indices that spanned the 44 years from 1870 to 1913. Seen in different

Table 6.4

Principal-Components Analysis of Selected Realized Rates of Return, 1870-1913

		1st PC 27.9%	2d PC 8.0%	3rd PC 7.5%	4th PC 6.3%	5th PC 5.9%	6th PC 5.3%
Domestic Equity	RWY	0.73	0.06	0.18	0.13	0.42	0.06
	BK	0.71	0.10	0.07	-0.30	0.03	0.28
	INS	0.64	-0.15	0.30	-0.04	-0.16	0.22
	TEX	0.34	0.39	0.29	0.05	0.18	-0.14
	DR	0.27	0.19	0.58	0.20	0.05	-0.26
	ISC	0.38	0.45	-0.23	0.16	0.26	0.31
	ME	0.28	0.15	0.37	0.07	0.12	0.41
	EE	0.21	0.13	-0.26	0.37	0.01	0.00
	CHEM	0.60	0.25	0.03	0.03	0.41	0.24
	GAS	0.66	0.28	0.22	-0.35	-0.24	-0.10
	C&D	0.65	-0.35	0.24	0.07	-0.05	-0.27
	SHIP	0.36	0.32	-0.31	0.14	0.18	0.14
	T&T	0.53	-0.09	0.08	0.01	-0.44	-0.16
	TRAM	0.11	0.22	0.05	0.25	-0.06	-0.48
Overseas equity	INRWY	0.74	-0.15	0.27	0.14	-0.29	-0.02
	WERWY	0.56	-0.45	0.18	0.12	-0.30	-0.16
	EERWY	0.44	0.16	0.11	0.56	0.01	0.05
	USRWY	0.27	-0.01	-0.47	-0.08	-0.33	0.48
	LARWY	0.60	0.17	-0.34	0.23	-0.27	-0.03
	A&ABK	0.40	0.20	-0.14	-0.37	-0.40	0.35
	SAFBK	0.60	-0.22	-0.11	-0.05	0.32	0.27
	CANBK	0.44	0.02	-0.23	0.05	0.15	0.42
	EMBK	0.34	-0.16	-0.23	0.74	-0.02	0.26
	LABK	0.53	0.04	-0.35	0.28	-0.11	-0.26
	NGAS	0.73	0.37	0.03	-0.18	-0.27	-0.12
	NTRAM	0.23	0.51	-0.38	0.32	-0.31	-0.15
	INSO	0.53	0.53	0.06	-0.09	-0.37	0.15
	WESO	0.68	0.23	0.14	-0.02	-0.30	0.09
	LASO	0.50	0.28	-0.39	0.01	-0.28	-0.26
	T&C	0.32	0.30	0.24	0.17	0.32	-0.14

Table 6.4 (con't)

		1st PC 27.9%	2d PC 8.0%	3rd PC 7.5%	4th PC 6.3%	5th PC 5.9%	6th PC 5.3%
Domestic debentures	CONR	0.09	0.07	0.08	-0.01	-0.01	0.00
	MNR	0.43	-0.32	-0.52	-0.28	0.05	-0.28
	RWYR	0.76	-0.34	-0.23	-0.22	0.11	-0.26
Domestic preferreds	PRWR	0.78	-0.05	0.23	-0.03	0.33	-0.23
	PMCR	0.55	0.11	0.36	-0.23	-0.24	0.05
Nondomestic debentures	FRR	0.21	-0.60	0.43	0.08	-0.10	0.39
	AUSR	0.80	-0.09	0.06	-0.22	0.19	-0.10
	CANR	0.72	-0.24	-0.45	-0.20	0.22	-0.18
	INDR	0.09	0.44	0.05	-0.61	0.23	0.10
	NZR	0.54	0.05	-0.15	-0.07	0.38	-0.24
	SAFR	0.74	-0.11	-0.08	-0.16	0.30	-0.01
	INRWR	0.79	-0.09	0.28	0.06	0.11	-0.08
	WERWR	0.44	-0.57	0.07	0.09	-0.23	0.31
	EERWR	0.46	-0.17	-0.09	0.53	0.15	0.11
	USRWR	0.40	-0.44	-0.52	-0.24	0.08	0.02
	LARWR	0.25	-0.34	0.07	-0.01	-0.26	-0.19

Note: The principal-components analysis is restricted to the 46 of 64 indices that spanned the full period, 1870-1913. The percent figures under the column titles give the percent of total variance accounted for by the given principal component. For meaning of abbreviations, see the spelled out entries in table 6.3.

light, almost two-fifths of the total variance of the individual return indices involved motion that had little connection with any other return index. Obviously, any concept of "the" rate of return on capital in dealing with annual movements of wealth accumulation and its return must be deemed somewhat artificial. This heterogeneity in the timing of returns suggests a highly complex complementarity and substitutability in the patterns of investment and financing of home and overseas economic activities. But importantly, when this more sensitive instrument of covariance analysis is employed, the regularities that characterized the movements of the aggregate indices remain in evidence. The general downward secular trend can be found in several components. To the degree that short-term fluctuations imposed parallel movements on industrial and regional returns, these, too, may be found. Upon closer inspection, with the aid of a principal-components analysis, the inverse movement between home and overseas returns found in the aggregate indices seems to be the product of several complex inverse motions. While there is clearly a home versus overseas locus, there is also a strong positive association between various overseas railway and social-overhead sectors' returns, on the one hand, and U.K. iron, coal, steel and heavy fabrication, mechanical equipment, and electrical equipment returns on the other. Obviously, the latter association draws on the important part the purchases of these overseas railway and social-overhead sectors played in the profitability of these home heavy-industry sectors.[7]

D. PRIVATE RATES OF RETURN: SUMMARY AND A SPECULATION ON THEIR ROLE IN LATE-NINETEENTH-CENTURY IMPERIALISM

On the basis of a sample of 566 first- and second-class equity, preference, and debenture securities, the principal conclusions of chapters 5 and 6 are the following:

1. On the average, for years 1870–1913, the United Kingdom's holdings of overseas portfolio investments realized a higher, price-deflated rate of return than their holdings of domestic portfolio investments.
2. A crude model investigating the relationship between realized returns and anticipated risks suggests that the overseas portfolio

had a slightly lower level of *ex ante* risk associated with it than the home portfolio but, relative to these *ex ante* risk measures, the overseas portfolio generated higher *ex post* returns.

3. Aggregate indices of both home- and overseas-realized, price-deflated rates of return were subject to slow secular decline, 1870–1913.

4. Aggregate indices for both home- and overseas-realized, price-deflated returns were also subject to long cycles of between 16 and 26 years in length; the home and overseas long cycles moved inversely and thereby produced alternating periods of home and overseas return dominance.

5. Throughout the years 1870–1913, aggregate overseas returns dominated their periods of ascendance more strongly than domestic returns did theirs and thus yielded the 1870–1913 average edge of overseas returns; the longest and strongest period of home or overseas dominance was the 1897–1909 period of overseas dominance, proximally owing to the strength of U.S. and Latin American returns but, more importantly, owing to an unusual weakness in nearly all sectors of the domestic portfolio.

6. Among several other patterns of stable covariance, there was a regular positive association between returns to the equity of overseas railway and social-overhead sectors and the U.K. suppliers of their capital goods.

7. A substantial portion of the variation of home and overseas industrial and regional returns was not subject to any stable pattern of covariation.

Before closing, it is worth speculating on one further association. As Rosenberg 1943 noted, there is a surprising similarity in the responses of many Western European governments to the serious depression that began around 1873. Among the most important responses were increased tariff protection and government encouragement to exporters and foreign investors. It was also the case that the willingness to engage in imperialist expansion abroad increased, and the late 1870s and early 1880s are well known as the first years of one of the most intense periods of nineteenth-century imperialist expansion. At one time, the course of domestic and foreign investment was emphasized as an underlying economic condition fostering this expansion.[8] Recent economic theories of late-nineteenth-century imperialism have stressed the conditions of domestic and overseas commodity trade

on the one hand[9] and the independent causal role of conditions
overseas on the other (Hopkins 1973, ch. 4). Without wishing to
diminish the importance of either commodity trade or the
political economy of the overseas nations threatened with
European rule, the evidence of this study suggests that the years of
accelerated overseas political acquisitions in the late 1870s and
early 1880s were also years in which the realized, price-deflated
rates of return to U.K. holdings abroad (the largest in Europe)
were well above the average return on domestic U.K. portfolio
assets. Granted, these returns were not from regions where the
United Kingdom extended its formal rule during these years, but
it is plausible to hypothesize that these optimistic investment
conditions abroad affected both the iedology and politics of the
groups most interested in expansion and lowered the resistance of
some of their opponents.

PART III: MACRO PROCESSES

CHAPTER 7: **DETERMINANTS OF AGGREGATE U.K. OVERSEAS INVESTMENT: AN INTRODUCTION**

ON AGGREGATION

So far, the motivation for Britain's massive overseas investment in the late nineteenth and early twentieth centuries has been discussed in terms of the diversity of U.K. and overseas lenders and borrowers in their specific industrial and regional settings. At this microeconomic level of observation, attention was focused on explaining the amount of foreign investment going to a specific region or industry and its rate of return. Alternative lending opportunities, the extent of British savings and wealth, alternative borrowing opportunities, and the extent of overseas savings and wealth are taken as exogenous, the "unmoved movers." Such simplification is useful in studying a single market. If, for example, the New Zealand colonial government wanted to tap U.K. savings, it is very likely these funds were raised without affecting the process determining total U.K. savings or the terms on which similar borrowing authorities from other corners of the globe and the United Kingdom could raise their funds in the United Kingdom.

However, what is true in the small may not be true in the large. In the late 1880s the net capital import of the United States was half of total U.K. net capital exports. During these same years total U.K. net capital exports were slightly less than half of total U.K. gross savings and investment.[1] In the years 1911–13 Canadian borrowing was perhaps a third of U.K. net foreign lending when U.K. net foreign lending was slightly more than half of total U.K. gross savings and investment. Furthermore, during these years Canadian net foreign borrowings funded around half of total Canadian investments.[2] During these short periods it is a strong possibility that the amount and return on U.S. and Canadian borrowing affected the processes dictating aggregate U.K., U.S., and Canadian savings, the terms on which alternative U.K. and overseas securities were funded in the United Kingdom and, in turn, feedback to affect the level and return to U.S. or Canadian borrowing.

Despite important differences in the timing of U.K. lending to specific overseas regions, the aggregate of U.K. lending exited the United Kingdom in three large surges. Measured trough to peak, these surges occurred, 1861–72, 1877–90, and 1901–13 (figures 2.1 and 2.2). Equally important, although the first long surge moved in rough parallel to domestic fixed investment, the second and third surges were somewhat larger and these coincided with low tides in domestic fixed investment.[3] In perhaps 34 of the 58 years between 1856 and 1913 net foreign lending was a third or more of total U.K. gross savings and investment (see appendix 1). In 10 of these 58 years it was a half or more. On the face of these facts it is a plausible hypothesis that the aggregate of net foreign lending may have had effects on the processes dictating the aggregate of U.K. savings and on the amount and terms on which domestic investment was funded and, in turn, have been affected by the processes dictating total savings and domestic investment.

Since Cairncross' justly famous Cambridge University dissertation was awarded in 1935, the principal context of discussions on the aggregate of U.K. foreign lending from 1850 to World War I has been its long-swing motion and its inversity to the long-swing motion of U.K. domestic fixed investment.[4] The central questions to these discussions have been what systematic and repeating social mechanisms caused annual U.K. home and overseas investment to cycle in this manner and what role these cycles played in the long-swing motion of output growth and investment on the frontiers of the regions of recent settlement in Argentina, Australia, Canada, New Zealand, South Africa, the United States, and elsewhere. Although it might have been possible to develop an explanation of why the *trend* in the United Kingdom's rate of net foreign lending rose across the 1850s and 1860s and then maintained a high (but variable) plateau until World War I, the issue was rarely raised; the focus was on the long cycles, not on the trend.

The purpose of Part III is to investigate and draw together the various microeconomic and macroeconomic threads necessary to understand the rise and high plateau characterizing the trend rate of aggregate U.K. foreign lending from 1850 to World War I. Economists and economic historians have long accepted that the forces shaping trends in investment and saving are often of a different kind and order than those shaping their cycles. To some degree the determinants of trends and cycles overlap, but only to a degree. It is accepted here that U.K. net foreign lending went through three long upswings and two intervening, long downswings between 1862 and 1913. Our principal interest is, however, with the forces that drove the U.K.'s net foreign lending rate over the long haul, that is, over the long swings.

To facilitate these investigations, a general model of national savings, overseas investment, and domestic investment is introduced in the next section. The principal theories offered to motivate the rise of overseas investment in the late nineteenth century are cast in terms of this simple model, and their aggregative behavioral underpinnings are discussed. In chapter 8 the character of U.K. national savings behavior, 1870–1913, is specified and Hobson's theory of oversaving as a cause of the period's capital outflow is tested. Chapter 9 examines the role of domestic investment and return patterns in aiding and abetting the flow of foreign lending. In chapters 10, 11, and 12 the influences of U.S., Australian, and Canadian growth and profits are investigated. The various threads are drawn together in a chronological survey in chapter 13.

A SIMPLE MODEL OF AGGREGATE ACCUMULATION

It is possible to posit a bare minimum of three behavioral relationships involved in the aggregate flow of capital abroad. Let aggregate annual savings desires be a positive function of the interest rate (i) and some income variables (Y), and a negative function of total U.K.-owned wealth at home and overseas (W), shown as line SS in figure 7.1:

$$S = h(\overset{+}{i}, \overset{+}{Y}, \overset{-}{W}). \tag{7.1}$$

Let the aggregate annual demand for domestic U.K. investment goods (line II^h in figure 7.1) be a negative function of the interest

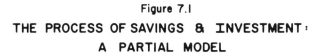

Figure 7.1

THE PROCESS OF SAVINGS & INVESTMENT :
A PARTIAL MODEL

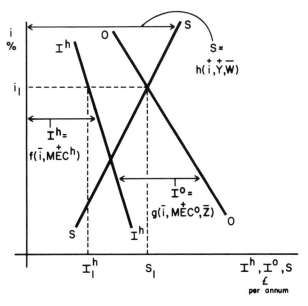

rate (i) and a positive function of the expected internal rate of
return on domestic capital goods, often termed the marginal
efficiency of capital (mec^h):

$$I^h = f(\overset{-}{i}, \overset{+}{mec^h}). \qquad (7.2)$$

Finally, let the net overseas investment demand be a negative
function of the interest rate (i) and those factors affecting the
recipient country's savings behavior (Z), and a postive function of
expected internal rates of return on overseas capital goods (mec^o):

$$I^o = g(\overset{-}{i}, \overset{+}{mec^o}, \overset{-}{Z}). \qquad (7.3)$$

Horizontally adding overseas and domestic investment yields
total U.K. investment demand, line OO in figure 7.1. Assuming

that there are strong tendencies toward equilibrium,

$$S = I^h + I^o, \tag{7.4}$$

the relationships in figure 7.1 interact to determine the market-clearing interest rate (i_1), total U.K. savings (S_1), U.K. domestic investment (I_1^h) and U.K. overseas investment ($I_1^o = S_1 - I_1^h$).

The interesting aspect of the behavior illustrated in figure 7.1 is what constellation of domestic push and overseas pull forces shifted the various curves during the late nineteenth and early twentieth centuries to raise the amount and rate of overseas lending to such unprecedented heights. Another way to capture this problem is to solve the three behavioral equations (1–3) and the equilibrium condition (4) for the equilibrium level of I^o,

$$I^o = \overset{-}{J}(\overset{+}{mec^h}, \overset{-}{Y}, \overset{+}{W}; \overset{-}{mec^o}, Z), \tag{7.5}$$

where the signs above the various exogenous-shift variables suggest the probable direction of their effect. Indeed, at the risk of some unnecessary repetition, it may be useful to cast the discussion of the great theories of Britain's capital export found in the introduction in terms of figure 7.1's curves and the shift variables identified in equation 7.5.

Discussion in chapter 1 identified four great theories of Britain's late nineteenth- and early twentieth-century massive capital outflow. Three of these theories favored a domestic explanation for outflow: unusually low U.K. returns, excessive U.K. savings, and biased U.K. capital market behavior; one theory favored an overseas stimulus for the outflow: unusually high overseas returns. In chapter 3, insufficient evidence was found to support the view that capital market biases could be held responsible for the massive outflow.

The view that unusually low returns to domestic investment were the motivating force behind the capital outflow is an argument that suggests II, the U.K. domestic investment demand curve, shifted out more slowly than a normally shifting savings curve (SS) due to a tendency for mec^h to fall. According to this theory, too few domestic investment projects appeared with high marginal efficiencies; this led to a tendency for the average mec^h to fall and thus slow aggregate U.K. domestic investment demand. This view was held by Smith, Ricardo, Wakefield, Marx, and Marshall among eighteenth- and nineteenth-century economists, and it is a direct inference from the work of many twentieth-century economic historians who have argued that either U.K. entrepreneurship or inventiveness underwent a "climacteric" beginning in the late 1870s or around 1900 (see chapter 1, notes 3 and 4). Evidence of these and other factors' affecting domestic investment and interacting with overseas investment will be sought in the trends and cycles of domestic demographic, productivity, extent of market, and profit variables, which are the principal factors thought to determine long-term levels of the marginal efficiency of investment and the rate of gross fixed investment.

Note, however, that the force of lowered domestic returns depends upon the interest sensitivity of savings desires. If SS was flat because savings were highly sensitive to movements in interest rates, a backward shift in the II^h curve due to a lower mec^h would lower the equilibrium I^h and total savings, S, but it would not affect the level of I^o (figure 7.2). At the other extreme, if SS was vertical because savings desires were insensitive to interest rates, any retreat of the I^h curve would leave the equilibrium level of total savings, S, unchanged; I^o would simply take up the slack (figure 7.3). A test of the interest sensitivity of savings is thus

Figure 7.2

HOME INVESTMENT, FOREIGN INVESTMENT & ELASTIC SAVINGS

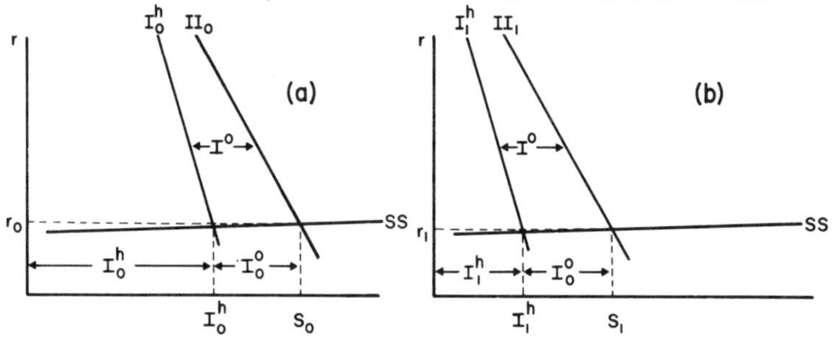

Figure 7.3

HOME INVESTMENT, FOREIGN INVESTMENT & INELASTIC SAVINGS

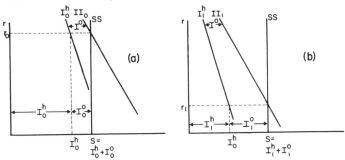

central to resolving the causes of the United Kingdom's augmented rate of foreign investment in the late nineteenth and early
twentieth centuries.

If unusually high overseas returns were the strongest force
increasing the level of U.K. capital exports, this would manifest
itself in figure 7.1 as the horizontal distance between OO and II
increasing much faster than the II and SS curves were shifting.
The cause of this rapid shift might be a long list of overseas
investment projects in land development, mineral resources,
transportation facilities, urban housing and distributional facilities, urban utilities, and many other activities, especially in the
regions of recent settlement, with high marginal efficiencies.
Unusually high overseas returns could attract more U.K. savings,
regardless of whether total U.K. savings were sensitive or insensitive to expected returns. If they were sensitive, the U.K.
savings rate would expand to accommodate any worthy overseas
project; if they were insensitive, the high-return overseas projects
would bump domestic projects with lower returns from the rank
ordering for access to the fixed pool of U.K. savings. Since in the
first case any worthy projects would not have to compete with
worthy home projects, the rate of U.K. foreign investment would
rise more strongly in the first case. Again, evidence for the
strength of the marginal efficiency of investment will be sought in
the trends and cycles of demographic, productivity, extent of
market, and profit variables.

Hobson's view that excess savings (or underconsumption) was

Figure 7.4

HOME INVESTMENT, FOREIGN INVESTMENT & HOBSONIST SAVINGS

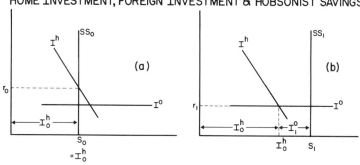

the strongest agent fostering the capital export translates into a tendency of the savings curve, *SS*, to shift out faster than a normally growing investment demand curve, *II*, particularly during or at the peak of the business cycle. Indeed, instead of savings behavior's being guided by the rate of interest, total income, and total wealth, as in equation 7.1, Hobson took the Ricardian and Marxian view that saving was principally a function of wage income and property income with the propensity of capitalists to save out of property incomes considerably higher than the propensity of workers to save out of wage incomes. During a business expansion, particularly near a peak, Hobson argued that the share of profits in U.K. national income tended to rise and the share of wage incomes tended to fall. Hobson assumed, not implausibly, that there was no reason to believe the availability of profitable domestic investment projects matched the timing of the shifting factor income shares. The excess savings then spilled over into foreign investment projects of dubious character (figure 7.4). Evidence for the presence of oversaving and its effect on the aggregate of foreign lending will be sought in trends in the distribution of U.K. factor incomes, the volatility of the factor income distribution, the volatility of U.K. business cycles, the sensitivity of U.K. aggregate savings to factor income movements, and the interaction of estimates of desired savings with domestic investment plans.

CHAPTER 8: STRUCTURE OF U.K. SAVINGS BEHAVIOR, 1850-1913, AND THE EVIDENCE ON OVERSAVING TENDENCIES

ESTIMATING DESIRED SAVINGS BEHAVIOR

Perhaps the most famous hypothesis concerning the massive outflow abroad of the United Kingdom's savings in the late nineteenth and early twentieth centuries was formulated by J. A. Hobson. Writing in the late 1890s, Hobson was concerned with the high tide of political and military imperialism characterizing the 1880s and 1890s and its domestic social foundations. The "taproot" of this augmented imperialism was an economic phenomenon, "oversaving." In what now seems a rather slim number of paragraphs for such an important element of his thinking, Hobson suggested that the United Kingdom "oversaved" at certain points in its periodic trade cycles and the unused excess drained abroad into various investment "sinks." Underlying his speculations was the assumption that U.K. desired savings behavior was largely tied to the cyclical behavior of profit incomes, which apparently were not well syncronized with, or otherwise adjusted to, the behavior of domestic investment plans.

But how and when did this phenomenon of oversaving start? Hobson was not clear. Was oversaving an old phenomenon and the new aspect its shift from domestic to overseas sinks? Or had oversaving recently worsened? If so, was the cause an intensification of the general U.K. trade cycle or, more specifically, the cycles in the share of profits in national income? Before taking on these questions, it seems best to verify whether U.K. private desired savings behavior was strongly related to U.K. profit incomes. Thus, this chapter begins with an econometric investigation into the structure of U.K. private savings behavior in the late nineteenth and early twentieth centuries. Having discovered whether the Hobson conception of U.K. desired savings behavior conforms to the known facts, it will then be possible to explore Hobson's line of reasoning further.

The shape of U.K. desired savings behavior is also central to a number of other hypotheses attempting to explain U.K. accumulation processes in the late nineteenth and early twentieth centuries. Abramovitz (1968) and Williamson (1964) have separately argued that the long-swing alternation of U.K. home and overseas investment in the late nineteenth and early twentieth centuries was in large degree the result of long swings in the U.S. demand for social-overhead capital acting on a "fixed pool" of U.K. savings. Brinley Thomas (1954) has suggested the reverse; the long-swing motion of the U.K. demand for social-overhead and urban residential capital acted on a "fixed pool" of U.K. savings. Evidence presented in chapter 2 made it quite clear that the ratio of national savings to national income was not fixed during these years, varying over a range of 10 percent to 17 percent (calculated from data in appendix 1). There remains, however, the important question of whether the savings rate expanded and contracted with the pressures of total investment demand or whether its variations were tuned to other phenomena.

The mechanism suggested by Smith, Mill, Marshall, and many other nineteenth-century economists for linking investment demand to aggregate savings behavior was interest rates. If savers were sensitive to expected returns, it was argued, the volume of savings would ride up and down depending on the pressures of total (home and overseas) investment demand. High total investment demand would tend to drive up interest rates and elicit more savings; slack total investment demand would leave interest rates low and so too the rate of savings.

Keynesian and post-Keynesian models of individual and corporate savings are often linked to the actions of provident households and large corporations with long planning horizons reacting to past, current, or expected income flows, almost totally ignoring any interest rate effects. Virtually simultaneous with the 1936 publication of Keynes' *General Theory of Employment Interest and Money*, the economic historian M. M. Postan (1935) surveyed the previous two centuries of savings and investment behavior. Although influenced by Keynes' new macroeconomics, Postan argued that the dominance of the provident household and the large self-contained corporation in British savings decisions was a relatively recent development. During the half century before World War I, the savings decision was largely guided by the actions and motives of the "pure investor." Unlike the provident household and corporate savers, the pure investor operated across the full range of British assets at home and abroad, often through public capital markets, with the sole criterion of maximizing expected return. Postan suggested that, with the passing of the pure investor's importance, the allocation of British savings across the spectrum of assets was less free and, quite possibly, an important cause of Britain's post-World War I economic difficulties. Another implication of this shift in the decision locus of the British savings decision, one that he skirted, is that the allocation of British income between savings and consumption had become less sensitive to expected returns.

If Postan is correct, that savings decisions were dominated by the pure investor before World War I, then it is appropriate to focus attention on the behavior of *total* private savings in our tests of the structure of savings behavior, 1850-1913. Available data permit us to estimate gross private savings by subtracting an estimate of government savings from total British accumulation.[1] Direct testing of the Keynesian view, however, is not possible. Separate estimates of the household and corporate components of gross private savings are not available. This is unfortunate. Whereas the share of corporate profits in British national income was low by modern standards during these years, the share was expanding rapidly across the period, particularly after the conversion booms of the 1890s. Perhaps 5 percent of total British incomes took the form of corporate profits in 1870, largely generated by railway and public utility companies.[2] By 1913, with the diffusion of limited liability to many industrial, commercial, and financial enterprises, the gross trading profits of companies had become perhaps 14 percent of total British incomes (Feinstein 1972:T44-45). If data limitations prevent a direct test of Postan versus Keynes on savings behavior in the late nineteenth century, it is still possible to achieve a strong test indirectly. If the shifting share of corporate profits is an index of the rise of new savings behavioral patterns, then any estimate of the structure of gross private savings behavior should shift across the years 1870-1913. Hence, a test for structural shift in the behavior of aggregate private savings represents a powerful test of the pure investor

versus separate behavioral patterns for household and corporation.

The approach employed here to investigate these various
hypotheses began with fitting a wide variety of modern savings
models to U.K. data on gross private savings, various kinds of
income streams, and wealth for the entire period, 1870–1913.
Estimates were made of the parameters of the Keynes, Duesen-
berry-Modigliani, Brown-Davis-Friedman, Mincer, Kaldor, and
Ando-Modigliani models of savings behavior in their original
forms and numerous alternatives.[3] The Kaldor model argues that
savings are a linear function of wage incomes and property
incomes, the latter possessing a substantially higher propensity to
save than the former. It is clearly a model embodying the ideas of
Hobson on savings behavior, although it may not be the only one.
Based on the standard error of the regression and Durbin-Watson
statistics, the best fitting models were the Brown-Davis-Friedman
and Kaldor lagged displayed in table 8.1, panel A.[4]

Next the yield on Consols was introduced to test the sensitivity
of aggregate private savings to expected returns.[5] Space limitations prevent presenting the results here, but the results were quite
straightforward. With one exception of an unlagged version of
the Kaldor model, the coefficient on the interest rate term was
insignificant in all simple formulations of the modern savings
models noted above. If we set aside for the moment the possibility
that structural shifts are affecting these results, it is conceivable
that the interest rate effect is hidden by the failure to comprehend
some other phenomena along with the interest rate. The exception of the unlagged Kaldor model suggests that these other
phenomena might be connected with the variation of the factor
income distribution, and, in turn, this suggests that the explicit
introduction of permanent and transitory income estimators
might also bring out the interest rate effect. Two hybrid equations
were thus introduced: a "classical" model, in which aggregate
private savings are a function of current and lagged values of the
level of income, the ratio of wage to nonwage incomes, and the
interest rate; and a "Friedman-Ando-Modigliani" model, in
which aggregate private savings are a function of permanent and
transitory income, private wealth, and the interest rate (table 8.1,

Table 8.1

Estimated Parameters of U.K. Aggregate Private Savings Behavior, 1872-1913

	s.e.r.	d.w.

A.   Some Simple Models

Brown-Davis-Friedman

$$GPS = -39.9 + .62\ Y - .55\ (Y-S)_{-1}$$
$$\quad\ (3.6)\quad (14.4)\quad (10.2)$$

s.e.r. 13.71   d.w. 1.49

Kaldor Lagged

$$GPS = -62.9 + .47\ W + .69\ NW - .50\ (Y-S)_{-1}$$
$$\quad\ (4.9)\quad (7.3)\quad (15.1)\quad (9.4)$$

s.e.r. 12.58   d.w. 1.92

B.   Hybrid Models: Levels

Classical

$$GPS = .56\ Y - 110.9\ (W/NW) + 14.9\ r - .46\ (Y-S)_{-1}$$
$$\quad (14.4)\quad (5.5)\quad\quad (3.3)\quad (9.3)$$

s.e.r. 11.46   d.w. 1.70

Friedman-Ando-Modigliani

$$GPS = -236.1 + .35\ Y^p + .74\ Y^t + 52.2\ r - .046\ A_{-1}$$
$$\quad (11.4)\quad (12.5)\quad (13.8)\quad (8.6)\quad (6.2)$$

s.e.r. 11.15   d.w. 1.30

C.   Hybrid Models: Levels, Corrected for Trend

Classical

$$GPS/Y = .50 - 163.9\ (W/NW)/Y + 20.9\ r/Y - .36\ (Y-S)_{-1}/Y$$
$$\quad (5.2)\quad (4.5)\quad\quad\quad (2.7)\quad (3.1)$$

s.e.r. .0107   d.w. 1.70

Friedman-Ando-Modigliani

$$GPS/Y = -233.9\ (1.0/Y) + .35\ Y^p/Y + .75\ Y^t/Y + 51.2\ r/Y$$
$$\quad (8.8)\quad\quad\quad (11.8)\quad (12.8)\quad (7.2)$$
$$\quad\quad - .048\ A_{-1}/Y$$
$$\quad\quad\quad (6.1)$$

s.e.r. .0068   d.w. 1.26

Abbreviations: Y = gross national product; Y^p = $(Y + Y_{-1} + Y_{-2})/3.0$; Y^t = $(Y^p - Y)$; W = income from employment; NW = (Y-W); A = net reproducible domestic capital stock + net accumulation of overseas assets + national government funded and unfunded debt; r = yield on consols. All variables except r are deflated by a consumer price index.

panel B). In using long time series from a growing economy, it is possible that the residual variance will grow larger over the sample period and result in biased coefficients. One way of correcting for this problem in savings studies is to divide the variables on both sides of our equations by current income. The regression equations using data transformed in this manner are shown in table 8.1, panel C.

The hybrid equations achieve much better statistical fits over the forty-four years than the "purer" models. But, before their coefficients are analyzed, it is necessary to perform one more statistical test. Three phenomena suggest that the underlying behavior of savings formation might have shifted in the middle of the 1870–1913 period. Prices generally fell in the mid-1890s and rose thereafter. Expectations of long-term deflation or long-term inflation, albeit quite slow, might have yielded different patterns of savings versus consumption. Interest rates also fell toward the mid-1890s and rose thereafter. Expectations of long-term interest rate decline or rise, again slow on an annual basis, might have depressed or raised the savings rate beyond the amount caught by our linear model. Finally, although the use of limited liability and increases in plant and firm size proceeded gradually across the years 1870–1913, there was an acceleration of these tendencies in the late 1890s through vertical and horizontal merger activity (Hannah 1976:8–28). By altering and probably enlarging the concentrations of mobile wealth in Britain, this acceleration may have altered the national savings rate as well. A Chow test was performed to investigate the possibility of structural shift between the years 1872–1895 and 1896–1913. The F-statistics for structural shift in the classical and Friedman-Ando-Modigliani savings models were .45 and 1.46, respectively, well below the 2.70 level suggesting statistical significance. Thus, whatever effect the alterations in the long-term direction of prices, interest rates, and incorporations had on savings behavior, they appear to have been substantially comprehended by table 8.1's models for the full period.

The interest rate coefficients are positive and statistically significant in table 8.1's hybrid savings models. The calculated *long-run* elasticities of the interest rate with respect to gross private savings implied by these coefficients are .41 for the classical model and .65 for the Friedman-Ando-Modigliani model. These elasticities are likely to be underestimates, owing to simultaneous equations bias. Investment demand is the most likely source for such bias, and the interest rate term in the investment demand relationship generally has a negative coefficient. Thus, the interest elasticity of gross private savings could be closer to 1.0 than these ordinarily least squares results suggest.[6]

This tendency has strong implications for the interdependence of domestic investment demand, overseas investment demand, the savings supplies. These implications will, however, be fully treated in chapters 9, 10, 11, and 12, when we examine the determinants of domestic investment demand and overseas investment demand. For the remainder of this chapter, discussion focuses on how the evidence of these statical tests bears on the Hobson oversaving hypothesis.

HOBSON TESTED

Hobson left a number of loose threads in his explanation of foreign lending and thus made precise testing difficult. In particular, the link between his mechanisms generating oversaving and the outflow of funds abroad is not very tight. Were there any domestic sinks for oversaving or were overseas investments the only sinks? This latter position is tantamount to assuming that oversaving was strictly a phenomenon of the period of foreign investment. If this is Hobson's view, then one test of his hypothesis is whether long-term trends in the share of nonwage incomes or its variability paralleled the rise in the rate of net foreign lending in the 1850s and 1860s and its trend stability thereafter to World War I. Tables 8.2, 8.3, and 8.4 assemble some data to examine this issue. It seems fairly certain that the share of nonwage incomes was either steady or falling, 1855–1913, and the trend in its volatility was downward. Thus, assuming Hobson thought foreign investments were the only sink and implicitly that oversaving was strictly a phenomenon of the period of foreign investment, Hobson's hypothesis flounders on the evidence of trends in the principal determinant of his oversavings.

Hobson may not, however, have believed that foreign invest-

Table 8.2

U.K. Savings, Investment, and Factor Income Shares, 1856-1913

Period (1)	GNA/Y (2)	GDFI/Y (3)	II/Y (4)	NFI/Y (5)	E/Y (6)	P_h/Y (7)	P_h^*/Y (8)	P_o/Y (9)
1856-64	--	.06	--	.03	.48	.49	--	.03
1860-69	--	.07	--	.04	.47	.49	--	.03
1865-74	--	.08	--	.06	.47	.50	--	.03
1870-79	.16	.09	.01	.05	.47	.48	--	.05
1875-84	.14	.09	.01	.04	.49	.46	--	.05
1880-89	.14	.07	.01	.06	.49	.45	--	.06
1885-94	.14	.07	.01	.06	.50	.43	--	.07
1890-99	.13	.08	.01	.04	.51	.42	.24	.07
1895-04	.13	.10	.01	.02	.51	.43	.26	.06
1900-09	.14	.10	.00	.04	.51	.42	.27	.07
1905-13	.16	.07	.01	.08	.50	.42	.27	.08

Abbreviations: Y = gross domestic income + net property income abroad. GNA = gross national savings
= gross national investment. GDFI = gross domestic fixed investment. II = change in
inventories. NFI = net foreign investment. E = income from employment. P_h = income
from self-employment + gross trading profits of companies + gross trading surpluses
of government enterprises + rent. P_h^* = gross trading profits of compnaies + rent.
P_o = net property income from abroad.

Source: Feinstein 1972 : Y (T4-5), GNA=GDFI+II+NFI, GDFI (T8), II (T8), E (T4-5), P_h (T4-5), P_h^*
(T4-5), P_o (T4-5). Appendix 1: NFI.

Table 8.3

The Distribution of United Kingdom Gross National Incomes, 1855-1913
(in average decade %s of GNI)

	Wages and Salaries (1)	Rents (2)	Mixed Incomes (3)	Gross Profits of Companies (4)	Gross Surplus of Gov't Enterprises (5)	(3)+(4) +(5) (6)	Net Property Income from Abroad (7)	(3)+(4) +(5)+(6) (8)
Deane and Cole Estimates								
1860-1869	48.5	13.7						38.9
1865-1874	47.6	13.0						39.4
1870-1879	48.7	13.1						38.2
1875-1884	48.8	13.9						37.3
1880-1889	48.2	14.0						37.9
1885-1894	49.2	13.0						37.8
1890-1899	49.8	12.0						38.2
1895-1904	49.6	11.6						38.8
1900-1909	48.4	11.4						40.2
1905-1914	47.2	10.8						42.0
Feinstein Estimates								
1855-1864	48.2	14.4				34.8	2.5	37.3
1860-1869	47.2	13.9				35.9	3.0	38.9
1865-1874	46.7	12.9				36.6	3.8	40.4
1870-1879	47.5	13.0				34.8	4.7	39.5
1875-1884	48.9	13.9				32.0	5.3	37.3
1880-1889	49.0	13.9				31.1	6.0	37.1
1885-1894	50.3	13.3				29.7	6.7	36.4
1890-1899	50.9	12.6	19.2	10.3	.4	29.9	6.5	36.4
1895-1904	50.7	12.4	18.0	12.0	.5	30.5	6.2	36.7
1900-1909	50.7	12.2	17.0	12.6	.7	30.3	6.8	37.1
1905-1913	50.1	11.6	16.5	13.1	.8	30.4	7.9	38.3

Sources: Deane and Cole 1969: 247, Feinstein 1972: T4-5.

Table 8.4

Trends in the Volatility of the Share of Non-Wage Incomes in U.K. GNP,
1855-1913

	m. (1)	s.d. (2)	c.v. (3)
1855-74	.5250	.0162	100.0
1860-79	.5268	.0130	80.0
1865-84	.5222	.0141	87.5
1870-89	.5176	.0143	89.5
1875-94	.5044	.0138	88.7
1880-99	.4999	.0131	84.9
1885-1904	.4942	.0121	79.4
1890-1909	.4911	.0084	55.4
1895-1913	.4948	.0068	44.5

Source: Data from Feinstein 1972: T4-5.

Notes: m. = mean value.   s.d. = standard deviation.
c.v. = s.d./m. (= coefficient of variation), 1855-74 = 100.0.

ment was the only possible sink for oversaving. It is possible that he thought oversaving was a fundamental aspect of the capitalist business cycle. Hence, it is possible he would see the railway booms of the second third of the nineteenth century as partly engendered by oversaving. From this perspective, foreign investment in the late nineteenth century may not have been the result of worse oversaving, as suggested and rejected above. Rather, it was a new form of sink. Again, Hobson's silence presents a problem. Political reasons for the shift can be ruled out for Hobson because oversaving was the "taproot" of imperialism, not vice versa. Another possible explanation is that *among all projects with abysmal returns*, foreign sinks offered better returns than domestic sinks in the latter half of the nineteenth and the early twentieth century.

Still, if the share of nonwage incomes was falling on trend from the mid-nineteenth century to World War I, the presumption must be that the problem of oversaving and its outcome, investment sinks, was worse *prior* to the period of heavy net foreign lending. One indication of this might be the violence of the U.K. business cycle. It is a strict inference from Hobson's writings that, if national income payments were shifted toward wage earners and away from profits, both the problem of business cycles and investment sinks would be mitigated. Thus, a plausible reading might suggest that a rising trend of investment sinks (at home or overseas) would be a result of increasing violence of the

Table 8.5

The Coefficient of Variation of U.K. Aggregate Income
and Output, 1830-1913

	Deane GNP Estimates		Feinstein GDP Estimates	
	Y (1)	Y/P (2)	Y (3)	Y/P (4)
1830-49	.1095	.1710		
1835-54	.1122	.1245		
1840-59	.1674	.1451		
1845-64	.1775	.1319		
1850-69	.2040	.1459		
1855-74	.1996	.1579	.1857	.1367
1860-79	.1558	.1441	.1522	.1366
1865-84	.0985	.1225	.1061	.1241
1870-89	.0565	.1058	.0652	.1114
1875-94	.0696	.1038	.0890	.1208
1880-99	.0941	.1802	.1335	.1506
1885-04	.1512	.1306	.1487	.1329
1890-09	.1465	.1235	.1286	.1071
1895-13	.1411	.1026	.1167	.0800

Sources:

    Cols. (1)-(2): Deane 1968: 104-7.
    Col. (3): Feinstein 1972: T4-5(9).
    Col. (4): Feinstein 1972: T18-9(3).

Notes: The coefficient of variations is the standard deviation divided
    by the mean of the observations. Y is current or nominal gross
    product. Y/P is real or price-deflated gross national product.

business cycle. Some information on the volatility of nominal and real aggregate U.K. output measures, 1830–1913, is offered in table 8.5.

Some common features emerge from the several indices of aggregate output variability of table 8.5. First, all four time series of aggregate output variability show a decline in volatility from the mid-nineteenth-century period toward World War I. Deane's longer time series indicates that the midcentury period of high volatility stretches back to the 1840s. Thus, as the rate of U.K. foreign investment was rising in the 1850s and 1860s and maintaining a high (but variable) plateau from the 1870s to World War I, the trend in volatility was on the decline. Second, Hobson was clear that the instability of the business cycle was contemporaneous with the foreign investment sinks. On this account, it is useful to point out that the contemporaneous correlation coefficients between the rate of net foreign lending (20-year averages) and each of the four time series of aggregate output volatility in table 8.5 are .06, .12, .48, and .03, respectively. The first, second, and fourth correlations suggest the absence of any relationship, especially for time series correlations, and, in any event, the relationship captured by all four correlations was consistently negative, precisely the opposite of Hobson's view. Third, a plausible alternative hypothesis might be that trends in volatility preceded the trends in investment sinks, but lagging the indices of variability by five, ten, or fifteen years behind the rate of net foreign lending yields equally poor correlations and, most important, negative relationships. Thus, the cyclical volatility evidence offers little support for the hypothesis that increased cyclical violence caused the rising trend of U.K. foreign lending, 1850–1913, or that foreign investment was a substitute sink for the railway opportunities of the midcentury era.

To briefly summarize the argument so far, trends in the rate of net foreign lending from 1850 to 1913 were not paralleled by clear signs that trends in the determinants of oversaving or other aspects of an oversaving economic system followed a similar course. Neither the share of nonwage incomes or its volatility, nor the volatility of the U.K. business cycle supports the hypothesis that there was a rise in the trend of oversaving. At best, these factors may help explain the foreign investment surge of the 1900s. This view demands, of course, an alternative explanation for the surges of net foreign lending in the 1860s and 1880s.

If Hobson's view of oversaving as a determinant of net foreign lending appears to flounder on the shoals of trends in certain variables, it may still be the case that oversaving was a product of more complex interactions with other phenomena that can be discovered in the annual variations of savings, income, and other variables. This is where the evidence of the models of desired savings presented in table 8.1 becomes relevant.

First, it must be asked where the factor income distribution of British product mattered in determining the annual variations in desired aggregate annual savings. One test of this hypothesis may be found in table 8.1, panel A. The sole difference between the Brown-Davis-Friedman model and the Kaldor lagged model is that the gross national income variable (Y) of the first model is disaggregated into its wage and nonwage income components in the second. The Kaldor lagged model achieves a superior fit to the data, suggesting that both the level and distribution of national income mattered to U.K. aggregate desired savings behavior to some extent.

Nevertheless, the classical model of table 8.1, panel C, which is statistically superior to the Kaldor lagged model in its capture of distributive and other effects, is itself inferior to the Friedman-Ando-Modigliani model, which totally ignores the factor income distribution. Why is this so? One possible explanation is that several important assumptions of the Hobson model are significantly violated. The Hobson model of savings assumes either that savings out of wage and salary incomes were trivial or that nonwage incomes fluctuated far more than wage and salary incomes over the cycle, and hence, nonwage incomes were the major determinant of cycles in total savings. The growth of small savings accounts at post office savings banks, trustee savings banks, building societies, and other small-saver institutions strongly suggests the existence of savings based on wage and salary incomes.[7] And the Kaldor lagged model demonstrates that there was a statistically significant propensity to save out of wage and salary incomes. Thus, the first assumption of the Hobson model does not meet the known facts. Furthermore, the second assumption, that nonwage incomes varied much more strongly than wage incomes over the business cycle, is also questionable. Although the variance of wage incomes about its time trend was about 60 percent of the variance of nonwage incomes about its time trend, 1870–1913, the partial correlation coefficient of the two variables was .961. To use the language of the Friedman-Ando-Modigliani model, wage as well as profit incomes appear to have had a transitory (cyclical) component. The FAM model, which disaggregates total income into its transitory and permanent components, thus provides a statistically superior account of savings behavior.

It is sometimes the case that, although one model is inferior to another model over the full set of year-to-year variations being studied, it might be superior in capturing behavior at major turning points. Table 8.6 shows the errors of the classical and Friedman-Ando-Modigliani models of table 8.1, panel C, across the estimation period. The numbers shown in col. 1 and 2 are the actual value of the gross private savings rate (col. 3) minus the gross private savings rate predicted by the indicated savings model.

The most important turning points for the Hobson hypothesis concerning the link between U.K. savings behavior and its foreign lending were the years 1877–79 and 1903–5. The years 1877–79 contain the extreme cyclical low point and first two years of the 1877–90 surge in the net foreign lending (figures 2.1 and 2.2). The great foreign investment surge of the 1900s may be thought to start from a trough in 1901, the extreme cyclical low point, but the years 1900–2 are clearly affected by the U.K. government's "dissaving" to fund the Boer War. Both domestic fixed investment and net foreign lending were affected by the government's debt financing.[8] Values of government savings returned to normal values in 1903, and so it seems fair to examine 1903–5 as the crucial opening years of the 1900s foreign lending boom. If the Hobson model of savings and foreign investment is correct, a model incorporating factor income movements should be able to account for aggregate savings movements better than alternative models during these crucial opening years of the great booms. The errors

Table 8.6

The Residual Errors of the Hybrid U.K. Savings Models,
Gross Private Savings Rates, Gross National Product,
and Share Prices, 1870-1913

Year	Residual Errors Classical Model (1)	F-A-M Model (2)	Gross Private Savings Rate (3)	GNP deflated (₤ mil.) (4)	Share Prices (5)
1870	--	--	.1156	1126	87
1871	--	--	.1503	1213	98
1872	.0080	.0088*	.1423	1218	110
1873	-.0028	.0022	.1245	1220	113
1874	.0260*	-.0001	.1509	1302	110
1875	.0008	-.0002	.1326	1295	104
1876	-.0051	.0040	.1162	1279	97
1877	-.0170*	-.0110*	.0943	1266	92
1878	-.0110*	-.0169*	.0945	1282	85
1879	-.0129*	-.0054	.0887	1258	78
1880	.0110*	-.0095	.1210	1370	92
1881	-.0029	.0020	.1175	1356	91
1882	.0053	.0086	.1206	1384	88
1883	.0013*	-.0023	.1247	1409	83
1884	-.0009	.0020	.1148	1429	79
1885	-.0070	-.0004	.1081	1432	78
1886	-.0044	.0069*	.1140	1445	79
1887	.0098	.0021	.1313	1533	76
1888	-.0023	.0052	.1271	1547	79
1889	.0043	.0016*	.1271	1577	89
1890	.0189*	.0166*	.1381	1628	89
1891	-.0009	-.0056	.1251	1677	88
1892	-.0035	.0016	.1054	1642	87
1893	-.0049	.0019	.0971	1631	88
1894	.0023	-.0034	.1117	1705	90
1895	-.0017	-.0038	.1137	1755	100
1896	.0029	-.0058	.1184	1837	121
1897	-.0068	.0010	.1119	1835	133
1898	.0059	-.0059	.1273	1946	133
1899	.0180*	-.0027	.1520	2072	136
1900	.0097	.0016*	.1495	2058	134
1901	.0120*	.0025	.1513	2116	127
1902	-.0095	-.0023	.1329	2087	125
1903	-.0081	-.0053	.1243	2082	122
1904	-.0102*	-.0114*	.1219	2099	115
1905	-.0008	-.0036	.1350	2148	122
1906	.0023	.0001	.1470	2217	124
1907	-.0062	-.0002	.1436	2241	122
1908	-.0285*	-.0012	.1159	2167	114
1909	.0021	.0077*	.1391	2226	114
1910	.0011	.0022	.1492	2299	124
1911	.0006	.0009	.1552	2386	130
1912	-.0149*	-.0003	.1440	2386	129
1913	.0101	-.0020	.1676	2542	128

Table 8.6 (cont.)

Sources:

Cols.(1)&(2): Col. (3) - "predicted" values of table 8.1, Panel
C's equations.

Col. (3) GPS/Y = (GNA-GS)/Y, see note 5.

Col. (4) Feinstein 1972: T10(9), T132(1).

Col. (5) Smith & Horne (1934).

The asterisks (*) denote the residual errors which exceed the respective equations' standard error of the regression (s.e.r.).

of the classical and FAM models reported in table 8.6 for the years 1877-9 and 1903-5 do not support this hypothesis. The two models are roughly equal in their inability to account for actual savings behavior during these turning points.

These errors at the beginning of the foreign investment booms deserve much more attention, however. The years 1877-79 and 1903-5 are the only years when substantial negative errors are clustered. To put the point bluntly, our savings models make their worst overestimates of actual savings just during those periods when the net foreign investment rate was climbing off its lowest levels. Importantly, this is not the case for the years when gross *domestic* investment was coming off its floor, for example, in the late 1880s and early 1890s. The FAM model shows almost no negative residuals during these latter years and the classical model's negative errors in the early 1890s are very small, well within the standard error of the regression.

In both the 1877-79 and 1903-5 periods, gross private savings, domestic investment, and gross national product were falling. The evidence of modern consumption and savings studies is that the actual and desired gross private savings rates should fall during cyclical downturns. On the assumption that the classical and FAM models estimated here capture *desired* savings behavior to some extent, the evidence of table 8.6 suggests a similar downward movement of actual and *desired* savings rates in 1877-79 and 1903-5.[9] What needs to be explained is why the actual savings rate fell more than the desired rate and why this occurred most severely only on the occasions when the net foreign investment rate was turning upward into a major surge.

Two explanations of the discrepancy between the actual and "predicted" savings rates during these years are plausible. First, our models of desired savings could be incomplete, leaving out an important factor that would indicate that desired savings should have fallen further 1877–79 and 1903–5. Second, the discrepancy could be the *ex poste* resolution of an *ex ante*, short-run gap between a relatively high rate of desired savings and a relatively low rate of desired domestic investment. This latter gap could easily be termed "oversaving," although not necessarily for the reasons that Hobson offered.

In taking up the possibility that our savings models are incompletely specified, the most obvious problems are that the factor income variable of the classical model may have missed some important element of cyclical income distribution behavior, and the wealth variable in the FAM model may not have fully captured the U.K. saver's idea of her or his current net worth.

The variable NW, which has been used so far to identify the forms of income most likely to have the largest propensities to save, consists of (1) income from self-employment, (2) gross trading profits of companies, (3) gross surpluses of public enterprises, (4) rents, (5) net property income from abroad. Unfortunately, sufficiently disaggregated data to break out these elements are not available before 1889. Table 8.7 presents the disaggregated factor income shares for the crucial years 1902–5.

In examining table 8.7 it is difficult to see internal shifting of the NW variable as a potential source of the 1903–5 discrepancy between actual and desired savings rates as shown in table 8.6. The most plausible assumption is that savers whose funds were likely to end up in foreign investment drew their incomes from gross profits of companies, rents, and net property income from abroad. The share of national income taking these forms over the years 1902–5 were .310, .310, .313, and .319, respectively. Since table 8.6's errors vary quite widely during these same years, the stability of the share of high saver incomes suggests the latter had little to do with the former's variation. Another possible source of

Table 8.7

The Share of Factor Incomes
in U.K. Gross National Product, 1902-5
(%)

Type of Income	1902	1903	1904	1905
Wages and salaries	50.7	52.0	51.5	50.3
Income from Self Employment	17.7	16.4	16.4	17.1
Gross Trading Profits of Companies	12.6	11.9	11.8	12.6
Gross Surpluses of Public Enterprises	0.6	0.6	0.8	0.7
Rent	12.2	12.7	13.0	12.5
Net Property Income from Abroad	6.2	6.4	6.5	6.8
	100.0	100.0	100.0	100.0
	(1772)	(1747)	(1734)	(1814)

Source: Feinstein 1972: T5. The figures in parentheses in the bottom row is gross national product (£ M.), estimated on the income side.

table 8.6's errors stemming from distributive movements might be that during cyclical downturns there was some tendency for profits to concentrate in the hands of a smaller and richer group of owners who were able to ride out the bad times. This hypothesis fails to explain table 8.6's errors on two grounds. First, it seems implausible that the extent of countercyclical concentration of ownership within gross trading profits would raise the savings rate enough to override the fall in the absolute size of profit incomes. Second, there is no plausible reason for this phenomenon to have its worst effects during the years 1877–79 and 1903–5. Other downturns of the period were far worse and presumably far more concentrating in the ownership of property incomes. In sum, neither redistributions among nonwage incomes nor the redistribution of profit incomes during downturns appears as a plausible explanation of the discrepancy between the actual level of gross private savings and the levels suggested by our models of desired savings.

Another source of misspecification of "desired" savings levels might be the wealth variable in the FAM model. This variable is based on the reproducible value of domestic machinery, buildings, inventories, etc., the accumulated value of U.K. capital exports, and the nominal value of the U.K. national government's debt. It seems fair to assume that, when savers examine their wealth positions to help determine their annual savings desires, their concern is likely to focus on the market values of the paper titles to these various assets, not on reproducible or nominal values. Since wealth enters the FAM model with a negative coefficient, the failure of desired savings to fall further during the 1877–79 and 1903–5 periods would have to be a consequence of the wealth variable's being undervalued. If stock prices, etc., were rising, the wealth variable would have risen further and caused desired savings to fall further and thereby eliminate the 1877–79 and 1903–5 errors of table 8.6, col. 2. The facts are, however, that U.K. stock prices were falling during these periods (table 8.6, col. 5). Hence, if the wealth variable were properly valued, it is likely the residual errors of the FAM model would be worse.

It is possible there are other variables or better data that might help better specify desired savings levels during the years 1877–79 and 1903–5, and that these variables would close the gap between the actual level of the gross private savings rate and the econometrically specified desired one. We have just considered two important potential sources of misspecification, and these only led to a larger gap. Let us thus assume that the classical and FAM models are fair representations of desired savings levels. In this case, as noted earlier, the discrepancy between actual and desired savings rates becomes an *ex ante* discrepancy between desired savings and desired investment, resolved *ex poste* by a forced drop in savings and perhaps a forced rise in investment spending.

It is widely accepted that the immediate context of a downturn in a capitalist economy is frequently a point in time when *ex ante* savings desires are greater than *ex ante* investment spending desires. For Keynesians and many other economists, this state of affairs has its primary short-run cause in the volatile movements of investment or export demand, rather than what are held to be the more stable savings desires. The immediate result is that inventories of goods pile up (and perhaps prices of goods fall a bit) and involuntary investment in inventories occurs.

The next stage involves producers' reducing rates of output and employment and thereby engendering falls in real incomes. In the initial reaction to the falls in real incomes, consumption and savings do not fall proportionately. In the short run, the drop in real incomes is treated as abnormal or transitory, and consumption demand holds up while savings levels drop sharply. Thus, in the short run, a fall in real income leads to a rise in the ratio of real consumption to real income and a fall in the ratio of real savings to real income. In the FAM model of U.K. aggregate private savings desires, 1870–1913, this means that, in the short run, a fall in real incomes leads to a big drop in savings and the savings rate because the marginal propensity to save out of transitory income is quite high (.75). This part of the FAM model works quite well; it is part of the FAM model's superiority over the other tested models. As income continues to fall, however, savers cease to view the fall as transitory; the fall in real income becomes embodied in their ideas of permanent incomes. According to the FAM model this takes two or three years. At this point, the lower marginal propensity to save out of permanent income (.35) comes into play and the desired savings rate begins to rise back toward its long-run level. Thus, when real incomes fall for some time, the desired gross private savings rate initially falls sharply and then begins to rise back to higher levels, even though real income may continue to fall. This means that, if the errors of the 1877–79 and 1903–5 periods were the result of a disequilibrium between desired savings and desired investment, the part of this disjuncture played by desired savings appears to be the immediate result of a long period of real income fall that went on so long that savers had begun to adjust toward their (higher) long-run desired savings rate.[10]

Another plausible source of the hypothesized *ex ante* discrepancy between desired savings and desired investment may have been a precipitous fall in investment demand. As will become clear in the next chapter, the long-run determinants of the rate of investment demand are only roughly understood. Something more is known about the short-run determinants of investment demand, the current and lagged values of stock prices and output levels being thought most potent. Certainly, the signs for investment prospects were quite bad by 1877. Exports in real and current values, new overseas portfolio issues, and net foreign lending turned down in 1873. Stock prices on domestic equity fell the following year. Real income peaked in 1873 when a broad-spectrum deflator is employed rather than the consumer price index used in table 8.6. Domestic investment spending on plant and machinery and residential dwellings held up despite these trends until 1876, presumably satisfying a gap between desired and actual levels of the relevant capital stock built up over a long period of time. Since real output and stock prices had been falling for several years and an important segment of aggregate spending (gross domestic investment spending) had just fallen, an inordinate drop in domestic investment *desires* becomes a plausible instability in the economic picture of the years 1877–79.

Thus, it would appear that there were two distinguishing characteristics of the 1877–79 and 1903–5 years. First, both periods were preceded by falls in real income that continued into the hypothesized years of oversaving. Real income began its fall in 1873 in the 1877–79 case and in 1901 in the 1903–5 case. The immediate result of these patterns was that desired savings rates, having fallen initially, responded to the continued downward movement of real incomes by readjusting themselves upward toward longer run values. Second, gross domestic investment spending fell off sharply in 1877 and 1904, and there is some evidence that investment spending desires may have fallen faster, 1877–79 and 1903–5, owing to falling output and stock prices for some years.

Exports, net foreign lending, and real income fell off precipitously in 1891, suggesting the possibility that oversaving might eventually underpin a domestic investment surge. However, real income turned up in 1894. Significantly, gross domestic investment had bottomed in 1887 and was on the rise before net foreign lending broke in 1891. In the 1877–79 and 1903–5 cases net foreign lending rose only *after* the gross domestic investment boom broke.

It seems fair to suggest from these data that, at least at their origins, the great foreign investment booms of the 1880s and 1900s began as something of a sink for a disjuncture between desired savings and desired domestic investment spending. If there is some value in temporizing on this conclusion, it is because large capitalist economies are not smoothly running machines; the patterns of output, income, savings, and investment have large random elements to them. The 1870–1913 period offers a sample of three occasions when home and overseas investment aggregates reverse their direction, tending to move against each other, and random elements may be the differentiating element in the specific timing of their paths. Nevertheless, the two net foreign investment booms start with evidence of a strong disjuncture between desired savings and desired domestic investment, and the same signs do not seem to be present for the strong domestic boom of the 1890s.

The data for the years 1850–69 do not allow estimation of regression equations that would specify U.K. desired savings behavior. This means, in turn, that it is difficult to determine whether oversaving was present at the beginning of the foreign lending surges of the late 1850s and the mid-1860s. Nevertheless, it is useful to see whether periods of stagnation preceded these U.K. foreign lending booms on the tentative hypothesis that such periods of stagnation would tend to depress domestic investment expectations but, if sufficiently long, involve an upward movement in desired savings rates as the latter return to their long-run values. Because Deane's estimates of gross national product accounts are the only annual estimates stretching over these years, it is her data that are employed in table 8.8's rates of net foreign lending and domestic fixed investment and the growth rates of real output.

The years 1856 to 1860 were the first time when rates of net foreign lending reached levels unusual for the preceding fifty years. However, according to Deane's estimates, the growth rates of real output in the early 1850s were either average or better for the mid-Victorian era. Unusually high rates of net foreign lending reappear in the mid-1860s, and in this case it is arguable that the years 1860–62 constitute a short low-growth period. The year 1860 was clearly a trade cycle depression year by all contemporary accounts. Output growth recovered in 1861, but 1862's output growth was as poor as 1860's. One might be inclined then to treat 1861 as a halting recovery with 1862 continuing tendencies inaugurated in 1860. The difficulty with this view is

Table 8.8

Annual Estimates of the Rate of U.K. Net Foreign Investment,
Gross Domestic Capital Formation,
and Growth of Aggregate Output, 1845-69

	NFI/Y (%) (1)	GDFI/Y (%) (2)	Annual Growth of Real GNP (%) (3)
1845	1.8	6.0	5.6
1846	1.4	8.6	6.6
1847	-0.2	10.1	0.5
1848	0.4	8.6	1.3
1849	0.7	7.1	1.6
1850	2.0	6.1	-0.9
1851	1.6	5.9	4.0
1852	1.4	6.7	1.7
1853	0.5	6.5	3.9
1854	0.9	6.4	2.6
1855	2.0	6.2	2.7
1856	3.0	5.7	4.5
1857	3.6	5.1	1.6
1858	3.2	5.4	-2.2
1859	4.7	5.1	6.2
1860	3.1	5.3	0.8
1861	1.8	5.4	3.1
1862	1.4	5.3	0.8
1863	3.1	6.4	3.8
1864	2.5	6.8	2.6
1865	3.6	7.9	6.0
1866	3.2	6.7	1.4
1867	4.1	6.0	1.1
1868	3.6	6.1	3.5
1869	4.5	5.9	1.8

Abbreviations: Y = nominal gross national product
              NFI = nominal net foreign investment
             GDFI = nominal gross domestic fixed investment

Sources:
    Cols. (1)&(2): Deane 1968: 104-5.
    Col. (3): Deane 1968: 106-7.

that 1861 was, in fact, a year of above-average output growth. This suggests that perhaps the 1862 downturn had a different cause than the 1860 downturn. Indeed, it is quite likely that the 1862 downturn was largely the result of trade disruptions and uncertainties attending the first years of the Civil War in the United States. From this perspective, the low growth of the 1860-62 period was due to the coincidence of two short-term shocks to the aggregate economy that temporarily depressed investment expectations in all directions but left underlying long-term investment expectations largely unaffected. Savings rates probably fell a bit in 1860 and 1862 owing to the transitory low-income growth of these years, whereas they were probably above trend in 1861 and 1863 owing to the transitory above-average income growth of those years. On this basis, it seems unlikely that any large disjuncture between desired savings and desired investment occurred prior to, or coincident with, the foreign investment boom that started in 1863. In sum, although good estimators of desired savings and investment behavior are lacking, it seems unlikely that Hobson-like effects were an important component of the foreign investment surges of the 1850s and 1860s.

SUMMARY

Let us recapitulate and conclude the findings on the Hobson hypothesis of oversaving and the United Kingdom's capital export of the late nineteenth and early 20th centuries:

1. Trends in the share of nonwage income, the volatility of nonwage income, and the volatility of the U.K. business cycle do not support the hypothesis that trends in oversaving were central to the rise in the trend rate of net foreign lending, 1850–1913.
2. Although the factor income distribution shows some evidence of determining annual variations in gross private savings, the Friedman-Ando-Modigliani model of gross private savings, which incorporates the concepts of transitory and permanent income without disaggregation to the factor incomes, achieves a superior fit to the available data.
3. At the major turning points for the Hobson oversaving hypothesis, 1877–79 and 1903–5, the years when the rate of net foreign lending moves off its lowest cyclical values into its major surges of the 1870–1913 period, 1887–90 and 1903–13, the best models of gross private savings desires make their worst overestimating errors; that is, predicted desired savings rates exceed actual savings rates. Some evidence seems to suggest that these errors may be interpreted as the *ex poste* resolution of an *ex ante* disequilibrium between desired savings and desired domestic investment spending, part of the resolution taking the form of savings, unwanted by domestic

investment decision makers, spilling over into foreign investment. Importantly, the evidence of desired savings' exceeding actual savings at the beginning of the domestic investment boom of the 1880s is quite weak.

4. At least one cause of these periods of oversaving is that real income falls preceded the period of oversaving for enough years so that, after an initial drop at the time of the real income fall, desired savings rates were moving back to long-term values. Thus, the cyclical evidence points toward the origins of the principal foreign investment booms in a longish slide in the total economy and its peculiar dichotomous effect on desired savings rates and desired domestic investment rates: the former tending to rise in longer term adjustment and the latter to fall.

5. Although Hobson's view of oversaving does not explain the trend or all cycles in net foreign lending in the years 1850-1913, a reformulated concept of oversaving does seem to fit the facts of particular episodes at the origins of the 1877–90 and 1903–1913 foreign investment surges.

CHAPTER 9: INFLUENCE OF DOMESTIC INVESTMENT CONDITIONS ON THE RATE OF OVERSEAS INVESTMENT

Within the framework of the simple four-equation macro-economic model of U.K. accumulation proposed in chapter 7, three propositions must be established to argue that domestic investment conditions were an important factor in raising or sustaining the high U.K. rate of overseas investment. First, it must be shown that the United Kingdom possessed an aggregate accumulation structure in which domestic investment conditions were capable of affecting the rate of overseas investment. Specifically, it must be established that aggregate U.K. private savings were not fully responsive to total (home and overseas) investment demand. If aggregate U.K. private savings were fully responsive to the total demand for investment spending, then any demander of investment goods could get as much or as little savings as wanted without imposing any interest or other constraint on other demanders (see figure 7.2). If, however, aggregate U.K. private savings were not fully responsive to total investment demands, then a decline in the demand for U.K. domestic investment goods would make room for more foreign investment, either through a lowered interest rate or some other mechanism. Clearly, chapter 8's evidence on aggregate U.K. private savings behavior is relevant here.

Second, given an aggregate transmission mechanism, it must be shown that the conditions for domestic investment were abating. Much is known about the short-term cyclical determinants of investment behavior in advanced capitalist economies, but little is known about the forces that determine national rates of capital formation over long periods. Long-swing research is one of the few sources of scholarship that are helpful, but this is oriented toward cycles, albeit growth cycles, not long-term averages. International evidence on rates of capital formation over long periods of time crudely suggests that differences in demographic and productivity variables are important (Kuznets

1966:220-84; Green and Urquhart 1976:233-40). International and long-term historical evidence on demographic and productivity trends will be the focus of our investigation of domestic investment long-term pressures.

Third and finally, it must be established that the important factors influencing trends in domestic investment were independent of the process of foreign investment. This point is quite important. Research over the last forty years into the long cycles that often characterized growth and development in the regions of recent settlement abroad and in the United Kingdom has produced some evidence to suggest that both U.K. foreign lending and U.K. domestic capital formation were determined to some degree within the interactions of an Atlantic economy. Thus, Brinley Thomas argues that U.K. domestic investments, particularly urban residential and other social-overhead capital investments, were affected by autonomous economic forces generated both at home and in the regions of recent settlement abroad (1972:137-39; 1954:155-90, 202-305).

Abramovitz and Williamson would agree that U.K. domestic investment, especially the types cited by B. Thomas, were endogenous to an Atlantic economy, but they would stress that any long swings in U.K. domestic investment aggregates were largely determined by autonomous overseas forces, particularly U.S. ones (Abramovitz 1968; Williamson 1964:208-16).

One prominent investigator, Habbakuk (1962), has disagreed quite strongly with the idea of an Atlantic economy affecting U.K. housing investment. But having ruled out the possibility of a causal path from overseas investment conditions to any domestic investment rates, Habbakuk did not close the door to domestic investment conditions influencing the United Kingdom's rate of overseas investment. Two types of evidence are relevant to test the exogeneity of U.K. domestic investment conditions affecting the rate of overseas investment. First, is the secular evidence for a slackening of domestic investment pressure in excess of an amount predictable from overseas influences? Second, do statistical tests of antecedence, sometimes called causality tests, give any enlightenment on the extent of influence among the various domestic and overseas savings and investment magnitudes?

MACROECONOMIC FOUNDATIONS

Could a fall in domestic investment spending pressure result in an augmented rate of foreign investment? The answer hinges on the character of U.K. aggregate private savings behavior. As discussed in the next section, it depends on the degree to which U.K. aggrevate private savings were responsive to the pressure of total (home and overseas) investment demand. Figures 7.2 and 7.3 show that, only if savings were partly or fully unresponsive to interest rates or some other transmitter of investment demand pressure, would a fall in U.K. domestic investment demand pressure result in more overseas investment.

Were U.K. private savings sensitive to interest rates or some other transmitter of investment demand pressure and to what degree? The evidence of table 8.1's regression tests suggests that, although U.K. private savings were responsive to interest rates, they were not enormously so. The Friedman-Ando-Modigliani model shows a positive and statistically significant interest rate coefficient. With the average values of gross private savings and interest rates, the elasticity of U.K. gross private savings with respect to interest rate movements was .65 in the long run. Thus, the shape of U.K. savings behavior was intermediate between figures 7.2 and 7.3. The savings curve was neither horizontal nor vertical.

Given this structure of aggregate private savings behavior, a hypothetical fall in domestic investment demand could cause a fall in interest rates and the gross private savings rate. On the reasonable assumption that overseas borrowers were sensitive to U.K. interest rates to some degree, the fall in the general level of interest rates in the United Kingdom would raise the rate of overseas investment.[1]

DEMOGRAPHIC PRESSURES FOR DOMESTIC INVESTMENT

On the basis of the pioneering research of S. Kuznets and many others, it is widely accepted that demographic pressures were an important determinant of national rates of investment in the late nineteenth century, particularly the rate of investment in residential housing and social-overhead capital. The case is sufficiently convincing that the latter types of investment are frequently termed "population-sensitive" investment. Green and Urquhart recently assembled international evidence showing the rough correlation between national rates of population growth, urbanization, and population-sensitive investment rates (1976:235, 237, 239). Table 9.1 differs from Green and Urquhart's insofar as it uses *all* years of each decade to indicate the long-term average rates of investment.

Although the fit is crude, it is difficult to deny that late nineteenth-century rates of investment in residential housing and social-overhead investment varied with rates of population growth and urbanization. From this international perspective, the U.K. rate of population-sensitive investment appears low because the U.K. rate of population growth was relatively low and the U.K. rate of urbanization was intermediate. To pursue this point, two questions must be addressed. First, did the behavior of U.K. demographic pressures after 1870 represent a break with previous U.K. experience? It is possible that U.K. demographic pressures were always relatively low. Second, is there evidence that any fall in demographic pressures was independent of overseas investment activity of the United Kingdom? If U.K. overseas investments helped to attract U.K. emigrants, persons who were typically in their maximal child-bearing years, then the lessening of domestic U.K. demographic pressures was not an independent cause of British foreign investment.

What was the long-term history of U.K. demographic pressures from the mid-nineteenth century to World War I? Table 9.2 presents decadal, per capita rates of change of population size, migration, marriage, and urbanization in England and Wales. Information on urbanization in Scotland and Ireland is limited, but this restriction is not important. Available evidence suggests that Scottish demographic trends were similar to those of England and Wales during this period, and there can be little doubt that population pressures abated in Ireland after the famine.

The evidence is quite strong for a decline in demographic pressures in England and Wales at some point after 1870 or so. Decadal rates of total population growth peaked in the 1870s and declined below pre-1870 levels over the next three decades. The

Table 9.1

Some International Evidence on the Long Term Determinants of Trend Rates of Domestic Capital Formation, 1870-1910

	Decadal Population Growth (%)	Population Change Accounted for by Urbanization (%)	Decadal Output per Capita Growth (%)	Ratio of Gross Domestic Capital Formation to GNP (%)	Ratio of Population-Sensitive Capital Formation to GNP (%)	Ratio of Productivity Sensitive Capital Formation to GNP (%)
	(1)	(2)	(3)	(4)	(5)	(6)
Highest GDCF/GNP						
Australia, 1870-1890	38.0	63.2	12.2	18.1	9.9	9.0
United States, 1870-1910	23.2	59.2	28.2	21.7	6.3	15.4
Canada, 1900-1910	34.4	61.9	25.7	19.2	9.1	10.1
France, 1870-1910	2.3	202.3	10.7	20.1	11.6	8.5
Intermediate GDCF/GNP						
Germany, 1890-1910	14.3	101.9	14.2	14.2	6.7	7.5
Italy, 1900-1910	9.0	--	18.5	14.1	2.0	12.1
Sweden, 1890-1910	7.2	63.2	30.0	11.5	4.4	7.1
Australia, 1890-1910	18.8	27.9	7.9	14.0	7.7	6.3
Canada, 1870-1900	13.4	72.4	19.3	14.6	8.0	6.6
Lowest GDCF/GNP						
United Kingdom, 1870-1910	9.5	102.9	9.5	8.7	4.6	4.1
Germany, 1870-1890	9.7	100.0	19.0	11.4	6.3	5.1
Italy, 1870-1900	6.4	--	7.7	9.0	1.8	7.2
Sweden, 1870-1890	7.1	66.8	16.9	10.3	4.4	5.9

Sources and Notes:

Columns 1, 2, 3. Green and Urquhart 1976: 235, 237.

Columns 4, 5.

    Australia: Butlin 1962: 6-7, 18-9, 24-5. Averages based on annual data, 1870-79, 1890-1909.

    Canada: Firestone 1958: 248, 281. Averages based on estimates for the years 1870, 1890, 1900, and 1910 only.

    France: Markovitch 1966: 93. The data presented by Markovitch are averages for the periods 1865-74, 1875-84, 1885-94, 1895-1904, 1905-13. The above estimates aggregated the 1865-74 and 1875-84 data for an estimate for the 1870s, 1875-84, and 1885-94 for the 1880s, etc.

    Germany: Hoffmann 1965: 259-60, 825-26. Averages based on annual data, 1870-89, 1890-1909, of net capital formation and net national product figures.

    Italy: Mitchell 1975: 782, 787 and Fua 1966: 60-3, 83-84. Averages based on annual data, 1870-99, 1900-09.

    Sweden: Mitchell 1975: 782, 789, and Kuznets 1961a: 87. Averages based on annual data for 1870-89, 1890-1909.

    United Kingdom: Feinstein 1972: T8, T85-6. Average for 1870-1909 based on annual data.

    United States: Kuznets 1961: 561, 572, 576-66, 599 and Ulmer 1960: 256-57. Kuznets' published data for a given year are five-year averages centered on the given data. Using his estimates for 1872 and 1877, it is possible to construct an accurate average for the years 1870-79, without overlapping, and so on for longer periods.

Population-sensitive capital formation is usually defined as (a) nonfarm, residential construction; (b) urban social overhead capital formation, and (c) railway capital formation. These sources are not sufficiently disaggregated in all cases to permit consistent use of this definition. The U.K., French, German, and Canadian data include all three components. The data for Sweden, the United States, and Canada include a and c only. The Italian data cover (a) only.

Column (6) = Column (4) - Column (5).

Table 9.2

Demographic Indicators of the Demand for Housing and Related Construction Investment, England and Wales, 1841-1911

Census Decade	Decadal Population Growth per 1000 (1)	Net Loss by Migration per 1000 (2)	Crude Rate of Natural Increase per 1000 (3)	Average Annual Marriage Rate per 1000 (4)	Net Gain of Towns and Colliery Districts per 1000 (5)	Net Gain of "Urbanized" Counties per 1000 (6)	Total Who Changed County Residence per 1000 (7)
1841-51	12.9	3.0	15.9	16.3	4.7	--	--
1851-61	11.9	7.7	19.6	16.8	3.4	10.2	7.1
1861-71	13.3	4.0	17.3	16.7	3.1	9.9	8.3
1871-81	14.3	4.1	18.4	16.0	3.0	24.7	9.2
1881-91	11.7	4.7	16.4	15.0	0.9	14.5	8.0
1891-01	12.1	3.5	15.6	15.6	2.1	10.4	8.0
1901-11	10.8	3.8	14.6	15.4	-0.6	19.7	7.5

Sources:

(1) Mitchell 1962: 9-10.
(2) Tranter 1973: 53.
(3) Col. (1) + (2).
(4) Mitchell 1962: 45-6.
(5) B. Thomas 1954: 124.
(6) Friedlander 1970: 431.
(7) Friedlander and Roshier 1966: 267.
All rates per 1000 are calculated on the initial population of the decade except Col. (4).

marriage rate peaks in the 1850s and 1860s, moved downward in the 1870s, and finds a low plateau in the 1880s, 1890s, and 1900s. The three indices of urbanization all show breaks in their per capita rates after the 1870s. Certainly, the demographic pressures for residential and social-overhead capital formation were not as strong in England and Wales after 1870 or so as they were before.

It is, however, a matter of some dispute about the extent to which these slowing demographic pressures were due to domestic developments or derived from overseas influences (Habbakuk 1962 versus B. Thomas 1954:202–3, 221–22). Our interest is, of course, strictly concerned with whether the United Kingdom's overseas investments induced the migration. In the latter case, the abating demographic pressures at home were not an independent cause of overseas investment.

Let us assume for the moment that all U.K. emigration was solely derived from overseas conditions created by U.K. overseas investments. We wish to know the extent to which the pace of U.K. population growth was affected by the outflow of people. In table 9.2 the decadal rate of population growth and the rate of emigration are summed in column 3 to give a crude idea of the rate of natural increase of the population of England and Wales.[2] This number peaks in the 1850s, 1860s and 1870s and declines thereafter. Table 9.3 presents birth rates, death rates, and the number of migrants over shorter time periods. The difference between the birth rate and death rate is the rate of natural increase; this is calculated in column 3. Again, it would appear that a decline set in after the 1870s. Clearly, variations in migration have some effect on birth rates, but table 9.3 makes it certain that this link is not the only force affecting birth rate trends. If, as was the case, trends in migration rates were constant or falling, the birth rate might fall for a period, but eventually it should stabilize. This is not the pattern of tables 9.2 and 9.3; birth rates continue to decline long after any adjustment for a smaller child-bearing population due to migration.

Thus, although the U.K. emigration had some effect on domestic U.K. demographic pressures, other important factors seem to have been involved in demographic trends. Indeed, there are excellent grounds for viewing the United Kingdom's demo-

Table 9.3

Birth Rates, Death Rates, and Migration
in England and Wales, 1841-1910

Period	Births per 1000 (1)	Deaths per 1000 (2)	Births minus Deaths per 1000 (3)	Net Loss by Migration (000s) (4)
1841-45	35.2	21.4	13.8	-301
1846-50	34.8	23.3	11.5	-182
1851-55	35.5	22.7	12.8	-787
1856-60	35.5	21.8	13.7	-581
1861-65	35.8	22.6	13.2	-373
1866-70	35.7	22.4	13.3	-434
1871-75	35.7	22.0	13.7	-388
1876-80	35.4	20.8	14.6	-543
1881-85	33.5	19.4	14.1	-706
1886-90	31.4	18.9	12.5	-525
1891-95	30.5	18.7	11.8	-389
1896-1900	29.3	17.7	11.6	-633
1901-5	28.2	16.1	12.1	-645
1906-10	26.3	14.7	11.6	-577

Source: Tranter 1973: 53.

graphic trends as part of the transformations of modern economic growth in advanced capitalist nations of the nineteenth and twentieth centuries rather than the peculiar outcome of the U.K. emigration history. At some stage in the modern economic growth of nations, it has been found that birth rates show downward trends that are faster than earlier falling death rates. In demographic histories it is generally agreed that the 1870s were the beginning of this trend for the United Kingdom (e.g., Tranter 1973: Ch. 4, "The 'Demographic Transition.'").

In addition, at some point during modern economic growth, the rate of urbanization slows because the redistribution of output and labor away from rural production and occupations ceases. The United Kingdom was at the tail end of this redistribution in the late nineteenth century. Table 9.4 shows the changing distribution of product of a number of advanced capitalist nations, 1860–1928. The United Kingdom (and Great Britain) had lower rates of redistribution out of agriculture than Germany, Italy, Sweden, and Canada. Moreover, the United Kingdom (and Great Britain) can be safely assumed to have much lower rates of residential housing investment in rural areas than the United States, Canada, and Australia; the rural population of the United Kingdom was virtually stagnant after 1870.

It may be beating a quite dead horse, but it is important to note that the earlier assumption that U.K. emigration was strongly connected to U.K. overseas investment in the long run is a weak one. First, the large British investments in Europe and Latin America were not paralleled by large-scale emigration to either region. Second, although it is true that both British capital and labor went to the United States, British capital in the United States was a very modest portion of total U.S. investment. Third, international evidence of a connection between international capital and population movements is weak. France exported capital at rates second only to the United Kingdom, and there were very few French emigrants in the nineteenth century. Italy exported virtually no capital but had a very high rate of emigration. Finally, some of the motivation of U.K. migrants was based on domestic U.K. labor market conditions, not overseas conditions. Indeed, recent migration studies have suggested that domestic U.K. labor market conditions may have had a dominant role (Williamson 1974b).

In sum, U.K. demographic and product events, stemming from patterns typical of the modern economic growth of nations, induced a decline in U.K. demographic pressures. These patterns are believed to be domestic in origin, and hence, the demographic pressures can be taken as largely domestic in origin. To the extent that the rate of investment in residential housing and social-overhead capital formation was population sensitive, it must be

Table 9.4

Distribution of National Product Among Three Major Sectors, Selected Countries, 1860-1928
Shares of National Product (%)

	Agriculture			Industry			Services		
	Initial Date (1)	Terminal Date (2)	Change (3)	Initial Date (4)	Terminal Date (5)	Change (6)	Initial Date (7)	Terminal Date (8)	Change (9)
United Kingdom, 1871 to 1907	15	6	-9	40	38	-2	45	56	+11
Great Britain, 1871 to 1907	14	6	-8	38	37	-1	48	57	+9
France, 1872 to 1909	43	35	-8	30	36	+6	27	29	+2
Germany, 1860-69 to 1905-14	32	18	-14	24	39	+15	44	43	-1
Italy, 1868-72 to 1908-12	58	44	-14	19	22	+3	23	34	+11
Sweden, 1868-72 to 1908-12	38	25	-13	19	32	+13	43	43	0
Australia, 1868-72 to 1908-12	25	26	+1	28	27	-1	47	47	0
Canada, 1870 to 1910	44	28	-16	23	30	+7	33	42	+9
United States, 1869-79 to 1919-28	20	12	-8	21	29	+8	59	59	0

Sources:

United Kingdom, France, Germany, Sweden, Italy: Mitchell 1975: 801-4.
Great Britain: Deane and Cole 1969: 166, 1975.
Australia: Butlin 1962: 12-13.
Canada: Firestone 1958: 281.
United States: Kuznets 1966: 90-1, 131.

Notes:

Agriculture also includes fisheries, forestry, and trapping.
Industry includes mining, manufacturing, construction, and power and light utilities.
Services include transportation and communication, trade, finance, real estate, personal, business, domestic, professional and government.

concluded that such capital formation was of declining profitability after 1870 or so.[3]

DOMESTIC PRODUCTIVITY PERFORMANCE AND OTHER INFLUENCES ON THE RATE OF U.K. MANUFACTURING INVESTMENT

Although population movements have been widely accepted as a major autonomous influence on long-term national rates of residential and social-overhead capital formation, the determinants of long-term national rates of manufacturing investment are less well established. In this section it is argued that two autonomous determinants—productivity growth and tariff policy—had a depressing influence on the profitability of U.K. domestic manufacturing investment and, given the structure of national savings behavior, thereby helped to raise the United Kingdom's rate of overseas investment in the late nineteenth century. That considerable care must be taken in establishing the logical and evidential grounds for the choice of these determinants of the rate of manufacturing investment is suggested by certain correlations of table 9.1's variables. The rank correlation between the growth rate of output per capita and "productivity-sensitive" (largely manufacturing) investment is .30. With the exclusion of France, with its static population growth but high urbanization rate, the bivariate Spearman rank correlation of national population growth and population-sensitive investment rate displayed in table 9.1 is .90.

Productivity Performance To establish that U.K. productivity performance had even a minimal connection with the rising rate of overseas investment in the late nineteenth century, it must first be shown that U.K. productivity growth rates were falling during this period. After all, it might be the case that U.K. productivity growth rates were low throughout the nineteenth century and hence unlikely to be the domestic agent causing the upsurge in overseas investment rates after the midcentury.

The latest data of Deane and Feinstein leave little room for doubt; U.K. productivity growth rates fell across the late nineteenth century.[4] Table 9.5 presents Deane's estimates of the growth rate of U.K. real gross national product per head from the

Table 9.5

Long-Term Rates of Growth in U.K.
Gross National Product, 1830-1914
(% rates of annual growth)

	Total G.N.P.	Average G.N.P.
1830/39 - 1860/69	1.97	1.61
1835/44 - 1865/74	2.36	1.85
1840/49 - 1870/79	2.42	1.85
1845/54 - 1875/84	2.31	1.59
1850/59 - 1880/89	2.15	1.46
1855/64 - 1885/94	2.13	1.33
1860/69 - 1890/99	2.05	1.17
1865/74 - 1895/04	1.98	1.07
1870/79 - 1900/09	1.94	1.05
1875/84 - 1905/14	1.88	1.00

Source: Deane 1968: 96

Notes: The aggregate measured is gross national product at factor
cost and at 1900 prices. The estimates presented are annual
percentage rates of compound growth calculated as between
averages for decades.

1830s to World War I in successive thirty-year segments. Although
this averaging procedure makes it difficult to date turning points,
it seems safe to suggest that sometime in the 1870s the growth rate
of national productivity began to decline from midcentury peaks
and fell below early nineteenth-century rates sometime in the late
1880s. Our interest, however, centers on manufacturing investment rates, and for these purposes Feinstein's estimates of U.K.
sectoral output and employment from the 1860s to World War I
are more appropriate than Deane's aggregate national data. Table
9.6 gives decadal growth rates of manufacturing and total
industrial product per worker. As with Deane's growth rates of

Table 9.6

The Growth of Labor Productivity in U.K. Manufacturing, Industry,
and Total Domestic Product, 1861-1911

| | % Decadal Growth Manufacturing Output per Worker | | % Decadal Growth Industrial Output per Worker | | % Decadal Growth Gross Domestic Product per Worker | Average Relative Price of Capital Goods |
	(1)	(2)	(3)	(4)	(5)	(6)
1861-71	26.1	23.4	23.5	24.7	14.6	95.3
1871-81	14.8	16.9	13.3	18.0	12.3	103.0
1881-91	10.9	9.6	6.8	8.5	9.0	101.0
1891-01	12.1	11.8	10.9	12.0	9.5	101.1
1901-11	6.9	6.6	3.9	4.4	5.4	100.0

Sources:

Cols. (1) & (3): Feinstein 1972: T111-2, T131. The index of
labor input includes both employed and unemployed workers.
Industrial output consists of manufacturing, mining, building,
gas, water, and electric output.

Cols. (2) & (4): Feinstein 1972: T111-2, T131, T125-26. In a
crude attempt to compensate for cyclical variations in the output data of Cols. (1) and (3), the output measures in Cols.
(2) and (4) have been adjusted to reflect "full employment"
output, utilizing an index of national labor unemployment.

Col. (5): Feinstein 1972: T51-52. The index of labor input and
material output both reflect cyclical capacity utilization
movements in these aggregate data.

Col. (6): An implicit gross domestic fixed investment goods price
deflator from Feinstein (forthcoming volume) is divided by an
implicit gross domestic product price deflator from Feinstein
1972: T10(9), T14(12), corrected for the new investment data
and prices.

total output per person, Feinstein's estimates of manufacturing
productivity appear to have sustained a sharp break downward in
the 1870s. A further fall takes place in the 1880s; a very small rise,
in the 1890s; and another sharp break downward, in the 1900s.
Feinstein's data sources do not permit annual estimates of sectoral
employment, and so it is impossible to date the turning points
more precisely.

Another noteworthy aspect of U.K. productivity performance involves the relative price of capital goods. U.K. goods markets were quite competitive over the long haul. If, through better equipment or skills, the pace of productivity growth in capital goods production exceeded that of other components of domestic product, the price of capital goods relative to the implicit deflator of gross domestic product probably would have fallen. There is, of course, the rough implication that entrepreneurs would be led to substitute capital for other inputs by such circumstances and thus raise the rate of domestic capital formation. Table 9.6 suggests that no such relative price movement occurred.

This static pattern in the U.K. price of capital goods relative to other components of gross domestic product was in sharp contrast to the downward course of the relative price of capital goods in the United States over these same years. In an investigation of the U.K. machine tool industry, the sector that makes machines to make machines, Floud found the same price pattern, static U.K. prices and falling U.S. prices (1976:113-14). These divergent price trends offer no evidence on whether the United States was at a higher or lower absolute productivity level than the United Kingdom in the production of either all investment goods or machine tools. As Floud points out, it is arguable that for most of the period 1850-1914 the United States could have been catching up from initially low productivity levels (1976:110-19, contra Landes 1969:308-23). What these comparative data do imply, however, is that, while the falling relative price of capital goods in the United States offered a strong impetus for the U.S. demand for investment goods behind its highly protective tariff barriers, the same was clearly not true for the U.K. demand for investment goods. In sum, with industrial productivity growth slowing and the cost of capital goods offering no firm price incentive, it seems very likely that the long-term pressures on the rate of U.K. industrial investment goods demand was either static or falling.

The causes of the downward trend in British productivity growth in the late nineteenth and early twentieth centuries have been debated for many years. This is not the place to present the many threads of this controversy. Nevertheless, some account of the productivity fall must be given. Three explanations of British productivity performance in the late nineteenth century evoke the smallest debate, the continued strength of certain large industries with relatively low potentials for large productivity advance, the relatively poor state of British science and technical education and research, and the low level of British tariffs. One explanation, entrepreneurial failure, is quite controversial but seemingly undefeatable.

It is widely agreed that, because British industry continued to specialize in textiles, iron, coal, and steam engine machinery, the potential gains from these large industrial sectors in the latter half of the nineteenth century were limited. International research has suggested that productivity growth in modern industrial sectors has a systematic pattern (Kuznets 1930; Burns 1934, esp. chs. 3, 4). One or a number of inventions create the basis for a strong burst of productivity and output growth. The sector grows rapidly, mostly by displacing other products or production methods. Inventive activity is also likely to increase.[5] On the demand side, technical bottlenecks make profit-maximizing entrepreneurs sensitive to new ideas. On the supply side, the rapid growth of sales and profits acts as a magnet for inventors; furthermore, the greater and greater experience with the initial process innovations yields considerable learning by doing (e.g., Zevin 1975; ch. 3; David 1975:95–168).

At some point, however, two events seem to slow the pace of productivity advance. First, the industry grows to the limit of its market (perhaps dictated by tariffs), and henceforth its output growth is limited by slower trends of income per head and population growth. This lessens its attractiveness to potential inventors and slows learning by doing. Second, after a generation or two of inventive activity and learning by doing, the basic physical processes of the initial inventions have been fairly thoroughly mined and the major technical bottlenecks eliminated, given the constraint of slowly growing basic scientific knowledge. Thus, the potential for big inventions and big leaps of learning by doing diminish and the industrial sector settles to a low rate of productivity advance resting on minor process inventions and slowed learning by doing. The worst instance of these trends manifested itself in the coal industry in the early twentieth century when a burst of international and domestic demand for coal involved the industry in much more difficult geological formations and the industry actually sustained diminishing returns to labor, that is, negative rates of labor productivity growth (Taylor 1969:46).

Another widely accepted source of British productivity decline is associated with the average (or worse) performance of British applied chemical and electrical science (Landes 1969:269-76; Musson 1978:194-95; 216-27). The explanation is widely taken to be the relatively limited support for education and primary research in the sciences by the public and private sectors. By the mid-nineteenth century, science was being effectively applied in the primary metals, metal fabrication, engine construction, and chemistry. British inventors made significant contributions in these areas. However, these contributions were not based on a broad and well-financed system of secondary school scientific education, university scientific education, and university science and technical research as was the inventive activity of a number of European and North American nations (Aldcroft 1975: 287-308; Robertson 1981) Chemistry and electricity were the burgeoning fields of science and technology by the late nineteenth century, and it is suggested that at this point Britain began to suffer from this underfunding. British scientists and technologists were involved in these burgeoning fields but not to the extent found elsewhere. The net result was that the United Kingdom did not hold its own in the heavy chemical and electrical engineering industries.

The absence of British tariffs becomes relevant to the experience of the new technologies appearing in chemicals, electricity, and automobiles in the very late nineteenth century. In each of these industries British exports were limited by high tariffs in the other leading industrial nations, whereas the domestic market was quite open because the United Kingdom had virtually no tariffs on foreign imports. Early in the industrial history of heavy chemicals, electrical generating equipment, and automobiles, foreign imports secured a strong British foothold. To put the matter simply, British firms involved or interested in adopting the new methods or products received no infant industry support.

Technical change is not balanced; it occurs in specific sectors at specific points in time. Many sectors for long periods are visited by little technical progress. A nation that wants to continue to grow fast must secure its share of inventive or imitative activity; tariffs may not be the most efficient way of performing this feat (David 1975:95–168); they are often set well above the level necessary to give infant support. Indeed, they usually go to old, large industries with political power. But, regardless of their efficiency or their political origins, most nineteenth-century nations protected their infant industries through this method and Britain did not. The absence of tariffs did not matter when British technology had a substantial lead early in the nineteenth century, but by the end of the century it probably did matter.

Entrepreneurial failure is the most debated cause of British productivity decline in the late nineteenth and early twentieth centuries.[6] Considerable scholarship over the past decade has suggested that British entrepreneurs were probably not statically inefficient (McCloskey 1971a; Sandberg 1974; Floud 1976); decisions on new technologies were based on a rational calculus of current input and output prices. Nevertheless, the whisper of entrepreneurial failure persists. In the steel industry, for example, the firms that accepted new technologies that were only marginally profitable on the static calculus tended to be led by a first generation of a family enterprise or the management of a new and broadly based joint stock company, not the second or third generations of a family enterprise (Allen 1978). On the assumption that the later generations of family enterprises tended to be less adventurous and risk taking, it might be argued that their presence acted as a drag on this sector's dynamic efficiency. This relative decline in adventurousness of an industry's enterpreneurship might be part of the reason for the systematically poor performance of the older U.K. industries, just described. True, the potential for big productivity change decreases as the basic physical processes have been mined with the constraint of slowly evolving scientific knowledge. But it is also true that hiring one's sons to continue the management of a firm hardly constitutes the broadest search procedure for a new generation of leadership. It may be the cheapest search procedure and it may be the one closest to one's heart. In any event, it lowers the probability of securing the kind of entrepreneurship that will be in the forefront looking for new products, new production methods, and new markets.

In sum, British productivity declines in the late nineteenth and early twentieth centuries are best explained by too much industrial output founded on older staples and too little output connected to a secure base for systematic scientific and technical education and research. The British could not, of course, hope to dominate industrial invention as other and larger nations became heavily involved in modern economic growth in the course of the nineteenth century. However, to claim its share of inventive activity and to import the inventions of others effectively, the stronger scientific, technical and educational base found elsewhere might have been advantageous for the late nineteenth-century United Kingdom.

By both international and historical standards the U.K. productivity growth rates in the late nineteenth century were low and declining, but it still must be asked to what degree productivity growth caused net investment rates rather than vice versa. Table 8.1's national data show a statistically significant, albeit moderate, correlation between the two variables, but this merely establishes association, not causal dominance. Furthermore, economic theory gives reasons for both paths of causation, productivity to investment and investment to productivity.

Net investment expenditures have two effects on national productivity growth. First, given the capital-using, labor-saving bias of much nineteenth-century technical change, net investment tended to put more and better capital in the hands of the existing labor force of the sectors where technical progress was occurring and thus tended to raise sectoral and national productivity. Second, net investment expenditures were not blind; they tended to go to sectors with the highest labor productivities, causing sectoral and national specialization in the most advanced methods and outputs. This second relationship between investment and productivity is important. Even if no sector was currently introducing new technologies, a rise in the investment rate might raise national productivity if previous allocations of net investment expenditures had not completed the specialization of national labor and capital resources into the highest productivity sectors. It is this specializing effect of net investment expenditures that makes it difficult to infer something about national manufacturing investment rates from tables 9.1's and 9.6's productivity growth rates. Use of their evidence thus hinges on whether this specialization effect is an important source of national productivity growth in an advanced capitalist nation such as the United Kingdom in the late nineteenth century.

Logic and some evidence would suggest that, the more backward a nation, the greater the chance that social, political, and economic barriers inhibit its ability to allocate capital and labor quickly and effectively to its highest productivity firms and sectors (Gerschenkron 1962, esp. ch. 1). The United Kingdom, however, had been engaged in mobilizing its resources into its highest productivity sectors for perhaps two centuries or more. Thus, it is unlikely that there were large reservoirs of productivity growth available from merely reallocating capital resources. This is, of course, a matter of degree. Any new technology will not only enhance the productivity of the existing labor force in the sector but will also attract entry of more capital and labor. The point is that an advanced capitalist nation in the late nineteenth century, having undergone considerable economic development and, with it, transfer of resources, is quite unlikely to have a large backlog of underspecialized industries. Only the sectors installing the very latest technologies will be underspecialized.

On the other hand, it is very likely that a considerable portion of, for example, Russian national productivity growth in the late nineteenth century stemmed from reallocating capital from agriculture to industry and, within industry, from handicraft to machine-powered factories (Kahan 1978:290). When Russia began to industrialize in the 1880s, perhaps two-thirds of national output was produced in its low productivity agricultural sector and perhaps half of the remaining nonagricultural commodity output was produced with handicraft methods (Crisp 1978:332–33). However, large gains from reallocation of capital and labor seem unlikely in the cases of the United Kingdom, Belgium, France, Holland, and the regions of recent settlement in the late nineteenth century.

If, for the moment, one accepts that France had reached a level of efficiency in transferring resources similar to the United Kingdom's, a comparison of French and U.K. data in table 9.1 affords an interesting example. The French rate of total savings and investment between 1870 and 1914 was probably around 20 percent, while the U.K. rate was in the range of 15 percent on average. The standard interpretation of this differential is that the French were thriftier. Note, however, that, although the French rate of productivity-sensitive capital formation was double the U.K. rate, the decadal growth of output per capita of the two countries was virtually the same. Hence, although the higher savings rate in this relatively advanced capitalist economy might have had some effect on the rate of manufacturing investment, it had little effect on national productivity growth. This conclusion, however, must be treated quite tentatively because table 9.1's estimate of France's productivity-sensitive investment includes agricultural capital formation and there is some evidence that French inheritance laws may have made it somewhat difficult to move savings and wealth out of the rural economy.

Perhaps a better example of the specialization effect of net investment is available in the German, Italian, and Swedish experiences in the early part of the 1870–1910 period seen at the bottom of table 9.1. Over the 1870–1890 years, these nations and the United Kingdom displayed the lowest rates of productivity-sensitive capital formation found in table 9.1. The German and Swedish decadal output per capita growth rates (col. 3) were considerably higher than those of the United Kingdom and Italy. Table 9.4 shows the changing distribution of national product among the agriculture, industry, and service sectors from 1860 to 1928. While Germany and Sweden were augmenting the share of the industrial sector during these years, the United Kingdom and Italy were not. It seems likely that Germany and Sweden thus had higher national productivity growth due to sectoral reallocations, while the United Kingdom, which was already highly specialized in industry in 1870, did not benefit as much from this factor.

One further example, the Australian case, is also suggestive. According to the data presented in table 9.7, Australian productivity growth and productivity-sensitive investment rates took

Table 9.7

Australian Productivity Growth and "Productivity Sensitive"
Investment Rates, By Decade, 1870-1910

Period	Output per Capita Growth (% per Decade) (1)	"Productivity Sensitive" Investment Rate (% GNP) (2)
1870-80	20.9	7.5
1880-90	4.2	8.6
1880-1900	-9.2	5.9
1900-10	28.4	6.6

Sources:

Col. (1): Butlin 1962: 33, OYCA 1920: 83.

Col. (2): Butlin 1962: 6-7, 18-19, 24-25. "Productivity sensitive investment includes industrial, mining, commercial,
shipping, pastoral and agricultural capital formation.

rather large swings lasting fairly long periods. Specifically, while productivity growth was a good indicator of the direction of productivity-sensitive investment rates one decade later, productivity-sensitive investment rates were not good indicators of the direction of productivity growth during either the same decade or the next one. The inference seems to be that if there was any relationship between the two variables it was that productivity growth may have influenced productivity-sensitive investment but not vice versa. The timing strongly suggests, for example, that the high rate of productivity-sensitive investment hit diminishing returns in the 1880s and, as a consequence, productivity-sensitive investment swung sharply downard in the next decade.

It thus seems likely that merely raising the investment rate of an *advanced* capitalist economy in the late nineteenth century might enhance national productivity growth rates for a short period but the gains would be limited. Unlike the undeveloped economies beginning the process of industrialization, there would be no large backlog of unadopted technical innovations and underspecialized sectors. The underspecialized sectors in an advanced economy would tend to be limited to those installing the very latest technical innovations. Since the specialization effect of net investment expenditures on productivity growth would thus be fairly small, it follows that an important element in the relationship between U.K. net investment expenditures and productivity growth would run from high productivity growth to high investment expenditures and low productivity growth to low investment rates. And, since the general path of U.K. productivity growth in the years from the 1870s onward was downward, it is plausible to hypothesize that an important determinant of the return to U.K. manufacturing was diminishing in strength and this was an influence tending to augment overseas investment.

Moving from this general hypothesis to the specific timing of U.K. productivity growth and capital formation rates in productivity-sensitive sectors is, however, problematic. The principal stumbling block is that annual data on sectoral employment are unavailable. In consequence, reliance must be placed on annual productivity data for total domestic product (table 9.8). Importantly, these data tend to reject the view that variations in investment rates have a large contemporaneous or leading influence on productivity growth, a view I have just suggested had substantial logical difficulties. The contemporaneous influence of productivity growth on productivity-sensitive investment rates is not very strong either. However, there is some correlation if, as in the Australian case, one assumes that productivity growth rates could influence investment rates five to ten years hence.

On this hypothesis, the rise of domestic manufacturing investment expenditures as a percent of gross national product in the late 1860s through the early 1880s finds explanation in the rise in the growth rate of productivity that starts in the first years of the 1860s or earlier, peaks in the early 1870s, and remains unusually high until the early 1880s. It follows that domestic productivity growth probably had little or no influence on the rising rate of overseas investment in the 1850s and 1860s. Declining manufacturing productivity and profits may have contributed to the surge of foreign investment in the 1880s, most likely as a sustaining element in the latter part of the decade. Poor productivity

Table 9.8

The Growth of Total U.K. Domestic Product per Worker
and Gross Fixed Industrial Investment Rates,
1856-1911

Period	Domestic Product per Worker (% Growth per Decade) (1)	Gross Fixed Industrial Industrial Rate (% GNP) (2)
1856-66	10.6	2.4
1861-71	14.6	2.7
1866-76	16.7	2.9
1871-81	12.3	3.2
1876-86	13.2	3.4
1881-91	9.0	2.7
1886-96	7.6	2.7
1891-01	9.5	2.9
1896-06	8.2	2.8
1901-11	5.4	3.3

Sources:

Col. (1): Feinstein 1972: T51-52.
Col. (2): Same sources as table 9.1.

performance may have constrained the rise of domestic manufacturing investment in the domestic investment boom that started in the mid-1890s, but it gives no explanation for the violent drop in overseas investment in the 1890s. The sustained low levels of productivity growth through the 1890s, however, may well have been a very important influence on the strength of the foreign investment boom that started in the early 1900s. Given the presence of many other influences on both productivity growth and investment rates, and the poverty of the relevant data base, it is unlikely that the case for trends in domestic productivity growth's influencing overseas investment rates can be made much stronger. It would be mistaken, however, to ignore its influence.

Tariff Policy   The United Kingdom's free trade policy may have been another factor affecting the long-term rate of manufacturing investment and, in turn, overseas investment rates. Trade policy was debated from the 1880s onward to World War I, but free trade was regularly reaffirmed by the various Conservative and Liberal governments. Given its regular debate, it is plausible to speculate on the effects of free trade on U.K. domestic investment rates.

What would be the consequence of a general tariff on manufactured importables? For the sake of simplicity, let it be assumed that the United Kingdom would have been able to impose a tariff on manufactured importables without retaliation.[7] The tariff would probably have a large short-run effect and a somewhat smaller long-run effect. The effects of a tariff are to raise the expected rate of return on plant and equipment producing manufactured importables and to lower the expected rate of return on plant and equipment producing exportables, mainly manufactured goods. The desired stock of capital producing importables is raised and the desired stock of capital producing exportables is lowered. If it is assumed that the disequilibrium between the desired and actual stock of capital producing the newly tariffed importables was large and, owing to a lack of retaliation, any shortfall in the desired stock of capital producing exportables was accomplished by normal wear and tear, the domestic rate of investment in all manufacturing could easily have risen for some time. Eventually, however, when the United Kingdom was specialized in the manufacturing sectors favored by the new tariffs, the rate of investment in manufacturing plant and equipment would fall, unless a second factor came into play.

In the long run the rate of desired investment expenditures in manufacturing would be higher than the pretariff investment rate only if the tariff-favored sectors were more capital intensive than the pretariff constellation. Rough estimation would, however, suggest that this is a plausible characterization of the actual situation. The sectors most likely protected under any late-nineteenth-century tariff would be the older industrial sectors threatened by competition from Germany and the United States. Iron, steel, fabricated metals, and machinery were prominent in this group, and these industries were surely relatively capital intensive (Aldcroft 1968). If infant industry protection was also part of the hypothetical tariff package, it is useful to note that the new electrical equipment, automobile, and heavy chemical sectors were also relatively capital intensive. Thus, it is reasonable to argue that the U.K. trade policy probably meant a less favorable environment for domestic manufacturing investment than a policy of manufacturing protection. And, given the nature of the United Kingdom's aggregate savings mechanisms, this probably meant a somewhat higher rate of overseas investment.

The fact that a significant amount of the United Kingdom's overseas investments returned to it in the form of orders for U.K. manufacturing exports would not change this conclusion. In the late nineteenth century, three-fifths of the United Kingdom's overseas investments went to regions in Africa, Asia, Australasia, Europe, and South America with small industrial sectors that did not export industrial goods to the United Kingdom, if anywhere. Of course, a very large portion of world trade was multilateral, and so it is probably inappropriate to isolate one component of the potential demand for U.K. exports. That being the case, one must deal with the average capital intensity of the United Kingdom's manufactured exportables and importables, and since the average group of potentially tariffed importables probably involved more capital per worker and per unit of output, the conclusion stands that a general tariff on manufactured importables would probably have resulted in a higher rate of desired investment in manufactures in the United Kingdom and, in turn, a somewhat lower rate of foreign investment.

ANTECEDENCE

So far, two areas of evidence have been offered to substantiate the influence of domestic investment conditions on the pace of overseas investment in the long run. First, it has been shown that U.K. savings behavior did not supply every investment demander from home or abroad with funds. The U.K. rate of savings was responsive to investment demand conditions only to a degree. Hence, if domestic investment conditions slackened, the general lowering of interest rates would tend to encourage overseas borrowers. Second, in the previous section evidence was offered to support the idea that demographic and productivity trends in the United Kingdom tended to depress long-term domestic investment conditions. Evidence was also offered to suggest that the discouragement to domestic residential and social-overhead construction from demographic trends was more than could be accounted for by overseas influences on U.K. demographic events. No evidence was offered to suggest that the discouragement to domestic manufacturing investment was domestic in origin, but it seems safe to assume that British trends in scientific and technical education and research had local origins.

The purpose of this section is to examine more closely whether overseas investment conditions had a prominent *independent* influence on long-term domestic investment conditions. Thus far, it could be argued we have offered a hypothesis of a causal pattern and some evidence on domestic demographic and productivity trends to substantiate the hypothesis. However, a skeptical reader could easily wonder whether the implied long lags between these determinants and the long-term rates of domestic investment should not be tested with a more powerful spotlight than tables involving averages of selected ten-year periods. The fundamental limitation is that annual quantitative data on demographic and productivity trends are not available—hence, the reliance on decadal census materials that are often arbitrarily timed vis-à-vis economic phenomena.

The most powerful statistical tool available to examine the issue of independent influence is a technique called, perhaps presumptuously, a "causality" test (Granger 1969; Sims 1972). In fact, the causality tests devised by Granger and Sims are really tests of antecedence. Of course, antecedence is one part of what most historians would require for proof of a causal pattern. It thus seem appropriate to use these tests here. Because of the aforementioned data limitations, the explicit economic model of domestic investment employed in the Granger-Sims tests must be quite crude. As will become clear shortly, this limitation is vitiated by the strength of the statistical results.

The first task is to present the theory of the Granger-Sims tests. Next the prominent hypotheses of U.K. domestic investment causality are reviewed. Given data limitations, a crude model of domestic investment is proposed that permits a rough test of these hypotheses. Finally, the results of these tests are presented and conclusions drawn.

In brief, the antecedence tests strongly suggest that antecedent overseas investment conditions had a very limited influence on the pace of domestic investment either directly or indirectly by affecting U.K. savings conditions. The slowing domestic investment conditions discussed earlier appear to have been unambiguously domestic in origin. The pattern of causality does not lead back to overseas events; abating domestic investment opportunities had an independent stimulating effect on the long-term rate of overseas investment.

Causality Tests as Tests of Antecedent Influence   Recently, Granger and Sims have developed tests for what they choose to term "causality." Let X and Y be two variables that may be related in some manner. Assume that the current values of X and Y, X_t and Y_t, are influenced by their own past histories, owing to a process of lagged adaptive adjustment or the way expectations are formed about current values. Suppose interest focuses on the phenomena that may influence the variation of current values of X; two models draw our attention.

$$X_t = f(X_{t-1}, \ X_{t-2}, \ X_{t-3}), \tag{9.1}$$

and

$$X_t = g(X_{t-1}, X_{t-2}, X_{t-3}; Y_{t-1}, Y_{t-2}, Y_{t-3}). \tag{9.2}$$

For simplicity; it is assumed that only values of X and Y from the previous three periods can influence current values of X. If the addition of past values of Y in the second model yields a statistically significant reduction in the unexplained variance of X_t, then the hypothesis that Y is an antecedent influence on X cannot be rejected. Since antecedence is one part of what most historians would demand as a test of causality for any long-lived social process, it is not hard to see why Granger and Sims came to call their tests causality tests.

Nevertheless, the Granger-Sims tests are really only a test of antecedent influence. First, there is probably a large number of Ys that might be antecedent influences on X, some of which may be far more important in influencing X than the Y under observation. Jointly tested, the specific Y under observation might be reduced to trivial statistical significance. Second, there is the possibility that both X and Y are deeply influenced by Z and Z happens to influence Y before Z influences X. The point is that a full causality test consists of at least two parts, a logical model based on reasonable behavioral assumptions that suggests a potential causal connection between X and a specific set of Ys, and evidence that the path of causality runs from the Ys to X, rather than vice versa. Given the long-lived manner in which most economic pressures work themselves out, evidence of antecedent influence is a strong test of the path of causality. But both a logical model and the tests of antecedent influence constitute a full test.

Hypotheses of U.K. Domestic Investment Causality   The most prominent hypotheses concerning the causal determinents of U.K. domestic investment stem from the research over the last forty years into the long cycles of 15 to 25 years characterizing the pace of growth and development in the regions of recent settlement abroad and parts of the U.K. economy. Much of this research has given support to the view that both U.K. foreign lending and U.K. domestic capital formation were determined to some degree within the interactions of an "Atlantic" economy comprising the United Kingdom, Canada, the United States, Argentina and several other Latin American economies, South Africa, Australia, and New Zealand. For Brinley Thomas U.K. domestic investment was endogenous to this Atlantic economy, determined partly by autonomous U.K. demographic and investment conditions and partly by autonomous overseas demographic and investment forces (1972:137–39; 1954:155–90, 202–305). Abramovitz and Williamson would probably agree that U.K. domestic investment was endogenous to the Atlantic economy, but they would argue that, at least in its involvement in the long-swing rhythm of Atlantic growth and accumulation, U.K.

domestic investment levels were largely dependent upon autonomous overseas forces, principally through the mechanisms of a
relatively fixed U.K. savings pool (Abramovitz 1968; Williamson
1964:208-16).

Disagreeing quite strongly, Habbakuk (1962) has argued that
U.K. housing investment, the component of U.K. domestic
investment with the most pronounced long swings, was largely
dependent upon domestic conditions, quite unaffected by overseas demands for U.K. savings and labor, except in the late 1880s.
Hence, to the extent that overseas investment and domestic
investment interacted, Habbakuk clearly rules out a causal path
from overseas investment conditions to domestic investment
rates, although he leaves open the possibility that domestic
investment conditions may have had an influence on the rate of
overseas investment.

In testing the force of these and any other causal hypotheses
there is one very strong constraint, the availability of data. Annual
data are required on the demographic, productivity, and other
phenomena that influence the marginal efficiency of home and
overseas investment, and these simply do not exist.

A crude alternative is to assume that the behavior of current and
past values of U.K. domestic and overseas investment embody
these missing exogenous data. Annual data for these variables are
available. Thus, the test of the influence of overseas phenomena
on current domestic investment rates is whether net foreign
lending itself constitutes a significant addition to the explanation
of U.K. domestic investment in the Granger-Sims sense. If it does
not, then it is likely that the exogenous determinants of overseas
capital formation and U.K. foreign lending do not either. Of
course, the path of influence of overseas exogenous phenomena
might be through their effects on U.K. domestic savings rates, and
so thoroughness dictates that the course of antecedent influence
from U.K. net foreign lending to U.K. savings to U.K. domestic
investment also be investigated. Furthermore, since B. Thomas,
Abramovitz, Williamson, and Habbakuk were often concerned
with population-sensitive investment, it is important to investigate U.K. dwelling investment rates, as well as the aggregate
investment rate, for antecedent overseas influences.

The crudity of this approach is that current and past values of net foreign lending may not be the strongest or most unambiguous proxy for exogenous overseas influences. Few would dispute, however, that it is one of the best candidates. Atlantic economy proponents have argued that, since long swings in U.K. net foreign lending tended to lag behind long swings in overseas capital formation rates, U.K. net foreign lending was causally connected to the demographic and other forces thought responsible for the long swing in overseas capital formation aggregates and rates. Furthermore, Ford (1965) has offered evidence that U.K. net foreign lending booms led U.K. export booms; this strongly suggests that net foreign lending also captures the influence of overseas export demand on U.K. domestic manufacturing investment.

The Results In table 9.9 and 9.10 F statistics are presented for tests of Granger-Sims antecedent influence among U.K. gross domestic investment (GDFI), U.K. net foreign lending (NFI), U.K. total savings (GNA), and U.K. gross fixed dwelling investment (DW). Table 9.9 assumes there was no current simultaneous interaction between the X and Y variables; table 9.10 assumes there was. Since some of the lag processes under observation were shorter than one year, the tests of table 9.10 pick up any simultaneous interactions, as well as any antecendent influence of less than one year's lead. Unfortunately, it is impossible to separate out these two parts from the annual data.

Antecedent influence is investigated with both aggregate data and rates of saving and investment per unit of gross national product. Various lag lengths are also tested. The logic of the Granger-Sims tests suggests that, if the given length of the lag does not produce a minimum of autocorrelation, then longer term processes may be involved. In many cases lags of two years produce relatively low serial correlation according to the Durban-Watson statistics. Still, the inference of much long-swing theorizing is that rather longer lag processes are involved in the mechanisms producing these fifteen- to twenty-five-year cycles. Since Abramovitz (1968), for example, argues that long-swing turning points were the cumulative result of relatively recent

Table 9.9

Tests of Antecedent Influence among U.K. Investment and Savings
Aggregates and Rates, 1868-1913: Non-Simultaneous Structure

$$(1)\ X_t = F(X_{t-1},\ \ldots)$$

Alternative Models:

$$(2)\ X_t = G(X_{t-1},\ \ldots:\ Y_{t-1},\ \ldots)$$

		2 Year Lags		8 Year Lags		12 Year Lags	
X	Y	F	D-W	F	D-W	F	D-W
				Levels, 1868-1913			
GDFI	NFI	1.72	1.94	1.88	1.88	1.29	1.93
NFI	GDFI	0.96	2.02	4.89**	2.22	3.29*	2.08
DW	NFI	0.91	1.85	1.45	2.00	1.01	2.09
NFI	DW	1.75	2.12	2.14	2.09	1.71	1.90
				Levels, 1882-1913			
GDFI	NFI	1.54	1.86	2.50	2.10	1.22	2.43
NFI	GDFI	1.73	2.08	2.94*	2.02	3.63*	2.08
DW	NFI	2.36	1.99	1.29	2.04	1.42	1.91
NFI	DW	1.31	2.13	3.23*	2.09	4.60*	2.44
GDFI	GNA	1.76	1.82	1.76	1.99	0.59	1.97
GNA	GDFI	0.31	1.88	2.41	1.61	2.19	1.76
NFI	GNA	3.39*	1.83	3.83*	2.15	4.62*	1.91
GNA	NFI	1.37	1.89	0.57	1.96	0.54	2.52
				Rates, 1882-1913			
GDFI	NFI	0.86	1.89	1.28	2.00	1.37	1.94
NFI	GDFI	1.62	2.19	1.70	2.06	5.07*	1.83
DW	NFI	4.47*	1.81	1.88	2.10	2.09	2.04
NFI	DW	0.84	2.13	0.93	2.14	1.82	2.62
GDFI	GNA	0.34	1.92	0.95	1.89	1.24	2.02
GNA	GDFI	5.19*	2.01	3.14*	1.86	1.71	2.06
NFI	GNA	5.29*	2.37	1.09	2.02	1.88	2.10
GNA	NFI	0.38	1.97	2.06	2.14	0.37	2.20

Table 9.9 (con't)

Abbreviations: GDFI = gross domestic fixed investment, NFI = net foreign
    lending, GNA = total savings, DW = gross fixed dwelling investment.

Data Sources: See Appendix 1.

Notes: The F-test statistical measures whether the additional variables
    found in Model (2) significantly reduce the variance of X_t, unex-
    plained by Model (1). (*) indicates that the additional variables
    reduce the unexplained variance of X_t at the .05 level of signifi-
    cance, (**) at the .01 level. The dates are the observation set of
    the X_t variable, the lags of the right-hand variables going back 2,
    8, and 12 years. Values of the Durbin-Watson statistic above 1.82
    or so indicate the hypothesis of first-order serial correlation can
    be rejected at the .05 level of significance.

events, our tests for long lag processes are limited to lags of less than half the length of the full long-swing cycle.

In analyzing these results, primary attention should be given to the lower panel of table 9.10 dealing with the rates of investment and saving. First of all, the focus of this chapter is on the question of why the *rate* of net foreign lending rose in the third quarter of the nineteenth century and maintained such a high level there-after to 1913. Second, it is quite likely that some amount of simultaneous interaction between investment and savings pro-cesses was an important part of the British economy during these years. Hence, the assumed simultaneous structure of table 9.10 is the most appropriate testing ground.

According to the tests reported in the lower panel of table 9.10, the rate of net foreign lending was not a statistically significant antecedent influence on either the rate of gross domestic invest-ment or its dwelling subcomponent. Furthermore, there was no significant path of antecedent influence flowing via the rate of total savings. The rate of net foreign lending (NFI/Y) had no significant antecedent influence on the savings rate (GNA/Y), which itself had no significant antecedent influence on the rate of gross domestic fixed investment (GDFI/Y). In brief, the rate of net foreign lending was not a strong, long-term antecendent in-fluence on the rate of domestic investment, directly or indirectly. These results do not contradict the view that U.K. domestic fixed

Table 9.10

Tests of Antecedent Influence Among U.K. Investment and Savings
Aggregates and Rates, 1868-1913, 1882-1913, Simultaneous Structure

$$X_t = f(X_{t-1}, \ldots; Y_t) \qquad (1)$$

Alternative Models:

$$X_t = g(X_{t-1}, \ldots; Y_{t-1}, \ldots) \qquad (2)$$

		2 Year Lags		8 Year Lags		12 Year Lags	
$\underline{X}$	$\underline{Y}$	$\underline{F}$	$\underline{D\text{-}W}$	$\underline{F}$	$\underline{D\text{-}W}$	$\underline{F}$	$\underline{D\text{-}W}$
				Levels, 1868-1913			
GDFI	NFI	1.66	1.86	1.74	1.88	1.33	1.93
NFI	GDFI	0.74	1.94	4.48*	2.22	2.97*	2.08
DW	NFI	0.52	1.81	1.50	1.99	0.96	2.09
NFI	DW	1.91	2.08	2.02	2.09	1.71	1.90
				Levels, 1882-1913			
GDFI	NFI	1.93	1.73	3.45*	1.97	2.37	2.77
NFI	GDFI	1.28	1.94	3.66*	1.88	5.29*	2.41
DW	NFI	1.12	1.90	1.20	2.03	1.29	1.88
NFI	DW	1.16	2.04	2.89*	2.08	4.19*	2.41
GDFI	GNA	3.50*	2.19	1.38	2.04	4.23*	2.27
GNA	GDFI	3.91*	2.25	3.39*	1.67	17.36*	2.06
NFI	GNA	2.95	1.92	1.86	2.17	1.99	1.91
GNA	NFI	5.78*	1.98	0.77	1.98	0.47	2.52
				Rates, 1882-1913			
GDFI	NFI	0.44	1.65	1.64	2.10	1.44	2.01
NFI	GDFI	3.70*	1.96	2.05	2.16	4.99*	1.90
DW	NFI	0.54	1.70	1.51	2.04	1.93	2.21
NFI	DW	1.72	1.94	1.09	2.07	1.43	2.79
GDFI	GNA	0.75	1.98	1.74	1.93	1.99	2.09
GNA	GDFI	7.04**	2.07	4.15**	1.89	2.65	2.13
NFI	GNA	5.70**	2.34	1.96	2.09	1.62	2.12
GNA	NFI	1.38	1.95	1.04	1.98	0.32	2.22

Abbreviations, Data Sources, and Notes: See table 9.9.

investment or dwelling investment was part of an Atlantic economy. What they do show is that if there was an Atlantic economy influence on GDFI/Y and DW/Y it was either simultaneous or involved lags of shorter than one year or so. While overseas influences might have had a simultaneous exogenous influence or an antecedent exogenous influence with a lag of less than one year, the usual formulations of long-swing-cycle generating and interaction mechanisms hypothesize much longer lag processes at work. These views are clearly not supported with the data on investment and savings rates found in tables 9.9 and 9.10.[8] In fact, these Granger-Sims tests make it quite difficult to avoid the conclusion that Habbakuk was essentially correct; domestic investment rates were largely a function of domestic phenomena with little long-run influence from overseas events.

Although the rate of net foreign lending does not appear to have been a strong antecedent influence on domestic investment rates, the reverse is clearly not the case. The rate of gross fixed domestic investment (GDFI/Y) had a significant antecedent effect on NFI/Y through both short and very long lag processes. Furthermore, there is strong evidence of an indirect link between these two variables through the total savings rate (GNA/Y). GDFI/Y had a significant antecedent influence on GNA/Y, and GNA/Y, in turn, had a strong short-lag influence on NFI/Y. There are, or course, two hypotheses for how domestic savings and investment conditions might affect overseas investment through the savings rate, one through Hobson-like oversavings effects and the other through a fall in the rate of domestic investment's lowering the general level of interest rates and thus encouraging more foreign borrowing. In the version of the oversaving hypothesis that found support in chapter 8, the lag structure was fairly short. In the case of falling domestic profit and investment rates' being the originating cause, the lags might be short or long. The models of saving and investment incorporated in tables 9.9 and 9.10 are too crude to separate the influence of oversaving from falling domestic returns, but the presence of both short- and long-lagged antecedent influences suggests that neither hypothesis can be causally rejected.

THE INFLUENCE OF DOMESTIC INVESTMENT CONDITIONS ON THE RATE OF OVERSEAS INVESTMENT SUMMARIZED

The logic and evidence of this chapter strongly suggest that domestic investment conditions had an important exogenous influence on the aggregate rate of overseas lending. First, it was noted that the behavioral structure of U.K. savings implies that any hypothetical fall in the rate of domestic investment would lead to a rise in the overseas investment rate through a general lowering in the market clearing interest rate. Second, evidence was marshaled to show that long-term demographic trends were such as to have a generally depressing effect on the rate of population-sensitive investment. The birth rate entered into a long downward slide sometime in the 1870s, more than could be predicted by the influence of U.K. emigration to overseas regions. Demographers are in broad agreement that these years saw the beginning of the falling birth rate phase of Britain's demographic transition, a transition found in nearly all advanced capitalist nations at some point in the history of their modern economic growth. Furthermore, there was a long-term slowing in the pace of British urbanization, probably related to a plateau in the nation's degree of urban industrialization. Third, it was suggested that exogenous productivity declines, starting in the 1870s, largely due to Britain's continued specialization in profitable but old industries, and too little private and public support for scientific and technical education and research, led to depressing conditions for domestic manufacturing investment. Finally, in the last section crude but relatively unambiguous tests of antecedent influence suggest that domestic investment conditions were not strongly affected by overseas phenomena. On the contrary, the strongest path of antecedent influence found in these tests was from domestic investment conditions to overseas investment rates. Thus, in brief, domestic investment conditions had an independent, exogenous effect on the United Kingdom's rate of net foreign lending, their ultimate origin probably resting with the long-term demographic and productivity phenomena just described.

CHAPTER 10: ACCUMULATION IN THE UNITED STATES AND ITS PULL ON U.K. SAVINGS

One of the most important facets of U.S. accumulation processes in the nineteenth century was the massive rise in the rate of both domestic investment and savings. Measured in current prices the rates of gross domestic capital formation and gross domestic savings rose from around 11 percent of gross national product in the late 1830s to around 20 percent in the 1890s (calculated from Gallman 1966:24, 36). Significantly, because the prices of capital goods fell relative to other components of U.S. gross national product, the rates of *real* investment and savings rose even more steeply. Measured in 1860 prices, the rates of real gross domestic capital formation and real gross domestic savings increased from around 9 percent of real gross national product in the late 1830s to 27 percent in the 1890s (table 10.1). Since this important feature of nineteenth-century U.S. economic development was only recently discovered (Gallman 1966), such explantations as have appeared must be treated as tentative (Davis and Gallman 1978; David 1977; Williamson 1979). Nevertheless, sufficient data exist to examine the role of U.S. net foreign borrowing in the light of this massive upward shift of domestic investment and savings rates and to suggest certain aspects of its determinants.

Viewed in terms of national aggregates, the contribution of net foreign investment to long-term U.S. accumulation patterns was fairly small. Using ten-year averages to smooth out short-cycle phenomena, table 10.1 shows that net foreign investment was probably never greater than 1½ percent of gross national product, and it is unlikely it ever exceeded 6 percent of gross domestic capital formation. Indeed, for most of the years before 1900 net foreign borrowing was closer to 0.6 percent of gross national product and 2 percent to 3 percent of gross domestic capital formation. Of course, some 60 percent to 70 percent of U.S. foreign borrowing took the form of U.S. railway bonds and equity. But applying these percentages to table 10.1's data shows

Table 10.1

United States Rates of Gross Domestic Investment,
Gross Domestic Saving and Net Foreign Investment,
Price Deflated, 1834/43 - 1899/'08
(1860 prices)

Periods	GDCF/GNP (1)	GDS/GNP (2)	NFI/GNP (3)	MFGCF/GNP (4)	CONCF/GNP (5)	RWYCF/GNP (6)	NFRCF/GNP (7)
1834-43	9.7	9.1	0.6	2.1	7.7	.8	-
1839-48	10.6	10.9	-0.3	2.3	8.3	.8	-
1844-53	12.9	12.5	0.4	2.9	10.0	1.6	-
1849-58	14.9	14.4	0.5	3.4	11.5	2.1	-
1854-63	-	-	(0.5)	-	-	-	-
1859-68	-	-	(0.9)	-	-	-	-
1864-73	-	-	(1.5)	-	-	-	-
1869-78	22.5	21.5	1.1	6.9	15.6	3.7	2.7
1874-83	20.9	21.0	-0.1	8.2	12.7	3.3	2.7
1879-88	22.7	22.0	0.8	10.2	12.5	3.0	3.8
1884-93	26.8	25.3	1.5	11.6	15.2	2.4	4.6
1889-98	27.9	27.4	0.5	12.5	15.4	1.8	4.2
1894-1903	26.1	26.9	-0.8	13.3	12.8	1.0	3.0
1899-1908	27.3	27.8	-0.5	15.6	11.7	1.5	2.7

Abbreviations: GDP = gross national product, GDCF = gross domestic
capital formation, GDS = gross domestic saving, NFI = net foreign
investment (- = outflow), MFGCG = producer durables gross capital
formation, CONCF = gross construction capital formation, RWYCF =
gross railway capital formation, NFRCF = gross non-farm residential
capital formation.

Sources:
  GNP, GDCF, MFGCF, CONCF: Gallman 1966: 26, 34.
  NFI: North 1960: 605) and Simon 1960: 699-705   deflated by the
    GDCF deflator of Gallman 1966: 26.   The estimates in parenthesis
    for 1854-63, 1859-68, and 1864-73 are deflated by the Warren-
    Pearson wholesale price index; the GNP estimates are crude ap-
    proximations from Gallman 1966 and Davis et al 1972: 34.
  GDS: GDCF minus NFI.
  RWYCF: Fishlow 1965: 399 and Ulmer 1960: 256.
  NFRCF: Kuznets 1961: 576-7(6) spliced to an 1860 base with Brady
    1964: 111.   This estimate of NFRCF/GNP is probably an underes-
    timate but using the older Kuznets 1961: 563 GNP estimates pro-
    duces the same time shape, 1869-1908.

that the impact of net foreign borrowing over the long haul was
still fairly small; on average, around 15 percent of U.S. gross
railway capital formation was funded with foreign lending before
1900. Finally, note that table 10.1's estimates of real net foreign
investment are deflated with Gallman's U.S. gross domestic
capital formation price index. Since the price of capital goods fell

relative to other elements of gross national product, this deflator yields the maximum rate of real net foreign investment. Still, if Gallman's gross national product price index is substituted, the share of net foreign investment would be only a few tenths of a percentage point less.

Simply stated, U.S. net foreign lending is given no role in the small literature so far developed on the accelerating rate of U.S. accumulation in the nineteenth century.[1] In a study rich with empirical findings, Davis and Gallman (1978) ignore U.S. foreign borrowing. Williamson relegates it to one among many factors that are part of a small, unexplained residual (1979:244). David finds a role for net foreign lending in the "disequilibrium dynamics" of the Kuznets 15 to 25-year cycles that punctuated the rising secular trend of domestic investment and saving rates (1977:521). Relying upon earlier work of Williamson, David argues that there are two ways in which net foreign lending was involved in these cycles.[2] First, David seems to suggest that domestic investment demands were particularly subject to the Kuznets' long cycles, with the inference that any gap with the more stable savings patterns would yield an excess demand for funds, potentially fillable by overseas borrowing. Second, David argues that foreign borrowing alleviated the periodic pressures on the U.S. balance of payments created by long cycles in import demands. Foreign borrowing thus forestalled an early end to domestic capital formation long-swing booms stemming from these balance of trade problems. In sum, David's analysis gives U.S. net foreign borrowing a strictly cyclical role, and he clearly sees U.S. forces as the dominant factor shaping the size of U.S. net foreign investment, not factors in the United Kingdom or other lending economies.

The year-to-year variations of U.K. lending to the United States from 1870 to 1913 were investigated in chapter 4. It was there concluded the U.K. forces were probably dominant in determining these annual variations. Since long cycles were a prominent feature of these annual variations in the U.K. capital export to the United States, it seems unlikely David's view that U.S. factors dominated the long cycles in U.S. foreign investment is correct, at least after 1870.

Nevertheless, this still leaves open the possibility that U.S.

factors were the dominant force affecting the long-term shape of the flow of funds from the United Kingdom to the United States. A simple test of the dominance of U.S. factors involves the long-term timing of U.S. net foreign investment relative to U.S. domestic investment. If U.S. foreign borrowing tended to rise as U.S. domestic investment rates surged to new *secular* heights, one would be inclined to treat the foreign borrowing as having been pulled by some of the same fundamental opportunities driving the domestic investment rate's acceleration. If U.S. borrowing tended to appear during periods of stability or decline in the rate of U.S. domestic investment, one would be inclined to look for some influence originating in the lending country or move to a sectoral model of the chapter 4 variety.

On this crude test, the data presented in table 10.1 certainly suggest that, between 1830 to 1900, the long-term trends of U.S. foreign borrowing were a response to the surges in the secular upward motion of U.S. investment demand. On each occasion when the rate of U.S. real domestic capital formation rose to new heights, the rate of U.S. net foreign borrowing also rose. When the rate of real domestic capital formation paused in its long-term upward march, the rate of net foreign borrowing fell off. Put differently, the rate of gross U.S. domestic savings rose as domestic investment rates surged but not as rapidly, catching up to the rate of domestic investment only after the latter reached a new, higher plateau. It would thus seem that net foreign borrowing was part of a "disequilibrium dynamic," to borrow David's phrase, of the rising *trend* of U.S. domestic investment and savings rates. Crudely, U.S. real domestic capital formation rates rose more rapidly than U.S. real domestic savings, owing to explosive investment demand and/or slower moving savings desires, and the gap was filled by net foreign borrowing. Once the slower moving savings desires reached their long-run target, net foreign borrowing disappeared.

The story alters, however, after the turn of the nineteenth century. In the late 1890s the United States became a net lender on international account. Gallman's product and investment accounts do not go beyond the years 1899–1908, but Kuznets' twentieth-century data are widely accepted (calculated from Kuznets 1961:563–64, var. III; 572–73; 599–600):

	GDCF/GNP	GDS/GNP	NFI/GNP
		(percent)	(− = outflow)
1899–1908	22.8	23.8	−1.0
1904–13	22.5	22.7	−0.3

According to Kuznet's numbers, the average rate of real domestic capital formation slowed slightly after the turn of the century. The negative sign on the net foreign investment rate indicates that the United States was a net lender, but the drop in the rate indicates that the gross flow of U.S. borrowing was increasing faster than the gross flow of U.S. lending (see USBC 1975:867 for estimates of the gross flows, which are available for 1900 and after). Thus, contrary to nineteenth-century trends, the early twentieth-century increase in the gross flow of U.S. borrowing did not coincide with a surge of U.S. real gross domestic capital formation. Within the context of our crude timing test of the secular forces guiding the macroeconomic dynamics of U.S. net foreign investment, the implication is that this post-1900 borrowing was somewhat more at the behest of foreign factors than the pre-1900 borrowing was.

The microeconomic analysis of U.K. lending to the United States in chapter 4 modeled the annual variations in this lending on the premise that the circumstances of the U.S. railway industry, not the entire U.S. economy, were central to the U.S. side of the international trade in these securities. This perspective seems reasonable when one views the year-to-year variation of U.S. borrowing. Nevertheless, seen from the point of view of U.S. national economic dynamics over long periods of time, one cannot help but note that U.S. railway securities were second only to the U.S. government debt issues in their marketability. The factors accounting for their return and risk depended on broad industrial, regional, and national phenomena that were regularly reported in the U.S. and London press.

U.S. railway securities often involved some form of local, state, or federal subsidies. U.S. railway and government securities had very deep U.S. markets. Furthermore, the evidence, shortly to be presented, suggests that agricultural, mining, and manufacturing enterprise paid even higher returns for given risk than U.S. railway enterprise. U.S. investors probably had better access to the

specifics of local demand and supply for the small-scale enterprises in these sectors. Hence, a combination of excellent return
and better information would tend to favor the export of the
relatively less attractive but more widely based and known railway
securities. The fact, reported in chapters 5 and 6, that the average
realized, risk-adjusted returns to U.S. railway securities was better
than those on U.K. railway securities still stands; the point is that
U.S. farming, mining, and manufacturing probably offered even
better returns but local investors got there first. Thus, if the
fundamental long-term cause of U.S. overseas borrowing was an
excess of total U.S. domestic investment demands over total U.S.
domestic savings desires, the evidence and logic suggest that U.S.
railway and government securities would be among the most
likely candidates for international marketing. From this perspective, the secular macrodynamics of the aggregate U.S. economy probably had an equal, if not more important, role in
shaping the long-term presence of the U. S. in international
capital markets than the microeconomic specifics of the U.S.
railway industry.

The task is now to try to locate the fundamental pressures
influencing aggregate U.S. domestic investment demands and
savings desires in order to gain a deeper sense of the trend of the
aggregate secular U.S. pull on U.K. savings. As noted earlier, the
secular timing of U.K. aggregate net foreign lending rate involved
a rise in the 1850s and 1860s and the maintenance of a high
average plateau thereafter to World War I. What was the role of
the U.S. accumulation pressures in these U.K. net foreign lending
trends? Did trends in U.S. opportunities help to create a gap
between U.S. and U.K. returns and thereby induce the trend flow
of U.K. funds to the U.S.? Our crude test suggested that this
secular pull was strongest at various points between 1830 and 1900
and weakest from 1900 to 1913. To gain a more precise sense of the
timing of this secular pull, it is necessary to survey the secular
determinants of U.S. aggregate domestic investment and savings
desires. By tracking the net pressure of their determinants, it
should be possible to specify more accurately the secular timing of
the U.K. pull on U.K. savings.

The demographic and productivity pressures on U.S. domestic
investment rates are displayed in table 10.2. As before, the rate of

Table 10.2

Determinants of U.S. Domestic Investment Demand: Some Demographic and Productivity Indicators, 1820-1910

Period	Change in Tot. Pop. as a % of Initial Tot. Pop. (1)	Change in Urban Pop. as a % of Initial Tot. Pop. (2)	Immigration as a % of Initial Tot. Pop. (3)	Output per Worker Growth Rate per Decade (4)	Output per Capita Growth Rate per Decade (5)	Relative Price of Investment Goods (6)
1820-30	34.1	4.5	1.3	-	-	-
1830-40	32.7	5.5	4.1	-	-	-
1840-50	35.9	9.9	8.8	10.3	18.1	105.3
1850-60	35.5	11.5	12.1	17.1	16.1	99.2
1860-70	26.6	11.7	6.6	10.1	0.0	-
1870-80	26.0	10.6	6.9	16.9	27.3	82.3
1880-90	25.5	15.9	10.9	11.8	17.3	84.5
1890-1900	20.7	12.8	5.9	8.7	12.0	77.3
1900-1910	21.4	15.6	10.8	17.8	25.4	73.4

Sources:

Col. (1): USBC 1975: 8.

Col. (2): USBC 1975: 8, 12-13.

Col. (3): USBC 1975: 8, 105-6.

Col. (4): Davis et al 1972: 34, the output estimates for each date are really period averages, e.g., 1840 is an average of 1834-43, 1850 is an average of 1844-53, etc.

Col. (5): Davis et al 1972: 34 and USBC 1975: 8. Dating as Col. (4).

Col. (6): Gallman 1966: 26, 34, the price of investment goods relative to all goods (including investment goods) entering into gross national product. The relative price for 1840-50 is an average of 1839, 1844 and 1849, and the estimate for 1850-60 is an average of 1849, 1854, and 1859. The 1870 estimates are based on period averages with the same dating as the output estimates of Cols. (4) and (5).

gross producers' durable investment is assumed to be especially sensitive to movements in productivity, and the rate of gross construction investment, to population growth rates. In these U.S. data, producers' durable investment expenditures include railroad engines and other rolling equipment, which are usually treated as social-overhead capital and therefore population sensitive. However, these rolling equipment expenditures were only 10 percent of total railroad investment spending over these years and, with an eye to Fishlow's estimates of total railway investment expenditures (table 10.1, col. 6), it does not appear that any major distortion of the concept of productivity-sensitive investment is involved in its inclusion in gross producers' durables. In any event, as the U.S. railway system approached its mature shape in the late nineteenth century, it is plausible to think of the rate of railway rolling equipment expenditures as being increasingly productivity sensitive.

Both productivity- and population-sensitive investment in the United States were under strong upward pressures across the years between 1830 and 1910. In examining population-sensitive investment first, it appears that about half of its upward movement between 1830 and 1910 occurred between 1834–43 and 1849–58. After the Civil War its average is clearly higher but subject to large swings. Surges appear in the early 1870s and in the late 1880s/early 1890s. The jump in the antebellum period is easily traceable in the demographic data presented in table 10.2. Total population growth rates in the 1840s and 1850s were somewhat higher than earlier, but the key pressures were the rising rates of urbanization, immigration, and interregional migration. Table 10.2 amply documents the acceleration in the rates of urbanization and immigration during these years. Evidence also exists to the effect that these years marked the highest nineteenth-century rates of interregional U.S. migration (Easterlin 1960:136). The movement into the East North Central (ENC) region that had been proceeding at rapid rates since 1800 was still quite strong in the 1840s and the movement into the West North Central (WNC) region was accelerating. In the 1850s, the immigration rate into the ENC region slowed somewhat, but movement into the WNC region again accelerated, as did immigration into the West South Central

(WSC) region. Between 1850 and 1860 something like 8 percent of the U.S. population moved interregionally. As Easterlin's data plainly show, the interregional movement, the movement to the agricultural and mining frontiers, was also an urbanizing movement. The fastest rates or urban population growth appear in these regions of recent settlement (1968:192–93).

After the Civil War the rate of urbanization again jumped and the rate of immigration was somewhat higher on average. However, the proportion of the U.S. population moving interregionally between decadal censuses was now closer to 5 percent on trend (Easterlin 1960:136). Viewed in terms of the rate of gross construction investment, the rise in the rate of urbanization and immigration seems to have more or less compensated for the fall in the rate of interregional movement. More concretely, it is likely that this switch in the sources of population pressure on investment spending reflects to some degree the slowing need of the agricultural economy for urban transportation and processing centers and the increasing role of U.S. cities as sites of manufacturing production. Because of the urban bias of manufacturing production, there can be little question that post-Civil War construction investments were significantly related to the high and rising rates of producers' durable investment and the resulting enlargement of U.S. manufacturing production and employment (Davis and Gallman 1978:18–19).

Although economic historians of the United States are not in full agreement on the pressures affecting the rate of U.S. producers' durable investment in the nineteenth century, the radical drop in the relative cost of capital goods is a central piece of evidence regularly cited (Davis and Gallman 1978:25–30; David 1977:208; Williamson 1979:234–38). All would agree that the innovations and learning by doing in the U.S. machine tool sector described by Rosenberg were a very important element in this cheapening (1976:9–31). The effect of the new "American system of manufacture" was quite widespread because the new lathes, etc., touched every enterprise that needed to fabricate wood and metal, whether for consumer or capital goods. Brady's detailed price research into machine tool and other capital goods provides a dramatic record of these innovations (1964:159–64). To some degree, the rapid rise in the rate of U.S. manufacturing investment must also be ascribed to scale effects of the vast and increasing U.S. domestic market and to consumer substitution toward manufacturing goods as per capita incomes rose across the nineteenth century. Still, in any history of nineteenth-century U.S. industrialization and manufacturing investment, the falling price of U.S. capital goods must appear as a central force.

The determinants of U.S. savings behavior are well surveyed in a study by Davis and Gallman (1978:34-65). The authors find three influences were the strongest determinants of the rising domestic savings rate: the upward shift in the share of property income in GNP, the downward movement in the proportion of the dependent population, and the rapid development of financial intermediaries. The last influence is difficult to index. Table 10.3 provides data on the share of profits in GNP and the share of the population under 10 and 15 years of age. Indices of real interest rates are also presented.

Although some combination of the increasing share of profits and the falling dependency ratio appears adequate to account for the rise in the U.S. domestic savings rate over the periods 1839-1854 and 1871-1913, this is not the case for the years 1854-71. An illustrative example that owes much to Williamson and David is useful. There is little research on U.S. savings behavior in the nineteenth century, but research on savings behavior across today's Western developed countries has suggested that the elasticity of the gross savings rate with respect to the share of the population under 15 years is around -1.4 (Leff 1969:891). In examining the years 1839-54 with the help of table 10.3, this would mean that, for the 3.7 percentage point fall in the population under 15 across these years, the gross savings rate should have risen $(-1.4) \times (-3.7)$ or 5.18 percentage points. Assume still further that all U.S. savings were derived from profit incomes. This suggests that the savings rate out of profit incomes was 9.1/25.0, or 0.364, in 1839. Applying this capitalist's saving propensity to the profit share of 1854, 0.32, implies that the gross savings rate of the United States would have been 2.55 percentage points higher in 1854 if the profit share had increased alone. In sum, the assumptions on parental and capitalist saving pro-

Table 10.3

Some Determinants of U.S. Domestic Saving Desires, 1835-1897

	GDS/GNP (%)	Share of Profits in GNP (%)	Share of Wh. Pop. Under 15 (%)	Share of Wh. Pop. Under 10 (%)	Real Interest Rate on Railroad Bonds 1840=100 (%)	Real Interest Rate on Municipal Bonds (%)	NFI/GNP (%)
	(1)	(2)	(3)	(4)	(5)	(6)	(7)
c. 1839	9.1	25	43.9	31.7	100	–	0.6
c. 1854	14.4	32	40.2	28.5	87	3.26	0.5
c. 1871	21.6	34	38.7	26.4	119	9.48	1.2
c. 1890	25.6	36	34.6	23.7	76	–	1.2
c. 1897	26.7	37	33.9	23.4	31	–	0.0
c. 1913	–	37	31.5	21.2	–	–	-0.3

Sources:

Col. (1): See table 10.1.

Col. (2): Abramovitz and David 1973: 431.

Col. (3): USBC 1975: 16. Age structure data for the black population is insufficiently detailed before the Civil War.

Col. (4): USBC 1975: 16.

Col. (5): Davis and Gallman 1978: 23, Index A(1). The index for expected price change is based on an average of the current and seven previous years, employing arithmetically declining weights.

Col. (6): Williamson 1974a: 656. The c. 1854 and c. 1871 estimates are actually 9-year averages of Williamson's estimates of the real interest rate, centered at 1854 and 1871. The index for expected price change is based on an average of the current and two previous years employed (6, 3, 1) weights.

Col. (7): See table 10.1.

pensities suggest that the U.S. gross domestic savings rate should have risen 7.7 percentage points (5.18 × 2.55) when the actual fact is it rose only 5.3 percentage points. It is thus not surprising that real interest rates and the rate of net foreign borrowing fell over these years.

On the other hand, during the years 1854–71 the increase in the actual savings rate was 7.2 percentage points and the increase implied by profit share and dependency ratio movements is only 3.4 percentage points. Note that over these years the real interest rate on railway and municipal bonds jumped sharply. The implication is that U.S. domestic savings were sensitive not only to profit shares and dependency rates but also to interest rates. And net foreign borrowing does not appear to have been indifferent to the rising real interest rates either; NFI/GNP rose by almost 1 percentage point.[3] After 1871 the movement of U.S. gross savings rates is again overdetermined by the behavior of the profit share and the dependency rate. And, as in the years 1839–54, the real interest rate fell and net foreign borrowing eventually disappeared.

The strongest point of these illustrative examples is that parental and capitalist saving propensities provide a plausible explanation for the increases in U.S. domestic savings rates during the years 1839–54 and 1871–1913, but they are not adequate to account for the rise across the 1854–71 period. If, as the preceding discussion suggested, one assumes that U.S. savings behavior was interest elastic, then a possible explanation for the "unaccounted" rise in the domestic savings rate is provided. That U.K. savings were interest sensitive is already documented in chapter 8. However this is not the end but the beginning of a problem in historical explanation. The question is now through what social arrangements did the rise in real interest rates mobilize savings?

Davis and Gallman place considerable emphasis on the leading character of financial intermediaries. Clearly, the accelerated development of financial intermediaries was part of the rise in the U.S. savings rate, the part induced by parental and capitalist propensities, as well as the remainder. But whether the rapid development of financial enterprise was a leading sector or whether financial entrepreneurs and their enterprises were responding to the same forces that pressured the savings rate is a matter of dispute.

Davis and Gallman do suggest that if the deficit sectors of the U.S. economy—the railroads and the rapidly developing agricultural and urban settlements on the frontiers—had interest-inelastic savings functions and the surplus industries and regions of the Northeast and old South had interest-sensitive savings functions, the movement from surplus to deficit sectors would have raised the national savings rate (1973:452). Certainly the pace of growth and profit on the frontier, its towns, and its transportation links to the East and international markets could easily have strained U.S. frontier savings possibilities to the limit. The Bogues and Swieranga found very high rates of return in Illinois and Iowa land speculation during these years (table 10.4). Whereas their methods of calculating rates of return to speculation differ, the result is undeniable; land speculation received a return well above alternative government railroad, and commercial financial assets. Moreover, it appears from their calculations that the greatest returns were obtained in the 1850s and 1860s. It seems likely that lower risk railway equities and bonds would have an even wider reach in the East and South, expecially with formal stock exchanges already trading the issues of Eastern U.S. railways. The high rates of return in the West could also have acted as a magnet for persons willing and able to perform the essential tasks of linking the deficit and surplus sectors and regions.

Note that this discussion assumes that the main function of the U.S. financial intermediaries during these crucial years was to make transfers of real resources between surplus and deficit, regions, industries, etc. However, there is an alternative view offered by J. Schumpeter, among others, that argues that, when there was an excess demand for loanable funds, the U.S. financial system created money to be used by the expanding sectors. In the ensuing inflation, it was the private entrepreneurs of the expanding sectors and the banks who captured the benefits of the "inflationary tax." Of course, the banks could not do this endlessly without impairing their solvency. A general shock to

Table 10.4

The Return on Western Land Speculation:
Average Annual Realized Returns, by Year of Sale
(%)

Period	Illinois: Three Small Investment Groups (1)	Nebraska: One Small Investment Groups (2)	SC Iowa: All Large Buyers (3)
1845-49	8.6	-	9.9[a]
1850-59	11.0	-	71.7
1860-69	32.6	-	31.0
1870-79	12.9[b]	10.6[c]	6.0
1880-89	-	13.3	3.9
1890-99	-	8.6	-

Sources:

Cols. (1) and (2): Bogue and Bogue 1957: tables 1 & 3.
Col. (3): Swieranga 1966: 21.

---

[a] 1846-49

[b] 1870-77

[c] 1877-79

the economy brought creditors to the doors of the businesses and banks, and they might not have had the specie to stem the tide. A general collapse ensued, and perhaps ownership of the real resources created in the expansion was transferred to more solvent capitalists. Still, and this is quite important, new real capital equipment had been added to the nation's stock.

Although there are a number of logical and empirical objections to this idea of forced savings, these in turn have weaknesses. In any event, this is not the occasion to debate these issues. The useful point in this context is that the same forces that promoted financial intermediaries to make real transfers from surplus savers to deficit investors, that is, the gap between expected rates of return prevailing among these groups, was the same force that encouraged the private creation of money. Hence, we are again led back to the view that Davis and Gallman's financial intermediaries were less a leading sector than part of the process that responded to the disequilibrium rates of return in the 1850s and 1860s and thereby helped to raise the U.S. domestic savings rate.

Needless to say, with the United States and Great Britain having by 1840 a long history of international trade, short-term international finance, and some experience with a trans-Atlantic trade in the Federal and state government issues that funded U.S. canals and other social-overhead capital, it seems entirely possible that long-distance lenders from Britain would be drawn into these U.S. activities almost as soon as long-distance lenders from the East and South of the United States.

Great Britain's railway system was also expanding in the 1850s and 1860s, doubling its trackage and the size of its total real capital stock (Hawke 1970:200). There is some evidence that the expansion of these decades was into lines generating less profit than the earlier railway investments of the 1840s, but industry-wide averages of the return on real and financial railway capital show no sign of any downward movement (Broadbridge 1970; Hawke 1970). The ratio of net profits to cost of construction appears to have been 2 percentage points higher in the Western U.S. railway networks than in the U.K. railway network as a whole in the 1850s, and the average yield on high-grade railway bonds displayed a similar spread.[4] Whereas table 10.3 shows clearly that U.S. railway bond yields rose in the 1850s and 1860s, no such movement occurs with U.K. railway equity and debenture yields. And, backed by a largely undisputed body of data, Hawke asserts very confidently that "the ratio of net private returns to accumulated expenditure on reproducible capital . . . shows no secular downward trend (1970:408).

Other evidence suggests that U.K. industrial rates of return were steady during these years. The trend growth rate of industrial output was at its peak for the nineteenth century during the 1850s and 1860s, fueled in no small part by rapidly expanding export markets. Competition was quite high among U.K. domestic manufacturers. Church's survey of the industrial profit picture, 1850-1973, is somewhat pessimistic, but it is largely based on a very slight fall in the share of profits inferred from price and wage rate movements (1975:40-42, 50-51, 53-54). The scattered evidence on rates of return does not show a similar downward trend. Deane's evidence suggests the U.K. price of capital goods was falling slightly relative to other prices over these decades.[5] Hence, a slightly falling profit share is not inconsistent with the scattered evidence that industrial rates of return were steady. In summary, it seems very likely that, if the surge of U.K. foreign investment in the 1850s and 1860s was motivated, in part, by a disquilibriating gap between U.S. and U.K. rates of return, the gap was created by newly high returns in the United States rather than by fading returns at home.

To summarize briefly, the strongest secular pull on overseas lenders from the United States appears to have occurred during the period 1854-1871. The rate of population-sensitive investment was then responding to a strong upturn in the rates of immigration, urbanization, and interregional movement. Productivity-sensitive investment was responding to sharp falls in the relative price of investment goods. At the same time, the determinants of domestic savings were moving upward only very slowly. The percentage of dependent children fell and the share of profits in U.S. GNP rose, but neither movement appears to have been adequate to produce sufficient savings to cope with the augmented rate of investment demand. The evidence points toward a sharp rise in the real interest rate across these years as a consequence of the differential between these investment and savings pressures. The evidence also suggests that both domestic and foreign savers responded to this rapid rise in interest rates. At other points between 1839 and 1900 the determinants of U.S. domestic savings desires moved in parallel with the determinants of U.S. investment demands, and this movement suggests that the secular pull of U.S. accumulation pressures on U.K. savings was quite small. After 1900 the secular pressure of U.S. investment demand plateaued or weakened while domestic savings determinants continued to pressure the savings rate. The aggregate secular pull for foreign borrowing by the United States seems to have disappeared after the turn of the century, if not well before. Viewed from the other side of the Atlantic, U.S. secular forces thus appear to have been an important determinant of the shape of U.K. lending in the 1850s and 1860s, but there is strong reason to doubt their force at other times before 1900 and very definitely thereafter.

CHAPTER 11: **AUSTRALIAN ACCUMULATION PRESSURES AND THEIR PULL ON U.K. SAVINGS**

From 1861 to 1891 Australia sustained a major accumulation boom. Averaging 12 percent of gross national product in the 1860s measured in current prices, gross domestic capital formation rose to 15 percent of total product in the 1870s and jumped again to almost 20 percent of total product in the 1880s (table 11.1). The fall of the domestic investment rate in the 1890s was quite sharp, although the average rate of almost 14 percent for the decade was above the average in the first decade of the 1860–90 boom period. After the turn of the century domestic investment rates again rose but mildly. There was no trend in the ratio of investment goods prices to the prices of other goods across these years. Investment goods prices rose and fell with greater cyclical amplitude than the gross domestic product deflator, 1861–1914, but even this cyclical movement was quite mild. Thus, there is little loss in generality in using current price indicators to present rates of investment, savings, net foreign investment, etc.

Compared with the United States, the role of foreign borrowing in the nineteenth-century Australian economy was substantial. From 1861 to 1899, net foreign borrowing averaged approximately 5 percent of gross national product and a third of gross domestic capital formation. This was five to six times comparable U.S. rates for any forty-year segment of the nineteenth century. Of course, there was considerable variation in the Australian use of foreign borrowing over the last four decades of the nineteenth century. It was most important in the 1860s and 1880s when it was almost half of Australian gross domestic capital formation, but it was 20 percent to 25 percent during the relatively low borrowing decades of the 1870s and 1890s, again well above the U.S. peak decadal rate of 6 percent found in the 1834–43 and 1864–73 periods. Like the United States, however, Australia became a net lender of small proportion around the turn of the century with some erosion in this new position in the years immediately preceding WW I.

Table 11.1

Australian Rates of Gross Domestic Investment, Gross Domestic Saving and Net Foreign Investment, 1861-1914

(%)

Periods	$\dfrac{GDCF}{GNP}$ (1)	$\dfrac{GDS}{GNP}$ (2)	$\dfrac{NFI}{GNP}$ (3)	$\dfrac{MFGCF}{GNP}$ (4)	$\dfrac{AGRCF}{GMP}$ (5)	$\dfrac{RWYCF}{GNP}$ (6)	$\dfrac{GOVCF}{GNP}$ (7)	$\dfrac{NFRCF}{GNP}$ (8)
1861-69	12.0	6.8	5.2	0.9	1.7	1.8	3.8	3.9
1865-74	12.2	9.6	2.6	1.1	2.2	1.5	3.2	3.7
1870-79	15.2	12.4	2.8	0.9	4.7	2.1	4.1	3.6
1875-84	18.4	12.8	5.6	1.1	5.1	3.5	5.9	4.3
1880-89	19.9	10.9	9.0	1.0	4.7	4.1	6.5	4.8
1885-94	17.8	10.1	7.7	0.7	4.2	3.8	6.1	3.9
1890-99	13.8	10.1	3.7	0.5	2.5	3.0	5.4	2.5
1895-1904	13.4	11.2	2.2	0.9	1.6	2.8	5.4	2.4
1900-09	14.2	15.2	-1.0	1.1	-.6	2.5	4.8	2.8
1905-14	15.4	16.1	-0.7	1.3	1.6	3.3	5.8	3.3

Abbreviations: GNP = gross national product, GDCF = gross domestic capital formation, GDS = gross domestic saving, NFI = net foreign investment (-= outflow), MFGCF = gross industrial capital formation, AGRCF = gross pastoral and agricultural capital formation, RWYCF = gross railway capital formation, GOVCF = gross government capital formation (incl. RWYCF), NFRCF = gross non-farm residential capital formation.

Source: Butlin 1962: 6-7, 20-21, 30.   GDS = GDCF - NFI.

Australian economic historians have never doubted the importance of foreign savings in the development of their economy in the nineteenth century. There is dispute concerning whether Australia or the U.K., the predominant Australian lender, called the tune for this flow. Discussion has taken two forms. Some investigators have sought to find the set of systematic Australian and U.K. determinants of the *annual* variations in Australian net foreign borrowing over the entire time span, 1860–1913 (Bloomfield 1968; Richardson 1972). This evidence was examined in chapter 4, and the conclusion was that there was a rough balance of Australian and U.K. influences. Other investigators (Butlin, Hall, Boehm, among others) have focused their attention on what they clearly thought were the crucial few years preceding the deep depression of the early 1890s, a depression that lasted until the turn of the century, in part due to the drought of the late 1890s (Butlin 1964; Hall 1963a; Boehm 1971). Were altered U.K. capital market conditions or flagging Australian investment opportunities the principal cause of the 1889–91 weakening of the long boom? It would be impossible to summarize briefly the complexities of this discussion. In any event, our focus is somewhat different.

Our general interest concerns the secular conditions that led to the persistent net flow of funds from the United Kingdom to Australia in the decades from 1860 to 1900. As discussed in chapter 4, the year-to-year variations of this transfer probably tell more about what nation's individuals and institutions were most responsive to these secular conditions, not what created them. It is the latter issue that concerns us here. In particular, in this chapter it is asked whether there is evidence of a strong net *secular* pull of Australian investment opportunities on U.K. savers; can the timing of this secular pressure be identified, and can the relative strength of this secular pressure be metered? Having found some tentative answers to these questions, it will then be possible to assess the Australian contribution to the secular rise and high plateau in U.K. total lending, 1850–1914. As in the previous discussion of the U.S. case, we begin by separately examining the influences of population-sensitive investment demand, productivity-sensitive investment demand, and then domestic savings desires. Finally, these influences are jointly discussed to determine the net secular pressure for the involvement of foreign lenders.

Perhaps the best way to describe the secular shape of population-sensitive investment spending in Australia from 1860 to WW I is in terms of its three surges in the early 1860s, the 1880s, and the decade before WW I (table 11.1, cols. 7 and 8). Of the three, the boom of the 1880s was the strongest by far. Both railroad and nonfarm residential construction spending show these three surges and the preeminence of the 1880s boom. The *nonrailway* component of government investment spending (table 11.1, col. 7 less col. 6) does not have this time shape. It averaged about 2 percent of GNP from 1860 to the late 1870s. It then jumped to around 2.5 percent of GNP, which it held to 1914. This component of government capital formation consisted of telegraphs, water and sewerage, public education buildings, roads, and bridges, clearly population-sensitive-type investments. Yet none of these subcomponents had the time shape of their aggregate (nonrailway, government investment spending), suggesting that their joint long-term shape was either fortuitous or the product of political, rather than economic or demographic, currents. In either event, it is clear from table 11.1 that railroads and nonfarm residential construction were the largest elements in the rate of population-sensitive investment spending and dominated its trends. Hence, the following discussion focuses solely on their trends and determinants.

Like early railway construction in the United Kingdom and the United States, the major portion of initial Australian railway trackage and investment spending linked established population centers. This point must be emphasized because discussion of Australian railway investment spending tends to dwell on the fact that the Australian network was constructed and owned by the colonial governments (e.g., Butlin 1964). Presumably owing to this fact, decision making was influenced by political and bureaucratic elements, perhaps to the exclusion of economic efficiency. Furthermore, the power of the fisc meant lower borrowing costs, a more elastic market for its debt instruments, and perhaps excessive borrowing and expenditures.

All these factors are said to have been present to some degree in the "overbuilding" of the 1880s. First, as will become clear when nonfarm residential construction is analyzed, there were fairly strong demographic pressures in the 1880s underpinning any optimism over interurban transport. Here one might note the rapid growth of small towns because the railroad network was pushing more strongly into the rural regions of the country by the 1880s (table 11.2, cols. 2 and 3). Second, the critique of government decision making and unusual access to capital markets does not compare Australian experience with other countries. Clearly, the privately built and owned U.S. network, though sometimes aided by government subsidies, etc., went to cyclical excess on occasion. Furthermore, after the American Civil War a number of western U.S. lines were probably built ahead of demand (Mercer 1974). Finally, it would be difficult to make the case that U.S. railway companies were hindered in finding funding in the late stages of their surges even after the growth rate of their revenues had been slowing for some years! In short, there were probably strong demographic determinants for a railroad construction boom in the 1880s and, if the boom rode a bit long into the late 1880s as revenues waned, the fact of government tutelage needs to be only one element in the "overinvestment," and not necessarily the dominant one.

Nonfarm residential construction movements clearly paralleled the swings in population growth, urbanization, and migration shown in table 11.2. What is not comprehended by table 11.2 is the reason why there should have been a particularly strong boom in the 1880s. The rate of urban growth for eastern Australian towns with more than 2500 in population and the rate of international immigration were higher in the 1880s than in the boom of the 1860s. However, the rate of total population growth and the rate of urban growth for eastern Australian towns of 500 or more were similar in the 1860s and 1880s.

What is missing in these indicators of demographic pressure is the influence of age-structure shifts on the demand for housing in Australia, 1850–1914. Widespread nineteenth-century evidence in the regions of recent settlement and Europe suggests that the peak years of housing demand were the peak years of family household formation, roughly the ages 20 to 34. The Gold Rush of the early

1850s nearly doubled the Australian population and, most importantly, the Gold Rush immigrants were predominantly young adult males (Hall 1963b; Kelley 1968). After the mining boom tailed off in the late 1850s some of the recent young immigrants left the colonies but most remained. This left the Australian age pyramid with a very strong kink that, all else held constant, would age and through marriage and family formation reproduce itself. Of course, the kink would eventually dissipate as inevitable climatic and economic shocks delayed or extended the periods of family formation for the "kinked" group and its descendants. In any event, for at least a half century Australia was likely to have a strong ebb and flow of persons in the years of maximal housing demand, which, in turn, would influence spending on housing investment and the aggregate economy. If these induced booms in the aggregate-economy attracted immigrants, again typically young adults, the new immigration would tend to amplify the wave of housing demand. Table 11.3 presents Hall's data on the growth rate of those aged 20–34 in Victoria and all Australia at census dates, 1861–1911.

It is unfortunate that the age-structure data begin only in 1861 because the boom in population-sensitive investment spending in the 1860s was influenced importantly by the age structure of the Gold Rush immigrants. The Gold Rush of the early 1850s involved a very rapid increase in the total population, which was highly concentrated, by all accounts, in the 20–34 age group. Most of these young miners lived in tents with equivalently temporary transportation and urban commercial facilities servicing their mining fields. Only when the mining boom began to slow in the late 1850s did the population growth of the early 1850s begin to have an impact on population-sensitive investment spending of a more permanent nature. As noted, some of the recent young immigrants left the colonies as the boom ebbed, and this is reflected in the negative growth of the 20–34 age group across the years 1861–1871. However, the 1851–61 inflow was much larger than this outflow, and it is the delayed marriages and child bearing of this older inflow that were crucial to the high rates of housing and other population-sensitive investment spending in the 1860s.

Table 11.2

Determinants of Australian Domestic Investment Demand:
Some Demographic and Productivity Indicators, 1830–1910

Period	Change in Tot. Pop. as a % of Initial Tot. Pop. (1)	Change in Urban Pop. as a % of Initial Tot. Pop. 500+ (2)	2500+ (3)	Migration as a % of Initial Tot. Pop. Inter-national (4)	Inter-regional (5)	gdp pop. Growth per Decade (6)	gdp l.f. Growth per Decade (7)	grp l.f. Growth per Decade (8)
1830-40	171.4							
1835-45	146.9							
1840-50	113.2		37.4					
1845-55	184.2							
1850-60	183.0		68.1	140.7				
1855-65	75.3							
1860-70	43.8	28.3	20.0	14.6	0.4	8.2	40.7	23.5
1865-75	36.5			10.2	0.4	33.7		
1870-80	35.4	19.4	17.0	11.7	1.0	20.9	18.6	41.8
1875-85	42.0			18.7	0.4	6.6		
1880-90	41.2	30.9	26.9	17.2	1.2	4.2	2.1	25.1
1885-95	29.6			6.8	2.8	-20.7		
1890-1900	19.5	7.8	8.9	0.8	4.2	-9.2	-10.6	-45.4[a]
1895-1905	15.5			-0.4	4.7	22.8		
1900-10	17.5			1.1	2.3	28.4	24.0	82.7[a]

Abbreviations: gdp = real gross domestic product, grp = real gross rural product, pop = population,
l.f. = labor force.

Sources:

Col. (1): OYCA 1920: 82.

Col. (2): Butlin 1964: 84-85, includes towns of 500 or more in Queensland, New South Wales, and Victoria. OYCA 1920: 82.

Col. (3): Jackson 1977: 93, includes towns of 2500 or more in Queensland, New South Wales, Victoria, and South Australia. OYCA 1920: 82.

Col. (4): OYCA 1921: 1142, OYCA 1920: 82.

Col. (5): Same as Col. (4), gross regional in-flows less international migration.

Col. (6): (7), (8): Butlin 1962: 460-61, Butlin and Dowie 1969 141, 144 Butlin 1964: 194. Butlin 1962: 460-61, Butlin and Dowie 1969 141, 144 Butlin 1964: 194.
The rural labor force estimate links the relative movements indicated in Butlin 1964: 194 for 1861, 1871, 1881 with the absolute levels given in Butlin and Dowie 1969: 144.

---

^agrp/l.f had no growth from 1891-1911.

Table 11.3

Secular Demographic Pressures
on the Australian Housing Market, 1861-1911

	Decadal Growth of Pop. Aged 20-34 (%)		Decadal Growth of the Total Pop. (%)	
	Victoria (1)	Australia (2)	Victoria (3)	Australia (4)
1861-71	-22.0	-	35.4	-
1871-81	13.6	-	17.9	-
1881-91	81.0	61.4	32.2	41.1
1891-1901	-8.5	12.2	5.3	18.9
1901-11	9.1	21.4	9.5	18.1

Source: Hall 1963b: 50-51.

What emerges much more clearly from the age-structure data is the solid foundation of the unusually strong housing boom in the 1880s in the colonies' kinked age distribution. Using various simulation techniques, Kelley was able to separate the impact of the earlier immigrations and the immigration of the 1880s on the pressure for housing in the 1880s (1968:261-62). In the early 1880s the pressure was largely an echo of the Gold Rush-induced age-structure kink, but by the late 1880s perhaps a half of the demographic pressure came from age-structure shifts related to the immigration of the late 1870s and 1880s.

The major component of productivity-sensitive investment in Australia was capital spending for pastoral and agricultural activity. Investment in manufacturing was about 1 percent of GNP throughout the 1860-1914 period, and it is well understood that this spending was linked to Australia's isolation, rather than to any cumulating comparative or tariff advantage. For most of this period, mining investment spending was even less important than manufacturing investment. Hence, the following discussion focuses exclusively on pastoral and agricultural investment demands.

The rate of rural investment rose from 1860 to a peak in the early 1880s. The rate fell off slowly in the late 1880s and then moved rapidly downward in the 1890s. Unlike most other components of Australian investment spending, private rural investment spending shows no sign of recovery in the decade before World War I.

From the beginning of white settlement in Australia, wool was a major product and export.[1] Britain first began to import wool in substantial quantities in the second quarter of the nineteenth century. By 1850 imports were a fourth of Great Britain's consumption. Over the next twenty years the share of imports rose to half of British consumption requirements and by the turn of the century it was 70 percent. France began to import wool in a serious way in the 1860s. In both the United Kingdom and France, this shift to external raw wool sources was largely due to rapid technical change in wool spinning and weaving, which reinvigorated the market for woolens and worsteds. Although tried early, European sources of raw wool proved less elastic than those in Australia, New Zealand, South Africa, and South America.

According to Barnard, pastoral settlement in Australia ran well ahead of organized transport and communication. In some regions, however, transport provision was vital to occupation. In particular, "the clearing of the Murray, Murrum brigee, and Darling River systems for navigation in the fifties and sixties opened up large areas of New South Wales" (1958:11). Most of the expansion of the wool industry up to the 1890s was in New South Wales (N.S.W.), and in terms of soil types, both in New South Wales and elsewhere, settlement was in semiarid regions lacking both transport and regular water supplies. Occupation certainly was nationally successful; from holding around 20 percent of Great Britain's small import market in 1840, Australia supplied around 70 percent of the import market in 1900 when, as just noted, some 70 percent of British raw wool needs were imported. In addition, Australian wools held a significant share of the continental European market through the British reexport trade.

Most of the capital-using technical change to aid wool production in Australia came after 1870 or so (Barnard 1958:13–18). The expenditures were for light stocking, sheep fencing, vermin fencing, and artesian water supplies. Fencing, however, was first introduced in Victoria in the late 1860s as a labor- and cost-saving device. It also increased the percentage of lambing, maintained the sheep and wool in better condition, and made heavier stocking of the pastures possible. It spread rapidly into N.S.W. in the 1870s. Mixed farming and machines for compacting wool also had substantial effects on sectoral productivity in these years.

The rate of pastoral investment shows a clear parallel with the productivity growth inherent in these innovations (tables 11.1 and 11.2). Separating the pattern of causality between investment and productivity growth rates is always difficult. Nonetheless, Australian economic historians are quite clear that anticipated profits based on these new techniques were a fundamental motive for the pastoral investment boom that began in the late 1860s and peaked in the early 1880s.[2] The productivity growth trends reported in table 11.2 suggest some degree of "overinvestment" in the 1880s, but this ignores the fact that climatic conditions were abnormally good (Butlin 1964:108-9). In any event, the precise margin of economic cultivation in these semiarid conditions could be discovered only by settlement over several years. Thus, the excellent climate and the optimism fostered by the high productivity and profits of the 1870s go some way to explaining the limited fall of the rural investment rate in the mid- and late 1880s. Thereafter, the deteriorating productivity levels amply motivate the rapid fall of investment spending in the 1890s and the low plateau of the early years of the twentieth century.

Savings rates in Australia between 1861 and 1914 were characterized by a slow trend and strong long-cycle phenomena. The domestic savings rate shows a slow upward trend, adding perhaps 1 to 1.3 percentage points per decade over the long run. This upward trend was interrupted by the low rates of saving in the late 1880s and 1890s. To some extent this reflects long-cycle phenomena, which will be discussed later. However, the Australian depression of the 1890s was abnormally long and severe. Taking this factor into consideration may still leave a pause in the upward trend in the late 1880s due to long-cycle phenomena, but it strengthens the view that there was a strong, if slow, secular upward trend in the domestic savings rate from 1861 to 1914.

Overlying the upward trend in Australian domestic savings rates were two long cycles. From an initial low point in the early 1860s, domestic savings rates rose to a peak in the late 1870s, hit a trough in the 1890s, and then rose to another peak in the decade before World War I. There was a high degree of cyclical inversion between these long swings of Australian domestic savings and net foreign borrowing. Net foreign borrowing was relatively high in the early 1860s, fell off in the 1870s, strengthened in the 1880s as domestic savings rates were ebbing, and then fell off steadily from a peak in the late 1880s, even as domestic savings recovered after the turn of the century.

Although Butlin has written an excellent account of sectoral fund raising from 1860 to the late 1890s, it is fair to say that aggregate Australian savings behavior is underresearched (1964: 111-65, 245-66, 334-51, 376-89). The influence of shifts in Australia's age-structure has been explored by Kelley (1968:233-41). Yet data are not available on the share of aggregate profits in gross national product. Fortunately, Butlin offers some evidence on the surplus generated in the important pastoral sector, 1860-91. Existing Australian interest rate series cover different types of assets and do not extend over the full period. However, the London borrowing rate of the colonial governments is well researched. Tables 11.4 and 11.5 assemble the known data.

There can be little doubt that age-structure shifts affected domestic savings rates of these years in Australia. The kinked age structure discussed earlier in connection with Australian housing demand had a strong, if differently timed, effect on savings behavior. In the United States the pattern of age-structure change was dominated by the trend toward fewer child dependents. Changes in the proportion of the population in the years of maximal income and savings, often given as 40-49, were the obverse of those in the younger ages (Davis and Gallman 1978:52). Hence, the dependency rate was really a proxy for both less dependency and more savers in the U.S. case. In the Australian case this would be an inappropriate assumption. The heavy young male adult immigration of the Gold Rush years, the partial exit of the younger ones in the late 1850s and early 1860s, the jump in family formation rates in the 1860s, and the very long

Table 11.4

Some Determinants of

Australian Domestic Saving Desires, 1861-1911

Date	GDS/GNP (%) (1)	Share of Cash Surplus in Pastoral Total Cash Revenue (%) (2)	Share of Total Pop. under 15 (%) (3)	Share of Total Pop. under 15 & over 65 (%) (4)	Share of Pop. Aged 40-49	
					Victoria (%) (5)	Australia (%) (6)
1861	5.1[a]	26.3[a]	36.3	37.3	9.3	–
1871	10.4	34.0	42.1	43.8	11.8	–
1881	12.6	37.5	38.9	41.4	11.0	10.1
1891	10.3	36.1[a]	36.9	39.8	7.7	8.3
1901	13.1	–	35.1	39.1	9.8	10.0
1911	15.2	–	31.6	35.9	12.6	11.5

Sources:

Col. (1): See table 11.1 sources.
Col. (2): Butlin 1964: 98.
Cols. (3) & (4): OYCA 1925: 916.
Cols. (5) & (6): Hall 1963b: 51-52.

[a]The estimates in Cols. (1) and (2) are five-year averages centered at the given date except the first entries which are an average of 1861-63 and the last entry in Col. (2) which is an average for 1889-92.

Table 11.5

Australian Interest Rates, 1861-1911

(%)

	Gov't of N.S.W. New Issues in London (1)	Rates of Interest Charged by N.S.W. Banks			AMLF Charge on Open Acc't (5)	AMLF 5 Year Debentures (6)
		12 Month Deposits (2)	Over-drafts (3)	3-Month Bills Disc. Rate (4)		
1861	-	-	-	-	c.10	-
1871	5.1	-	-	-	9-10	5
1881	4.0	5	10	7-9	7.8	4.2
1891	3.7	4½	9	7	7.2	3.5
1901	3.2	3	6-7	5-5½	-	-
1911	3.8	3	6-7½	5.6	-	-

Sources:

Col. (1): Hall 1963b: 208, 5-yr. averages, centered at given data.
Cols. (2), (3), & (4): Hall 1963a: 134, rough point estimates for 1880, 1890, 1900 and 1910.
Col. (5): Bailey 1966: 60, Australian Merchantile Land and Finance Co.'s charge on open account at given date.
Col. (6): Bailey 1966: 60, rate paid by AMLF on 5-yr. debentures.

depression of the 1890s all meant that, even without the shocks of further age-biased immigration in the late 1870s and 1880s, the dependency percentage and the percentage in the maximal income and savings years would probably not move in a U.S.-like, inverse secular pattern. Rather, the dependency rate and the proportion in the maximal adult savings years might move in a less connected pattern. Kelly's work on the implications of the shifting proportion of persons in the maximal income and savings years demonstrated that, all else held constant, the shifts in this proportion led to long cycles in the savings rate but no trend (1968:240). The trendlessness of the proportion in the years 40–49 displayed in table 11.4 is indicative of this result. Hence, while the dependency rate might be affecting both the trend and the cycles in the aggregate domestic savings rate, it seems likely that the share in the years of maximal income and savings was influencing only the long cycles.

Perhaps the best way to capture the path of Australian domestic savings behavior is to emphasize its interplay with the secular course of aggregate investment demands. Starting in the 1860s investment demand rose to a peak in the mid-1880s, fell to a trough stretching across the 1890s, and was on the upswing again in the last decade before WW I. If one looks at domestic savings rates in the mid-1860s, the mid-1880s, the turn of the century, and early 1910s, the long slow trend of the domestic savings rate was well in evidence; that is, more and more of domestic investment demand was being funded by domestic savings sources and less and less by foreign savings. Importantly, the upward trend of Australian domestic savings rates was nicely paralleled by the falling dependency rate of the young and elderly.

Yet, as noted earlier, Australian savings rates and behavior were also subject to strong cyclical movements. In particular, savings rates were probably below trend in the early 1860s, in the late 1880s, and throughout the 1890s. They were above the trend in the late 1870s and early 1880s. Again, as noted earlier, since the cycles in the rate of overseas borrowing were inverse to these cycles in domestic savings rates, it is vital to see whether there were domestic determinants for these long swings in domestic savings.

If domestic savings rates were cyclically low in the early 1860s (when the data begin), the interesting element is that the dependency rate was also quite low. Ordinarily, a low rate of dependency implies a high rate of savings. The best explanation appears to be that the low dependency rate of the early 1860s was aberrent. The Gold Rush brought in a disproportionate number of young male adults. There are no age-structure data for the pre-Gold Rush population, but it is very likely that the child dependency ratios in the first half of the nineteenth century were at least 40 percent to 41 percent. It was a frontier, rural, and urban population with relatively little problem supplying its heirs with the principal sources of wealth and income.[3] Hence, it is not necessary to abandon the secular story of slowly falling dependency rates across the nineteenth century's causing an underlying upward trend in the savings rate.

Still, given the lurch downward in the dependency rate in the 1850s due to the Gold Rush shock, why were savings rates so low in the early 1860s? The answer probably lies in the cyclically low proportion of the population in the years of maximal saving (see table 11.4, col. 5) and the relatively low share of profits in national income during these years. Mining profits had been dropping off from the mid-1850s as the easily accessible lodes disappeared. Pastoral profits (table 11.4, col. 2) had yet to recover from the Gold Rush decade. The 1850s represent a pause in Australia's climb to dominance of the British raw wool market (Barnard 1958:218). It is not so much that money and men left pastoral activities, although some did, but rather, little new resources arrived in the 1850s and alternative sources of raw wool for Britain were available. In short, with a low proportion of adults in the maximal savings years and a likely low share of profits in national income, the savings rate of the early 1860s was well below trend, despite the aberrently low dependency rate.

By the late 1870s and early 1880s the domestic savings rate was probably above its long-term trend. Again, the explanation is a compound of age-structure and profit share phenomena. The share of the population aged 40–49 was at a cyclical peak during these years, and Butlin's data on pastoral surplus incomes leave little doubt about the radical upward shift of profit incomes in the 1870s.

In the late 1880s and throughout the 1890s savings rates were clearly below trend. The cyclical lurch downward in the 1880s and its further fall in the 1890s require, however, somewhat different explanations. Across the 1880s there was a radical fall in the proportion of the population aged 40–49, the maximal savings years. It is also likely that a falling national profit share contributed some downward pressure on national savings rates. Pastoral surplus incomes fell somewhat across these years, but more importantly the locus of national production and incomes during the 1880s was shifting toward government, railway construction, and urban economic activities, particularly residential construction, manufacturing, and service activities. Butlin's national production and income evidence strongly suggests that the wage bills in these construction and urban activities were a larger proportion of income-generated than in pastoral activities. Thus, neither demographic nor profit share determinants were propitious for a sizable advance in the domestic savings rate in the 1880s, precisely when productivity and demographic determinants of investment demand were still pressuring for an accumulation boom.

The proportion of the population in the years of maximal savings cycled upward in the 1890s; furthermore, owing to the sharp fall in real wages, there may also have been some upward movement in the national profit share. Nevertheless, as noted earlier, the length and severity of the depression and drought in the 1890s probably dominated these movements and kept the domestic savings rate well below trend until the end of the drought and the beginning of recovery in the last years of the decade.

It is now possible to draw the threads of Australian investment and savings desires together and analyze the net secular pull of Australian opportunities on overseas lenders, 1860–1914. Dominated by pastoral investment needs, productivity-sensitive investment rates moved into a long boom in the late 1860s that peaked in the early 1880s. Fading slowly in the 1880s, productivity-sensitive investment fell abruptly in the 1890s and hardly recovered before 1914. The innovations that permitted the opening of the semiarid regions of eastern Australia had diffused, reaching their limit with the falling productivity growth rates of the 1880s. Investment demands sensitive to demographic pressures went through surges in the 1860s, 1880s, and the last decade before WW I. Total population growth rates, urbanization rates, and international migration rates go some way toward explaining these surges, but these forces are better captured by focusing attention on the proportion of the population in the years of peak family formation and housing demand, ages 20-34 (Kelly 1968:263, 267). Owing to the kinked age structure induced by the massive inflow of young male adults in the Gold Rush of the 1850s, Australia was bound to undergo several waves of housing demand as the kinked age structure worked itself through at least two or three generations. However, the resulting waves of residential construction demand kicked off more general economic expansions. The general expansions tended to draw immigrants from abroad who, in turn, were also in the years of maximum household formation and housing demand.

While the underlying demographic forces pressured for a higher savings rate across these years, the same kinked age structure had what can only be described as perverse cyclical effects on the gently rising savings rate trend. In the 1850s and the 1880s the kinked age structure yielded a rapid increase in the proportion of the population in the years of maximal housing demand, 20-35, but a simultaneous decrease in the proportion of the population in the years of maximal savings, 40-49. The pull on overseas savings resources was thus quite strong during these two episodes but most strong in the 1880s.

The extent of the pull on foreign savers in the 1880s is worth careful note, for this decade was the high tide of Australian foreign borrowing in the century before World War I. First, on the investment demand side, demographic pressures were unusually strong. Whereas productivity pressures were past their peak values of the 1870s, the rate of productivity growth during the 1880s was at the same high pace as it was in the first stages of the pastoral investment boom in the 1860s. Second, both age-structure shifts and profit share movements suggest domestic Australian savings potentials were decreasing. Into this yawning gap came a massive British capital export. The movement was fairly rapid. Interest rates in Australia, for example, moved in lock step with British rates.

This discussion does not eliminate the possibility that a portion of the British foreign investment in Australia in the 1880s was insensitive to Australian profitability conditions. It only argues that there were good Australian grounds for both a strong investment boom and flagging domestic savings. Thus, some part of the British capital export response was warranted by the Australian macrodynamics of the 1880s. The argument that British savings were excessive is usually based on the view that there was overinvestment in Australia, particularly in the late 1880s. Whatever the grounds for this view, it must be balanced with the fact that Australian climatic conditions were abnormally good, fueling continued rural settlement and some urban develop- ment. The continued strength of settlement could have easily underpinned government railway investment policy, despite declining receipts. Certainly, the demographic pressures, aug- mented by recent immigration flows, were propitious for both residential and railway construction spending extending into the late 1880s. Still, the incremental productivity of some of these investments was declining (particularly pastoral and railway spending), and it is this that raises the specter that some of the late 1880s boom was insensitive to profitability and, hence, excessive.

The rapid withdrawal of foreign investment in the 1890s was also to an important degree based on secular Australian accumu- lation events. Australian age structure and productivity trends were such as to sharply curtail domestic investment demand. Domestic savings, but for the sharp depression and the drought, might have moved upward. The South African gold mining boom started in the 1890s and drew considerable U.K. funds, even as the U.K. was undergoing a domestic investment boom. It thus cannot be argued that good overseas ventures were missed by British savers in the midst of their own boom.

As the twentieth century began, Australian population-sensi- tive investment demands reawakened. However, the net pull on overseas savings resources was quite weak. First, although the demographic pressures on investment demand stemming from age-structural effects were positive, they were quite moderate. Second, the pressure on the rate of investment demand arising from the rate of immigration was at its lowest level of the entire 1850–1910 period. Third, the upward trend of the domestic savings rate due to the secularly falling dependency rate was reaching sizable proportions. Finally, unlike the previous periods, when the shifting age structure yielded a wave of relatively high demand for housing, the years before WW I display a conforming, rather than an opposing, wave in the proportion of the Australian population in the years of maximal savings. Thus, while population-sensitive investment demands rose in the decade or so before WW I, fostering a moderate upward movement in total investment demand, easily accountable increases in Australian savings desires appear to have met these augmented investment demands.

In summary, the net secular pull of Australian opportunities on overseas savings resources was strongest in the 1860s and 1880s, and more so in the latter than the former. After the turn of the nineteenth century there was virtually no net secular pull. If one remembers that the British overseas lending rate rose in the 1850s and 1860s and maintained a high average plateau from the 1870s to 1914, the net secular pull of Australian opportunities in these British trends seems clear. It helped augment the U.K. rate of overseas investment in the 1860s and was probably a strong, independent, and sustaining element in the 1880s. However, there is sufficient suspicion of overinvestment in Australia in the late 1880s to moderate any conclusion that the 19 percent to 20 percent rate of Australian domestic investment during these years had a purely domestic Australian origin. Granted the favorable demographic trends of these years, the falling but still high productivity growth rates, and the fortuitously beneficial climatic conditions, it seems fair to attribute one, at most two, percentage points of that 19 percent to 20 percent rate of domestic investment during the late 1880s to overly abundant U.K. savings. Still, and this must be emphasized, the vast bulk of the Australian secular investment boom that ended in the early 1890s was warranted by Australia's clear comparative advantages and its unique population pressures. In any event, there can be little doubt that there was no Australian net secular pull on overseas savings sources operating during the last big surge of U.K. foreign investment, which began in the early 1900s and ended with World War I.

CHAPTER 12: CANADIAN ACCUMULATION PRESSURES AND THEIR PULL ON U.K. SAVINGS

Apart from the United States and Australia, four international borrowers deserve study in any investigation of the net secular pull of overseas opportunities on U.K. savings in the late nineteenth and early twentieth centuries: Argentina, Canada, India, and South Africa. According to Bloomfield, the net international borrowing of each of these nations over the years 1881–1913 was on rough par with Australian levels and these four became more important borrowers from Britain as the flows to the United States and Australia tailed off at the turn of the century (table 12.1). Unfortunately, balance of payment data and national income accounts do not exist for Argentina, India, and South Africa over sufficiently lengthy time spans to permit an analysis of *secular* trends in their accumulation processes. Moreover, good time series of the demographic, productivity, profit share, etc., determinants of these nations' investment and saving rates do not exist. In the Canadian case, the data base is much better, although it is not as good as the data for the United States and Australia. The existence of the Canadian data, however, is crucial for our investigations.

So far, the U.S. and Australian evidence suggests that there was a strong secular pull from abroad operating on U.K. savers in the 1850s, 1860s, and 1880s, though perhaps less so in the 1880s in the U.S. case.[1] After the turn of the century, the evidence for a strong secular pull from these two regions of the globe disappears. Since Canada was far and away the principal colonial or national borrower from the United Kingdom in the twenty years before World War I, it is essential that Canada's experience be carefully examined for evidence of a strong pull in this era.

Investigation of the secular trends in the Canadian accumulation experience from the mid-nineteenth century to WW I is inhibited by two data problems. First, breakdowns of national expenditure into its investment, consumption, etc., components are available only for the years 1870, 1890, 1900, and 1910

Table 12.1

Net International Capital Movements for Selected Periods, 1881-1913
in Millions of Pounds

	1881-85	1886-90	1891-95	1896-1900	1901-05	1906-10	1911-13
Creditor Countries (net outflows):							
Great Britain	307.8	437.9	260.2	201.6	245.2	729.0	618.4
France	7.7	135.4	106.4	181.8	257.9	313.0	131.1
Germany	134.8	150.2	84.7	100.1	153.5	145.1	207.9
Debtor Countries (net inflows; -= net outflows):							
United States	53.2	214.8	80.5	-165.9	-150.0	48.9	-13.9
Canada	34.4	49.7	41.5	25.5	65.7	170.5	237.6
Australia	75.4	109.0	20.6	27.6	6.2	-38.7	18.5
Sweden	16.7	16.9	7.0	12.7	21.6	22.8	2.0
New Zealand	17.0	7.2	1.2	3.0	n.a.	n.a.	n.a.
South Africa	n.a.	13.7	25.3	32.9	81.3	-7.7	7.1
Argentina	33.0	133.6	n.a.	34.8	n.a.	n.a.	n.a.
India	n.a.	n.a.	n.a.	n.a.	38.6	55.5	19.6
Norway	-1.9	-2.1	6.7	16.3	15.5	14.8	6.8
Russia	47.1	-25.4	40.6	125.1	21.3	100.7	115.7

Source: All countries except Russia, Bloomfield 1968: 47; Russia, Gregory 1979: 382-83 for flow in
rubles, and Bloomfield 1963: 95 and Gregory 1979: 392 for exchange rate to pounds.

(Firestone 1958:248, 275). In the analyses of the United States and Australia, estimates of secular trends were based on averages of five- to ten-year periods and thereby reduced the variance due to minor business cycle phenomena. Fortunately, the author of the Canadian national product accounts, Firestone, also provides estimates of the rate of unemployment for these years, 4 percent in 1870, 5 percent in 1890, 4 percent in 1900, and 3 percent in 1910 (1958:58). By adjusting the analysis with these data, a better approximation to long-run behavior is possible.

The second problem with the Canadian data involves the detail of the investment expenditure data. Firestone provides a breakdown of gross fixed investment expenditures for two categories—construction expenditures and machinery and equipment expenditures. There is no further detail on residential construction, railway construction, etc. Buckley's 1955 study of Canadian investment expenditures is more detailed, but it starts in 1896.

These two problems combine to make it difficult to analyze the secular trends in Canadian investment and savings before the turn of the century. However, our interest is less concerned with pre-1900 variations in investment and savings trends than it is with the contrast between the pre-1900 and post-1900 years. In particular, we wish to understand the sharp rise in the rate of Canadian foreign borrowing after 1900; it is this surge that dominates British overseas lending in the decade or so before World War I started.

That an important break occurred in Canadian accumulation patterns around 1900 is easily verified (tables 12.2 and 12.3). For this purpose it is best to substitute the Buckley-Ankli averages for 1901–15 for Firestone's 1910 estimate. Too much of Firestone's 1910 estimate is absorbed by the highly unusual amount of inventory investment in 1910. In contrasting 1870, 1890, 1900 with the averages for 1901–1915, it emerges that the rate of gross *fixed* domestic capital formation nearly doubled. In current and constant prices the average rate rose from around 13 percent of gross national product to 24 percent. In current prices most of this increase took the form of a rise in the rate of gross construction spending, but deflation brings out an important subordinate role for the rate of gross machinery and equipment spending. Fire-

Table 12.2

Canadian Rates of Gross Domestic Investment,
Gross Domestic Savings, and Net Foreign Investment,
1870, 1890, 1900, 1910

Current Prices
(%)

	$\dfrac{GDCF}{GNP}$ (1)	$\dfrac{GNS}{GNP}$ (2)	$\dfrac{NFI}{GNP}$ (3)	$\dfrac{CONCF}{GNP}$ (4)	$\dfrac{M\&ECF}{GNP}$ (5)	$\dfrac{INV}{GNP}$ (6)
1870	14.8	7.2	7.6	7.2	4.6	3.1
1880	-	-	-	-	-	-
1890	15.5	8.6	6.9	9.1	4.8	1.6
1900	13.5	9.4	4.1	7.7	4.6	1.3
1910	26.4	13.4	13.0	11.3	6.9	8.2

Constant Prices
(%)

1870	14.6	7.1	7.5	9.6	2.4	2.7
1880	-	-	-	-	-	-
1890	15.4	8.5	6.9	10.6	3.3	1.6
1900	12.7	8.9	3.8	8.3	3.1	1.3
1910	26.4	13.4	13.0	11.3	6.9	8.2

Abbreviations: GNP = gross national expenditures, GDCF = gross domestic
capital formation, GDS = gross domestic saving, NFI = net foreign investment (- = outflow), CONCF = gross construction capital formation,
M&ECF = gross machinery and equipment capital formation, INV = inventory investment; CONCF + M&ECF + INV = GDCF.

Source: Firestone 1958: 100, 101, 248, 275.   The price deflators are
reset so that 1910 = 100. GNS and NFI are deflated by the relative
price of capital goods.

stone's estimates suggest that from 1870 to 1900 gross domestic
savings rates were rising and the net foreign borrowing rate was
falling.

It might be argued that point estimates from the years 1870,
1890, and 1900 are not the best dates for examining trends in the
net foreign borrowing rate. Hartland's five-year moving averages
of net foreign borrowing, 1868-72 through 1898-1902, and
annual estimates thereafter to 1913, show long cycles that peak
1871-75, 1888-92, and 1909-13 with troughs 1877-81 and 1895-99.
However, the pre-1900 downward secular trend in the rate of net

Table 12.3

Canadian Rates of Gross Domestic Investment,
Gross Domestic Saving, and Net Foreign Investment,
1901-5, 1906-10, 1911-15

Current Prices
(%)

	1901-05	1906-10	1911-15
GDCF/GNP	19.5	24.7	27.1
GDS/GNP	14.9	16.2	14.6
NFI/GNP	4.6	8.5	12.5
CONCF/GNP	12.1	17.0	16.5
M&ECF/GNP	6.7	6.9	7.5
NFRCF/GNP	2.9	4.4	4.3
RWYCF/GNP	4.9	7.6	7.7
POPCF/GNP	10.5	15.5	16.0
PRDCF/GNP	8.3	8.4	8.0

Abbreviations and Definitions: GNP = gross national product, GDCF = gross domestic capital formation, NFI = net foreign investment, GDS = gross domestic saving, CONCF = gross construction capital formation, M&ECF = gross machinery and equipment capital formation, GDFCF = gross domestic fixed capital formation (= CONCF plus M&ECF), NFRCF = gross non-farm residential capital formation, RWYCF = gross railway capital formation, POPCF = gross population-sensitive capital formation (= NFRCF + RWYCF + non-railway transport and non-transport government capital formation), PRDCF = gross productivity-sensitive capital formation (= GDFCF - POPCF).

Source: Investment data are from Buckley 1955: 129-39; the estimates of gross national product are those of Ankli 1980: 270.

foreign borrowing is affirmed if one employs Hartland's estimates (1960:718) of net foreign borrowing at the 1871-75 and 1888-92 peaks and any plausible guess about Canadian nominal income levels. While Hartland's estimates suggest a peak-to-peak rise of around 6 percent in net foreign borrowing, it seems likely nominal national product rose by 60 percent to 70 percent. In the boom years after 1900 both domestic savings and net foreign borrowing rates rose. Buckley's data suggest that, on trend, domestic savings rates rose earlier than net foreign borrowing rates in the post-1900 boom. Nevertheless, the important points are that there were substantial differences among Canadian rates of domestic investment, domestic savings, and net foreign borrowing during the 1870–1900 and 1900–1915 eras and that their radical rises fully warrant our attention. Discussion, as in the U.S. and Australian cases, will proceed by covering productivity-sensitive investment demands, population-sensitive investment demands, domestic savings behavior, and, finally, the net effect of these trends on the Canadian pull on foreign savings.

The division of gross fixed investment into construction expenditures, on the one hand, and machinery and equipment outlays, on the other, does not afford good estimators of, respectively, population-sensitive and productivity-sensitive investment spending. Railways require rolling stock, as well as road bed, and factories consist of both plant and equipment. It is impossible to make direct estimates of population- and productivity-sensitive investment from Firestone's data. Buckley's data from 1896 to 1915 do yield a good estimator of population-sensitive investment, leaving productivity-sensitive investment as the residual from gross fixed investment. And by employing a number of ratios from Buckley's data, it is also possible to guess at the size of these variables before 1900. On this crude basis, it would appear that the rate of productivity-sensitive investment spending rose from around 5 percent of gross national product, 1870–1900, to 8.2 percent, 1900–1915. Over the same periods, the rate of population-sensitive investment spending rose from 7½ percent to 15 percent of gross national product. However, once it is necessary to discuss the components of each of these rates, the paucity of the data forces us back to the approximation afforded by the rates of machinery and construction spending for, respectively, productivity- and population-sensitive investment.

In constant prices the rate of gross machinery and equipment spending rose from around 3 percent of gross national product before 1900 to around 7 percent in the years 1900–1915. All components of machinery and equipment spending increased, but the rate of spending on industrial, electrical, and mining machinery and equipment moved up faster than other components (Buckley 1955:132). Farm machinery and equipment spending, which claimed a third of gross machinery and equipment expenditures in the initial years of the boom, 1896-1900, fell to between a fifth and a fourth in the years 1911-15.

Most Canadian economic historians attribute the beginning of the pre-WW I boom, and an important sustaining influence, to the rapid expansion of the wheat economy in the Canadian plains that started in the late 1890s.[2] A steadily increasing international demand for wheat, the approach of full utilization of more fertile regions of the United States and Argentina plus pressures to substitute more profitable crops in closer proximity to burgeoning urban markets, and the introduction of heartier seed varieties suitable for the Dakotas and the Canadian plains all contributed to the settlement boom. According to Firestone, the 1890s were marked by a sharp rise in agricultural productivity, but a distinctly slower productivity growth rate appeared during the years 1900-1910 (table 12.4). Thus, it is not surprising that Buckley's data show that the percentages of gross agricultural machinery and equipment spending in gross national product were as follows (1955:132, 135):

1896-1900	1.5
1901-5	2.1
1906-10	1.8
1911-15	1.7

In manufacturing there is little evidence of a rising rate of productivity in the 1890s or 1900s to support the sector's augmented rate of capital spending. Although the value of fixed plant and equipment in constant dollars per worker rose from $1,112 in 1890, to $1,365 in 1900, and then again to $2,044 in 1910, real value added per worker in manufacturing rose only 6.5 percent, 1890-1900, and 3.5 percent, 1900-1910.[3] The explanation for the augmented investment rate in manufacturing would appear to lie elsewhere.

First, Canadian patent and tariff laws were written to ensure that a sizable proportion of any rising demand for manufactures would be satisfied by Canadian production. The Canadian Patent Acts of 1872 and 1903 made it very difficult to claim patent rights

Table 12.4

Determinants of Canadian Domestic Investment Demand,
1851-1911

Demographic Indicators

	Change in Tot. Pop. as a % of Initial Tot. Pop. (1)	Change in Urban Pop. as a % of Initial Tot. Pop. (2)	Net Int. Immigrat. as a % of Initial Tot. Pop. (3)	Growth Rate of Pop. Aged 20-34 (4)
1851-61	32.6	-	7.5	38.0
1861-71	14.2	-	-8.5	12.3
1871-81	17.2	10.5	-3.2	21.3
1881-91	11.7	9.9	-6.5	15.9
1891-1901	11.1	9.9	-5.0	9.2
1901-11	34.2	23.7	17.4	47.2

Productivity Indicators

	gnp/pop (5)	gnp/n (6)	gap/n (7)	gmfgp/n (8)	gminp/n (9)
			(% growth per decade)		
1870-80	15.7	13.1	8.7	9.4	-
1880-90	19.8	13.2	13.2	34.8	5.7
1890-1900	19.0	18.1	40.8	6.5	82.5
1900-10	26.8	10.5	5.3	3.5	-1.2

Abbreviations: gnp = real gross national product, gap = real value-added in agriculture, gmfqp = real value-added in manufacturing, gminp = real value-added in mining, pop = population, n = persons working.

Sources:
Cols. (1) - (4): Urquhart and Buckley 1965: 14, 16, 25.
Col. (5): Firestone 1958: 240, 275.
Col. (6): Firestone 1958: 58, 275.
Col. (7): Firestone 1958: 199.
Col. (8): Firestone 1958: 221.
Col. (9): Firestone 1958: 184, 281, 304.

in Canada without local production. The tariff of 1879 and its revision in 1897 were clearly intended to foster and expand Canadian manufacturing against British, American, and other competition. From this perspective, the rising rate of manufacturing investment in the late 1890s and thereafter was probably more strongly linked to the rapidly increasing size of Canadian total product and population, and possibly the 1897 tariff revision, rather than to an increasing comparative advantage based on Canadian productivity growth.

Canadian capital and entrepreneurs were not alone in reading the profit prospects embedded in the altered political economy. Given the Canadian patent law and tariff protection, particularly the revision of 1897, which had a built-in British preference, direct investment by American manufacturing and mining corporations in Canadian plant and equipment was the only way the Americans could hold and expand their large Canadian markets (Wilkins 1970:142-45). Again, particular Canadian productivity strengths probably did not have much to do with U.S. direct investment plans (Wilkins 1970:76-77, 87-88, 91, 97, 103, 142-46). The motivation was simply to gain as large a share of the expanding Canadian market as possible; that is, the motivation was partly a preemptive one. Wilkins notes that both Canadian and American savings participated in the establishment of these American manufacturing firms north of the border; indeed, there was no sign that funds were scarce in the least (1970:147).

In mining, a sharp rise in productivity occurred in the 1890s, and then, rather strikingly, productivity growth was slightly negative across the years 1900-1910 (table 12.4). It could be that augmented capital and labor inputs in this industry were so plentiful that the industry was driven to diminishing returns. If so, one might question whether here too financial resources might not have been somewhat overabundant.

To summarize, productivity considerations appear to have had some influence on augmented investment rates in agriculture and mining. With regard to the increased rate of manufacturing investment, patent laws, tariff rates, American corporate investment strategies, and the burgeoning size of the Canadian market appear to have been the prime motivators, not enhanced productivity growth rates. Finally, the evidence that productivity levels were largely unaffected by the investment rate in manufacturing and that diminishing returns were a result of augmented spending in mining raises the strong possibility that funds for these sectors were certainly not scarce and may have been, at least in some sense, overabundant.

As noted earlier, a rough calculation would suggest that the rate of population-sensitive investment in Canada rose from around 7 percent to 8 percent, 1870–1900, to 14 percent, 1900–1915. Nonfarm residential construction and railway investment expenditures were the most important elements in this increase. The demographic data are uniform in suggesting a basis for the pre- and post-1900 behavior of nonfarm residential construction. The growth rate of total population, the international net migration rate, the decadal change in the urban population, and the growth rate of the population in the years of maximal family formation and housing demand all show a dramatic rise after 1900.

It is interesting to contrast these Canadian boom data for 1900–1915 with the Australian boom experience during the 1880s. All indicators of Australian demographic pressure for the 1880s were at a higher pitch than the Canadian ones for the 1900–1915 era. The largest differential was between the rates of growth of those in the years of maximal housing demand in the two countries while the smallest differential was between their boom years' rates of international migration. It was Buckley's impression that the key Canadian demographic indicator was the rate of international migration, since this was the best indicator of the spatial redistribution of the Canadian population, to the Western prairie, and to the cities in both the West and East (1955:44, 47). The fact that the Australian rate of nonfarm residential construction in the 1880s was 4.8 percent of gross national product while the Canadian rate for 1906–15 was 4.4 percent, only slightly lower, tends to bear out his insight.

Although the jump in the Canadian rate of nonfarm residential investment spending at the turn of the century appears to be well linked to the period's augmented demographic pressures, the same cannot be said of the rapid increase in the rate of railway investment spending. Clearly, the increased demographic pressure from the surging prairie and urban economies would have led to some increase in the national rate of railway investment spending and in transportation and communication expenditures. But the 7 percent to 8 percent rate of Canadian railway investment spending, 1906–15, has no precedent in either the United States or Australian case, for any decade of the nineteenth or early twentieth century. Comparing the various indices of Canadian demographic pressure during the 1900–1915 era with

U.S. and Australian data shows several periods of similar levels of U.S. and Australian demographic pressures. Yet neither the United States nor Australia ever generated decadal rates of railway investment above 5 percent.

A major portion of Canadian railway expenditures during the early twentieth century went to finance Canada's second and third transcontinental railways. The guiding force behind these expenditures was the persistent lobbying of railway construction interests and the decisions of the Canadian Parliament, not private investment decisions. Following a long line of Canadian economic historians, Ankli remarks, "there is no question but that a second transcontinental was needed, but it was questioned even then if a third line was necessary (especially by the opposition to the government) and most certainly the National Transcontinental between Winnipeg and Moncton, New Brunswick, would never have been built if the government had not done it itself" (1980:259-60). In a leading textbook of Canadian economic history, Easterbrook and Aitken note that there was "an atmosphere of optimism and nationalistic self-confidence in which these later transcontinentals were born; it was not an atmosphere that encouraged precise calculation of risks and returns, nor perhaps, with the knowledge and experience available, would attempts at calculations of this kind have yielded unambiguous counsel" (1956:443). Yet they go on to say:

The alternatives that were in fact open between 1900 and 1905 received very inadequate consideration. Granted that the national interest required one transcontinental railway north of Lake Superior, did it require three? Granted that the Canadian Pacific Railway's monopoly in the west presented certain dangers, were the possibilities of government regulation fully explored? Granted even the desirability of competition in through traffic, would not one strong competitor, adequately equipped with feeders and branch lines in the east and west, have proved at least as effective as two weak ones? . . . The impression that remains is one of haste and overconfidence, of large commitments assumed with little deliberation . . . (1956:443-44).

That these lines were not self-supporting once built is attested to by the fact that after 1910, when agricultural exports from the prairies were a major force in Canadian aggregate growth, both lines faced bankruptcy. And in 1920 both lines were government owned.

The cash and credit offered by the Canadian government to these two transcontinentals in the crucial years between 1905 and 1915 amounted to perhaps a quarter of railway gross capital formation (Buckley 1955:71, 136). Furthermore, since government land grants, interest guarantees, and dividend guarantees characterized much of the privately raised capital, this rough estimate of the impact of government decisions on the extent of railway spending is probably an underestimate.

That there was little constraint on these ambitious plans and expenditures from Canadian and overseas capital markets is widely agreed upon by Canadian economic historians. As Buckley remarked, "government intervention rather than the profitability of railroading in Canada was responsible for the large flows of foreign capital attracted to the railway field" (1955:34). The dividend and interest guarantees, the land grants, and the Canadian government's own expenditures fostered the feeling that Canadian railway equity and debentures were a very sound venture.

Yet one point that must be added to this assessment is that the same means of attracting local and overseas funds were often used by the state and national governments in Australia and the United States, in many cases involving railway lines with far better immediate revenue prospects, without eliciting quite the same response from the United Kingdom's capital markets. The comparative evidence strongly suggests that there was a large amount of U.K. savings during these years that was somewhat unconcerned with return and risk, needing only the hint of Dominion guarantees to drown Canada with sterling. Thus, it is not enough to point to the Canadian government's debt guarantees, to rationalize the unusual flow of U.K. savings into Canadian railways after the turn of the nineteenth century. The yields of Canadian government and railway securities being at the lower end of the spectrum of U.K. home and overseas returns, one cannot escape the strong suspicion that the supply of U.K. savings to Canada was overabundant and in its absence the rate of Canadian railway investment spending would have been considerably smaller.

Like the domestic investment rate, the Canadian gross domestic savings rate jumped around the turn of the century. From 1870 to 1890 the gross domestic savings rate rose gently from around 7 percent to 9 percent of gross national product.[4] Then, the gross domestic savings rate sharply increased to 14.9 percent, 1901-5, moved up again to 16.2 percent, 1906-10, and fell back to 14.6 percent, 1911-15. After the turn of the century government deficits became sizable for the first time. This meant that the gross domestic *private* savings rate varied somewhat from the gross *total* domestic savings rate. According to Buckley's data on government investment and saving, the gross domestic private savings rate averaged 14.1 percent for 1901-5, 16.3 percent for 1906-10, and 17.3 percent for 1911-15 (1955:63).

The demographic determinants of savings behavior give slight indication of this dramatic rise in Canadian savings rates in the early twentieth century (table 12.5). From 1851 to 1911, the proportion of the population under 15 had a fairly steady downward trend. Child dependency was trending downward, presumably permitting an increased savings rate. But there was

Table 12.5

Some Determinants of Canadian Domestic Saving Desires,
1851-1911

Date	Share of Total Pop. under 15 (%) (1)	Share of Total Pop. under 15 & over 65 (%) (2)	Share of Total Pop. Aged 40-49 (%) (3)	Share of Wage Incomes in Manufacturing Value-Added (%) (4)
1851	45.0	47.8	7.5	-
1861	42.4	45.4	7.6	-
1871	41.6	45.3	8.1	50.0
1881	38.7	42.8	8.5	53.6
1891	36.0	40.5	8.9	52.9
1901	34.4	37.6	10.0	48.9
1911	33.0	37.7	10.1	42.1

Sources:
   Cols. (1) - (3): Urquhart and Buckley 1965: 16.
   Col. (4): Firestone 1958: 207, 221.

no sharp drop in child dependency after 1890 or 1900 to explain the post-1900 behavior of the savings rate. If one adds the proportion of the population over 65 to the proportion under 15, the drop in the proportion of child and elderly dependents from 1891 to 1901 was certainly the biggest for the 1851–1911 period. However, the 1891–1901 drop was only slightly larger than the decreases of 1851–61 and 1871–81. Across the years 1891–1901, the proportion of the population 40–49, the years of maximal savings, registered its biggest increase, but again the increase is not so different from previous decadal changes as to rationalize the sharp post-1900 increase in the savings rate.

Suppose, for the moment, that the only influences on Canadian savings rates, 1870–1900, were demographic ones. If one accepts that the demographic determinants did shift somewhat more than previously across the years 1891–1901 and their effect on savings took some time, the Canadian gross domestic savings rate might have been 10 percent to 11 percent by 1910. Given that the gross domestic savings rate averaged 15.2 percent, 1901–15, and the gross domestic private savings rate averaged 15.9 percent over the same years, the bulk of the shift in the Canadian savings rate after the turn of the century remains to be explained.

At least one important element that is likely to have influenced the surge of the savings rate after 1900 is the share of national income accruing to the owners of land and capital. There are no aggregate national data on the shares of Canadian national income going to wages, profits, rents, etc., before World War I. Nevertheless, data from the manufacturing and agricultural sectors give strong testimony for a significant upward shift in the share of nonwage incomes after 1890, most of the shift occurring after 1900.

Firestone found that, between 1890 and 1910, the share of wages in manufacturing value added fell from 52.9 percent to 42.1 percent (1958:207). The share of manufacturing value added in gross national product remained fairly stable, 1890–1910, at between a fifth and a quarter. Thus, the shift toward nonwage incomes in manufacturing represented an increase of 2 percentage points of gross national product.

The *proximal* cause of this movement in nonwage incomes in manufacturing was that the individual worker did not do very well during the turn-of-the-century boom. Nominal hourly wage rates and annual earnings both advanced between 1890 and 1910 but not by very much (Firestone 1958:207). Real hourly wage rates and real annual earnings also advanced very little, if at all. Indeed, real wage rates and annual earnings probably rose to 1900 and then fell back very close to 1890 levels by 1910. This pattern suggests that the heavy post-1900 immigration may have held wages down, but, as noted earlier, average productivity in manufacturing did not advance very much between 1890 and 1910, and so the situation was probably more complicated than first meets the eye.

Whatever the causes of this movement, it seems unlikely that wage rates could fall behind in manufacturing during the boom without this phenomenon's being somewhat more widespread. Firestone's data on wage costs, employment, and value added in construction tend to confirm this inference. The approximation is crude, but his data indicate that the construction wage bill doubled between 1890 and 1910 while value added in construction tripled (1958:185, 281, 304).

Canadian economic historians have produced several estimates of the amount of rent generated by prairie agriculture in 1901 and 1911 in connection with estimating the impact of the period's wheat economy boom (see footnote 2). Perhaps the best estimates of the actual change in prairie rents are those constructed by Bertram, who decapitalized the census' valuations of land in 1901 and 1911 with average mortage interest rates. This method suffers from limited mortgage interest rate evidence, but it avoids the more serious problem of ignoring share tendency rents that results from employing the Census' cash rental data. On this basis, Bertram found that rents increased from $9.6 million in 1901 to $98.6 million in 1911 (1973:548). By using Firestone's gross national product estimates, it appears that prairie rents rose from 0.9 percent to 4.6 percent of national income.[5]

Thus, data from manufacturing, construction, and prairie agriculture all point toward a significant increase in the share of nonwage incomes in Canadian national income. Since there are no estimates of aggregate factor payments, no precise estimate of its effect on Canadian savings rates is possible. Simply combining the manufacturing and prairie agriculture data yields a rise of 5 to

6 percentage points in the share of nonwage incomes, 1890-1910, and most of that after 1900. If we take the evidence from the construction sector as indicative of a widespread wage lag, noting that manufacturing and prairie agriculture constituted perhaps a third of Canadian gross national product, it seems plausible to argue that the 5 to 6 percentage point shift is an understatement. In any event, if it is assumed that the marginal propensity to save out of nonwage incomes was between a quarter and a third, at least 2 to 3 percentage points of the advance in the gross domestic private savings rate are easily attributable to the post-1890 factor income trends and perhaps more.

Canadian interest rates trended down from 1870 to the mid-1890s and then rose (Edelstein 1970:297-98). If it is assumed that Canadian savings were somewhat interest rate sensitive, some portion of the rise in the savings rate after the mid-1890s was also due to this factor.

One additional point warrants attention. The evidence on rising manufacturing wage shares and falling interest rates prior to 1900 suggests that the falling dependency rate of the 1870-1900 period was not the only influence impinging on the savings rate during that period. Indeed, the reported factor share and interest rate trends would tend to depress the effect of the falling dependency rate. Thus, our earlier estimate of the effect of demographic pressures on post-1900 savings rates based on the relationship of pre-1900 demographic and savings rate trends is clearly biased downward.

If the latter point is taken into consideration, it appears that favorable demographic trends, income distribution shifts, and interest rate movements can account for the rise in the savings rate from 9 percent in the late 1890s to its average of 15 percent to 16 percent, 1900-1915. Certainly, given the size of these determinants of movements and any plausible elasticities, tendencies for greater movement in the Canadian domestic savings rate, 1900-1915, seem quite unlikely.

When Canada gained Dominion status in 1867 and data permitting national income accounting began to be collected, perhaps half of Canadian gross domestic capital formation was funded by foreign savings. By the 1890s, when the domestic investment rate was at about the same level as 1870, domestic savings rates had risen a bit and net foreign borrowing was down to about a third of Canada's gross domestic capital formation. In the first stages of the turn-of-the-century investment boom, both the gross domestic capital formation rate and the gross domestic savings rate rose 6 percentage points of gross national product. As the boom continued and the gross domestic investment rate rose still further, foreign savings became more and more significant. Almost half of the nation's gross capital formation was funded by the British and, to a lesser extent, American savings during the 1911–15 quinquennium.

The Canadian use of foreign savings in the early twentieth century was a compound of several elements. The prairie wheat boom and associated urban developments stemmed from a newly acquired comparative international advantage. The settlement of the prairies and towns raised the pressure for residential construction and other population-sensitive investment projects. Since there is little evidence of a blossoming comparative advantage in Canadian manufacturing, it is likely that, within the protective environment set by Canadian tariff and patent laws, a major portion of manufacturing investment was also population sensitive. Given the very strong force of the agricultural comparative advantage and its associated demands for rural and urban social-overhead capital and manufactured goods, it seems likely that investment good demands emanating from these specific elements would have outstripped any plausible response of the domestic savings rate to the period's demographic and factor income trends. Some rise in foreign borrowing was thus likely.

Nevertheless, there are signs that an overabundance of foreign savings probably fostered a portion of the early twentieth-century investment boom. First, although the prairie wheat boom and its population pressures would have raised the demand for railroad investment spending to some extent, the railway investment rate seems inordinately large. On the demand side, railway investment appears to have been some combination of rather farfetched popular and parliamentary ideas about Canadian development potential and the persistent lobbying of railway construction interests. The outcome of these forces was capital expenditure plans to construct Canada's second and third transcontinental railway systems, a portion of which the government built itself, the remaining portion being heavily subsidized with government land grants, loan guarantees, and other aid. British capital was the major source of finance for both types of railway projects. The extent of British involvement was certainly influenced by the Canadian government's direct and indirect participation. Still, British savers had received similar inducements from other regions of the globe, including the United States and Australia, without exporting quite so much sterling per decade to any one of these regions. Thus, a sizable proportion of railway investment in Canada after 1905 rested on overenthusiastic government tutelage and an extremely liberal source of funding in Great Britain, rather than on well-considered estimates of future revenues.

Manufacturing and mining investments also appear to have been an arena for excessive investment expenditure. Both sectors received funds at an augmented rate during the boom, and the slow or negative growth rate of productivity in these two sectors indicates signs of diminishing returns, 1900-1910. In this connection, it is interesting to note Paterson's recent judgment on the quality of Britain's direct investment in these sectors after 1890 (1976:103-14). Paterson found a record of poor profit performance for these pre-1914 direct investments and overwhelming evidence that these British direct investments were attended by inadequate enterpreneurship and management. Paterson's evidence also suggests that overly abundant British financial resources permitted, if not fostered, this condition.

If one remembers the time shape of British foreign lending, the Canadian case adds vital evidence. Canada was the largest borrower in the last great surge of British lending that started 1902-3, absorbing perhaps a third of British net lending in the years before World War I. Canada certainly exerted a secular pull on British savings in these years, but there also appears to be strong evidence that British savers were not taking care with a portion of their Canadian investments. It thus seems likely that either diminishing returns to domestic British investments or a portion of British savings insensitive to any return was an important element in the last years of Britain's high rates of foreign investment.

CHAPTER 13: **A CHRONOLOGICAL SURVEY**

The purpose of part III has been to provide an explanation for the rising trend in the rate of aggregate U.K. lending in the 1850s and 1860s and its uniquely high plateau from the 1870s to World War I. The logic of economic analysis led to an examination of the principal hypotheses for this pattern: U.K. oversaving in chapter 8, declining U.K. domestic investment opportunities in chapter 9, and the net secular accumulation pressures for overseas borrowing in three major receiving regions in chapters 10, 11, and 12. The investigation suggested that each hypothesis had some bearing on the massive outflow of U.K. savings. However, the force of each explanatory factor varied across the 64 years. It thus seems useful to conclude part III with a summary of the macroeconomic determinants of U.K. foreign lending, emphasizing their chronological interplay.

The model for examining the secular determinants of the unprecedented U.K. trend rates of foreign lending from 1850 to World War I in this, as in previous chapters of part II, is straightforward. Trends in desired savings rates are taken to be linked to changes in a nation's age structure, the distribution of factor incomes, and rates of return. Short-term variations are linked to transitory, as well as permanent, income, wealth, and rates of return. Changes in desired investment rates are separated into movements in desired housing and social-overhead capital formation, on the one hand, and movements in desired agricultural and industrial capital formation on the other. Trends in desired housing and social-overhead investment rates are shown to be strongly linked to population pressures—especially the growth rate of the young adult population, regional and international mobility, and urbanization rates. Trends in the desired rate of agricultural and industrial capital formation are sensitive to productivity growth, as indicated by output per worker growth rates and the relative price of capital equipment.

If somewhat crude, the model does have an extensive empirical base in the many studies of modern economic growth authored by Kuznets, Cairncross, B. Thomas, Abramovitz, Easterlin, Williamson, Green, Urquhart, and many others. Given the known strength of these few determinants of national savings and investment rate behavior and the tested weakness of many other variables, it is defensible to have kept our attention narrowly focused, seeking to push this simple model to its limits. Each nation, however, had its own accumulation pattern with some determinants unique to its evolving social and economic structure. In Canada, for example, national railway development policy, patent laws, and tariff schedules provide examples of such unique circumstances, circumstances we have sought to incorporate to strengthen the bare bones of our model.

It might, of course, be argued that trends in a nation's factor income distribution, population pressures, and productivity growth are not entirely independent of national savings and investment rates. There can be no doubt that this point has some merit. Still, studies of modern economic growth suggest that there are many elements determining trends in the income distribution and in demographic and productivity determinants other than the feedbacks from accumulation trends. If, for example, the factor income distribution represents to some degree the outcome of a capital-using bias in technical change, embodied in new capital equipment, it also represents an outcome of a somewhat autonomous history of struggles between labor and capital, as well as the influence of demographic trends. The downward shift in birth rates characterizing the later stages of modern economic growth was independent of accumulation processes, since there is no evidence that its timing in various nations had anything to do with a particular trend in savings and investment rates. Finally, some of the roots of productivity growth were quite independent of accumulation rates; a nation's penchant for scientific and technical research and education in any particular era, national tariff policy, and the evolving state of labor-management relations also had impacts. Given that one book cannot deal with the ultimately unmoved movers in economic history, it seems plausible to take our determinants as proximally exogenous to the accumulation processes and, hence, to the secular macroeconomic dynamics of nineteenth- and early twentieth-century foreign lending and borrowing.

TRENDS IN THE 1850S AND 1860S

There seems little doubt that the most important underlying cause of the upward trend in the United Kingdom's rate of foreign investment in the 1850s and 1860s was the burgeoning opportunities for U.K. savers abroad. In the United States, the net secular accumulation pressures for overseas borrowing were strongest in the years 1854–71. The U.S. rate of population-sensitive investment rose sharply then, a response to accelerated rates of immigration, urbanization, and interregional migration. The rate of productivity-sensitive investment was rising even faster, heavily influenced by a sharp fall in the relative price of investment goods. In contrast to these strong movements in the determinants of aggregate U.S. demand for investment goods, there appears to have been a much slower movement in the determinants of aggregate U.S. savings. The U.S. dependency rate fell and the U.S. profit share rose, implying that the U.S. had a larger pool of income for saving purposes. The size of these movements, however, was not adequate to produce sufficient savings to fund the very large increase in investment demand pressure. There was a sharp rise in the U.S. real interest rate over these years, and it seems fair to attribute this to the pressures created by the differential between the long-term increased demands for U.S. investment and the lesser increase in domestic savings desires. The evidence indicates that U.S., U.K., and other foreign savers responded to this rapid rise in U.S. real interest rates and thereby supplied extra savings to fund the high investment demands.

Little is known concerning the quantitative dimensions and determinants of foreign investment in Australia in the 1850s. It is well established, however, that the immense Gold Rush immigration of the early 1850s did not immediately generate an equivalent rise in the rate of housing and other population-sensitive investments. The miners lived in tents, and the transportation and urban commercial trades that serviced the mining boom also employed temporary equipment and structures. As the gold mining boom ebbed in the second half of the 1850s a surge in more permanent, population-sensitive investment structures got underway. Good quantitative data begin in 1860, and it is apparent that the late 1850s surge in the demand for population-sensitive investment goods continued into the 1860s. Productivity-sensitive investment demand was not a major factor in aggregate investment demand in the early 1860s. In the late 1860s the rate of investment in agriculture rose, based on the excellent and, to an important degree, unanticipated experience with more capital-intensive pastoral farming methods in Victoria. It thus appears that these various secular pressures led to a strong aggregate demand for investment goods throughout the 1860s.

The secular pressures operating on the supply of Australian savings, however, were not similarly strong. First, total agricultural profits were low because of the diversion of resources toward the mining economy in the 1850s and the ebbing productivity of pastoral operations under the older technology. Second, mining profits were well past their 1850s peaks. It thus seems likely that the share of national income paid to capitalists was at a reduced level during the 1860s. Third, the same age-structure kink that was boosting the demand for housing in the 1860s was also lowering the proportion of the population in the age group crucial for savings, the age cohort 40–49. In brief, while the pressure for installing capital goods was strong in the 1860s, local Australian savings pressures were probably ebbing. The aggregate net secular pressure for overseas borrowing was thus quite high.

Of course, the United States and Australia were not the only regions that were undergoing investment booms in the 1850s and 1860s and that relied upon U.K. savings to help fund the accelerated pace of their capital accumulation. After the mutiny of 1857, the British Raj became highly interested in extending the Indian railway system to move troops and emergency foodstuffs. Indian government guarantees of dividend and interest payments on railway equity and debenture securities were offered to draw British funds. With U.S. cotton exports disrupted by the Civil War, railway lines to the cotton-producing regions of India briefly became a lucrative venture. According to Habbakuk (1940) some 40 percent of the 1850–75 surge in overseas investment went to the British Empire, with Australia and India as major recipients.

Europe also offered an excellent field for British savers. Scattered evidence suggests that the bulk of the United Kingdom's European investments during these two decades went into the

French and Russian railway systems (Jenks 1927:413, 421–23). In the 1850s the French railway system added more trackage than any other Continental nation and in the 1860s France shared leadership in this respect with the burgeoning Russian railway system (Mitchell 1975:581–83). The railway systems of the various German states were also growing very rapidly during these years, but such foreign investment as took place in aid of the German railway construction and industry seems to have come largely from the French (Cameron 1961).

These factors suggest that aggregate investment demand was high in India, France, and Russia at various times during the 1850s and 1860s. However, so little is known about aggregate savings rates and behavior in these countries during these years that it is not possible to make even rough guesses at the aggregate net pressure for foreign borrowing. One might search for evidence of profligate investment spending to test for overborrowing from the United Kingdom, induced by its declining returns or oversaving. But, without the solid foundation of data on rates of investment, rates of savings, demographic indicators, and productivity growth rates, it would be difficult to pinpoint the extent of such profligacy.

There is little evidence that the determinants of U.K. investment demand were exerting an unusually strong pressure on the rate of U.K. accumulation during the 1850s and 1860s. First, U.K. demographic pressures for population-sensitive investment, and productivity growth pressures for productivity-sensitive investment, were either slightly higher in the second quarter of the nineteenth century or about the same. The downward trend in U.K. demographic pressures and productivity growth begins only after 1870. Secondly, the scant evidence on U.K. profit rates during the 1850s and 1860s presented in chapter 10 suggests long-term stability. Great Britain's railway system was expanding in the 1850s and 1860s, doubling the trackage of the British railway network and the size of its real railway capital stock. There is some evidence that the expansion of these decades was into lines generating less profit than the earlier railway investments of the 1840s, but industry-wide averages of the return on real and financial railway capital show no sign of any downward movement. The ratio of net return to cost of construction appears to have been 2 percentage points higher in the western U.S. railway networks than in the U.K. railway networks as a whole in the 1850s, and the average yield on high-grade railway bonds displayed a similar spread. But, importantly, while western U.S. railway net returns on cost of construction show a rise in the 1850s, the U.K. ratio, as well as returns on U.K. equity and debentures shares, show steady returns between 1840 and 1870.

Furthermore, U.K. industrial profit rates were more or less unchanged during the 1850s and 1860s. The growth of industrial output was at its nineteenth-century peak during these decades, fueled in no small part by buoyant export markets. Competition was quite keen among U.K. domestic manufacturers. A recent survey of the period's industrial profit picture is somewhat pessimistic, but its conclusion is largely based on a slight fall in the share of profits, which is inferred from industrial output price indices and wage rate patterns. Scattered evidence on rates of return do not show a similar downward trend. Since there also appears to have been a slight fall in the price of capital goods relative to the implicit deflator for gross national product from the mid-1840s to the mid-1860s, the slightly falling profit share for industry is not incompatible with the evidence that industrial rates of return were steady.

The possibility that the increased levels of the U.K. net foreign investment rate of the 1850s and 1860s were motivated by cyclical U.K. oversaving tendencies does not appear very strong. Precise tests for the presence of disjunctures between desired savings and desired domestic investment levels are not possible, owing to a lack of important data series. However, study of the years 1870–1913 suggested that disjunctures between rising domestic savings desires and falling domestic investment desires, which occasioned the early stages of long net foreign investment surges of the 1870–1913 period, were usually preceded by three or more years of stagnant aggregate output growth. There were two surges in the U.K. net foreign investment rate in the 1850–69 period, one occurring in the late 1850s and the other in the mid-1860s. The late 1850s surge in overseas lending was preceded by average or stronger aggregate output growth rates. The surge of the mid-1860s was preceded by poor growth in 1860 and 1862; 1860 was clearly a trade cycle depression year. Aggregate output recovered strongly in 1861. Because 1862 was as bad as 1860 in output growth, one might view 1861 as a halting recovery with 1862 continuing the tendencies inaugurated in 1860.

An alternative hypothesis with somewhat more empirical weight would attribute the poor growth in 1862 to the trade disruptions and uncertainties attending the first years of the American Civil War. From this perspective, the low growth of the 1860–62 period was due to the coincidence of two short-term shocks to the aggregate economy that temporarily depressed investment expectations in all directions but left underlying long-term investment expectations largely unaffected. Savings rates probably dipped in 1860 and 1862 owing to the transitory low-income growth of these years, whereas they were probably fairly high in 1861 and 1863 owing to the transitory above-average income growth of those years. Thus, it is unlikely that any large disjuncture between desired savings and desired investment occurred prior to, or coincident with, the foreign investment boom that started in 1863. In brief, the evidence that *cyclical* oversaving led to the augmented overseas investment rates of the 1850s and 1860s appears to be slight.

Note that the rising trend of the U.K. net foreign investment rate during the 1850s and 1860s coincided with a rising trend in the share of nonwage incomes in national income. Between 1855–64 and 1865–74, nonwage incomes rose 1.5 percentage points as a share of gross national product. This evidence has been largely ignored because between 1865–74 and 1905–13, when the rate of net foreign lending was roughly stable on trend, the share of nonwage incomes in gross national product was steadily falling, 3.0 percentage points of gross national product. Hence the hypothesis that a positive, causal relationship connected trends in profit shares with trends in net foreign lending rates fails to fit the full sweep of the 1850–1913 period.

Still, each period might have a separate set of trend variables, and so it will be useful to estimate the upper limit of the effects of the U.K. factor income shift of the 1850s and 1860s. Even if all 1.5 percentage points of the factor income shift toward nonwage incomes from 1855–64 to 1865–74 went to net foreign lending, this would constitute not even half of the 3 to 4 percentage point rise in the net foreign investment rate over these years. Second, on the more plausible hypothesis that capitalists save somewhere between a quarter and a third of their nonwage incomes, the contribution of the shift in the factor income distribution becomes quite small. In the limit, if one assumes the 51.8 percent share of nonwage income in gross national product, 1855-64, was the entire source of the nation's 13.4 percent savings rate of the 1840s, 1850s, and 1860s, the implied capitalist savings rate was 25.9 percent. In turn, this implies that only 0.4 percentage point (0.259×1.5) of the 3 to 4 percentage point trend rise in the net foreign investment rate might be attributable to trends in the factor income distribution.

In summary, both cyclical and trend evidence from the years 1850–1869 suggest that U.K. oversaving was, at best, a very minor element in the period's rising overseas lending rates. With the secular determinants of U.K. domestic investment demand steady, it appears that the weight of the evidence favors rising net pressures for foreign borrowing from overseas regions as the principal cause of the period's rising rate of U.K. foreign investment.

TRENDS IN THE 1870S AND 1880S

Certainly by the beginning of the 1880s, and most likely earlier, all three causes of U.K. overseas investment—U.K. oversaving, declining U.K. domestic investment opportunities, and the net pressures from overseas—had become involved in sustaining the U.K. foreign investment rate at its uniquely high level.

In the United States, net secular pressures for foreign borrowing were probably not very strong between 1871 and 1896. First, although demographic pressures, productivity gains, and the declining relative price of capital goods continued to push the U.S. rate of aggregate investment demand upward, their force was somewhat less than in preceding decades. Second, declining U.S. dependency rates and augmented U.S. profit shares now appear to have been more than adequate to generate the savings necessary to meet the increased investment demand. These movements in the determinants of U.S. domestic investment demand and savings desires would suggest that real interest rates should have been either steady or falling (to some degree depending on the savings offered by foreign lenders) and foreign borrowing should have been either steady or falling (to some degree depending on the behavior of U.S. real interest rates). In the event, real interest rates fell strongly between 1871 and 1890 and the rate of net foreign borrowing held steady at about 1 percent of U.S. gross national product. In the 1890s, real interest rates fell strongly but now the rate of net foreign borrowing fell to zero. Given the shift in the determinants of U.S. savings behavior, 1871–1897, and the dramatic fall in U.S. real interest rates, one is inclined to treat U.S. borrowing of this period as motivated more by events in the lending countries, principally the United Kingdom, than as the result of net investment and savings pressures in the United States. This is not to say that U.S. opportunities were not better than comparable ones in the United Kingdom, but rather that the margin was not increasing and, indeed, was very likely decreasing.

Cursory data on Argentinian events and extensive evidence on Australian accumulation pressures suggest somewhat the reverse was the case elsewhere among the United Kingdom's principal borrowers during the 1870s and 1880s. Productivity growth in the Australian rural economy was very high in the 1870s and, while lower in the 1880s, it was still at rates quite high by international standards. Population-sensitive investment spending was low in the 1870s but quite strong in the 1880s, responding to the very rapid growth of the population aged 20–34, the age bracket of those with the highest rates of household formation and housing demand. The latter pressure was the joint product of a demographic echo from the Gold Rush-induced, kinked age structure and high rates of immigration, strongly linked to the pastoral investment and output boom that started in the late 1860s, accelerated in the 1870s, and continued well into the 1880s.

In the midst of this gathering boom for investment goods, the impact of the determinants of domestic savings behavior was not sufficient to match the increase of domestic investment pressures. Profit shares may have risen across the 1870s but held steady or fell in the 1880s. The share of the dependent population fell, 1871–91, but the share of the population in the years of maximal savings, ages 40–49, fell just as dramatically. Thus, while there was some pressure for savings rates to rise in the 1870s, the reverse was probably the case in the 1880s. And, as it worked out, domestic savings rates rose somewhat in the 1870s but fell in the 1880s, just as the domestic investment rate was reaching its peak nineteenth-century values. With extensive trade and other links to the United Kingdom, and a successful period of heavy domestic investment and borrowing from the United Kingdom in the late 1850s and early 1860s, it seems quite appropriate that the secular disjuncture between rising domestic investment demand pressures and falling domestic savings pressures would lead to a massive import of U.K. savings into Australia from the late 1870s to the early 1890s.

Toward the end of the 1880s with productivity growth rates falling in agriculture and population pressures abating slightly, there appears to be some ground for worrying about the match between some of the pressures for Australian domestic investment and the high rate of Australian foreign borrowing, particularly when a substantial portion was borrowed by Australian governments whose revenues from new railway construction hardly matched even the low expectations of many politicians bent on subsidizing regional growth. Still, the memory of the great pastoral profits of the 1870s was not *strongly* falsified by the rural profits of the 1880s, and climatic factors were very propitious, albeit abnormally so, as became clear in the drought-ridden 1890s. In short, the bulk of the explanation for Australia's heavy foreign borrowing in the 1870s, and still more in the 1880s, appears Australian in origin, although perhaps by the late 1880s a small piece of the explanation might lie with the U.K., not Australian, conditions.

So little is known about the aggregate Argentinian economy during the 1870s and 1880s that no strong statements can be made about the domestic macroeconomic foundations of its heavy foreign borrowing during these years. The fact that Argentina was the third heaviest international borrower during the 1880s is well documented, but the Baring Crisis of the early 1890s, caused by the inability of the London firm of Baring Brothers to market its large inventory of Argentinian municipal debentures, has long suggested to some observers that the whole Argentinian boom of the 1880s was founded on the profligacy of U.K. lenders, rather than on objective Argentinian opportunities. This point of view is clearly exaggerated and possibly quite misplaced. Rural

Argentina offered excellent opportunities for extensive agricultural development from the 1850s onward, first in wool and then in wheat.

But several political changes altered conditions for this type of economic development in the late 1870s and 1880s. First, a government came to power that was sympathetic to large-scale emigration from Europe. Second, in the late 1870s the Indians who threatened settled European agriculture and pasturage in several choice rural areas were either killed or run off to the western mountains. Thus, it seems quite likely that both productivity-sensitive and population-sensitive investment demands jumped in the 1880s in this new political-economic environment. Nothing is known about profit shares or demographic structure, but given the size of the immigration, it is probable that there was a decline in the share of the population in the maximal saving ages, 40–49. International competition was high in the 1880s for both wool and wheat, and so it also seems plausible that Argentinian, as well as Australian, rural profit shares were high but not increasing. In brief, there are some reasonable, albeit not strong, grounds to suggest that at least part of the Argentinian foreign borrowing boom in the 1880s had solid domestic roots in the trend disjuncture between augmented domestic investment demand pressures and less auspicious savings circumstances. However, it seems quite improper, given the weight of the evidence on the shaky character of some Argentinian investment projects in the late 1880s, to entirely dismiss the possibility that some part of the explanation for the heavy inflow of U.K. savings in the late 1880s relied upon secular U.K., not Argentinian, conditions.

The United States, Australia, and Argentina, in that order, were the largest borrowers from the United Kingdom during the 1870s and 1880s, with U.S. borrowing about a third less than Australian and Argentinian combined. Judged by our brief survey there were strong overseas currents beckoning U.K. lenders in the Australian and Argentinian cases but not in the U.S. case. And even in the Australian and Argentinian cases there were grounds for judging a minor role for influences of a nondomestic character for the late 1880s.

At some point subsequent to the early 1870s, U.K. pressures for U.K. domestic investment began to abate, and this influenced the subsequent high level of U.K. overseas lending in the 1870s and 1880s. Virtually all measures of population growth and urbanization show long-term trend declines beginning in the 1870s or 1880s. Some portion of these declines was probably due to the effects of overseas migration on the size of the child-bearing population of the United Kingdom, but since the trend rate of emigration was steady or falling, this could account for only a small proportion, if any, of the falling birth rates, etc. The simple fact is that, starting in the 1870s and 1880s, U.K. demographic pressures were affected by two secular phenomena that are a standard feature of the experience of nations that have undergone the sustained high rates of per capita income growth and the other associated phenomena characterizing modern economic growth. First, as elsewhere, at some point after sustained high per capita income growth appears, birth rates begin to fall at rates faster than any death rate declines. The reasons for this widespread phenomenon among the nations characterized by modern economic growth have yet to be settled by demographic and economic historians, but the net result is well known—a nation's rate of natural population increase declines. The 1870s date the beginning of this trend for the United Kingdom. Second, modern economic growth typically involves a substantial shift in the proportion of the labor force and output away from agriculture toward the manufacturing and service sectors. Given nineteenth-century technologies of land and sea transportation, energy generation, and energy transmission, this meant that manufacturing and service employment and output growth took place in rapidly expanding urban areas. However, as specialization in manufacturing and service reached its economic limits, rates of urbanization were bound to slow. For the United Kingdom the pace of redistribution out of agriculture slowed in the fourth quarter of the nineteenth century, as did the rate of urbanization.

It also appears to be the case that U.K. productivity growth rates began to fall off in the 1870s, falling below early nineteenth-century rates in the late 1880s. The reasons for this phenomenon are not altogether clear, but several lines of reasoning have gained a certain currency. First, in the late nineteenth century the U.K. continued to specialize in the same industrial products it had developed and pioneered in the late eighteenth and early nineteenth century—textiles, iron, coal, steam engines, etc. Such specialization may have been steadily profitable, but much evidence suggests that the pace of productivity growth slowed in these old industries, a pattern for aging industries well known from the economic histories of the developing capitalist nations of the nineteenth and twentieth centuries. Second, the United Kingdom was not as quick as other late-nineteenth-century growing economies to develop private and public support for education and research in the sciences and technology. Whereas elsewhere new industries boomed in applied chemistry and electrical equipment, this was not the case in the U.K., and the poor scientific education and research base is frequently cited as an important cause of this limited growth. Thus, in addition to the large, older sectors exhibiting slowed productivity growth. the U.K. was not quick to develop some of the new products that had rapid productivity growth rates. In the 1870s and 1880s, however, the slowed productivity growth rates were probably much more tied to the slowed productivity growth in the old sectors rather than to failures to develop science-based new industries. This latter problem really becomes important only in the 1890s and 1900s.

To the list of U.K. factors tending to sustain the U.K.'s high rate of foreign investment in the 1870s and 1880s must be added at least one fairly well-delimited incident of "oversaving." The best evidence on the behavior of factor incomes and their volatility suggests that *trends* in these variables were not a cause of a trend toward persistent oversaving, with the possible outcome of an augmented rate of investment in overseas "sinks." However, some fairly good evidence points toward at least one incident of *cyclical* oversaving, and this coincided with the beginning of the strong foreign investment boom of the 1880s. Oversaving may be defined as a disjuncture between savings pressures and domestic investment pressures, at least in part created by savings behavior, and it appears that such an incident took place in the years 1877–79. Econometric specification of U.K. desired savings behavior in chapter 8 suggests that the U.K. rate of desired savings responded to periods of slowed aggregate income growth by first falling and then after a few years regaining its long-term rate, even if the slowed growth persisted. Such slowed aggregate income growth began in the mid-1870s. Given the lag structure of U.K. desired savings behavior, this meant that, by 1877–79, desired savings rates were returning upward to their long-term norms. At the same time, there are excellent reasons, both on the side of slowed real output growth and of stock prices, for believing that U.K. desired domestic investment plans were coincidentally being curtailed. In short, with cyclical savings pressures rising and cyclical investment pressures static or declining, it seems plausible to hypothesize some tendencies toward oversaving. And, since these years coincide with a sharp rise in the rate of foreign investment, it seems equally reasonable to view the augmented capital outflow of 1877–79 as part of the resolution of this temporary disjuncture.

In brief, then, the high trend rate of U.K. foreign investment in the 1870s and 1880s involved a variety of domestic and foreign factors. Net secular accumulation pressures for offshore borrowing were quite high in Australia and Argentina. The United States was a substantial U.K. borrower in these years, but the U.S. evidence points toward U.K. accumulation forces as a more important determinant of this flow than U.S. savings and investment pressures. Declining U.K. demographic and productivity pressures probably led to a slackening of U.K. domestic investment demands. Given that the United Kingdom's desired savings function was interest-rate sensitive to a limited degree, the declining U.K. investment pressures led to more foreign investment. Finally, there is at least one instance in the late 1870s when a combination of cyclical forces probably led to a short period of U.K. oversaving, and it is likely that the disequilibrium underlying this phenomenon was to some degree resolved by increased overseas lending during those years.

THE 1890S AND 1900S

Although U.K. oversaving, diminished U.K. domestic investment pressures, and the net secular accumulation pressures from overseas opportunities all played a role in the high sustained rate of U.K. overseas investment in the 1890s and 1900s, domestic factors, particularly diminished U.K. investment opportunities, were probably the dominant element in the period's massive capital outflow.

In examining the strength of the secular pull from major overseas borrowers, the sense emerges that less of the borrowing was due to burgeoning overseas investment opportunities facing temporary or long-term local savings constraints and more was due to factors emanating from U.K. investment and savings behavior. The United States became a net lender on international account in the 1890s, but this net position eroded after 1900 as gross borrowing grew somewhat faster than gross lendings. This augmented borrowing after 1900 took place at the same time the U.S. rate of domestic investment was either constant or falling somewhat. One would thus be hard pressed to view the rise of U.S. gross foreign borrowings as due to the pull of U.S. investment opportunities since the actual rate of U.S. investment, the outcome of such opportunities, was not rising. More specifically, U.S. investment conditions were subject to two divergent tendencies: productivity-sensitive investment appears to have continued to be subject to strong upward pressures from productivity growth, and the falling relative price of capital goods. And although immigration rates rose in the 1890s, trends in total population growth, urbanization rates, and interregional migration rates were clearly decreasing. In the event the ebbing demographic pressures were stronger than the strengthening pressures for productivity-sensitive investment, and total rates of U.S. domestic investment fell. At the same time the U.S. profit share was constant and U.S. dependency rates continued their century-long downward path. With this constellation of forces, it is hard to see the period's augmented gross foreign borrowing (and reduced net foreign lending) as the result of net secular U.S. accumulation forces; more likely, it was the outcome of U.K. investment and savings pressures.

In Australia the constellation of forces in the 1890s and 1900s was somewhat different, but the outcome with regard to the net secular pressure for foreign borrowing must be judged similar to that in the United States. As the economy recovered from the severe depression and drought of the 1890s, there was upward pressure on Australia's gross investment demand, but it was entirely due to demographic pressures, and of a fairly weak variety at that. Productivity growth rates after 1900 were high, but they merely reflected a recovery from the drought period as land was reoccupied and the climate improved. They were not due to a heavy spurt of new technologies or new natural resource discoveries. More significantly, domestic savings determinants pointed strongly toward a rise in the nation's savings rate. The dependency rate was falling and the percentage of the population in the years of maximal savings was rising. It therefore seems quite likely that Australian investment and savings forces were such as to strongly reduce the secular pressure for overseas borrowing and that increase in gross foreign borrowing that did take place at the start of the twentieth century was strongly affected by U.K. conditions.

South Africa and Argentina were two important borrowers of U.K. savings during this period—South Africa in the 1890s and early 1900s, and Argentina after 1900. Unfortunately, there are few aggregate data to formulate precise pictures of their aggregate accumulation experiences. Nevertheless, economic histories of South Africa leave little doubt about the net secular causes of the foreign borrowing boom that characterized South Africa's accumulation experience in the 1890s and early 1900s. Very significant gold and diamond mining opportunities were discovered in the 1880s and 1890s and the white settler population was simply too small to generate sufficient savings to meet the immensity of the investment opportunities. Early realized returns to equity in gold mining were exceptionally high, and these could have served only to attract mobile capital (Frankel 1967).

The Argentinian domestic investment and foreign borrowing boom of the 1900s is somewhat better documented with aggregate statistics than the previous development surges. And there is good evidence that there were strong pressures for overseas borrowing resulting from Argentinian investment and savings determinants. Population-sensitive investment, particularly housing and railroads, was the strongest element in Argentinian investment demand during this period (Diaz Alejandro 1970:7). This element of aggregate investment demand was responding to unprecedented rates of total population increase, urbanization and immigration, and a decided increase in the percentage of the population in the age groups of family formation and maximal housing demand (Diaz Alejandro 1970:421–24). Of course, at the foundation of this boom in population-sensitive investment was the renewed growth in mining and in agriculture, especially wheat and corn, following the low levels of the early 1890s. But it appears that productivity growth was not very strong in the rural sector, and the falling percentage of investment spending going to agriculture was probably a response to this fact (Diaz Alejandro 1970:6–8).

Argentinian savings conditions were not anywhere near as dynamic. The dependency rate fell by a percentage point, but the percentage of the population in the ages of maximal savings, 40–49, also fell (Diaz Alejandro 1970:26). There are no aggregate factor income data, but to the extent that movements in real wage rates versus per capita real incomes reflect trends in labor incomes versus total income, their similar growth patterns do not suggest any shift away from wage incomes toward profits in the early twentieth century (Diaz Alejandro 1970:42).

In brief, the economic history of Argentina from the late 1890s to 1914 suggests a divergence between investment demand's responding to the pressures of rapid extensive development and the inauspicious conditions for domestic savings rates to meet this pressure. The United Kingdom's lending to Argentina during the early twentieth century thus seems largely the result of Argentinian investment and savings pressures rather than of domestic U.K. forces.

By a large margin the most significant borrower from the United Kingdom in the 1890–1913 years was Canada. And, although there is good evidence that part of this flow was engendered by strong Canadian accumulation pressures, there are also data to suggest that some portion of its foreign borrowing came as a result of either U.K. diminishing returns or U.K. oversaving. The Canadian prairie wheat boom and associated urban developments that started in the late 1890s stemmed from a newly acquired international comparative advantage. The settlement of the prairies and towns raised the pressure for residential and other population-sensitive investment products. Since there is little evidence of a blossoming international comparative advantage in Canadian manufacturing, and the force of Canadian tariff and patent laws is well established, it seems plausible to treat a major portion of the period's augmented manufacturing investment as essentially population sensitive. With its new comparative advantage in wheat very strong and prairie urban and rural settlement quite rapid, there seems little question that Canada's rate of investment demand was under considerable upward pressure.

Canadian pressures for raising the domestic savings rate were not slight by any means. Indeed, favorable demographic trends and income distribution trends give a plausible explanation for the substantial jump in the savings rate that characterized these years. Nevertheless, the force of the demographic determinants of population-sensitive investment demands appears to have been such as to easily outdistance the savings rate increases. Hence, Canadian pressures for foreign borrowing were quite high after 1900.

Some portion of the early twentieth-century Canadian investment boom was, however, probably fostered by an overabundance of foreign savings. Post-1900 Canadian railway expenditures were quite large relative to other nineteenth- and early twentieth-century regions of recent settlement around the globe. Although some amount of railway investment was warranted by the prairie wheat boom and its associated rural and urban population expansion, a portion seems to have been fostered by a combination of popular and parliamentary ambitions about Canadian development potential that were quite optimistic and by the persistent lobbying efforts of railway construction interests. Government involvement was all pervading, and various direct and indirect inducements and subsidies were offered to attract foreign lenders to support railway construction.

Government construction and aid to private construction were not unique to the railway development of Canada. Other colonies and independent nations made extensive use of these methods for similar purposes. What is striking is the response of British savers to these Canadian appeals in the early twentieth century. In Canadian manufacturing and mining there is evidence of investment in the face of declining returns, measured by either productivity or profits. It thus seems fairly certain that the

Canadian case was a mix of well-founded, net secular Canadian accumulation pressures for foreign borrowing and an overabundance of U.K. savings seeking overseas outlets.

To sum up the evidence on net secular accumulation pressures overseas, the data from a number of major U.K. foreign borrowers in the 1890s and 1900s suggests some portion was built on strong overseas accumulation pressures but a large portion found its motivation elsewhere. Furthermore, it would seem that the role of these latter forces was much stronger than they were in the 1850–70 or 1870–90 periods.

With regard to the secular course of U.K. domestic investment opportunities, 1890–1914, the evidence is much less ambiguous. Both the secular determinants of population-sensitive and productivity-sensitive investment and the behavior of realized returns to U.K. domestic portfolio investment point in the same direction—investment opportunities at home were certainly not expanding rapidly and were quite likely contracting.

Nearly all demographic indicators of population pressure in the years 1890–1913 show the continuation of downward trends that started in the 1870–90 period. The long-term downward pressures on birth rates continued to influence the rate of natural increase. Urbanization rates and intercounty migration rates were lower on trend, again influenced by the slowing transfer of labor and capital out of rural employments into the urbanized industrial and service sectors.

Without any question the long-term rates of productivity growth in U.K. manufacturing, industry as a whole, and domestic output as a whole were distinctly below those in the 1870–1890 period. Productivity growth rates were lower in the home boom of the 1890s than in that of the 1870s and distinctly lower in the decade of heavy overseas investment of the 1900s than in the previous decade of heavy foreign investment in the 1880s. U.K. realized returns and overseas realized returns showed inverse long swings, with average home returns slightly dominant in the early 1870s, average overseas returns clearly dominant in the very late 1870s and early 1880s, average home returns dominant in the very late 1880s and early 1890s, and average overseas returns dominant in the very late 1890s and 1900s. But, quite significantly, home returns were substantially weaker in the period of overseas dominance in the 1900s than they were in the previous period of overseas dominance in the 1880s. And this relative weakness in the 1900s runs right across the industrial and transportation sectors.

These trends were the product of continued reliance on older industries; one might remember the negative productivity growth rates in coal mining as an outstanding example of an old industry of some profit but clearly diminishing physical productivity. In addition, the absence of well-established scientific and technical education and research facilities, directed toward application in industry, comes into play in this period. These years were when new, science-based industries in the United States, Germany, and elsewhere began to have an important impact on their respective industrial sectors. And it was also now that the United Kingdom's lack of tariffs on manufacturing imports hurt most, with France an early and serious competitor to U.K. producers in automobiles, Germany and the United States in electrical equipment, the United States in machine tools, and several nations in heavy chemicals.

In turning to the possibility of oversaving in the 1890–1913 era, two facts are compelling. First, the factor income distribution was virtually static during these years. The proportion of nonwage incomes might have risen by a half a percentage point of gross national product as between the 1870–1890 and the 1890–1913 years. If all saving was done by nonwage income earners, perhaps 0.25 percentage point of gross national product was newly available for foreign investment in the 1890–1913 period from this source, hardly important when the trend rate of foreign investment was close to 5 percent of gross national product. Second, although there was probably another cyclical incident in 1902–5 when the desired domestic savings rate was rising and the desired domestic investment rate was contracting, the degree of the discrepancy, at least as measured in chapter 8 by the divergence of the desired savings rate from the actual savings rate, was less than in the 1877–79 oversaving incident.

In summary, the trends of the 1890–1913 period point toward the lessened importance of net secular accumulation pressures from the overseas receivers of U.K. savings, the static or falling influence of oversaving, and the ascendent influence of failing domestic opportunities.

Coda Between 1850 and 1913 foreign assets became a substantial part of the United Kingdom's accumulated wealth. This process involved a dramatic and unprecedented rise in the share of national product devoted to foreign investment. From around 1 percent to 1½ percent of gross national product in the late 1840s and early 1850s, it rose to around 4½ percent to 5 percent of gross national product in the late 1860s and early 1870s and stayed at that uniquely high level, with some fluctuation, until World War I. In the initial twenty years, the primary force impelling the increased rate of accumulation of foreign assets was the augmented attractiveness of opportunities in the United States, Australia, India, and Europe.

There is little evidence that during these decades the domestic U.K. economy was subject to declining investment opportunities or tendencies toward oversaving. In the years from 1870 to 1890, however, the pattern changed. The high rate of U.K. foreign investment was now sustained by both overseas and domestic U.K. forces. As in the 1850–70 period, the pressures of local investment demand far exceeded those for local savings in a number of overseas areas, and the net result was pressure for long-distance borrowing. The United Kingdom responded to these opportunities, but it was also driven toward foreign lending by domestic conditions. U.K. pressures for productivity-sensitive and population-sensitive capital formation began a secular decline in the 1870s and thereby lowered domestic opportunities for U.K. capitalists. Given this U.K. aggregate savings behavior, which was only partly sensitive to rates of return, the smaller scope for domestic U.K. investment opportunities yielded heightened pressures for foreign investment.

In the late 1870s, just at the beginning of what was to become a major surge of U.K. overseas lending, there is also evidence of U.K. oversaving. The episode was brief, based on the divergent reactions of U.K. domestic investment demand and savings desires to the slow output growth of the mid-1870s. It appears not to have been very closely associated with cyclical or trend movements in the share of profits in gross national product as suggested by J. A. Hobson.

In the years from 1890 to 1913, the rate of foreign investment continued at a high level, and, as in the 1870–90 period, it was the product of both overseas and domestic forces. While many overseas regions again manifested strong net pressures for offshore borrowing, other overseas regions received U.K. savings somewhat in excess of needs indicated by the juxtaposition of local investment demand and savings pressures.

This evidence is not surprising, for the downward trend of U.K. productivity-sensitive and population-sensitive investment demands continued and probably grew worse during these years and, in turn, increased domestic U.K. pressure for overseas lending. Again, in the years 1903–5 there appears to have been a brief episode of U.K. oversaving, resolved by augmented foreign investment flows. By comparison with the 1877–79 episode of oversaving, the 1903–5 oversaving incident was less extensive. Thus, it seems fair to conclude that the high rate of overseas lending by the United Kingdom in the two decades before World War I was the result of some augmented overseas opportunities, a brief episode of oversaving, and secularly declining domestic U.K. investment opportunities, with the latter definitely more important in these decades than at any earlier point.

In discussions of U.K. imperialism in the late nineteenth and early twentieth centuries, U.K. foreign investment and its determinants are often given a prominent role. This is not the place to start a discussion of the complex threads that guided the United Kingdom's involvement in the high tide of European overseas imperialism. Still, the importance that many historians attach to the link between the United Kingdom's overseas investments and the expansion of its political empire certainly warrants some comment.

To argue that the 1850–1913 period's uniquely high rates of overseas investment were not involved in this concurrent extension of the United Kingdom's overseas empire seems fundamentally implausible. At the very least, U.K. ownership of overseas assets was so broadly based among the wealthy and politically powerful classes of Great Britain by the late nineteenth century that to suggest that this ownership did not influence the structure, goals, and policies of imperial trends amounts to arguing that the extensive landholdings of the British aristocracy in the early modern era had little to do with the structure of Tudor-Stuart political life. Thus, insofar as the structure and patterns of U.K. foreign investment formed part of the background, and sometimes part of the foreground, of the "age of high imperialism," it was far more the upsurge in overseas opportunities and, after 1870 or so, the additional and mounting pressures of ebbing domestic U.K. investment opportunities that determined the 1850–1913 period's uniquely high involvement in overseas investment, rather than Hobson-like or other tendencies toward oversaving. Granted that the African & Asian regions where the United Kingdom principally extended its formal and informal rule during these six decades were not usually the regions where the United Kingdom's overseas investment and profits were heaviest. Nevertheless, the gap between investment opportunities in many overseas areas, a high proportion of them older colonial areas, and those at home could not help but affect the politics of those most interested in imperialist expansion, raise the interest of a broader public, and lower the resistance of some of its opponents.

Another area of U.K. history in the late nineteenth and early twentieth centuries where the high rate of U.K. overseas lending is sometimes given a prominent role is in the slowing growth rates of the aggregate U.K. economy. This study has taken the view that one of the important pressures impelling the high rate of foreign investment after 1870 was the slowing opportunities for domestic U.K. investment. These opportunities were static or contracting because population and productivity growth pressures were slowing. Some have argued, however, that the causality was not entirely one way, that eventually the high rates of foreign lending operated to constrain certain high-productivity U.K. domestic investment projects and hence U.K. output and income growth rates. By international standards the United Kingdom was late in moving into a number of new industries in the 1890s and early twentieth century (e.g., heavy chemicals, electrical equipment, automobiles), and perhaps a larger pool of U.K. savings available for domestic investment might have speeded things somewhat.

More important, however, were two fundamental aspects of U.K. political and social economy. These were, on the one hand, the nation's policy of free trade with its corollary of no infant industry protection and, on the other hand, the aspects of U.K. social and political structure that fostered the relative public and private neglect of education and research in science and technology. It is these features of the U.K. social, political, and economic structure that most differentiate the United Kingdom from its major competitors, not any inherent institutional or structural bias toward foreign lending.

The United Kingdom was an advanced capitalist economy with some experience in mobilizing resources toward specialization in its most productive sectors, the ones with the strongest regional and international comparative advantages. Indeed, this study has offered evidence that new opportunities for domestic capital formation in the late nineteenth and early twentieth century were not stymied by any lack of funding. Insofar as the organized capital markets were concerned, there was probably even a slight bias in favor of domestic opportunities after 1890. Thus, within the constraints placed on the United Kingdom's evolving comparative advantages by its tariff, education, and research environment, it seems dubious that there were large amounts of high-productivity domestic investment opportunities in underspecialized sectors waiting to be taken up with consequent large effects on the nation's per capita output growth rates. Rather, to the extent that the United Kingdom's aggregate savings behavior led U.K. overseas lending to cut off some U.K. domestic investment projects, it was probably low-return domestic projects that were neglected, ones with lower returns than the typical lowest return overseas projects actually taken up.

APPENDIX 1: OVERSEAS AND HOME INVESTMENT, TOTAL ACCUMULATION AND GROSS NATIONAL PRODUCT, ANNUALLY, 1856-1913

Table A1.1

Year	Overall Balance on Current Account (OBCA) (1)	Net Foreign Lending (NFI) (2)	Gross Domestic Fixed Investment (GDFI) (3)	Inventory Invest- ment (II) (4)	Gross National Accumu- lation (GNA) (5)	Gross National Product (at Factor cost) (Y) (6)
1856	22	24	61	15	100	826
1857	27	20	56	-5	71	789
1858	22	32	55	-5	82	778
1859	36	37	58	15	105	831
1860	24	21	61	15	97	866
1861	14	12	63	5	80	875
1862	12	14	68	15	97	917
1863	27	31	83	15	129	953
1864	23	28	97	20	145	1002
1865	35	41	99	15	155	1034
1866	33	46	91	15	152	1076
1867	42	52	81	-15	118	1011
1868	37	42	79	0	121	1025
1869	47	51	77	5	133	1043
1870	44	55	83	25	163	1100
1871	72	76	101	40	217	1204
1872	98	97	114	10	221	1267
1873	81	86	117	5	208	1308
1874	70	78	132	35	245	1348
1875	51	57	138	20	215	1313
1876	23	31	148	15	194	1298
1877	13	10	143	10	163	1274
1878	17	23	130	5	158	1258
1879	35	31	109	-5	135	1180
1880	36	33	115	40	188	1324
1881	66	60	114	10	184	1297
1882	58	61	117	15	193	1339
1883	48	49	121	30	200	1382
1884	72	70	111	0	181	1333
1885	62	62	97	0	159	1294

Table Al.1 (cont.)

	OBCA (1)	NFI (2)	GDFI (3)	II (4)	GNA (5)	Y (6)
1886	79	78	84	5	167	1287
1887	87	88	83	30	201	1355
1888	92	91	89	20	200	1376
1889	81	83	101	25	209	1425
1890	98	107	108	15	230	1474
1891	70	72	113	25	210	1517
1892	60	63	115	5	183	1488
1893	53	57	109	0	166	1468
1894	39	50	114	30	194	1519
1895	40	55	114	30	199	1545
1896	56	50	129	35	214	1612
1897	42	41	151	15	207	1636
1898	23	29	178	35	242	1740
1899	37	47	206	35	288	1865
1900	26	34	225	0	259	1952
1901	13	19	221	25	265	2013
1902	19	24	219	5	250	1988
1903	43	43	220	-5	258	1999
1904	53	52	206	5	263	1996
1905	82	88	202	15	305	2055
1906	119	121	197	20	338	2117
1907	157	162	176	10	248	2171
1908	157	150	146	-30	266	2098
1909	135	142	153	20	313	2169
1910	167	174	160	30	364	2263
1911	198	204	159	30	393	2353
1912	198	203	164	20	387	2421
1913	222	234	194	45	474	2576

Sources:

Col. (1): OBCA. NFI (Col. 2) less net additions to bullion. Imlah 1958: 70-75.

Col. (2): NFI. 1856-1898: Imlah 1958: 70-75. 1899-1913: Feinstein 1972: T37-38.

Col. (3): GDFI. Feinstein 1972: T8, revised according to Feinstein 1979.

Col. (4): II. Feinstein 1972: T8 and use of Feinstein methods and gross domestic product data to derive rough estimates for 1856-69.

Col. (5): GNA. Col. (2) + Col. (3) + Col. (4).

Col. (6): Y. 1856-1869: Y is defined as gross domestic product (GDP) + net property income from abroad (NPIA). NPIA is derived from Feinstein 1972: T4. The estimate of GDP, 1956-69, derives from Feinstein's 1972: T18(4) compromise estimate of real GDP and the implicit deflator calculated from Feinstein 1972: T4-5, T18-19, scaled to the GDP estimator underlying Y, 1870-1913, and revised upward according to Feinstein 1979. 1870-1913: Feinstein 1972: T8, revised upward according to Feinstein 1979.

APPENDIX 2: **ESTIMATING THE LEVEL OF GOVERNMENT SAVINGS, 1861-1913**

THEORY AND METHODS

The simplest definition of government savings is total government receipts (excluding debt creation or redemption) minus total government expenditures. National accounting methods, however, permit two ways of treating government accounts, and these two treatments have implications for estimating government savings. One method of national income accounting treats all government expenditures as if they were consumption expenditures, that is, giving service immediately, with no life beyond the calendar year. A second method separates government expenditures into public consumption and public investment expenditures, the latter yielding services over a number of years.

Apart from the various reasons for this latter separation found in the literature of public finance theory, when government investment becomes a large share of a nation's capital formation, the analysis of national accumulation behavior dictates that government investment be separated from the government account and possibly merged with the investment account. This definitional change in the government and investment accounts forces a further change in the definition of government savings.

Let C = private consumption expenditures, I = private investment expenditures, G = total government expenditures, $(X-M)$ = exports minus imports (or net foreign lending), S = private savings, and T = total government receipts. The standard GNP identity holds that

$$C + G + I + (X\text{-}M) = GNP = C + S + T. \qquad (A2.1)$$

Eliminating C from both sides of the equation and moving G to the right-hand side leaves the familiar savings-investment identity,

$$I + (X\text{-}M) = S + (T\text{-}G), \qquad (A2.2)$$

315

where $(T\text{-}G)$ is government savings.

This framework ignores government capital formation behavior, however. Let G^i = government investment expenditures and G^c = public consumption expenditures for current goods and services. The equation (A2.1) becomes

$$C + I + G^i + G^c + (X\text{-}M) = GNP = C + S + T. \qquad (A2.3)$$

Eliminating C from both sides and isolating *all* capital formation on the left side, we have

$$I + G^i + (X\text{-}M) = S + (T\text{-}G^c), \qquad (A2.4)$$

where $(T\text{-}G^c)$ is now government savings.

Feinstein 1972 correctly views government investment as an important component of U.K. national capital formation and gives estimates of both public and private capital formation from 1856 forward. Hence, he compels us to redefine government savings to be that of equation 4, that is,

government savings (GS) = total government receipts − current government expenditures. (A2.5)

One method of estimating GS is to build up the accounts directly from (a) the various taxes, trading surpluses, rent, interest, and dividends accruing to the government, yielding total government receipts and (b) the various current expenditures, subsidies, grants, and debt interest payments, yielding the current government expenditure estimate. Feinstein 1972:T31-35 presents most of the data series for an estimate via this *direct* method covering the years 1900-1965. The only missing series is death duties, and this is available from several sources.

A second method of estimating the level of GS builds on changes in the financial liabilities and assets of the central and local government authorities. Definitionally, capital expenditures must equal capital receipts, thus

$$GFCF^g = GS + (dL\text{-}dA), \qquad (A2.6)$$

where $GFCF^g$ = gross fixed capital formation of central and local
governments

GS = gross government savings

L = government liabilities (Bank of England note issue, advances from the Bank of England, treasury bills, national savings, government securities, etc.)

A = government assets (Bank of England gold, lending to the private sector, etc.)

d = an operator, meaning "change in."

Rearrangement of this definition yields an *indirect* method of estimating GS,

$$GS = GFCF^g-(dL-dA).$$
(A2.7)

Unfortunately, Feinstein's estimates of the government capital account begin only in 1920 (1972:T79, T81).

ESTIMATION PROBLEMS: THE DIRECT METHOD

Although data series on taxes and government expenditures are available from Feinstein and the government accounts, neither source offers readily usable estimates of trading surpluses, rent, interest, dividends, subsidies, grants, and debt interest payments for the years 1860–99. The pieces are perhaps fifty separate government accounts, requiring considerable time and effort to rescue. For example, the main grants during the period 1860–1900 were educational, but creating the correct data series requires digging deeply enough to isolate the grants to persons and nongovernmental entities and netting out intragovernment transfers. Again, data on debt interest payments are available, albeit rather poor for local government, but it is quite difficult to ascertain how much of these sums accrued to various government entities and how much was actually paid to persons or nongovernmental entities.

ESTIMATION PROBLEMS: THE INDIRECT METHOD

Fortunately, nearly all the important components of the *indirect* estimator are readily available. First, national savings can be ignored because nearly all the Post Office Savings Banks and Trustee Savings Banks holdings are government debt of one sort or another. (Correct estimation would require reducing the estimate of government debt instruments by inside holdings and presenting the deposits of the Post Office and Trustee Savings Banks as a separate entity.) Second, there was little lending to the private sector in this period, and so this item can also be safely ignored. Government records yield immediately employable series on Bank of England note issue, net creation of national government debt, and Bank of England gold acquisitions.

The principal difficulty in building up an estimate of government savings with the indirect method is construction of an accurate series on net creations of local government debt. Although previous investigations of the local government accounts have generated excellent estimates of capital expenditures, little work has been done on carefully stipulating the loans going for capital formation purposes. Thus, while Mitchell 1962:414-5 has a series built up from the annual *Local Taxation Returns* on receipts from loans, it is quite unusable; it does not stipulate the ultimate purpose of the loans, public consumption or public investment. The annual *Local Taxation Returns* from the turn of the century offer a series that is restricted to "productive" outstanding loans, "productive" loans being those committed to projects that generate income for local government bodies. Included are loans to construct baths, warehouses, cemeteries, electric lighting, gasworks, harbors, docks, piers, quays, canals (except the Manchester Ship Canal), light railways, markets, tramways, and waterworks. Estimates of the quantity of outstanding "productive" loans are available for 1879-80, 1884-85, 1889-90, and 1891-92 to 1913-14 (table A2.1). An alternative estimate of local debt movements can be constructed from the figures on publicly issued municipal and county debt found in the annual *Burdett's Official Intelligence*, 1883-1898, and *The Stock Exchange Official Intelligence*, 1899-1913 (table A2.2).

ESTIMATION

Two attempts are made here to estimate government savings by the indirect method, distinguished by their method of estimating net local debt creation.

Table A2.1

Outstanding Productive Loans of U.K. Local Governments, 1879-1914

(millions of pounds)

Years	England & Wales		Scotland
1879-80	59.0[a]		
1884-85	81.7		
1889-90	93.7		
1891-92	97.5		
1892-93	99.6		
1893-94	102.4		
1894-95	106.5		25.1
1895-96	108.9		
1896-97	112.5		
1897-98	117.7		
1898-99	124.5		
1899-1900	135.3		32.8
1900-01	145.8		35.2
1901-02	159.8		37.0
1902-03	175-4		37.9
1903-04	187.1		39.5
1904-05	246.8[b]	200.8[b]	40.6
1905-06	256.3	208.9	41.8
1906-07	262.3	215.1	41.9
1907-08	268.6	220.5	43.2
1908-09	274.2	225.3	43.6
1909-10	301.7[c]	252.2[c]	43.6
1910-11	303.8	254.1	43.6
1911-12	307.4	257.8	43.7
1912-13	308.3	258.7	43.7
1913-14	310.2	260.4	

Source: Great Britain 1880-1914.

Notes: Productive loans are loans raised for baths, warehouses, cemeteries, electric lighting, gasworks, harbors, piers, quays, docks, canals (excluding the Manchester Ship Canal), markets, tramways, waterworks, and light railways.

[a]Great Britain 1880-1914 provides an estimate for 1879-80 of 54.2 million, but this excludes baths, warehouses, markets and tramways. These excluded items were 8.13 percent of the total in 1884-85, and so the 1879-80 estimate is increased accordingly.

[b]Includes the Metropolitan Water Boards' outstanding debt of 45.9 million.

[c]Includes the Port of London Authorities' outstanding debt of 23.2 million. Any net creations figure must exclude this sum and the 45.9 million of the Metropolitan Water Boards.

Table A2.2

Accumulated U.K. Municipal and County Debt, Publically Issued,
at Nominal Value, 1883-1913, £m

Year	Amount Issued
1883	46.00
1884	55.51
1885	60.77
1886	65.99
1887	69.71
1888	71.65
1889	74.05
1890	75.20
1891	78.57
1892	82.08
1893	91.44
1894	96.28
1895	106.14
1896	108.57
1897	118.25
1898	123.21
1899	125.50
1900	134.90
1901	138.68
1902	154.22
1903	165.98
1904	199.51
1905	208.28
1906	224.04
1907	230.46
1908	237.20
1909	263.40
1910	269.21
1911	275.96
1912	276.82
1913	277.08

Sources: Burdett's Official Intelligence, 1883-1898;
The Stock Exchange Official Intelligence, 1899-1913.

Method I. On the assumption that the nation's stock exchanges paid particular attention to debt generated for capital expenditure and ignored debt destined for nonproductive, consumption purposes, the stock exchange series on outstanding local debts can be used to estimate net local debt creations. Importantly, the stock exchange and local taxation information of tables A2.1 and A2.2 do not disagree strongly on changes in the level of outstanding

Table A2.3

Elements of the U.K. Government Capital Account, 1861–1913

(millions of pounds)

Decade	GPCF^g p.a. (1)	Death Duty Taxes p.a. (2)	Note Issue Increase p.a. (3)	Bullion Increase p.a. (4)	Net Central Govt Debt Creation p.a. (5)	Net Local Govt Debt Creation p.a. (6)
1861-70	5.70	5.15	0.35	0.99	-2.56	--
1871-80	12.60	5.71	0.32	0.13	-2.23	3.15
1881-90	11.55	7.87	-0.12	-0.06	-6.29	4.17
1891-00	21.00	13.55	0.47	0.44	-0.43	5.67
1901-10	32.10	18.93	-0.12	0.34	5.32	13.43
1911-13	25.80	25.84	0.03	0.13	-10.33	2.62

Sources:

(1): GFCF^g: Feinstein 1972: T85-86.

(2): Death Duty Taxes: Mitchell 1962: 393-94, interpolated to calendar years.

(3): Note Issue: Banker's Magazine, 1860-1913; a monthly periodical that published a statistical compendium (including estimates of the outstanding stock of notes) on a weekly basis. These stock estimates were differenced to get the increase (or decrease) in the note issue, based on year-end stocks. For example, the 1861-1870 estimate represents the difference between the stock in the last week of 1860 and the last week of 1870, divided by ten to get the annual average.

(4): Bullion Increase: Same source and method of estimation as number 3.

(5): Net Central Government Debt Creation: Mitchell 1962: 404-08; creations minus redemptions, interpolated to calendar years.

(6): Net Local Debt Creation: Burdett's Official Intelligence, 1882-1898, and The Stock Exchange Official Intelligence, 1899-1913, displayed in Table A2.2 above. The 1881-1890 estimate assumes that the average annual creations, 1884-1890--4.17 million--also hold for 1881-83. The 1871-1880 estimate is the difference between the implied stock estimate at the end of 1880, resulting from the previous calculation--33.5 million (75.2 [1880] - 41.7)--and the total municipal debt listed in The Investor's Monthly Manual, December 1869, that is, £2 million.

debt. Table A2.3 presents the estimates of government capital formation, note issue, bullion increase, net central government debt creation, and net local government debt creation. Table A2.4, column (4), shows the resulting estimate of government saving, defined in equation (A2.7).

Method II. One means of checking the accuracy of Method I's net local debt creation series is to generate a second series, based on the proportion of local government capital formation funded by net local debt creation in the years 1900–1913 and 1920–1939.

(a) 1900–1913. Since the Feinstein tables on current account surplus (1972:T35) and information on death duty taxes give us an excellent estimate of GS, 1900–1913, and all other components of the government capital account are fairly well known (table A2.3), the amount of net municipal debt creation can be estimated as a residual, 1900–1913. The average ratio of net municipal debt creation to $GFCF^g$ was .40, 1900–1913 (central government capital formation was a trivial sum, 1900–1913 and before).

(b) 1920–1939. A series of local government debt creations minus redemptions can be constructed from Feinstein's capital

Table A2.4

U.K. Government Savings, 1861–1913

(annual averages, by decade, millions of pounds)

Decade (1)	GCFC^g p.a. (2)	Transactions in Financial Instruments & Bullion p.a. (3)	GS p.a. Method I (4)	GS p.a. Method II (5)	GS Feinstein-Based Estimate (6)
1861–70	+5.70	−3.20	+8.9	+6.7	--
1871–80	+12.60	+1.11	+11.5	+9.6	--
1881–90	+11.55	−2.18	+13.7	+12.7	--
1891–1900	+21.00	+5.27	+15.7	+13.0	--
1901–10	+32.10	+18.29	+13.8	+14.8	+12.5
1911–13	+25.80	−8.68	+33.5	+24.9	+36.8

Sources: Cols. 1–5: see text. Col. 6: The current account surplus (Feinstein 1972: T35), plus death duties (Mitchell 1962: 393–94), interpolated to calendar years.

account tables (1972:T79, T81), and this averages 46 percent of local government capital formation, 1920–1939.

Note that the implication of these ratios is that GS was the principal means of raising funds for local government capital formation.

Multiplying gross government capital formation, 1860–1913, by .40 yields a series on net local debt creation, and combining this estimator with the other series of table A2.3 yields the Method II estimate of GS found in table A2.4, column 5.

A Direct Estimate. For the years 1900–1913 GS can also be estimated by adding Feinstein's surplus on current account (1972:T35) and death duty collections (table A2.3). It will be remembered that Feinstein constructed the current account surplus series by directly estimating the various taxes, other receipts, expenditures, grants, etc. Importantly, the Feinstein-based direct estimate found in table A2.4, column 6, and the indirect Method I estimate of column 4 are quite close in the overlapping years. Given their independent data bases, this result is encouraging for the quality of the pre-1900 Method I estimates. The estimates of GS employed in the text are Method I estimates, 1861–1900, and Feinstein-based estimates, 1901–1913.

NOTES

1. The Background

1. Calculated from Feinstein 1972:T4-5, T37-38. See also chapter 2.
2. Feinstein 1978:88. See also chapter 2.
3. A. Smith 1776:354; Malthus 1803:2:79-81; Ricardo 1817:139-40; Malthus 1836:271-82, 414-15; Wakefield 1849:75; Mill 1848:728-39, Marx 1894:211-66; Marshall 1887-88, 49.
4. Phelps Brown and Handfield-Jones 1952; Coppock 1956; Saville 1961; Ames and Rosenberg 1963; Richardson 1965; Ashworth 1965; W. A. Lewis 1978; McCloskey 1970; Kennedy 1974.
5. Studies by Flux 1910 and Lehfeldt 1913-14 are concerned only with debentures after 1890 and Nash 1880 is limited to the years 1870-1880.
6. Sismondi 1819:1:105, 263, 270-72; Marx 1894:ch. 15 (esp. pp. 242-44), 484.
7. Landes 1969:249-50. Contra Ricardo (1817:155) and Marshall (1887-88:9-11), who envisaged the investor's bias to run toward domestic assets.
8. Abramovitz 1961, 1964, 1968; Williamson 1964; Butlin 1964:31, 34; Richardson 1972.

2. Overseas Investment During the Pax Britannica

1. Feinstein 1978:71. Note that Feinstein's estimates are clearly for the total of overseas assets held by those residing in Great Britain. The total stock of British West Indian capital and land owned by residents of the B.W.I., Great Britain, and others was around £30 million, c.1775 (Sheridan 1968:56).
2. Deane and Cole 1969:82-89; Hartwell 1971:109-57; Hobsbawm 1969:26-38; Landes 1969:52-55; Mathias 1969:92-106.
3. Eagly and Smith 1976:206 find a coherence with London-Amsterdam interest rate movements in the late eighteenth century, but this could be a high correlation of big interest rate movements in the two financial centers due to war time conditions, not big movements in capital. Furthermore, Eagly and Smith's 1976:208 regression results testing whether British or Dutch conditions dominate London bill yields show fairly clear dominance of British conditions, 1773-1789.
4. Fogel and Engerman 1974:1:25; 2:30-31, correcting some computational errors in the sources used by Curtin 1969:140 for these dates.
5. Postan 1935; Mathias 1969:145-46; Crouzet 1972:185-88. The London-Amsterdam connection was probably stronger than any intra-British connection in the eighteenth century. The country banks that tied the short-term capital markets of Great Britain into a fairly cohesive national short-term market were a development that lagged the accelerations in the pace of industrial development (Pressnell 1956).
6. Much has been made of the fact that a certain amount of the profits from overseas investment funded the creation of the famous "Georgian" estates (Davies 1960). Several points must be made with respect to these allocations of

planter profits. First, only some of the money went to net capital formation in the form of new buildings; the land purchase involved a transfer, not an act of net capital formation. Furthermore, much of the planter profits going into real estate took the form of purchasing existing buildings, again a transfer, not an act of net capital formation. If, for example, the person who sold the estate to the "nabob" was heavily indebted and the proceeds of the sale ended up in the pockets of his creditors, it is quite possible that the net capital formation attributable to the "nabob's" profits took the form of additions to inventories or long-term investments outside the housing sector.

7. Cameron 1967:65 and P. Ford 1929:192–96 suggest links from the overseas tobacco merchants to cotton and coal.

8. There can be no question about overseas profits' being a central cause for the event itself. Spain, Portugal, and Holland received substantial amounts of overseas profits in the sixteenth to eighteenth centuries without inducing an industrial revolution.

9. Paish 1909, 1911, 1914; C. K. Hobson 1914:217–20. C. K. Hobson's table on new capital issues in London contains an important but unnoted definitional shift. From 1870 to 1902 the annual series is the sum of monthly *IMM* "money calls"; from 1903 to 1913, the annual series is the sum of monthly *IMM* "creations."

10. I am taking into consideration the definitional break in Hobson's new capital issues series mentioned in footnote 9:

	Hobson	Simon
Total money calls, 1870–1902	£1734.7 m.	£2131.8 m.
Total creations, 1903–1913	£1272.7 m.	£1628.3 m.

Clearly Simon found considerably more new colonial and foreign offerings than Hobson, but the difference is easily explained by Simon's wider search for new issue data at home and abroad.

Using various stock exchange sources, Paish estimated that the stock of British-held securities was £3714 m. in 1914. Feis 1930:27 corrected Paish's Russian and Turkish totals and increased the 1914 total to £3763.3. Both of these estimates are nominally valued so that their differences with Simon are due either to some repatriation of Simon's new issues before 1914 or to Simon's efforts to collect data from sources other than those associated with the London Stock Exchange.

11. Imlah 1958:42–81. Cottrell 1975:13 notes that Imlah probably under-estimated overseas insurance earnings, 1870–1914, and also suggests consider-able caution in using the 1815–1854/5 estimates of the OBCA. The latter fall within the error margins on the import and re-export component series.

12. Feinstein 1978:72 suggests that about £10 m. more was accumulated in gold and silver, 1830–1860, than recorded by Imlah 1958:70–72, basing his argument on contemporary sources. On the assumption that Imlah got the amount of NFI correctly over these years, this argument implies a reduction in

the amount of OBCA. We have thus reduced Imlah's accumulated sum of OBCA, £124 m., 1831-1854, by 8 million.

13. Feinstein 1972:T37-8 diverges from Imlah 1958:70-75 in estimating NFI in 1899. Imlah's data on bullion accumulation being assumed, this divergence implies some minor revision to the OBCA estimate for these years. Imlah's estimate of the OBCA accumulation, 1865-1913, is £3535 million.

14. This figure includes Feinstein's 1972, 1978 revisions and assumes with him that the stock of overseas assets stood at 10 m. and bullion at 45 m. at the end of 1815. See table 2.5 for fuller documentation (Simon 1967:52-53).

15. The bibliography in this field is very rich. Central recent contributions with excellent bibliographies are Abramovitz 1964, 1968; Butlin 1964; Cairncross 1953; Easterlin 1968; Gottlieb 1976; B. Thomas 1954, 1972; Williamson 1964. A compendium of several important monographs with an excellent introduction can be found in Hall 1968.

16. Adler 1970:170-89 presents a picture of substantial activity to control the behavior of a number of U.S. railways by British equity and debenture owners. It is, however, mainly a story of attempts rather than successes and, in view of the record of financial difficulties of nearly all U.S. lines at one time or another, the attempts seem to be rare relative to the provocations.

17. Simon 1967:58-59. Simon's text suggests it is reasonable to assume that the overwhelming portion of his government and mixed borrowers used their funds in social overhead investments, not extractive, financial, or manufacturing enterprise. On this assumption 85 percent of social overhead capital issues were government or mixed government-private enterprises, 1865-1874. At the end of the period, 1900-1914, the proportion had dropped to 48 percent. The average for the entire period, 1865-1914, was 65 percent.

18. For the mixture of law and order, stable commercial justice, and private profit, the Argentine case is fairly well analyzed. See Ferns 1973:37-52 and Ford 1962:86-87.

3. The British Capital Market, 1870-1913

1. Moreover, 33 percent of all companies registered were immediately abortive; 60 percent of all remaining public limiteds dissolved within ten years. See Shannon 1933:306-09.

2. The spread between yields on home industrials and home social-overhead debentures narrowed by about 20 percent into the 1890s and widened slightly after interest rates generally turned up in the decade or so before the war. In comparison to overseas railway yields, only Indian railway yields remained below home industrial debentures. The yield on home industrial debentures fell below Western European, United States, Canadian, and Latin American railway debenture yields. There was some reversal of this spread between home industrial and overseas railway yields in the years immediately preceding World War I, but here too the relative position did not fall back to that prevailing in the 1880s.

3. Gerschenkron 1962; Cameron 1963, 1967; and Fremdling and Tilly 1976 present generally positive views on the German investment banks. Neuberger and Stokes 1974 suggest there were substantial parts of the German economy that the big banks did not serve.

4. The model of capital asset pricing used in this essay comes from a study which clarified the earlier work of Lintner and Sharpe; Fama 1968.

5. Insurance companies and the financial trusts operated in both home and overseas markets; see Hall 1963a:47–56. The holdings of industrial companies reveal a regional and industrial diversity as well. See Sigsworth 1958:229; Hyde 1956:144–47; R. Smith 1954:130–203.

6. Shannon 1933. A discussion of aggregate default and bankruptcy in government railway and other company securities is presented in chapter 5, but nonrailway company defaults abroad are treated by assumption.

7. It is possible to show that if r_m, a common underlying factor affecting all assets, is used instead of R_M^m, the return to all assets, equation 3.3 may still be used to test propositions concerning equation 3.2, for both sides of 3.3 are off by the same constant. See Fama 1968:39–40.

8. The data are described in chapter 5 and fully tabulated in Edelstein 1970:238–91.

9. Insufficient data exist to construct an index incorporating annual changes in the level of each industry's equity. Hall 1963a is the basis of the rough estimates of the weights, 1900–1910. This index is fully described in chapter 5, and the data are presented in Edelstein (1977).

10. A dummy variable for security denomination was also tested in order to investigate the possibilities of asymmetry in "entry" costs; the variable proved even less significant than those discussed in the text.

11. The assumptions of the Sharpe-Lintner model are fairly strong. In a number of studies of the Sharpe-Lintner model, it has been reformulated to comprehend the possibilities that the capital market may not be in continuous equilibrium and that there are different prices of risk for various kinds of assets. These modified models were estimated with our British data along with the simpler model underlying table 3.3. The tests based on these modified models show the same statistical insignificance reported in table 3.3. See Friend and Blume 1970 for these modified models.

12. Corporate profits from nonrailway limiteds jumped from, at most, 8 percent of nonagricultural profits, 1870–79, to 49 percent, 1910–14. See Feinstein 1968:116 for estimates of domestic profits from nonagricultural enterprise, and corporate profits. Estimates of railway profits are from Cairncross 1953:138. The estimate of nonrailway profits, 1870–79, is £30 million, an upper bound estimate that assumes a rate of return of 13 percent (Brown 1968:412) on the average stock of long-term securities from domestic, nonrailway companies, 1870–79, or £230.

13. The figure for provincial brokers is a rough estimate based on trade directories for the entire United Kingdom. In addition to the approximate levels implied by table 3.1 the estimate above involves a small number of Irish brokers and the much larger numbers of provincial brokers who were not members of any stock exchange.

14. Little is known about the types of collateral acceptable by British banks in this period. The only mention of the subject in the secondary literature suggests use of industrial securities as collateral as early as the 1860s, and this in London. See Sayers 1957:107, 184.

15. For an excellent introduction to the role of externalities in the growth of Britain, 1870–1913, see Kindleberger 1964:chapters 3 and 7.

4. Micro Processes

1. For Britain, see Cairncross 1953; B. Thomas 1954, 1972; and J. P. Lewis 1965. For the regions of recent settlement, see Abramovitz 1961, 1964; Bloomfield 1968; Easterlin 1968; Hall 1963a; Butlin 1964; Dowie 1963, 1966; and Williamson 1964.

2. Having tried a number of ways of aggregating proxies for the annual variation in overseas returns, Bloomfield 1968:40 stated that "with few exceptions, the results of these various tests proved negative. . . . these unsatisfactory results no doubt reflect in part the simple character of the underlying models, which do not take account of the many other influences acting upon capital flows." J. M. Stone 1971 attempted to test some of Cairncross' aggregative hypotheses and found little evidence for the influence of the terms of trade. However, data problems seem to have limited his ability to test other hypotheses. Furthermore, t-statistics and beta coefficients are not reported, and so it is difficult to assess and weigh the merits of his proxies.

3. See Abramovitz 1961, 1964; Williamson 1964; Butlin 1964; Hall 1963a, 1968; Paterson 1976; Dowie 1963; and Ford 1971. Bloomfield 1968 and Richardson 1972 examine a number of regions individually. Among the very few industrial studies are Frankel 1967 on South African mining and Adler 1970 on American railways.

4. E.g., Williamson 1964:ch. 4; Ford 1971; Richardson 1972; Paterson 1976:32–36.

5. In both level and fluctuation the yield on U.K.-held U.S. investments was closely related to that on Latin American assets, and, to a lesser extent, those on Western and Eastern European assets. See Edelstein 1970:198–202.

6. For an excellent empirical investigation of the small proportion of British investment in Canada that was direct, see Paterson 1976.

7. Williamson's study of movement in the U.S. balance of payments is the only previous econometric work that deals directly with the push-versus-pull problem in the U.S. context. A "reduced form" methodology is employed. In two separate regressions, one with U.K. and U.S. domestic investment as the independent variables and the other with U.K. and U.S. domestic stock prices, the U.K. variables accounted for most of the variance of net U.S. capital imports. Unfortunately, even though Williamson thought both U.S. and U.K. financial market behavior was critical to the U.K.-U.S. flow, his use of purely domestic U.K. variables carries the implicit assumption that non-U.K., non-U.S. accumulations and returns were irrelevant to the U.K. decision to invest in the United States. As noted in the text, this is a highly tenuous assumption. Williamson 1964:ch. 4.

8. Miller and Whitman 1970 tried the level of national income as a proxy for cyclical risk patterns. When a similar variable was employed in our preliminary tests (not reported here), the sign on the regression coefficient varied across assets and the regression coefficients were often insignificant. This inconsistency and other evidence suggest that national income is a bad proxy for risk, and it was therefore dropped from consideration.

9. To further test this conclusion, the exogenous variables from the U.S. investment functions of Kmenta and Williamson, and of Neal, were introduced separately into the reduced form equation in the yield on U.S. railway bonds in the London market. This equation was derived from the portfolio demand and asset supply relations shortly to be presented. In general, the exogenous variables from the U.S. investment demand equation were not significantly related to the London yield variable.

10. The partial correlation of N.Y. and London yields on first-class U.S. railway bonds was .98, 1871–1913; for changes in their levels, the partial correlation coefficient was .77.

11. While the interpretation of the estimated U.S. wealth elasticity is fairly unambiguous for most years of the 1870–1913 period, it is likely that in the six or seven years just before World War I the wealth variable is, to some important degree, an instrument for both the general U.S. demand for railway assets and the surging influence of railway corporate savings. Unfortunately, owing to the presence of multicollinearity, it was impossible to give separate econometric expression to these two influences.

12. The effects of $e/g + e$ and $g/g + e$ are directly analogous to the involvement of the price elasticities in a model of a commodity demand and supply. The amount the equilibrium quantity increases when, for example, income increases and the demand curve shifts, depends on the relative elasticity of the supply curve and the demand curve. If the own-price elasticities of the demand and supply curves are equal, the rise in the equilibrium quantity bought and sold is only half the relative rise in incomes. If g is very large relative to e, the relative rise in the equilibrium quantity is very close to the relative income rise.

13. The series on the money calls for U.S. securities issued in London was prepared by the late M. Simon and kindly provided by I. Stone, Baruch College, City University of New York. To arrive at annual stock estimates, the Simon series was cumulated from an estimate of £50 million in U.K. holdings of U.S. portfolio issues in 1870. See table 3.1.

14. U.K. domestic fixed investment (Feinstein 1961:374) and net foreign lending are cumulated from an interpolated estimate of 4632.4 million pounds of U.K. reproducible wealth in 1870 (Deane and Cole 1969:274).

15. Money calls on total overseas long-term security issues (Simon 1967:52–53) are cumulated from the estimated stock of overseas issues held in the United Kingdom in 1870 given in table 3.1. Money calls on domestic long-term security issues (Hall 1957:62) are decumulated for the estimated stock of home securities outstanding in 1913 given in table 3.1. The stock of commercial bank loans and advances derives from Sheppard 1971:116.

16. $W2$ may possibly be affected by double-counting. Short-term commercial loans were extended to holders of long-term portfolio investments, and the totals for domestic and overseas portfolio investments include the equity of home and foreign banks. To test for possible bias arising from this factor, a third U.K. wealth variable, $W3$, was constructed that consisted of domestic and overseas portfolio investments alone. Regressions run with $W3$ as the U.K. wealth variable yielded coefficients that were not significantly different from those run with $W2$.

17. This series was prepared for Kuznets 1961 and kindly provided by the author.

18. A crude approximation of domestic U.S. holdings may be obtained by subtracting U.K. holdings of U.S. assets, A, from the series on the total outstanding debt of the U.S. railway found in U.S. Bureau of the Census 1960.

19. See Edelstein 1970:Appendix IV for r_A and r_{UK}. The source of r_{US} is USBC 1960:656.

20. For the principal components analysis, see Edelstein 1970:200. In the first attempts to estimate the structural equations, indices of equity rates of return that incorporated capital gains were utilized as estimators of the expected rate of return on home and overseas assets, both by themselves and alongside the estimators of debenture yields noted in the text. These early tests suggested that the debenture yield series was the best indicator of year-to-year movements in the expected return to financial assets. While the regression coefficients on the equity return variables were statistically insignificant, this was rarely the case with the coefficients on the debenture yield variables. The low explanatory value of equity rates of return incorporating capital gains is consistent with studies of recent financial behavior, a result that is generally attributed to the inability of equity return estimators to effectively capture investor views of corporate retained earnings and the tendency of dividend yields to move inversely with expected changes in earnings. See, for example, C. Wright 1969:286–92.

21. See Malinvaud 1966:473–96 for an excellent discussion of this model of lagged behavior and its econometric problems. The specific technique employed to estimate these equations is that of Fair 1970:507–15.

22. While the problem of multicollinearity allows only the most tentative statements on differences in lagged behavior, the lags in the excess supply equations tended to be somewhat longer than those in the demand relations and lags in both relationships were longer in the years 1874–1894 than during 1895–1913. The latter movement suggests that both asset demanders and suppliers underwent a familiarization or learning process as the period progressed. Since the relative risk on American assets held in the U.K. probably fell across the period, it may also be that stock adjustment was more rapid because these assets were becoming more liquid. It would, however, be quite difficult to distinguish these two hypotheses, for risk is, in part, a subjective judgment; thus familiarity may have led to lowered risk premiums and lowered risk premiums to greater familiarity.

23. The cost of this adjustment is that, while the estimates of the remaining

structural parameters are larger than they would be if their current influence on LA_t was isolated, they are underestimates of the true long-run parameters. However, these underestimates never seriously affect our basic conclusion when the estimated equations are employed to analyze the relative influence of U.S. and U.K. participants and other historical issues.

24. While the central focus of our model of U.K. investment in the U.S. is the long run, it is useful to ask how well the model captures market behavior immediately subsequent to the period's financial panics. Given the sudden downturn of expectations on these occasions, it is reasonable to hypothesize that, in the year following a financial panic, the estimated demand and excess supply equations would tend to overestimate the level of U.S. securities held in the U.K. The financial panics of 1875, 1878, 1882, 1890, 1895, and 1907 either engulfed the London market or were so important to the New York market that it can be assumed that the American segment of the London market was substantially disturbed; see Morgenstern 1959:546-48. Inspection of the sign on the residuals from Table 1's equations in the year immediately following these panic years (nearly all of the panics occurred late in the calendar year) confirms the overestimation hypothesis, but it is important to note that the magnitude of the average residual in the postpanic year is quite small relative to the standard error of the regression. To the extent that our model effectively captures the secular tendencies of market participants, the latter finding suggests that the postpanic year did not involve large amounts of aberrant behavior, and it seems reasonable to attribute this to the relative maturity of the London capital market. The relatively largest residuals tended to occur at major peaks and troughs of A, which, as Morgenstern carefully notes, were often not years of financial panics.

25. Needless to say, the sign on r^{US} in the 1874-1894 excess supply equation is incorrect if r^{US} is assumed to be a variable reflecting alternative returns for U.S. investors. Inspection of the correlation matrices suggests that the yields on U.S. industrial and railway equity tended to move together during the first subperiod; thus, r^{US} may have acted as a measure of the cost of U.S. railway funding. However, to the extent that a much higher proportion of U.S. railway equity was marketed and held in the U.S. than in the U.K., it still seems safe to continue to treat r^{US} as approximately exogenous to the trans-Atlantic capital migrations.

26. Rates of price change in the United States and United Kingdom were roughly similar and fairly small on an annual basis for both 1874-1894 and 1895-1913. It therefore seems plausible to assume that expected rates of price change in the two countries were based on similar and lengthy past price histories and thus may be safely ignored. See Neal 1969:126-27 on lowered risk premiums.

27. Although there is some debate over the precise extent of the shift to the use of external long-term financial instruments, there is little doubt concerning the fact of the shift. See Hall 1957, 1958 and Cairncross 1958.

28. The average yield on first-class U.S. railway and U.K. industrial debentures listed on the London stock exchange, 1892-1913, were 3.94 percent and 4.06 percent respectively.

29. It is sometimes suggested that the industrial and geographic distribution of British wealth was suboptimal during the years 1870–1913, because of certain dynamic institutional or technological inefficiencies connected with Britain's largely private processes of savings and investment. Since Britain was the major international long-term lender during these years, it would be interesting to assess Britain's power to affect market interest rates and clearings and to calculate the foregone income potentially available to compensate the nation for these suspected inefficiencies. Given that the own-interest elasticities of the U.S. excess supply and U.K. asset demand relations, g and e, respectively, were less than unity and roughly equal, 1895–1913, it follows that, all else held constant, a stamp tax on American assets held in Britain would probably have raised the interest income (tax included) paid by the American borrowers and that the burdens of the tax would have been shared equally by the Americans and private British lenders. Of course, "all else" most certainly would not have remained constant. It seems probable that a large portion of these direct gains would have disappeared owing to, first, U.S. shifts to alternative European and domestic U.S. funding sources, and second, the effects of a likely diminished rate of U.S. railway capital formation on the price of British imports from the United States. It is, of course, somewhat artificial to hypothesize a tax on only U.S. holdings when Britain's market power probably was greater elsewhere abroad. However, an attempt to assess the effects of a stamp tax on all overseas holdings would require an aggregative general equilibrium model specifying, among other relationships, Britain's aggregate savings behavior.

30. Bloomfield 1968:38; Williamson 1964:148, 152, 155. In tests not shown here a reduced-form version of our U.S. model was estimated in both stock and flow form, and the rank order of beta coefficients in the two resulting equations was quite similar.

31. Beta coefficients are the outcome of a regression where each variable has been divided by its standard deviation. Normalizing the variables by their standard deviations avoids the problem of differences in the scale of each variable. Beta coefficients are thus a "pure" number that indexes how much of a right-hand variable's variance "accounts for" the variance of the left-hand variable. See Hanushek and Jackson 1977:78–79 for its sampling properties.

5. Private Realized Rates of Return

1. Fieldhouse 1967 provides a convenient compendium of the views summarized in this paragraph.

2. For example, Kennedy 1974 argues that, since most U.K. overseas investments were held in the form of low-risk debentures, overseas investment may have earned a lower average return than home investments, which were placed in equity and preference shares, as well as debenture instruments. In addition, the timing of home and overseas returns differed and thus overseas investment afforded the opportunity to diversify out of the British business cycle.

3. Flux 1910 and Lehfeldt 1913–14 are concerned with debentures, whereas

Nash 1880 covers only the years from 1870 to 1880, and Cairncross 1953 provides a modern discussion.

4. See Nerlove 1968. For a variety of reasons, "insiders" may withhold some of their knowledge from the public. It seems implausible, however, that such information monopolies can be maintained for more than a few years. Some individuals will find a leak profitable, if only to facilitate the public issue of a firm's securities. In any event, modern studies show a very strong relationship between equity prices and earnings; see Brealey 1969:77–114.

5. As noted in chapter 3, Saville 1965, Landes 1969, and Kennedy 1974, 1976, argue that there was an institutional or investor bias in favor of overseas investment. Writing at the beginning of the nineteenth century, Ricardo 1817:151 suggests that savers preferred home assets.

6. Stigler 1963 studies rates of return to real capital, for example. Examples of studies of the rates of return to financial capital include Frankel 1967 and Merrett and Sykes 1963.

7. A full discussion of selection procedures and sources, as well as listings of the securities in each industrial and governmental grouping, may be found in Edelstein 1970:238–74. The principal sources consulted include Nash 1880, Flux 1910, Lehfeldt 1913–14, and Smith and Horne 1934.

8. Several equity groupings warrant special comment. First, the Oldham cotton spinning grouping is the product of "oversampling" in a branch of the textile industry. The grouping "all textiles" includes cotton spinning firms, but most of the securities in the Oldham sample are not used in the aggregate index, in order to avoid serious distortion. Second, roughly half of the securities in the "mechanical equipment" grouping are equity instruments of railway equipment manufacturers.

9. See Nerlove 1968:316–17 for a discussion of the estimator adopted here and several alternatives. In Nerlove's tests, all estimators produced similar results in the long run.

10. The text rightly stresses that r_{ijkt} is literally an index of "realized" return, the net wealth accumulation of a 1-year holding pattern. It is possible, however, to treat r_{ijkt} as an estimator of expected returns, too. Such a view involves assumption that the rate of capital gain, dividend (or interest) payout, and price change will be the same in the forthcoming period as they have been over the previous year.

11. Hall 1958 demonstrates the substantial errors in the new issue information. These errors were often carried over to "old" issue data in *The Investors Monthly Manual* and elsewhere.

12. The principal alternative to the method adopted in the text is to continue weighting each security equiproportionately, this time with the securities in national or supranational groupings. The U.K. pattern of purchase was not, of course, equiproportionate, and hence, the method described in the text is relatively superior. However, equiproportionate national and supranational indices were constructed and tested against the indices presented in the text. Differences in level, trend, and timing were not statistically significant.

13. As a further qualification, note that this method of aggregation introduces a form of the classic index number problem. The employment of 1913 weights in some sense assumes that U.K. investors had full presentiment. If the weights are taken from earlier dates, the implicit assumption is that U.K. investors could not recognize a good thing. To test the importance of this difficulty, aggregate indices with both 1890 and 1913 weights were constructed. Although the two weighting systems generated small differences in the absolute level, trend, and timing of the aggregate home and overseas indices, the gross comparative statements that are the focus of this study were largely unaffected. For economy of presentation, only one set of aggregate indices is employed here. The 1913 weighted indices were chosen because the quality of their data base is somewhat better than that of the 1890 weights. The 1890 and 1913 weights are based on data found in Hall 1963:4, 11, 13, 16, 20 and Edelstein 1970:229-37. Underlying these studies are the data found in *Burdett's Official Intelligence* 1882-98, *The Stock Exchange Offical Intelligence* 1899-1914, and *The Investors Monthly Manual* 1864-1914. The weights are available upon request from the author.

14. See Phelps Brown 1968:40 and Bowley 1937:appendix D for a description of the series and reservations respectively. In theory, Phelps Brown's cost-of-living index is inappropriate for a study of wealth allocation and rates of return, because it is based on worker, not wealth-owner, budgets. Unfortunately, a cost-of-living index for wealth owners is not available. Whether use of a worker's cost-of-living index substantially misrepresents either the absolute level or trends of our indices is unknown, although it does seem doubtful. In any case, since Phelps Brown's index is appropriately applied to all series, any bias due to this problem does not affect any comparative statements.

15. As of 1913 the included sectors were at a minimum 66.8 percent of the total overseas portfolio, while overseas extractive and manufacturing, and foreign government were, at most, 20.0 percent and 13.2 percent, respectively. Since the latter are definitely overestimates, which thus exaggerate their importance, the test of the impact of omitting them is biased in their favor. As may be seen, however, this rebounds in favor of table 5.5's evidence on the overseas–home return gap.

16. Frankel 1967:27 finds that the realized return to *all* classes of South African gold-mining equity, 1887-1913, was 2.1 percent per annum. This estimate includes, however, a considerable amount of third-class and failed equity. The average return on *all* South African gold-mining equity, 1887-1967, was 5.2 percent per annum. The text assumes that this is a good *lower* bound estimate of the realized return on first- and second-class overseas extractive and manufacturing, 1870-1913. Tables 5.3 and 5.4 lend support to this 5.2 percent per annum assumption. The returns to first- and second-class South African banking equity, and tea and coffee equity, 10.53 percent annum and 9.34 percent per annum, 1870-1913, respectively, were considerably higher than the assumed 5.2 percent per annum, and these groupings derived their profits from similar sources. Note also that the assumed 5.2 percent is below the aggregate return on domestic equity, 6.37 percent per annum.

17. Let DD = domestic company defaults, d = the default rate, and DK = the paid-up capital in domestic companies. Mathematically, $DD = \Sigma_{1870}^{1913} d(DK_t)$, where d is assumed to equal 2.7 percent per annum. To estimate DD, a time series of DK must be estimated. The paid-up capital in U.K.-registered, nonrailway companies in 1913 was £2.4 billion, but this estimate contains an unknown amount of capital for overseas enterprise (Great Britain, 1871-1914). The nominal capital of domestic, nonrailway companies listed by London Stock Exchange publications was approximately £1.5 ± 0.1 billion at the same date (table 3.1). By 1913 most domestic companies listed on the London Stock Exchange required fully paid-up shares, but the estimate based on the stock exchange fails to include capital traded on provincial stock exchanges and privately held and exchanged capital. The best estimate of domestic paid-up capital is probably £1.9 billion. The estimate of net insolvency losses in the text assumes that the timing of domestic accumulation was that of all U.K.-registered companies, 1870-1913, and the initial value of domestic paid-up capital in 1870 was £0.1 billion.

18. Bankruptcy losses from partnerships and other, noncompany organized enterprises are thus ignored. According to Macgregor 1929 these losses were about a quarter of nonrailway company losses, 1893-1902.

19. (£billion/0.61) − £1 billion = £0.64 billion approximately.

20. Let OVD = total nondomestic company defaults, 1870-1913, d = the default rate, and OVK = the paid-up capital in nondomestic companies. Mathematically $OVD = \Sigma_{1870}^{1913} d(OVK_t)$, where d, is assumed to equal 2.7 percent per annum. OVK is estimated by taking the 1870 and 1913 values of overseas company capital from table 2.1 and interpolating the intervening year's values with the aid of Simon 1967:52-53.

21. This £500 million is the sum of £50 million in foreign government defaults and £450 million in overseas company defaults.

22. See Sharpe 1970, esp. chaps. 5, 6, for an excellent introduction to modern portfolio pricing theory. The Sharpe-Lintner model of asset pricing suggests that, in a fairly competitive market, where each investor acts on the basis of predicted returns, standard deviations of return, and the correlation coefficient of return, the equilibrium-expected return to any security (or portfolio) will be a linear function of the expected covariance of the security's (or portfolio's) return and the market rate of return. The covariance term as a measure of risk takes into consideration both the existence and the desirability of diversification. The model involves a number of rather stringent assumptions concerning investor preferences, the extent of investor agreement, and market institutions, assumptions that were met only crudely by the U.K. capital market 1870-1913.

23. See Sharpe 1970:117-86 and Brealey 1969:123-32 and their respective bibliographies for an introduction to recent empirical work. Use of the covariance measure of risk implicitly assumes that factors such as the difficulty of contending with foreign legal systems in the event of bankruptcy reflect themselves in the relative volatility of a securities earnings and market price and thus in our realized rates of return. The assumption is explicitly examined in the

latter part of this section. One of the cruder aspects of our covariance measure of *ex ante* measure of risk is that it is calculated over the same 44 years as the average return data. Our only excuse is that there were opportunities for diversification resulting from long swings in numerous home and overseas groupings and only with a large span of years would the covariance measure incorporate these phenomena.

24. As mentioned in note 22, use of the covariance term assumes that U.K. investors were sensitive to gains from diversification. On the alternative assumption that they were not very sensitive to the gains from diversification, the standard deviation (a measure of own-variation rather than covariation) of tables 5.3 and 5.4 groupings was also tried as a measure of risk. The r^2's of these regressions were somewhat lower than those using the covariance measure, but the behavior of their residuals was substantially the same as that reported in tables 5.3 and 5.4 for the covariance measure.

25. Only those groupings in tables 5.3 and 5.4 whose returns span the years 1870–1913 or 1871–1913 are included in table 5.6's data base.

26. The indices of the "risk-premium" predicted by table 5.6's equation for U.K. railway equity and preference shares are 2.30 percent and −1.40 percent, respectively.

27. See Saul 1968, Taylor 1969, and Burn 1940 for views suggesting technological backwardness; see McCloskey 1971b and Floud 1971 for recent contrary views.

28. Clearly, no U.K. investor held either the national portfolio or the home and overseas segments being examined here. In some sense, the national portfolio is "representative" of the aggregate of all investors' interaction for return and diversification. It is important to note here that, according to modern portfolio theory, the values of the coefficients in table 5.6's regressions (the unit prices of risk) are presumed to be invariant according to whether one is examining individual securities, nonoptimal portfolios such as those in table 5.3 and 5.4, or optimally diversified portfolios.

29. Implicit in the covariance measure of risk are two motives for acquiring new assets. The assets may offer a better combination of return and own-risk than ones current set, or the new asset may offer opportunities for diversification, regardless of own-risk and return, because the new assets' return is not highly correlated with ones current set. Both motives are guiding investors in our model and it is reasonable to suppose both motives were responsible for acquiring overseas assets. Table 5.5 shows that overseas returns were higher than home returns for approximately the same standard deviation of return and, importantly, the correlation coefficient of aggregate home and overseas returns was 0.562.

30. Kennedy 1974 hypothesized that the rate of return on overseas assets was lower than that for all home assets owing to the very high proportion of low-risk debentures in the overseas holding. Our evidence suggests that for portfolio assets the gross rate of return was higher abroad (table 5.5's). However, Kennedy's hunch that overseas assets carried a lower level of risk, albeit small,

appears to find some support here. Kennedy's remarks dealt, or course, with all home assets, rather than just those sold across the nation's stock exchanges. Yet, it is an open question whether the assets left off the nation's exchanges principally small businesses, large family-held businesses, and agricultural and urban real estate were, on average, riskier than those that were traded on the exchange.

6. Trends and Cycles in Private Realized Rates of Return

1. The validity of this periodization is roughly confirmed by testing the actual proportion of the years of home (or overseas) dominance during each subperiod against the null hypothesis that the proportion should be one-half if there were no distinct subperiods; the null hypothesis fails at levels of significance of 0.001, 0.168, 0.001, and 0.317; home dominance in the first subperiod, 1870–76, is not statistically significant. However, home returns exceeded overseas returns in 4 of this subperiod's 7 years and, as shown in table 6.2, the average of home returns exceeded overseas returns during these years. On this basis, it was concluded that the years 1870–76 were a period of home dominance, albeit mildly so.

2. The year 1872 is the first year of the detrended and smoothed data and the first long-swing peak for domestic returns, but it is obviously not the peak year when annual unsmoothed data for 1870 and 1871 are inspected. The year 1911 is the last year of the detrended and smoothed data, but it is clear from the annual unsmoothed data for 1912 and 1913 that overseas aggregate returns continue to decline beyond 1911 to the end of the data presented here. In consideration of the possibility that 1913 may not be the actual trough year, the data are placed in parentheses in the text.

3. Cairncross 1953. For a good compendium of the various views on long-swing investment behavior, see Hall 1968; also valuable are Abramovitz 1968 and Easterlin 1968.

4. A discussion of how realized rates of return may have acted with other factors as causes of long swings in home and overseas investment is too complex a topic to be considered here. However, a regression analysis employing polynomial-distributed lags suggests that current and past values of home portfolio investment are stronger determinants of current home-realized returns than current and past values of home-realized returns are of current investment flows, and similarly for overseas investment and realized return variates. Thus, concentrating on the role of realized returns as an outcome of the investment process rather than as a cause has some empirical support.

5. There are two important products of an analysis of principal components: first, a set of new and statistically distinct variables, the x_i's or principal components, usually fewer in number than the original set of variables (the y_j's) and which to a known degree "explain" the total variance of the original multivariate system; and second, the a's, the weights that are used to build the first, second, etc., principal components. Through an examination of each

component's weights, it is possible to grasp the central character of the regularities in the original multivariate system. See Morrison 1967:222-34 for a rigorous treatment.

6. The statistical results of a principal-components analysis are quite detailed and thus only the principal conclusions are summarized here.

7. It is a well-known characteristic of this period that U.K. national income and expenditure fluctuated much less widely than either domestic or overseas investment expenditures Mathews, 1957:216-21. One reason offered for this phenomenon is that the inverse long-swing movement of home and overseas investment expenditures yielded a roughly constant share of total investment in national expenditures. Section B's analysis of the inverse motion of home- and overseas-realized returns indicates that a similar substitution and possible constancy in the aggregate may have characterized the share of national income accruing to U.K. wealth holders as well. Section C's principal-components analysis suggests the existence of several other important inverse relationships among various home and overseas sectors and adds another basis for the relative smoothness of aggregate U.K. income and expenditure.

8. Most prominently in the works of J. A. Hobson 1902, Hilferding 1910, Lenin 1916.

9. Owen and Sutcliffe 1972, and Hopkins 1973, esp. ch. 4. For an opposing view, see Fieldhouse 1973, esp. ch. 2.

7. *Determinants of Aggregate U.K. Overseas Investment*

1. According to Bloomfield 1968:47 net capital imports into the United States were $1045 million, 1886-90, and British net capital exports were $2131.2 million over the same years. U.K. gross national accumulation, 1886-90, was $4506.8 million, an exchange rate of $4.867 to the pound being assumed; see appendix 1.

2. Canadian net capital imports, 1911-13, were $1157 million, while U.K. net capital exports were $3009.3 million according to Bloomfield 1968:42. U.K. gross national accumulations, 1911-13, were $5670.1 million at $4.867 to the pound; see appendix 1. Firestone 1958:248 gives the Canadian gross domestic investment rate at 26.4 percent of national product in 1910 and the Canadian net borrowing rate as 13.0 percent.

3. Reflecting both short- and long-cycle influences, the partial correlation coefficient of Feinstein's rate of gross domestic fixed investment (GDFI/Y) and net foreign lending (NFI/Y) was .41, 1856-1873. From 1873 to 1913, their partial correlation coefficient was −.77. For data see appendix 1.

4. Cairncross 1953 is a revised version of the original, widely read dissertation, which was entitled, *Home and Foreign Investment in Great Britain, 1870-1913* (Unpub. Ph.D. dissertation, Cambridge, England, 1935). The compendium of essays assembled by Hall 1968 is a fair rendering of the long-swing emphasis in U.K. foreign lending studies after Cairncross.

8. Structure of U.K. Savings Behavior, 1850-1913, and the Evidence on Oversaving Tendencies

1. The principal data source is Feinstein 1972. Gross private savings is estimated by adding gross fixed domestic investment, inventory change, and net foreign lending to obtain gross national savings (T8-9[3-4], T37-39[16]), and then an estimate of government savings is subtracted from gross national savings to obtain gross private savings. The estimator of government savings is "rates and taxes on expenditures" minus "current expenditures on goods and services" (T8-9[2,8]). This estimate leaves out a number of insignificant receipts and expenditure items that have not been estimated for the years prior to 1900. The omitted items tend to cancel each other out in the scattered available evidence. The correct total is available (T35[12]) after 1900, and the correlation between our estimator and the true figure is .87. The income estimate of these regression tests is gross national product at factor cost (T8-9[12]). Wage income is estimated by income from employment (T4-5[1]), and nonwage income is gross national product less wage incomes. The estimate of private assets is derived from Feinstein's estimate of the net domestic capital stock at current replacement value (T103-05[9]), the accumulated stock of overseas lending (T37-38[16], T110), and the outstanding stock of the U.K. government's debt from Mitchell 1962:403; all of these components of the wealth estimate are deflated by Feinstein's consumer price index (T132-33[1]). The estimator of interest rate movements in Homer's 1963:196-97, 409 yield on Consols.

2. For railway profits, see Cairncross 1953:138. For gross national product, see appendix 1.

3. In the functions incorporating Koyck-type lag structures, $(Y-S)_{-1}$ is employed to embody the idea that the short-run marginal propensity to save is larger than the long-run marginal propensity to save. A direct proof of this assumption may be found in the estimators of the hybrid Friedman-Ando-Modigliani model, introduced later.

4. The S.E.R.s of the rejected models were all greater than 22.5. Their Durbin-Watson statistics indicated statistically significant negative serial correlation as well.

5. The interest rate employed here is not deflated by an index of expected price change, p^e. At an early testing stage an estimator of p^e was introduced that was based on price change over the previous ten years with geometrically declining weights. The regression coefficient on the deflated interest rate, $r - p^e$, was insignificantly different from that on the nominal interest rate. Since long-term price change before 1913 was very small on an annual basis, it seems reasonable to assume that expected price change would also be small on an annual basis, and hence, most of the play in the real interest rate would be from the nominal interest rate.

6. Two-stage least squares estimates of the classical and Friedman-Ando-Modigliani models were prepared with r and y treated as endogenous variables. The remaining right-hand variables in the savings functions were treated as exogenous, as well as lagged values of national output and the domestic capital

stock, current stock prices, and current high-powered money. The resulting estimates of the interest rate coefficient were slightly higher than the ordinary least squares estimates but insignificantly so.

7. Horne 1947. The best data compendium can be found in Sheppard 1971:141-72.

8. During the years 1899-1902 the average annual government savings rate (GS/Y) was −2.11 percent of gross national product. The average GS/Y for 1870-98, 1903-13 was .81 percent. If the years 1870-98, 1903-1913 are assumed to be a rough measure of what would have prevailed, on average, in the absence of the Boer War, some interesting points can be made on the effect of the only large government deficit on savings behavior in a period of generally small and mildly surplus government budgets. The gross national rate of accumulation (GNA/Y) in the non-Boer War years was 13.32 percent, and the gross private savings rate (GPS/Y) was 12.51 percent. During the Boer War, the GNS/Y was 12.53 percent and the GPS/Y was 14.64 percent. If the effect of the Boer War was the change in the rate of government saving, that is, 2.92 percent of gross national product (= .81 − [−2.11]), then a quarter of the expense of the war took the form of reductions in new national capital formation and wealth, and three quarters took the form of a rise in the gross private savings rate. Patriotism may have been involved in the latter result; capital controls were not. In any event, the higher GPS/Y was rewarded, for it was accompanied by above-trend interest rates. Unfortunately, no strong conclusion on the effect of government borrowing can be made, because the economy peaked in 1900 and unemployment rates were rising.

9. Predicted Desired Savings Rate = Actual Savings Rate minus Residual Error.

10. Note that the hypothesis of an *ex ante* disequilibrium gap resolved through output movements implicitly denies that the interest rate was an important force for equilibrition of savings and investment over periods of a few years. In fact, the principal involvement of the interest rate in the savings models estimated here was their role in accounting for the U shape of the savings rate, 1874-1913, and certain other fairly long-run movements.

9. Influence of Domestic Investment Conditions on the Rate of Overseas Investment

1. Econometric estimates of the interest sensitivity of U.K. net foreign lending have not been very successful (e.g., Bloomfield 1968:39-40; Richardson 1972:107). Experimentation suggests that negative interest rate coefficients appear only when the U.K. net foreign lending equation is estimated on the assumption that it was simultaneously determined within a structure like the one presented in chapter 7. The best two-stage, least-squares regression equation yields a calculated interest elasticity of net foreign lending as −.53 (i.e., a 1.00 percent change in the Consol interest rate led to an opposite 0.53 percent change in the level of net foreign lending).

2. The crudity of the approximation is due to the fact that some emigrants

would have died if they had remained in England and Wales across the given decade. The emigrants were, however, quite disproportionately not from age groups with the highest death rates, that is, infants and the elderly. The true rate of natural increase would be somewhat higher, therefore, but not by very much.

3. Population-sensitive investment demand, especially residential housing investment demand, is clearly also a function of family income levels. Hence, if average family income accelerated its growth at the same time that population growth and urbanization slowed, it is possible that the latter effects might be nullified. However, income per capita growth rates are not an independent variable. Proximally, it depended on productivity growth trends and, as will be shown in the next section of this chapter, growth rates of income per capita and output per worker were slowing in the United Kingdom from the 1870s onward to World War I.

4. The measures of productivity presented in the text and tables are output per unit labor or population. Measuring productivity by output per unit of weighted labor and capital, McCloskey 1970:457–58 arrives at quite similar trends. Curiously, the downward trend of total factor productivity is neglected in McCloskey's general defense of the Victorian economy.

5. See Schmookler 1966, esp. chs. 6, 7, for the interaction between extent of market and invention.

6. Aldcroft 1964 surveys the evidence for entrepreneurial failure; McCloskey and Sandberg 1971 survey the opposing viewpoint.

7. The plausibility of no retaliation in the late 1870s and 1880s, when other industrialized nations raised their tariffs but the United Kingdom did not, hinges on the fact that the British market was probably a small share of the output of the exporting U.S., German, and others' industrial sectors. Its implausibility depends on the weight one wishes to give the heightened nationalism of these years, reflected to some degree in the period's well-known rise in European imperialism in Africa and Asia. In the U.S. case, retaliation might have been limited by the politicians from the Cotton South and the Wheat Midwest.

8. In the lower panel of table 9.9 the F-test statistic indicates a significant influence of NFI/Y on DW/Y when the equation structure ignores simultaneous interactions and the lag length is two years. It will also be noticed that the Durban-Watson serial correlation statistic is 1.81, indicating the possibility of some serial correlation in the residuals. Extending the lags to reduce the serial correlation removes the significant influence of NFI/Y on DW/Y. The implication is that, when longer lag processes for DW/Y are incorporated in the model of DW/Y, both the short- and long-term influence of NFI/Y become insignificant.

10. Accumulation in the United States and Its Pull on U.K. Savings

1. Discussions predating the discovery of the accelerating accumulation rate were also quite skeptical of the contribution of U.S. net foreign borrowing to U.S. development; see Knapp 1957:433–34 and Kravis 1972:403–4.

2. Williamson 1964 is the classic study of long swings in U.S. international commodity and payment flows. Indeed, it clearly presages the later development of the monetary approach to the balance of payments. It is not a study of trends, as is Williamson 1979; in the 1964 work Williamson deliberately detrends his time series to focus on the long cycles.

3. Much debate surrounds the effects of the U.S. Civil War on U.S. accumulation patterns. Evidence of a lag of wages behind prices during the Civil War is offered by DeCanio and Mokyr 1977, but, as the authors note, wages began to catch up with prices as soon as the war ended and thus reversed any rise in the profit share stemming from the Civil War wage lag. Significantly, the catchup took much longer than the period of inflationary shift, and so the profit shift of the Civil War may have lasted for some years beyond 1865. Using the DeCanio-Mokyr estimates of the average annual Civil War redistribution less the average annual post-Civil War reversal suggests that perhaps 1 percent of GNP was in the hands of profit owners in 1871 that was not there in 1854. By using the text methods, this means perhaps 0.45 percent of GNP in 1871 was devoted to savings that was not so allocated in 1854. Engerman 1966 noted that the interest on the Civil War debt was redistributive, since the typical owner of the debt was relatively wealthy and the average taxpayer was not. He found perhaps 1 percent of GNP devoted to savings in the late 1860s and 1870s that was not there before the Civil War. Williamson 1974a noted the displacement effect of Civil War financing and the reverse effect after the war ended and the debt was repaid. He did not, however, show why the effect of these movements should be on the size of the private savings rate as opposed to its composition if, as Williamson argued, the debt was raised at competitive interest rates. Indeed, the high nominal and real interest rates of the post-Civil War years raise a logical problem, If we sum the effects of shifting age structure, profit shares, wage lags, and debt financing, there is a very strong overdetermination of U.S. domestic savings behavior. Why then were nominal and real interest rates so high, 1866–72? One possibility is that the Civil War had some negative effects on national thrift that have yet to be explored.

4. For the U.S., see Fishlow 1965:178 and Homer 1963:287–88, 318–20. For the United States, sec Hawke 1970:200, 406 and Broadbridge 1970:65.

5. Deane 1968:104–7. The implicit price of domestic fixed investment goods relative to the implicit price of gross national product was 90.4, 1841–50; 87.8, 1851–60; 83.3, 1861–70; and 95.2, 1871–80.

11. Australian Accumulation Pressures and Their Pull on U.K. Savings

1. Barnard 1958:3–47 is the basis for the discussion in this paragraph and its two successors.

2. E.g., Barnard 1958:13–18; Butlin 1964:85. However, Sinclair 1976 has suggested that the major break that occasioned the long boom from the 1860s to the 1880s was a rise in the U.K. savings rate in the 1850s and 1860s beyond the now slowing demands of Britain's domestic industrial revolution. According to

Sinclair the productive potential of the Australian continent was known in the early nineteenth century. The techniques of fencing, artesian wells, etc., were sufficiently well known. Hence, the settlement of the semiarid regions in the 1860s, 1870s, and 1880s was a matter of new savings sources.

Although Sinclair is certainly correct that the fencing technology introduced in Victoria in the late 1860s was part of the stock of knowledge of European agronomy, there is little doubt that its Australian potential was seriously underrated before its Victorian debut. Whatever the expected saving from fewer shepherds, the effects on animal survival rates, the size of the clip, etc., were certainly imperfectly perceived. Hence, to an important degree, the benefits of semiarid settlement were not known but once experienced became a powerful incentive for higher rates of pastoral investment. Furthermore, since the United Kingdom was investing in government and private ventures in the United States, Latin America, and Europe before 1850, some of them quite risky, one cannot help but wonder why Australia did not receive sizable funding before the late 1850s if the production potential of the colonies was as well known and highly rated as Sinclair suggests. It seems, therefore, more likely that the important break occasioning the long boom was the sharp expansion in the demand for raw wool in the United Kingdom and Europe in the middle of the nineteenth century.

3. See Easterlin 1976 for a study of the interaction between inheritable wealth and population change in nineteenth-century United States.

12. Canadian Accumulation Pressures and Their Pull on U.K. Savings

1. In terms of the absolute amount of funds entering a region from abroad, Argentina was the third heaviest international borrower of the 1880s, behind the United States and Australia. Just as some Australian economic historians suspect that an excess of British savings supplies caused some degree of overinvestment in Australia in the late 1880s, so too do many historians of the same years in Argentina. As in the Australian case it would be important to know the secular path and force of the Argentinian investment and savings determinants before making a judgment on this issue, but these data do not exist. *Ex poste* it might appear that Argentinian municipalities borrowed too heavily because it was their financing difficulties that were the immediate precipitent of the Baring Crisis of 1890 and the abrupt end of the domestic Argentinian boom and its foreign borrowing. Several Argentinian railway companies were also in grave difficulty in the late 1880s, as became clear during the sharp downturn. At a somewhat technical level, it is widely agreed that the Baring Crisis and subsequent financial difficulties involved a problem of timing. Monies were raised abroad in the form of fixed-interest securities for municipalities and the railways. The social-overhead investments using these funds had long gestation periods before sales taxes and tariff revenues swelled, but interest payments were, of course, due immediately. Note that this explanation does not question the view that the secular investment determinants of the late 1880s were objectively

strong. Furthermore, as long as *ex poste* evidence is being used, it should be pointed out that unlike the Australian case the Argentinian economy and its foreign borrowing began a strong recovery in the late 1890s when the defaulting Argentinian borrowers agreed to make good on their debts and a more realistic set of government guarantees and subsidies was enacted. Yet this type of evidence is no substitute for data on productivity, etc., with which to meter the underlying secular pressures for investment and savings.

2. The view that the expansion of the wheat economy propelled the post-1896 Canadian economic boom was well accepted by Canadian historians until quite recently; see, for example, Buckley 1955:4; Easterbrook and Aitken 1956:400–405. Writing in 1966, Chambers and Gordon constructed some simple general equilibrium models of the 1901–1911 period and concluded that perhaps 10 percent of the per capita income growth of these years was attributable to the wheat boom. Subsequent critics found numerical mistakes, which raised the 10 percent figure somewhat, but perhaps more importantly challenged the realism of Chambers and Gordon's models. Indeed, when models incorporating the critic's suggestions were used to make empirical estimates, the uniform result was the restoration of the role of the wheat export boom, e.g., Dales et al 1967; Caves 1971; Bertram 1973; Grant 1974; F. Lewis 1975. More recently, Ankli 1980 has argued that the evidence is more complex than the critics of Chambers and Gordon supposed. Using the Kravis 1972 criteria for export-led growth, Ankli finds that, although the wheat economy's expansion was a strong stimulant for the national economy from 1896 to 1900, the continuation of the national economic boom to 1910 was largely propelled by domestic investment spending rather than by wheat exports. However, Ankli believes that most of the investment expenditures were made in anticipation of heavy immigration from abroad and expansion of the Canadian wheat economy. After 1910 the capital for such expansion was in place and then exports again carried the national economic boom forward. As is argued in the text, Ankli believes that politics and political visionaries, rather than profitability and productivity, were the criteria propelling much of the 1900–1910 boom in railway investment expenditures.

3. Firestone 1958:221. Firestone 1958:178, 304–5 also finds that the price of machinery and equipment relative to all final demand product prices dropped 53.2 percent between 1870 and 1910, about half occurring in the 1880s and the remainder across the years 1900–1910. This price drop might provide some explanation for the higher rate of investment in machinery and equipment for industrial uses during these decades. However, Firestone's index is largely based on raw materials and semifabricated items, not sophisticated machinery. It thus seems best to remain agnostic concerning the role of machine prices in the rising investment rate in manufacturing in the early 1900s.

4. Three somewhat separated sources confirm the 1870–1900 increase and the 9 percent rate in the late 1890s: 1. Firestone 1958 on gross domestic capital formation, net foreign borrowing, and gross national product processed in table 12.3. 2. Hartland's 1960:718 net foreign borrowing estimates for 1871–75 and 1888–92, the peak years of domestic investment and foreign borrowing, 1870–

1900. 3. Buckley's 1955 nearly complete estimates of gross domestic capital formation, 1896–1900, combined with Hartland's 1960:718 and Firestone's 1969 recent estimate of nominal gross national product for 1896 and 1900.

5. Firestone 1958:248. With a more complex model of the national economy F. Lewis 1975 tried to incorporate the effects of the shift of labor to the prairie, which probably tended to raise nonprairie wages and lowered nonprairie rental incomes. Lewis' calculation 1975:1254 suggests that this negative effect on national rents totaled around $10 million in 1911. This more conservative estimation suggests a net shift toward rental incomes of 3.3 percentage points of gross national product instead of the text's 3.7 percentage points.

REFERENCES

Periodicals

Banker's Magazine, 1860-1913. London.
Burdett's Official Intelligence. 1883-1898. London.
The County Brokers Directory. 1875. London.
Dundee Year Book. 1882-1890. Dundee.
The Investor's Monthly Manual. 1864-1914. London.
Ralph's Stock and Share Brokers Directory. 1852-1858. London.
The Stock Exchange Official Intelligence. 1899-1913. London.
The Stock Exchange Yearbook. 1875-1914. London.
The Stockbroker's Directory of Great Britain and Ireland. 1873-1874. London.
The U.K. Stock and Sharebrokers' Directory. 1882. London.

Articles and Books

Abramovitz, M. 1961. The Nature and Significance of Kuznets Cycles. *Economic Development and Cultural Change*, 9:225-48.
Abramovitz, M. 1964. *Evidences of Long Swings in Aggregate Construction since the Civil War*. Occasional Paper 90. New York: NBER/Columbia University Press.
Abramovitz, M. 1968. The Passing of the Kuznets Cycle. *Economica*, 35:349-67.
Abramovitz, M. and P. David. 1973. Reinterpreting Economic Growth: Parables and Realities. *American Economic Review, Papers and Proceedings*, 63: 428-39.
Adler, D. R. 1970. *British Investment in American Railways 1834-1898*. Charlottesville: University Press of Virginia.
Aldcroft, D. H., ed. 1968. *The Development of British Industry and Foreign Competition 1875-1914*. London: George Allen and Unwin.
Aldcroft, D. H. 1964. The Entrepreneur and the British Economy, 1870-1914. *Economic History Review*, 2nd Ser., 17:113-134.
Aldcroft, D. H. 1975. Investment in and Utilization of Manpower. In B. M. Ratcliffe, ed., *Great Britain and Her World 1750-1914*. Manchester: Manchester University Press.
Allen, R. C. 1978. *Entrepreneurship and Technical Progress in the Northeast Coast Pig Iron Industry: 1850-1913*. Discussion Paper No. 78-13. Vancouver: University of British Columbia, Department of Economics.
Ames, E. and N. Rosenberg. 1963. Changing Technological Leadership and Industrial Growth. *Economic Journal*, 73:13-29.
Anderson, B. L. 1972. The Attorney and the Early Capital Market in Lancashire. In F. Crouzet, ed., *Capital Formation in the Industrial Revolution*. London: Methuen.
Anderson, B. L. 1975. Law, Finance, and Economic Growth. In B. M. Ratcliffe, ed., *Great Britain and Her World 1750-1914. Essays in Honour of W. O. Henderson*. Manchester: Manchester University Press.

348 REFERENCES

Ankli, R. E. 1980. The Growth of the Canadian Economy, 1860–1920. Export Led and/or Neoclassical Growth. *Explorations in Economic History*, 17: 251–74.

Arrow, K. J. 1971. *Essays in the Theory of Risk-Bearing*. Chicago: Markham.

Ashworth, W. 1960. *An Economic History of England, 1870–1939*. London: Methuen.

Ashworth, W. 1965. Changes in Industrial Structure: 1870–1914. *Yorkshire Bulletin of Economic and Social Research*, 17:61–74.

Bailey, J. D. 1957–58. "Australian Company Borrowing, 1870–1893. A Study in British Overseas Investment." Ph.D. dissertation, Oxford University.

Bailey, J. D. 1966. *A Hundred Years of Pastoral Ranking. A History of the Australian Mercantile Land and Finance Company. 1863–1963*. Oxford: Clarendon.

Barnard, A. 1958. *The Australian Wool Market, 1840–1900*. Melbourne: Melbourne University Press.

Bertram, G. W. 1973. The Relevance of the Wheat Boom in Canadian Economic Growth. *Canadian Journal of Economics* 6:545–66.

Bloomfield, A. I. 1963. *Short-Term Capital Movements Under the Pre-1914 Gold Standard*. Princeton Studies in International Finance No. 11. Princeton: Princeton University, Department of Economics, International Finance Section.

Bloomfield, A. I. 1968. *Patterns of Fluctuation in International Investment Before 1914*. Princeton Studies in International Finance, No. 21. Princeton: Princeton University, Department of Economics, International Finance Section.

Boehm, E. A. 1971. *Prosperity and Depression in Australia 1887–1897*. Oxford: Oxford University Press.

Bogue, A. G. and M. B. Bogue. 1957. "Profits" and the Frontier Land Speculator. *Journal of Economic History*, 17:1–24.

Bowley, A. L. 1937. *Wages and Income since 1860*. Cambridge: Cambridge University Press.

Brady, D. S. 1964. Relative Prices in the 19th Century. *Journal of Economic History*, 24:145–203.

Brealey, R. A. 1969. *An Introduction to Risk and Return from Common Stocks*. Cambridge: MIT Press.

Broadbridge, S. 1970. *Studies in Railway Expansion and the Capital Market in England 1825–1873*. London: Cass.

Buckley, K. A. H. 1955. *Capital Formation in Canada, 1896–1930*. Toronto: University of Toronto Press.

Burn, D. L. 1940. *The Economic History of Steel-Making, 1867–1939*. Cambridge: Cambridge University Press.

Burns, A. F. 1934. *Production Trends in the U.S. Since 1870*. New York: NBER.

Butlin, N. G. 1962. *Australian Domestic Product, Investment and Foreign Borrowing, 1861–1938/39*. Cambridge: Cambridge University Press.

Butlin, N. G. 1964. *Investment in Australian Economic Development, 1861–1900*. Cambridge: Cambridge University Press.

Butlin, N. G. and J. A. Dowie. 1969. Estimates of the Australian Work Force and Employment, 1861-1961. *Australian Economic History Review*, 9:138-53.

Cameron, R. 1961. *France and the Economic Development of Europe*. Princeton: Princeton University Press.

Cameron, R. 1967. *Banking in the Early Stages of Industrialization: A Study in Comparative Economic History*. London: Oxford.

Cairncross, A. K. 1953. *Home and Foreign Investment 1870-1913*. Cambridge: Cambridge University Press.

Cairncross, A. K. 1958. The Capital Market Before 1914. *Economica*, N.S., 25:142-46.

Caves, R. E. 1971. Export-Led Growth and the New Economic History. In J. N. Bhagwati, et al., eds., *Trade, Balance of Payments and Growth*. Amsterdam: North Holland.

Chambers, E. J. and D. F. Gordon. 1966. Primary Products and Economic Growth: An Empirical Measurement. *Journal of Political Economy*, 74: 315-22.

Church, R. A. 1975. *The Great Victorian Boom, 1850-1873*. London: Macmillan.

Clapham, J. 1968. *An Economic History of Modern Britain*. 3 vols. Cambridge: Cambridge University Press.

Coleman, D. C. 1969. *Courtaulds: An Economic and Social History*. 2 vols. Oxford: Clarendon.

Coppock, D. J. 1956. The Climacteric of the 1890's: A Critical Note. *Manchester School of Social and Economic Studies*, 24:1-31.

Corporation of Foreign Bondholders. 1871-1913. *Annual Reports*. London.

Cottrell, P. L. 1975. *British Overseas Investment in the 19th Century*. London: Macmillan.

Crafts, N. F. R. 1976. English Economic Growth in the 18th Century: A Re-Examination of Deane and Cole's Estimates. *Economic History Review*, 2nd ser., 29:226-35.

Crisp, O. 1978. Labour and Industrialization in Russia. In P. Mathias and M. M. Postan, eds., *The Cambridge Economic History of Europe*, vol. 7, part 2, ch. 7. Cambridge, England: Cambridge University Press.

Crouzet, F. 1972. Capital Formation in Great Britain During the Industrial Revolution. In F. Crouzet, ed., *Capital Formation in the Industrial Revolution*, ch. 6. London: Methuen.

Curtin, P. D. 1969. *The Atlantic Slave Trade: A Census*. Madison: University of Wisconsin Press.

Dales, J. H., et al. 1967. Primary Products and Economic Growth: A Comment. *Journal of Political Economy*, 75:876-81.

David, P. 1975. *Technical Choice Innovation and Economic Growth*. Cambridge, England: Cambridge University Press.

David, P. 1977. Invention and Accumulation in America's Economic Growth: A 19th Century Parable. In K. Brunner and A. H. Meltzer, *Carnegie-Rochester Conference Series on Public Policy*, vol. 6. Amsterdam: North Holland.

Davies, K. G. 1960. Empire and Capital. *Economic History Review*, 2nd ser., 13:105-110.

Davis, L. E. 1957. Sources of Industrial Finance: The American Textile Industry, A Case Study. *Explorations in Entrepreneurial History*, 9:190-203.

Davis, L. E. 1958. Stock Ownership in the Early New England Textile Industry. *Business History Review*, 32:204-22.

Davis, L. E. 1966. The Capital Markets and Industrial Concentration. *Economic History Review*, 2nd ser., 19:255-72.

Davis, L. E., et al. 1972. *American Economic Growth: An Economist's History of the United States*. New York: Harper & Row.

Davis, L. E. and R. E. Gallman. 1973. The Share of Savings and Investment in Gross National Product During the 19th Century in the U.S.A. In F. C. Lane, ed., *Fourth International Conference of Economic History*. Paris: Mouton.

Davis, L. E. and R. E. Gallman. 1978. Capital Formation in the United States During the 19th Century. In P. Mathias and M. M. Postan, eds., *The Cambridge Economic History of Europe*, vol. 7, part 2, ch. 1. Cambridge: Cambridge University Press.

Davis. L. E. and H. L. Stettler. 1966. The New England Textile Industry, 1825-1860: Trends and Fluctuations. In D. S. Brady, ed., *Output, Employment and Productivity in the United States After 1800*. New York: NBER/ Columbia University Press.

Deane, P. 1968. New Estimates of Gross National Product for the United Kingdom, 1830-1914. *Review of Income and Wealth*, 14:95-112.

Deane, P. and W. A. Cole. 1969. *British Economic Growth 1688-1959*, 2nd ed. Cambridge: Cambridge University Press.

DeCanio, S. J. and J. Mokyr. 1977. Inflation and the Wage Lag During the American Civil War. *Explorations in Economic History*, 14:311-36.

Diaz Alejandro, C. F. 1970. *Essays on the Economic History of the Argentine Economy*. New Haven: Yale University Press.

Dobb, M. 1947. *Studies in the Development of Capital*. New York: International Publishers.

Dowie, J. A. 1963. Inverse Relations of the Australian and New Zealand Economies, 1871-1900. *Australian Economic Papers*, 2:171-79.

Dowie, J. A. 1966. The Course and Character of Capital Formation in New Zealand, 1871-1900. *New Zealand Economic Papers*, 1:38-58.

Eagly, R. V. and V. K. Smith. 1976. Domestic and International Integration of the London Money Market. *Journal of Economic History*, 36:198-212.

Easterbrook, W. T. and H. G. J. Aitken. 1956. *Canadian Economic History*. Toronto: Macmillan.

Easterlin, R. A. 1960. Interregional Differences in Per Capita Income, Population, and Total Income, 1840-1950. In W. N. Parker, ed., *Trends in the American Economy in the 19th Century*. Princeton: Princeton University Press.

Easterlin, R. A. 1968. *Population, Labor Force, and Long Swings in Economic Growth. The American Experience*. New York: NBER/Columbia University Press.

Easterlin, R. A. 1976. Population Change and Farm Settlement in the Northern United States. *Journal of Economic History*, 36:45-75.

Edelstein, M. 1970. "The Rate of Return on U.K. Home and Foreign Investment, 1870-1913." Ph.D. dissertation, University of Pennsylvania.

Edelstein, M. 1977. Realized Rates of Return on U.K. Home and Overseas Portfolio Investment in the Age of High Imperialism, *Explorations in Economic History*, 13:283-329.

Edwards, M. M. 1967. *The Growth of the English Cotton Trade, 1780-1815*. Manchester: Manchester University Press.

Engerman, S. L. 1966. The Economic Impact of the Civil War. *Explorations in Entrepreneurial History*, 3:178-99.

Fair, R. C. 1970. The Estimation of Simultaneous Equation Models with Lagged Endogenous Variables and Serially Correlated Errors. *Econometrica*, 38: 507-15.

Fama, E. 1968. Risk, Return and General Equilibrium: Some Clarifying Comments. *Journal of Finance*, 23:29-40.

Feinstein, C. H. 1961. Income and Investment in the U.K., 1856-1914. *Economic Journal*, 71:367-85.

Feinstein, C. H. 1968. Changes in the Distribution of the National Income in the United Kingdom Since 1860. In J. Marchal and B. Ducros, ed., *The Distribution of National Income*. London: Macmillan.

Feinstein, C. H. 1972. *National Income, Expenditure and Output of the United Kingdom, 1855-1970*. Cambridge: Cambridge University Press.

Feinstein, C. H. 1978. Capital Formation in Great Britain. In P. Mathias and M. M. Postan, eds., *The Cambridge Economic History of Europe*, vol. 7, part 1, ch. 2. Cambridge: Cambridge University Press.

Feinstein, C. H. 1979. "New Estimates of Domestic Capital Formation, 1860-1920." Unpublished manuscript. University of Hull.

Feis, H. 1930. *Europe, The World's Banker 1870-1914*. New Haven: Yale University Press.

Ferns, H. S. 1973. *The Argentine Republic 1516-1971*. Newton Abbot, England: David and Charles.

Fieldhouse, D. K., ed. 1967. *The Theory of Capitalist Imperialism*. New York: Barnes and Noble.

Fieldhouse, D. K. 1973. *Economics and Empire 1830-1914*. London: Weidenfeld and Nicolson.

Firestone, O. J. 1958. *Canada's Economic Development, 1867-1953*. London: Bowes and Bowes.

Firestone, O. J. 1969. *Industry and Education*. Ottawa: University of Ottawa Press.

Fishlow, A. 1965. *American Railroads and the Transformation of the Ante-Bellum Economy*. Cambridge, Mass.: Harvard University Press.

Fishlow, A. 1966. Productivity and Technological Change in the Railroad Sector, 1840-1910. In D. S. Brady, ed., *Output, Employment and Productivity in the United States After 1800*. New York: NBER/Columbia University Press.

Floud, R. 1971. Changes in the Productivity of Labour in the British Machine Tool Industry, 1856-1900. In D. N. McCloskey, ed., *Essays on a Mature Economy: Britain After 1840*. London: Methuen.

Floud, R. 1976. *The British Machine-Tool Industry 1850-1914.* Cambridge: Cambridge University Press.

Flux, A. W. 1910. The Yield on High Class Investments, 1896-1910. *Transactions of the Manchester Statistical Society.* Manchester: Manchester Statistical Society.

Fogel, R. W. and S. L. Engerman. 1974. *Time on the Cross.* 2 vols. Boston: Little Brown.

Ford, A. G. 1962. *The Gold Standard, 1880-1914: Britain and Argentina.* Oxford: Clarendon.

Ford, A. G. 1965. Overseas Lending and Internal Fluctuations. *Yorkshire Bulletin of Economic and Social Research,* 17:19-31.

Ford, A. G. 1971. British Investment in Argentina and Long Swings, 1880-1914. *Journal of Economic History,* 31:650-63.

Ford, P. 1929. Tobacco and Coal: A Note on the Economic History of Whitehaven. *Economica,* 9:192-96.

Frankel, S. H. 1967. *Investment and the Return to Equity Capital in The South African Gold Mining Industry, 1877-1965.* Oxford: Basil Blackwell.

Fremdling, R. and R. Tilly. 1976. German Banks, German Growth, and Econometric History. *Journal of Economic History,* 36:416-24.

Friedlander, D. 1970. The Spread of Urbanization in England and Wales, 1851-1951. *Population Studies,* 24:423-43.

Friedlander, D. and R. J. Roshier. 1966. A Study of Internal Migration in England and Wales, part 1. *Population Studies,* 19:239-79.

Friend, I. and M. Blume. 1970. Measurement of Portfolio Performance Under Uncertainty. *American Economic Review,* 60:561-75.

Fua, G. 1966. *Notes on Italian Economic Growth.* Milan.

Gallman, R. E. 1966. Gross National Product in the United States, 1834-1909. In D. W. Brady, ed., *Output, Employment and Productivity in the United States After 1800.* New York: NBER/Columbia University Press.

Gatrell, V. A. C. 1977. Labour, Power and the Size of Firms in Lanchashire Cotton in the Second Quarter of the 19th Century. *Economic History Review,* 2nd ser., 30:95-129.

Gerschenkron, A. 1962. *Economic Backwardness in Historical Perspective.* Cambridge: Harvard University Press.

Gottlieb, M. 1976. *Long Swings in Urban Development.* New York: NBER/Columbia University Press.

Granger, C. W. J. 1969. Investigating Causal Relations by Econometric Models and Cross-Spectral Methods. *Econometrica,* 37:424-38.

Grant, D. 1974. The Staple Theory and Its Empirical Measurement. *Journal of Political Economy,* 82:1249-53.

Great Britain. 1871-1914. *Parliamentary Papers. Annual Reports on Joint Stock Companies.*

Great Britain. 1878. *Parliamentary Papers. Royal Commission on the London Stock Exchange,* vol. 19.

Great Britain. 1880-1914. *Parliamentary Papers. Annual Local Taxation Returns.*

Great Britain. 1914-16. *Parliamentary Papers. Returns of the Capital, Traffic, Working Expenditure, Etc., of the Railway Companies of the U.K.*, vol. 60.

Great Britain. 1931. *Report of the Committee on Finance and Industry* (Macmillan Report).

Green, A. and M. C. Urquhart. 1976. Factor and Commodity Flows in the International Economy of 1870-1914: A Multi-Country View. *Journal of Economic History*, 36:217-52.

Gregory, P. R. 1979. The Russian Balance of Payments, the Gold Standard, and Monetary Policy: A Historical Example of Foreign Capital Movements. *Journal of Economic History*, 39:379-400.

Habakkuk, H. J. 1940. Free Trade and Commercial Expansion of the British Empire. In J. H. Rose, A. P. Newton, and E. A. Benians, eds., *The Cambridge History of the British Empire*, vol. 2. Cambridge: Cambridge University Press.

Habakkuk, H. J. 1962. Fluctuations in House-Building in Britain and the United States in the 19th Century. *Journal of Economic History*, 22:198-230.

Hall, A. R. 1957. A Note on the English Capital Market as a Source of Funds for Home Investment Before 1914. *Economica*, N.S., 24:59-66.

Hall, A. R. 1958. The English Capital Market Before 1914: A Reply. *Economica*, N.S., 25:339-43.

Hall, A. R. 1963a. *The London Capital Market and Australia 1870-1914*. Canberra: The Australian National University.

Hall, A. R. 1963b. Some Long Period Effects of the Kinked Age Distribution of the Population of Australia 1861-1961. *Economic Record*, 39:43-52.

Hall, A. R., ed. 1968. *The Export of Capital from Britain 1870-1914*. London: Methuen.

Hannah, L. 1976. *The Rise of the Corporate Economy. The British Experience*. Baltimore: Johns Hopkins University Press.

Hanushek, E. A. and J. E. Jackson. 1977. *Statistical Methods for Social Scientists*. New York: Academic Press.

Hartland, P. 1960. Canadian Balance of Payments since 1868. In W. N. Parker, ed., *Trends in the American Economy in the 19th Century*. Princeton: NBER/ Princeton University Press.

Hartwell, R. M. 1971. *The Industrial Revolution and Economic Growth*. London: Methuen.

Hawke, G. R. 1970. *Railways and Economic Growth in England and Wales 1840-1870*. Oxford: Clarendon.

Henderson, W. O. 1972. *Britain and Industrial Europe 1750-1870*. Leicester: Leicester University Press.

Hilferding, R. 1910. *Finanzcapital, Marx-Studien*, vol. 3. Vienna: Verlag der Wiener Volksfuchhandlung, 1923.

Hobsbawm, E. J. 1969. *Industry and Empire*. London: Weidenfeld and Nicolson.

Hobson, C. K. 1914. *The Export of Capital*. London: Constable, 1963.

Hobson, J. A. 1894. *The Evolution of Modern Capitalism*. London: Walter Scott.

Hobson, J. A. 1902. *Imperialism: A Study*. London: Nisbet.

Hoffmann, W. G. 1965. *Das Wachstum Der Deutschen Wirtschaft Seit Der Mitte Das 19. Jahr-hunderts*. Berlin: Springer-Verlag.

Homer, S. 1963. *A History of Interest Rates*. New Brunswick: Rutgers University Press.

Hopkins, A. G. 1973. *An Economic History of West Africa*. London: Longmans.

Horne, H. O. 1947. *A History of Savings Banks*. Oxford: Oxford University Press.

Hyde, F. E. 1956. *Blue Funnel*. Liverpool: Liverpool University Press.

Imlah, A. 1958. *Economic Elements in the Pax Britannica*. Cambridge: Harvard University Press.

Jackson, R. V. 1977. *Australian Economic Development in the 19th Century*. Canberra: Australian National University Press.

Jeffreys, J. B. 1938. "Trends in Business Organization in Great Britain Since 1856." Ph.D. dissertation, London School of Economics.

Jenks, L. H. 1927. *The Migration of British Capital to 1875*. New York: Knopf.

John, A. H. 1953. Insurance Investment and the London Money Market of the 18th Century. *Economica*, N.S., 20:137-58.

Joslin, D. M. 1954-1955. London Private Bankers, 1720-1785. *Economic History Review*, 2nd ser., 7:167-86.

Kahan, A. 1978. Capital Formation During the Period of Early Industrialization in Russia, 1890-1913. In P. Mathias and M. M. Postan, eds., *The Cambridge Economic History of Europe*, vol. 7, part 2, ch. 6. Cambridge: Cambridge University Press.

Kelley, A. C. 1968. Demographic Change and Economic Growth: Australia, 1861-1911. *Explorations in Entrepreneurial History*, 2:207-77.

Kennedy, W. P. 1974. Foreign Investment, Trade and Growth in the United Kingdom, 1870-1913. *Explorations in Economic History*, 11:425-34.

Kennedy, W. P. 1976. Institutional Responses to Economic Growth: Capital Markets in Britain to 1914. In A. D. Chandler, Jr., ed., *Management Strategies and Business Development*. Mystic, Conn.: Lawrence Verry.

Keynes, J. M. 1924. Foreign Investment and the National Advantage. *The Nation and the Athanaeum*, 15:584-87.

Keynes, J. M. 1936. *The General Theory of Employment, Interest and Money*. New York: Macmillan.

Killick, J. R. and W. A. Thomas. 1970. The Provincial Stock Exchanges, 1830-1870. *Economic History Review*, 2nd ser., 23:96-111.

Kindleberger, C. P. 1964. *Economic Growth in France and Britain*. Cambridge: Harvard University Press.

Kmenta, J. and J. G. Williamson. 1966. The Determinants of Investment Behavior: United States Railways, 1872-1941. *Review of Economics and Statistics*, 58:172-81.

Knapp, J. 1957. Capital Exports and Growth. *Economic Journal*, 67:432-44.

Kravis, I. B. 1972. The Role of Exports in 19th Century U.S. Growth. *Economic Development and Cultural Change*, 20:387-405.

Kuznets, S. 1930. *Secular Movements in Production and Prices*. New York: Houghton Mifflin.

Kuznets, S. 1961. *Capital in the American Economy: Its Formation and Financing*. Princeton: NBER/Princeton University Press.

Kuznets, S. 1961a. Quantitative Aspects of the Economic Growth of Nations: 6. Long-Term Trends in Capital Formation Proportions. *Economic Development and Cultural Change*, 9 (no. 4).

Kuznets, S. 1966. *Modern Economic Growth. Rate Structure and Spread*. New Haven: Yale University Press.

Landes, D. 1969. *The Unbound Prometheus*. London: Cambridge University Press.

Lavington, F. 1921. *The English Capital Market*. London: Methuen.

Leff, N. 1969. Dependency Rates and Saving Rates. *American Economic Review*, 59:886-96.

Lehfeldt, R. L. 1913-14. The Rate of Interest on British and Foreign Investments. *Journal of the Royal Statistical Society*, 76:196-207, 415-6; 77:432-35.

Lenin, V. I. 1916. *Imperialism: The Highest Stage of Capitalism*. Moscow: Foreign Languages Publishing House, 1947.

Lewis, F. 1975. The Canadian Wheat Boom and Per Capital Income: New Estimates. *Journal of Political Economy*, 83:1249-57.

Lewis, J. P. 1965. *Building Cycles and Britain's Growth*. London: Macmillan.

Lewis, W. A. 1978. *Growth and Fluctuations, 1870-1913*. London: George Allen and Unwin.

Lindert, P. H. 1969. *Key Currencies and Gold 1900-1913*. Princeton Studies in International Finance No. 24. Princeton: Princeton University, Department of Economics, International Finance Section.

Lintner, J. 1965a. Security Prices, Risk, and Maximal Gains from Diversification. *Journal of Finance*, 20:587-615.

Lintner, J. 1965b. The Valuation of Risk Assets and the Selection of Risk Investment in Stock Portfolios and Capital Budgets. *Review of Economics and Statistics*, 47:13-37.

Lowenfeld, H. 1909. *All About Investment*. London: Financial Review of Reviews.

McCloskey, D. N. 1970. Did Victorian Britain Fail? *The Economic History Review*, 2nd ser., 23:446-59.

McCloskey, D. N., ed. 1971a. *Essays on a Mature Economy: Britain After 1840*. London: Methuen.

McCloskey, D. N. 1971b. International Differences in Productivity? Coal and Steel in America and Britain Before World War I. In D. N. McCloskey, ed., *Essays on a Mature Economy: Britain After 1840*. London: Methuen.

McCloskey, D. N. and L. G. Sandberg. 1971. From Damnation to Redemption: Judgements on the Late Victorian Enterpreneur. *Explorations in Economic History*, 9:89-108.

Macgregor, D. G. 1929. Joint Stock Companies and the Risk Factor. *Economic Journal*, 39:491-505.

Malinvaud, E. 1966. *Statistical Methods of Econometrics.* Chicago: Rand McNally.

Malthus, T. R. 1803. *An Essay on Population*, 2nd ed., 2 vols. Dent, England: Everyman's Library.

Malthus, T. R. 1836. *Principles of Political Economy*, 2nd ed. Oxford: Blackwell, 1951.

Markovitch, T. J. 1966. *L'Industrie Française de 1789 à 1964.* Paris: Cahiers de l'I.S.E.A.

Markowitz, H. 1959. *Portfolio Selection: Efficient Diversification of Investments.* New York: John Wiley.

Marshall, A. 1887-1888. Testimony Before the Gold and Silver Commission of 1887-1888. *Official Papers.* London: Macmillan, 1926.

Marx, K. 1894. *Capital*, vol. 3. In F. Engels, ed., *The Process of Capitalist Production as a Whole.* New York: International Publishers, 1967.

Mathews, R. C. O. 1957. *The Business Cycle.* New York: Cambridge University Press.

Mathias, P. 1969. *The First Industrial Nation.* London: Methuen.

Mercer, L. J. 1974. Building Ahead of Demand: Some Evidence for the Land Grant Railroads. *Journal of Economic History*, 34:492-500.

Merrett, A. J. and A. Sykes. 1963. Return on Equities and Fixed Interest Securities, 1919-1963. *District Bank Review*, December.

Mill, J. S. 1848. *Principles of Political Economy.* Edited by W. J. Ashley. London: Longmans, 1936.

Miller, N. C. and M. v. N. Whitman. 1970. A Mean-Variance Analysis of U.S. Long-Term Portfolio Foreign Investment. *Quarterly Journal of Economics*, 84:175-96.

Minchinton, W. E. 1954. Bristol—Metropolis of the West in the 18th Century. *Transactions of the Royal Historical Society*, 5th ser., 4.

Mitchell, B. R., ed. 1962. *Abstract of British Historical Statistics.* Cambridge: Cambridge University Press.

Mitchell, B. R. 1975. *European Historical Statistics 1750-1970.* New York: Columbia University Press.

Mokyr, J. 1976. *Industrialization in the Low Countries, 1795-1850.* New Haven: Yale University Press.

Morgenstern, O. 1959. *International Financial Transactions and Business Cycles.* Princeton: NBER/Princeton University Press.

Morrison, D. F. 1967. *Multivariate Statistical Methods.* New York: McGrawHill.

Musson, A. E. 1978. *The Growth of British Industry.* New York: Holmes and Meier.

Nash, R. L. 1880. *A Short Enquiry into the Profitable Nature of Our Investments.* London: Effington Wilson, Royal Exchange.

Navin, T. R. and M. V. Sears. 1955. The Rise of the Market for Industrial Securities, 1887-1902. *Business History Review*, 24:105-38.

Neal, L. 1969. Investment Behavior by American Railroads: 1897-1914. *Review of Economics and Statistics*, 51:126-35.

Nemmers, E. E. 1956. *Hobson and Underconsumption*. Amsterdam: North Holland.

Nerlove, M. 1968. Factors Affecting Differences Among Rates of Return on Investment in Individual Common Stocks. *Review of Economics and Statistics*, 50:312-31.

Neuberger, H. and H. H. Stokes. 1974. German Banks and German Growth, 1883-1913: An Empirical View. *Journal of Economic History*, 34:710-31.

North, D. C. 1960. The U.S. Balance of Payments 1790-1860. In W. N. Parker, ed., *Trends in the American Economy in the 19th Century*. Princeton: NBER/Princeton University Press.

North, D. C. 1962. International Capital Movements in Historical Perspective. In R. F. Mikesell, ed., *U.S. Private and Government Investment Abroad*, ch. 2. Eugene: University of Oregon Books.

Organization for Economic Cooperation and Development. 1974. *National Accounts Statistics*. Paris: OECD.

O'Hagan, H. O. 1929. *Leaves from My Lives*. 2 vols. London: Lane.

OYCA. 1920. *Official Yearbook of the Commonwealth of Australia*.

OYCA. 1921. *Official Yearbook of the Commonwealth of Australia*.

OYCA. 1925. *Official Yearbook of the Commonwealth of Australia*.

Owen, R. and B. Sutcliffe, eds. 1972. *Studies in the Theory of Imperialism*. London: Longmans.

Paish, G. 1909. Great Britain's Capital Investment in Other Lands. *Journal of the Royal Statistical Society*, 72:465-80.

Paish, G. 1911. Great Britain's Capital Investment in Other Lands. *Journal of the Royal Statistical Society*, 74:167-187.

Paish, G. 1914. Export of Capital and the Cost of Living. *The Statist*, 79.

Paterson, D. G. 1976. *British Direct Investments in Canada, 1890-1914*. Toronto: University of Toronto Press.

Payne, P. L. 1967. The Emergence of the Large Scale Company in Great Britain, 1870-1914. *Economic History Review*, 2nd ser., 20:519-42.

Phelps Brown, E. H. 1968. *A Century of Pay*. London: Macmillan.

Phelps Brown, E. H. and S. J. Handfield-Jones. 1952. The Climacteric of the 1890's: A Study in the Expanding Economy. *Oxford Economic Papers*, 4:266-307.

Phillips, G. H. 1887. *Phillip's Investors Annual*. London: Effingham Wilson.

Pollard, S. 1964. Fixed Capital in the Industrial Revolution. *Journal of Economic History*, 24:299-314.

Pollins, H. 1957. Railway Contractors and the Finance of Railway Development in Britain. *Journal of Transport History*, 3:41-51; 103-10.

Postan, M. M. 1935. Recent Trends in the Accumulation of Capital. *Economic History Review*, 6:1-12.

Pressnell, L. S. 1956. *Country Banking in the Industrial Revolution*. Oxford: Oxford University Press.

Price, J. M. 1973. *France and the Chesapeake*. Ann Arbor: University of Michigan Press.

Reed, M. C., ed. 1968. *Railways in the Victorian Economy. Studies in Finance and Economic Growth.* New York: Kelly.

Reed, M. C. 1975. *Investment in Railways in Britain, 1820-1844. A Study in the Development of the Capital Markets.* London: Oxford.

Ricardo, D. 1817. *On the Principles of Political Economy and Taxation.* Edited by R. M. Hartwell. London: Penguin, 1971.

Richardson, H. W. 1965. Retardation in Britain's Industrial Growth, 1870-1913. *Scottish Journal of Political Economy,* 12:125-49.

Richardson, H. W. 1972. British Emigration and Overseas Investment, 1870-1914. *Economic History Review,* 2nd ser., 25:99-113.

Robertson, P. L. 1981. Employers and Engineering Education in Britain and the United States. *Business History,* 23:42-58.

Rosenberg, H. 1943. Political and Social Consequences of the Great Depression of 1873-1896 in Central Europe. *Economic History Review,* 8:58-73.

Rosenberg, N. 1972. *Technology and American Economic Growth.* New York: Harper and Row.

Rosenberg, N. 1976. *Perspectives on Technology.* Cambridge: Cambridge University Press.

Sandberg, L. G. 1974. *Lancashire in Decline.* Columbus: Ohio State University Press.

Saul, S. B. 1968. The Motor Tool Industry in Britain to 1914. *Business* 5:22-44.

Saul, S. B. 1968. The Machine Tool Industry in Britain in 1914. *Business History,* 10:22-43.

Saville, J. 1961. Some Retarding Factors in the British Economy Before 1914. *Yorkshire Bulletin of Economic and Social Research,* 13:51-59.

Sayers, R. S. 1957. *Lloyds Bank in the History of English Banking.* Oxford: Oxford University Press.

Schmookler, J. 1966. *Invention and Economic Growth.* Cambridge: Harvard University Press.

Shannon, H. A. 1933. The Limited Companies of 1866-1883. *Economic History Review,* 4:290-315.

Sharpe, W. F. 1964. Capital Asset Prices: A Theory of Market Equilibrium Under Conditions of Risk. *Journal of Finance,* 19:425-42.

Sharpe, W. F. 1970. *Portfolio Theory and Capital Markets.* New York: McGraw-Hill.

Sheppard, D. K. 1971. *The Growth and Role of U.K. Financial Institutions, 1880-1962.* London: Methuen.

Sheridan, R. B. 1968. The Wealth of Jamaica in the 18th Century: A Rejoinder. *Economic History Review,* 2nd ser., 21:46-61.

Sigsworth, E. M. 1958. *Black Dyke Mills.* Liverpool: Liverpool University Press.

Simon, M. 1960. The U.S. Balance of Payments, 1861-1900. In W. N. Parker, ed., *Trends in the American Economy in the 19th Century.* Princeton: NBER/ Princeton University Press.

Simon, M. 1967. The Pattern of New British Portfolio Foreign Investment,

1865-1914. In J. H. Adler, ed., *Capital Movements and Economic Development*. London: Macmillan.

Simon, M. 1970. New British Investments in Canada, 1865-1914. *Canadian Journal of Economics*, 3:238-54.

Sims, C. A. 1972. Money, Income and Causality. *American Economic Review*, 62:540-52.

Sinclair, W. A. 1976. *The Process of Economic Development in Australia*. Melbourne: Cheshire.

Sismondi, J. C. L. S. de. 1819. *Principes D'Economie Politique*. Paris: Jeheber, 1951.

Smith, A. 1776. *The Wealth of Nations*. Edited by E. Cannan. New York: Modern Library, 1937.

Smith, K. C. and G. W. Horne. 1934. *An Index Number of Securities, 1867-1914*. London: London and Cambridge Economic Series, Special Memorandum 37.

Smith, R. 1954. "The Lancashire Cotton Industry and the Great Depression, 1873-1896." Ph.D. dissertation, Birmingham University.

Stigler, G. J. 1963. *Capital and Rates of Return to Manufacturing Industries*. Princeton: NBER/Princeton University Press.

Stone, I. 1968. British Long-Term Investment in Latin America, 1865-1913. *Business History Review*, 42:311-39.

Stone, I. 1972. British Investment in Argentina. *Journal of Economic History*, 32:546-47.

Stone, I. 1977. British Direct and Portfolio Investment in Latin America Before 1914. *Journal of Economic History*, 37:690-722.

Stone, J. M. 1971. Financial Panics: Their Implications for the Mix of Domestic and Foreign Investments of Great Britain, 1880-1913. *Quarterly Journal of Economics*, 85:304-26.

Swieranga, R. P. 1966. Land Speculator "Profits" Reconsidered: Central Iowa as a Test Case. *Journal of Economic History*, 24:1-28.

Taylor, A. J. 1969. The Coal Industry. In D. Aldcroft, ed., *The Development of British Industry and Foreign Competition, 1875-1914*. London: Allen and Unwin.

Thomas, B. 1954. *Migration and Economic Growth. A Study of Great Britain and the Atlantic Economy*, 2nd ed. Cambridge: Cambridge University Press, 1973.

Thomas, B. 1972. *Migration and Urban Development*. London: Methuen.

Thomas, R. P. 1968. The Sugar Colonies of the Old Empire: Profit or Loss for Great Britain. *Economic History Review*, 2nd ser., 21:30-45.

Thomas, W. A. 1973. *The Provincial Stock Exchanges*. London: Frank Cass.

Tobin, J. 1958. Liquidity Preference as Behavior Towards Risk. *Review of Economic Studies*, 25:65-86.

Tranter, N. L. 1973. *Population Since the Industrial Revolution*. London: Croom Helm.

Ulmer, M. J. 1960. *Capital in Transportation, Communications, and Public*

Utilities: Its Formation and Planning. Princeton: NBER/Princeton University Press.

Urquhart, M. C. and K. A. H. Buckley, eds. 1965. *Historical Statistics of Canada.* Cambridge: Cambridge University Press.

United States. Securities and Exchange Commission. 1939. *Investment Trusts and Investments Companies: Report of the S.E.C. Pursuant to Sec. 30 of the Public Utility Holding Company Act of 1935, Supplementary Report: Investment Trusts in Great Britain.*

United States. Bureau of the Census. 1960. *Historical Statistics of the United States.* Washington: Government Printing Office.

United States. Bureau of the Census. 1975. *Historical Statistics of the United States.* Washington: Government Printing Office.

Wakefield, E. G. 1849. *A View of the Art of Civilization.* London: Parker.

Wilkins, M. 1970. *The Emergence of Multinational Enterprise: American Business Abroad from the Colonial Era to 1914.* Cambridge: Harvard University Press.

Williamson, J. G. 1964. *American Growth and the Balance of Payments 1820–1913.* Chapel Hill: University of North Carolina Press.

Williamson, J. G. 1974a. Watersheds and Turning Points: Conjectures on the Long-Term Impact of Civil War Financing. *Journal of Economic History,* 34:636–61.

Williamson, J. G. 1974b. Migration to the New World: Long-Term Influences and Impact. *Explorations in Economic History,* 11:357–390.

Williamson, J. G. 1979. Inequality, Accumulation and Technological Imbalance: A Growth-Equity Conflict in American History? *Economic Development and Cultural Change,* 27:231–53.

Wilson, C. H. 1968. *The History of Unilever: A Study in Economic Growth and Social Change.* New York: Praeger.

Woodruff, W. 1966. *Impact of Western Man.* London: Macmillan.

Wright, C. 1969. Savings and the Rate of Interest. In A. C. Harberger and M. J. Bailey, eds., *The Taxations of Income from Capital.* Washington: Brookings Institution.

Wright, G. 1974. Cotton Consumption and the Post-Bellum Recovery of the American South. *Journal of Economic History,* 34:610–35.

Wright, W. R. 1974. *British-Owned Railways in Argentina.* Austin: University of Texas Press.

Zevin, R. B. 1975. The Growth of Manufacturing in Early 19th Century England. New York: Arno.

INDEX